LINCOLN'S
Scapegoat General

A Life of Benjamin F. Butler, 1818–1893

Benj. F. Butler

LINCOLN'S
Scapegoat General

A Life of Benjamin F. Butler
1818–1893

BY

RICHARD S. WEST, JR.

illustrated with maps
and a frontispiece

HOUGHTON MIFFLIN COMPANY BOSTON
The Riverside Press Cambridge
1965

First Printing **w**

To
Victor F. White

"Let me get a chance to shake my boar's head at them!"

MIRABEAU

ACKNOWLEDGMENTS

AMONG the Librarians whose suggestions have helped this book the author especially thanks the following:

Dr. David C. Mearns and Dr. C. P. Powell, of the Division of Manuscripts, the Library of Congress

Dr. Vernon Tate, Librarian of the U. S. Naval Academy

Mr. Stephen C. Riley of the Massachusetts Historical Society

Mr. Hugh F. Downey, of the Public Library of Lowell, Massachusetts

Mr. Elmer M. Hunt, Director of the New Hampshire Historical Society.

Mr. John Hall Jacobs of the New Orleans Public Library

Mr. V. L. Bledsole of the Department of Archives, Louisiana State University

The staff of the Public Library of the City of Boston

Miss Helen Northrop, of the University of Wisconsin Library

Miss Dorothy C. Barck, of the New York Historical Society

Mr. Dennis Dooley, of the Massachusetts State Library, the State House, Boston

Miss Barbara Dunsford, the Middlesex County Law Library, Lowell, Massachusetts

Bibliographical data were supplied by Mr. Charles V. West of the Library of Congress, Mr. Alvin O. West of Arlington, Virginia, Mr. Richard Townsend of Annapolis, Captain Walter D. Sharpe, USN (Ret.) of Annapolis, and by the following of my colleagues at the U.S. Naval Academy: Dr. Paolo M. Coletta, Dr. Robert W. Daly, Dr. W. W. Jeffries, Dr. Rocco M. Paone, and Professor Neville T. Kirk.

Friends who have read the manuscript in whole or in part include

Mr. Victor F. White of Dallas, Texas, and Taos, New Mexico; Dr. Kent Roberts Greenfield of Baltimore, Miss Mary Carter-Roberts of Annapolis, and Mr. David Legerman of New York City. To Mr. Craig Wylie of the Houghton Mifflin Company I am indebted for suggesting a more extended treatment of Butler's postwar battle for the civil rights of the Freedman. Mrs. Blanche Ames Ames very kindly permitted the use of material from her book *Adelbert Ames, 1835-1933* (North Easton, Massachusetts, 1964). To Mrs. Jessie Ames Marshall of Jamaica Plain, Massachusetts, I am especially grateful for making available to me the later papers of General Butler. Throughout the making of the book my wife, Marie McElreath West, has served as a second author.

RICHARD S. WEST, JR.

PREFACE

To DISENTANGLE Ben Butler from the myths that have grown up about him is the aim of this book. The businessman who drove his coach and four so furiously across the Massachusetts countryside was not the seven-times millionaire that the press proclaimed. The politician, despite his formidable reputation, was not the vote-grubbing, salary-grabbing epitome of all that was bad in the political rings of the "Dreadful Decade." The lawyer was sharp enough, but, folklore to the contrary, he did not attach the great waterwheel of a Lowell, Massachusetts, mill to force the operators to pay a poor girl's wages. His Woman Order at New Orleans won him denunciations by Northern Copperheads, an official ban of outlawry by Confederate President Jefferson Davis and gratuitous abuse even in the British Parliament, but only in Southern propaganda did it subject the ladies of New Orleans to insult by his soldiers. Nor was the wartime rumor true that when he left New Orleans he carried off as part of his baggage a coffin filled with silver spoons.

The man beneath the legend was an intensely puritanical idealist who after studying for the ministry switched to law in the belief that there he could better help his fellowmen. Himself born on the wrong side of the tracks, he championed the rights of the Lowell factory girls against the textile tycoons. In the Massachusetts legislature he agitated for a shorter working day in industry and for the secret ballot to take the voter out from under the monitoring eye of his employer at the polls.

By the outbreak of the Civil War, when his business investments and his law practice had made him independently wealthy, he launched himself upon the national scene as a crusader to preserve the Union. Irregular in his military habits, he nevertheless succeeded in leading Massachusetts troops to the relief of Washington. His seizures of Annapolis and Baltimore — if not his whimsical confiscation of the Great Seal of Maryland — possibly prevented Maryland from seceding. At New Orleans he dealt with a more complex administrative problem than any other Union general was faced with. To obtain funds to carry on emergency relief Ben Butler levied contributions upon wealthy Secessionists in proportion as they had contributed funds to the Confederate cause, on the Butlerian theory that the hunger-pinched little people, poor whites, Negroes, indigents of foreign extraction impoverished by the war, were not themselves morally responsible for the "crime" of secession, but that the leaders were so responsible. Ironically it has not been the little people who have shaped the views about General Butler in the history books, but the wealthy whose silver plate was confiscated.

Lincoln, reacting to the pressure of foreign consuls, recalled Butler from New Orleans in December 1862 and in November of 1863, reacting to public opinion throughout the North, he put Butler in command in Virginia and North Carolina. Here Butler fought the War Department, the newly established civilian government of Virginia, and the complex administrative problems around Norfolk as well as the Confederate enemy before Richmond. He identified himself with the cause of the Negro, whom he enlisted, trained, and sent into battle. To care for the families of Negro troops who streamed into his lines he set up an Office of Negro Affairs which became a prototype of the postwar Freedmen's Bureau. His rugged individualism brought him into conflict with General Halleck, and to a lesser extent with General Grant. But as a soldier he was forever handicapped by his own legend. West Pointers, considering him a "lawyer in shoulder straps," ungenerously magnified the importance of an early skirmish at Big Bethel, and kept him under close leash, with too few troops for offensive campaigns. His grand strategic moves at Bermuda Hundred, Dutch Gap, and Fort Fisher became the subject of some of the war's bitterest controversies.

In Congress after the war he became a natural leader of the Radical Republicans. He led the prosecution of Andrew Johnson in the Impeachment. As Chairman of the House Committee on Reconstruction he made history by maneuvering through Congress the first Civil Rights Bill and the bill to curb the Ku Klux Klan.

In politics he boxed the compass, moving from Jacksonian Democracy to Republican, back to Democrat and finally to Greenback-Labor. He was an independent idealist who shifted — as he claimed — his party allegiance as party ideals themselves shifted.

In 1882 he was swept into office as reform Governor of Massachusetts and in 1884 he culminated his career as a liberal political crusader by a Herculean, one-man campaign for the presidency of the United States. Although his picturesque effort to found a third party failed, many of the liberal ideals of his so-called "People's Party" have later been woven into the fabric of American liberalism.

CONTENTS

PART ONE: THE LAWYER

    1. Never Pull a Journalist's Nose   3
    2. Cross-Eyed   7
    3. Juliet   17
    4. Radical Reform   25
    5. Ten-Hour Day   30
    6. Political General   39

PART TWO: THE POLITICAL GENERAL

    7. Relief of Washington   51
    8. Butler Seizes Baltimore   64
    9. Butler's Fugitive Slave Law   76
    10. Enough Rope   87
    11. Recovery After Big Bethel   97

PART THREE: ADMINISTRATOR OF NEW ORLEANS

    12. Launching the New Orleans Expedition   111
    13. New Orleans Campaign   119
    14. The Woman Order   129
    15. Military Government Reforms   144
    16. Shoestring Offensive   158

17. Reconstruction 171
18. Commerce, Consuls and the Recall 186
19. Politics Behind the Lines 205

PART FOUR: THE RICHMOND CAMPAIGN

20. The Virginia Front 219
21. Bermuda Hundred 232
22. Prisoners and the Exchange 251
23. Military Vs. Civil Government 263
24. Finale at Fort Fisher 279

PART FIVE: THE REFORMER

25. The Legend of the Spoons 295
26. Return to the Law 309
27. The Radical Congressman: The Impeachment Trial 320
28. The Radical Congressman: Reconstruction 334
29. The Radical Congressman: Civil Rights 352
30. The Reform Governor 366
31. Nomination for President: 1884 379
32. The People's Party Campaign 391
33. *Butler's Book* 408

Bibliographical Notes 423

Index 455

ILLUSTRATIONS

FRONTISPIECE

The frontispiece shows Benjamin F. Butler in his uniform as a brigadier general of the Massachusetts Militia. This photograph was taken by Mathew B. Brady about the time of Butler's seizure of Baltimore. It is reproduced from the Collections of the Library of Congress.

MAPS

The Relief of Washington and Seizure of Baltimore   66

The Lower Peninsula and Fortress Monroe   78

Approaches to the Lower Mississippi River   124

The Push up the River   162

Bermuda Hundred: General Butler's Entrenched Camp below Richmond   233

Fort Fisher, Wilmington, N.C.   286

PART ONE

The Lawyer

1

NEVER PULL A JOURNALIST'S NOSE

ON JULY 6, 1842, a young lawyer named Ben Butler was trailed to the courthouse in Concord, Massachusetts, and up the stair to the Court of Common Pleas by an ascetic and bespectacled young journalist named William S. Robinson. Lawyer Butler was to defend a shifty youth, one Elbridge G. Record of Lowell, charged with passing counterfeit money. Although a number of persons in Lowell had been swindled, the initiative in this prosecution had been taken by a Mrs. Sarah Emma Wilkins, the plaintiff. Constable Zachariah Shed of Lowell, the arresting officer, and possibly one of the many who had been cheated, was among the citizens who had made the eighteen-mile trip over to Concord to see justice done.

Butler led off by discovering two flaws in the indictment and asking the Court to direct the jury to bring in a verdict of acquittal. The indictment, as drawn, charged the prisoner with defrauding "Sarah Wilkins." The plaintiff now acknowledged that her full name was "Sarah Emma Wilkins" and that she had a husband living. Under Massachusetts law, Lawyer Butler pointed out, it was the husband who should have brought the charge.

Like two boxers backing a referee into a corner, the district attorney and Lawyer Butler belabored the judge with their explanations and contentions.

The case having come to trial, Butler would consent to no modification of the indictment's wording. It was his habit to catch at every point in the faults of his opponents. A good point of law in his client's favor was as much the property of his client as a good point of fact.[1] Butler believed that he had no right to waive any technicality that might help his client. He, Butler, had not phrased the laws. His job as lawyer was to defend his client by bringing to his aid every defense known to the law.

The Court overruled the district attorney's objections and directed the jury to bring in a verdict of acquittal. The jury did so.

Aware that the Wilkins charge was only one of several against his client, and that if he were indicted on one of the other counts he would have to sit in jail until the succeeding term of the Court, Lawyer Butler immediately moved that the prisoner be discharged.

The Court nodded. And before the clerk had repeated the order for discharge, Butler himself opened the door of the prisoner's box and with a "Go along, and go as quick as you can!" hustled his client out of the building.

Ben Butler was twenty-four, a stocky five feet four inches tall, with heavy barrel chest, short arms and legs and an enormous head. He had a mane of uncut red hair which curled in ringlets over his white-skinned neck. He was cross-eyed, and had come up from the wrong side of the tracks. An underdog outside the charmed precincts of Beacon Hill and famous for his hair-trigger temper and willingness to beat up anyone who dared whisper the sobriquet "Old Cockeye" — Lawyer Butler possessed an uncommon ability to identify himself with his client. To the astonishment, and often the disgust, of people in the courtroom, he was able to uncork a flow of tears as easily as an ordinary man might operate the handle of the town pump. He was clever, he was crafty, he was sometimes crude. Some opposing lawyers considered him unscrupulous. He could think circles around them, and few were able to match his high-pitched, rasping staccato delivery which could outshout the noisiest opponent.

A few minutes after he had freed the prisoner, word came that the latter had been rearrested. Butler, leaving behind his hat and papers, dashed downstairs and across the street to his rescue. Uninhibited here by decorum of the courtroom, Lawyer Butler rained fire and brimstone upon Constable Shed for arresting without a warrant and exercising in Concord an authority which did not extend beyond Lowell.[2]

In his write-up for the Lowell *Courier,* Reporter Robinson berated Ben Butler for "very scaly and disreputable" courtroom trickery and concluded, "Perhaps his greatness is not of the highest order: neither was Bonaparte's but who will dispute the claim of the latter to be called great? The opening of the prison doors by Mr. Butler, without permission, might be called a somewhat outrageous proceeding, but it would be called so only by those who would blame Cromwell for dissolving the Rump Parliament." [3]

The same night that Robinson's article appeared, Lawyer Butler stormed into the *Courier* office to demand retraction of its inaccuracies and personal abuse. Finding Reporter Robinson recalcitrant, he called him "a liar and a scoundrel" and pulled his nose.

Editor William Schouler, seizing Butler by the wrists, sought to put him out of the office. Butler shook himself free. Then he brandished his walking stick and stood near the door in posture of defense, trembling and red with excitement. After a few minutes, finding himself unopposed, he left.

As was to be expected, the *Courier* enjoyed a field day, comparing Butler to Napoleon, describing his lamblike manners, his voice "mild as an Eolian harp," and his flourishing his cane "like a monkey going through the small sword exercise." Robinson, indeed, retracted several inconsequential details but adhered to his opinion that "the man who has reduced impudence to a science, certainly has an element of greatness, and should have the credit of it." [4]

To this Butler struck back in a letter to the Lowell *Daily Advertiser:*

> In the matter of the trial of Elbridge G. Record, of which an untrue, garbled and malicious account was given by the Courier of Thursday last, I have only to say, that I used my best efforts, as I always intend to, for the acquittal of my client, and gave him the best advice I could as to his future course. *After* he had been discharged by the Court, and was as free as any man, I opened the door of the box where he was placed during the trial, and told him to go and not to wait to be again *arrested* — thus to avoid the long imprisonment to which he would be subjected, if taken by another warrant. I did not then "rush out of the house in a comfortable state of excitement," but calmly remained attending to my

business, until word was sent me by my client, that he was arrested again. I went out as soon as sent for, and found Record arrested by a *constable of Lowell,* who had *no authority to act* out of the city, and *without a warrant.* At the time I left the Court-room I supposed Record to be in the lower part of the house, consequently did not take my hat; but finding him across the street at the Hotel, I sent for my hat and went to Record. I used there harsh and peremptory language to the *person* who was thus exceeding his authority and doing *an uncalled for and illegal act* — but I was not "declaiming to the crowd," as the Courier correspondent represents . . . I am confident that I did in no thing exceed what was my *sworn duty to do,* and if I acted promptly and zealously in the matter, and my client has not suffered thereby, I am content; and no one shall abuse me thereafter, either in a public or private manner.

As to the editorial which appeared in the Courier of Saturday last, I have no fears that any one will believe it to be a *true or candid* account of a personal altercation, of which the public at present knows and cares nothing, and of which I shall only say that after asking Mr. Robinson, the "Concord correspondent," to retract his offensive observations, and his refusal to do so, I wrung his nose.

Mr. Schouler then assaulted me and was repelled and shaken off, with some violence. He then attempted to put me out of the door of his office, but I repelled the attack and forced him again from me. After remaining a few minutes and seeing no disposition manifested to renew the attempt to repell me by force, I told Mr. Schouler where I was always to be found, and quietly walked out . . . Benjamin F. Butler, July 11, 1842.[5]

2

CROSS-EYED

THE sharp young lawyer who scoffed at newsmen lived in an unfashionable part of Lowell, Massachusetts. He lived in a boardinghouse for textile mill employees that was run by his mother.

He had been born in the frontier village of Deerfield, forty miles west of Portsmouth, New Hampshire. The day, November 5, 1818, as English-bred neighbors might have reminded the Butlers, was Guy Fawkes Day, and associated with political conspiracies since it was the anniversary of an abortive effort to blow up King James I and his Parliament. The Butler ancestors would scarcely have been caught weeping had Guy Fawkes succeeded in his attempt to blow up the Houses of Parliament, for they were Irish. Obscure Irish. In later years, when it became a fad to hunt up one's ancestors, Ben Butler was intrigued by the etymology of his name from "botler," bottle carrier or cup bearer. To Charles Neumeyer he wrote:

> I trace my family from the Ormonds of Ireland, whose family name was Butler, and whose ancestors, I suppose held the wine cup for some barefooted Irish king. And the traditional family crest was a covered wine cup with the motto "Comme je trouve." [1]

And to F. W. Butler:

> When Kings of Ireland drank claret, but hardly wore breeches, one of them had a butler, and whether he had any breeches I know not. He was accustomed to bring his master his stirrup cup. He was annoyed by having the flies and other vermin get into it, and so he carried it to his master covered. Now there was a tradition that any poison put into the drink would make it foam and boil up, and the drinker would be

warned by the appearance of the wine. Using a cover to his cup was denounced to the King as a contrivance by which he was to be poisoned, and on a given day he was informed that the stirrup cup would be brought to him covered, and not to drink the contents of the cup. Whereupon when the butler presented it the King charged him with the crime he was about to commit. The butler dashed off the cover of the cup and drank its contents to the dregs, saying "Comme je trouve" — as I find it. His safety proved his innocence, and the King knighted him, his crest to be the covered wine cup and his motto to be his claim to innocence, with the right that he and his descendants as butler to the King might always bring the wine to him in a covered cup.[2]

Nicholas Butler, six generations removed from Ben, immigrated to America in 1637 from Kent. Ben's grandfather Zephaniah Butler, born in Connecticut in 1728, fought at Quebec in the French and Indian War and at Bunker Hill in the Revolution. Zephaniah married Abigail Cilley, daughter of the Revolutionary General Joseph Cilley. Ben's father John Butler was born on May 17, 1782.[3]

Ben's father, twice married, had three children by each marriage. Ben was his youngest child. That the father, a small farmer from Nottingham, New Hampshire, was resourceful is indicated by the fact that he saw to it that William Graves, M.D., got through the snowdrifts of hilly Deerfield Parade in time to bring his youngest son Benjamin Franklin into the world.[4] That he was a hero worshiper is suggested by the names he gave his sons, Andrew Jackson and Benjamin Franklin Butler.

Upon the outbreak of war in 1812 Ben's father recruited from among his neighbors a company of light dragoons and was commissioned as captain on July 23, 1812. He fought on the Canadian frontier until invalided home with a broken leg, the improper setting of which retired him with a permanent limp. With the aid of friends he now fitted out a vessel as a privateer, and several times carried messages to General Jackson at New Orleans. After the war he continued the freebooter life under a letter of marque from Bolivar, although his commerce-raiding scarcely made him a living.

At home in Deerfield the forthright veteran of 1812 once took the lead in riding a fellow citizen out of town on a rail, a high-handed act which netted him a fine of $200 that he could ill afford to pay.[5]

Five months after Ben's birth, Captain John Butler died of yellow fever in the West Indian port of St. Kitts. The news was not received by his family for a long while after, and the precise date of his death was never learned — a situation which gave currency to a rumor that he had been hanged as a pirate.[6]

During the next nine lean years Ben's mother, Charlotte Ellison Butler, was compelled to rely upon her own toil and the good will of relatives. Her late husband's brother, William Butler, took Ben's older brother, Andrew Jackson, to live on his farm outside of Nottingham, and the widow with her daughter Charlotte and Ben divided her time between Ellison relatives in Deerfield and Butler relatives in Nottingham. Charlotte Ellison's father was an old-country believer in primogeniture who left his farm to his eldest son and cut off Charlotte with an inheritance of $1. The Widow Butler, healthy and able, hired out to work for neighbors, leaving Ben in the care either of his twelve-year-old half-sister Betsy Morrill or of a Mrs. Rundlett, with whom she sometimes boarded.[7] Charlotte Butler was a devout Baptist who impressed upon Ben her hope that he would become a preacher.

Ben was reading the Bible and *Robinson Crusoe* before he was old enough to enter Nottingham District School. Though his preferred interest was *Robinson Crusoe,* his mother required him to read a chapter of the Bible for every chapter of the fictional story she helped him with. Having a photographic memory he was soon able to recite the four Gospels, including, he once boasted, the "begats" in St. Matthew.[8]

At his paternal grandmother's in Nottingham Ben learned about Grandfather Zephaniah Butler's war experience at the siege of Louisburg and at Bunker Hill. A proud possession which Ben eventually acquired was Zephaniah's carved powder horn. The headstone on Grandfather Zephaniah's grave in Deerfield noted that he had died in 1800. Grandmother Abigail was as thin and straight as a sapling. Ben loved to bring his plate to her special table and hear her stories.[9]

By 1827, when Ben was nine, a Deerfield neighbor wrote to the President and Board of Trustees of Phillips Exeter: "At the request of Widow Charlotte Butler I have examined Benjamin Butler, her son, and find him to be a promising youth and forward scholar for his age, and his age is short of ten years. His talents bid fair for distinguished usefulness, could he be favored with the means of obtaining an education. I am informed that he is remarkably steady and his habits are of a studious turn of mind and of a fair moral character." [10] Awarded a scholarship, young Ben in the fall went to Exeter, where President Nathaniel Appleton Haven laid a hand on Ben's red head and admonished, "My boy, you can do anything that any man can do in this world if you will work." [11]

The nine-year-old scholarship student, directed toward the ministry and having "a fair moral character," shortly developed his father's disposition to fight. A schoolfellow at Phillips Exeter wrote that Ben was "a reckless, impetuous, headstrong boy, of remarkable precociousness and not particularly civil when his grain was crossed." He left his mark upon the skull of the school's chief wit for exercising his talent at Ben's expense; and got into all sorts of fights, "but having inherited some, aye, a good deal of the pluck of his father, who was a gallant officer in the War of 1812, always came off first best." [12]

Concerning Phillips Exeter, the most important thing Ben himself recalled in his autobiography was compulsory attendance at the Unitarian Church. "I was confused by the new doctrine of one God as opposed to the doctrine of the triune God, — Father, Son and Holy Ghost. I had been taught the latter, and I could not permit myself to have any doubts concerning it." [13]

In 1828 Ben's mother accepted a position as boardinghouse keeper in the thriving new industrial city of Lowell, Massachusetts, a situation which would enable her to unite her family under one roof. Consequently in January, at the close of his first term at Phillips Exeter, Ben set out for Lowell.

The slender ten-year-old boy in fox-skin cap drawn tight over his ears and linsey-woolsey jacket buttoned to his throat made the trip as companion to an elderly snuff-dipping countryman who was traveling to Lowell in a sleigh. Early rains had left bare patches on the road over which the sleigh's metal runners ground on granite pebbles. Leaving the old man, Ben ran ahead when they reached Dracut to look across the river at the city which was to be his home.

The long covered bridge spanned the Merrimack River over low piers that rose just above the rapids of the "fall." On a hill beyond the bridge stood Dr. Ayer's stone house, with its wide verandas, the finest home in Lowell. To the left lay a sprinkling of huts with mud walls and slab roofs — Shanty Town — where lived the families of immigrant Irish canal diggers. Next came the red brick, two-story boardinghouses, one of which his mother was to manage. Behind the boardinghouses ran a row of detached cottages, the "Johnny Bull's Row," assigned as homes to the blockprinters who had been imported from England as finishers of the new American-manufactured calico. Then in succession the brick buildings of the Lowell Machine Shop and the steeples of St. Anne's Episcopal Church and the First Baptist Church, where Ben and his family would worship, and whose minister would become one of Mrs. Butler's future boarders. On a bluff below the town stood the residence of Judge Livermore with its trimmed lawn, stately poplars and its view of the falls of the Merrimack, precisely the kind of place the ambitious youth would one day covet for his own.

Ben overtook the sleigh, which had mushed past him, and climbed in beside the old man as it crossed the bridge, to save paying a separate toll. His entry into the boom town with its population of 4000, Ben Butler recalled vividly in his oration on the fiftieth anniversary of the city,[14] but what impressed him more than water-power canals which were being blasted across the Chelmsford meadows or red, steeple-crowned factory buildings were the tricks of a magician in Carter's Tavern and his own successful struggle to eat his first oysters.

The typical textile company boardinghouse when the Butlers moved to Lowell lodged from twenty-four to thirty girls, with four girls in a room. Each morning the boarders were aroused in time to reach the mill at five o'clock, for a predawn warm-up of looms and spindles. At 7 A.M. and at noon all the factory bells in town would "ring out" and the girls would dash home for meals. At long tables in the common room on the ground floor, they ate flapjacks, plum cake and hash and coffee for breakfast, and the same with the addition of vegetables and hot meat dishes, for dinner and supper. Exactly half an hour after the bells had "rung out," they would "ring in," and the girls would scurry back to the mills. The girls, ranging in age from twelve to thirty, worked from twelve to fourteen hours a day. From the evening meal at seven until curfew at nine they were free to read, sew, write letters or go shopping on Merrimack Street. Mrs. Butler was expected to look to their morals and enforce the curfew.

Although by Lowell's statutes a man could still be jailed for being a common fiddler, commerce had so elbowed puritanism aside as to devote Lowell's principal street to ladies' hats, dresses and other fripperies. The city's steeple-topped factories reminded a French visitor of convents.[15] New England's less sophisticated poet John Greenleaf Whittier, who edited one of Lowell's seven newspapers, was pleased with "Acres of girls . . . fair unveiled Nuns of Industry, Sisters of Thrift . . . who shall sneer at your calling? Who shall count your vocation otherwise than ennobling?" [16]

President Andrew Jackson visited Lowell in 1833, when Ben was fifteen, to be welcomed by a parade of 2500 factory girls in white dresses and silk stockings and twirling gay silk parasols. Charles Dickens noted Lowell's fresh buildings of bright red brick and painted wood. The humanitarian novelist was delighted with working conditions in the factories and with living conditions in the boardinghouses. "The owners of the mills are particularly careful to allow no persons to enter upon the possession of these houses, whose characters have not undergone the most searching and thorough inquiry. Any complaint that is made against them, by the boarders, or by any one else, is fully investigated; and if good ground of complaint be shown to exist against them, they are removed, and their occupation is handed over to some more deserving person." [17]

Life in Lowell for the short, wiry, cross-eyed, and redheaded boy was seldom dull. There were chores at the boardinghouse. In fights with other boys on the commons Ben and his brother Andrew developed a lifelong understanding. They were together in the Lowell Public School under Joshua Merrill, who sat at a high pulpit behind his students and who flailed with a leather strap.

When Ben's teacher recommended that he be expelled, Ben appeared before the School Board determined to defend himself, but the young minister of St. Anne's Episcopal Church who was a member of the Board quietly took him to one side and reasoned him into apologizing to the teacher. From 1832 to 1834 Ben Butler attended the newly established Lowell High School, where his friends and classmates included George L. Balcom, E. A. Straw, and Gustavus V. Fox, who later became wealthiest man in Vermont, Governor of New Hampshire, and Assistant Secretary of the Navy in Lincoln's Government. Fox especially, whom Ben called Old Reynard, was a close friend. Their favorite sport was sailing on the Merrimack, which above the dam was as smooth as a millpond. Thomas M. Clark, the first principal of the Lowell High School, testified that whatever trouble Ben Butler may have given other teachers, "he never gave me the slightest . . . Benj. F. Butler was a boy who might be led, but could not be driven." [18]

The Reverend E. W. Freeman, pastor of the Free Will Baptist Church in Lowell, who boarded at Mrs. Butler's, was influential in sending Ben to the Baptist college at Waterville, Maine, where he could prepare for the ministry according to his mother's wish, and also work his way through school.

Waterville College stood on the west bank of the swift Kennebec River, its campus with three four-story brick buildings hemmed in between the town and the river. The central structure, containing chapel, administrative offices and classrooms, was flanked by North and South Dormitories. Young Butler's room during this first year was Number 18 in North Dormitory. Tuition, room rent, and the use of the library for a year cost him $31; repairs and incidentals $6; board $1.50 per week; firewood $2.50 per cord. [19] Ben worked four hours a day in the student shops, at woodworking, printing and painting for ten cents an hour.

One of Ben's essays during his first year denounced abolitionists for distributing incendiary publications throughout the South, "thus exciting the slaves to rebellion and the master to Desperation."

In the debating society Ben declaimed with irony on the inconsistencies of human nature. He was interested in alchemy, medicine, and history, and speculated at length on the different advantages of law, medicine, and the pulpit. [20]

In September of 1835, at the beginning of his second year, Ben rebelled against compulsory chapel attendance with its sermons by students. Yet whenever he cut chapel he had to pay a fine of ten cents or work an extra hour in the shop. He now decided against becoming a minister and asked his mother to apply to Congressman Isaac Hill of New Hampshire for an appointment to West Point.

In Ben's behalf William Graves, M.D., certified on January 22, 1836, "that I was present at the birth of Benjamin Butler, and that he is eighteen years of age. I am well acquainted with the young man. He is an excellent scholar, a young man of industrious habits and would make, in my opinion, an excellent scholar at West Point. His moral character is good and he is highly respected in the town — young Butler has a claim upon the charities of the government — His father served as Captain of a company of Dragoons during the last war with England and soon after its termination died — leaving a widow and several young children upon the mercies of their country — and if any young man deserves the assistance of friends to obtain him a place in the above named Seminary it is Benjamin Butler." [21] Dr. Theodore Edson of St. Anne's who had helped Ben out of his trouble in high school, wrote: "Mr. Benjamin F. Butler is a young gentleman of good moral character so far as I know and believe that during a residence of several years in this town he has been esteemed as a person of interesting and promising talents." [22]

Representative Hill, in whose district Ben was born, advised Mrs. Butler to apply to the representative from the Lowell District where she was now resident. But again the mother's application was turned down. The Honorable Caleb Cushing explained by letter that his appointment to the Military Academy had been committed to other nominees who had applied earlier.

The blow, a bitter one, left Ben with a sharp prejudice against West Pointers, and a fixed determination to get ahead despite his lack of money or political influence. For the moment it doomed him to remain two more years as a poor working student in a college whose theological atmosphere he despised.

Ben while in college also taught in a district school near Waterville. As the neighbors took turns giving him board he was shunted from

farm to farm. He disliked these shifts because he felt they deprived
him of the chance to develop close friendships. In December of 1836
he wrote:

> The weather is blue without, the fire burns blue within, and the blue
> devils are dancing gallapades [sic] through my brain, or rather in my
> scull [sic], for the brain would not be a very extensive place for their
> antics.
>
> I have been thinking of home, and all its joys in winter season, when
> the cold biting frost causes one to draw closer to the fire, and in the
> long winter when the nuts, apples, cidor [sic], and the social chat goes
> 'round.
>
> Then the living parties and merry "blind man's bluff," the Jovial skate
> and coast down hill under "the pale cold moon, the inconstant moon,
> which monthly changes in his circled orb." And for what am I to ex-
> change the privilege of being a pedagogue, of teaching "the young idea
> how to shoot" or in other words to institute erudition into one end of a
> thick sculled [sic] boy, by beating on the other.
>
> Can anyone blame me for being homesick under such circumstances?
> If he does, let him place himself in my situation, and use the Turkish
> phrase. Please God we shall see! B. F. Butler.[23]

At Waterville Ben Butler learned that he could trouble theology
students with agnostic arguments. If he were elected to be saved, he
would argue, chapel attendance would do him no good, except, perhaps, to make heaven somewhat more pleasant. "But where I was to
go could not be changed, yet I was to pray God's mercy wherever I
might be, that is I must ask that He, in His mercy for a single person,
would alter His divine laws made from the beginning and unalter-
able. It was my duty to make these useless trials and hear these teachings, the result of which might be to add to the miseries of the torment of the lake into which I was to be cast." [24]

At length Ben petitioned the faculty of the college to be relieved
from going to prayers and church. The faculty reprimanded him and
left his situation unchanged. Henceforth he skipped as many sermons
as he could afford to pay for and, to his chagrin, for he prided himself on his intellect, his academic grades declined with his chapel attendance. "What stronger principle is there," he wrote in a student

theme about this time, "than that of returning blow for blow, injury for injury and wrong for wrong?"[25] If he differed from the school authorities he was no less vehement in his insistence on an-eye-for-an-eye and a-tooth-for-a-tooth. He possessed, too, a talent for sarcasm which appeared in his paper on collegiate manners read before the Erosophian Adelphii Society at Waterville:

> I like to see the person carving help himself to the best piece in the dish. It shows that he wants pay for his trouble. I like to see a gentleman ask for a thing at the other part of the table in this manner: "Hallo! scull that sugar down this way." It shows that he was once a log driver . . . I like to see a student take a knife from the table to scrape the dirt off a seat and lay it back on his neighbor's plate . . . I like to see a man feel all the cakes in a plate to find which is the warmest; it shows that he is sure his hands are clean . . . I like to see a student instead of using the appropriate knife wipe his own on his tongue to cut the butter with . . . Lastly, I like to see a man pull the beam out of his own eyes before he tugs at his neighbors.[26]

3

JULIET

CLEARLY Ben Butler at Waterville was headed for politics and the law. Some Whig students aroused his Democratic ire by raising their campaign banners on the campus. Ben seized them and ran off down the riverbank. Eluding his pursuers by swimming the river, he buried the offensive emblems in the woods. Another time a prankster had hidden in Ben's room a signboard from a Waterville shop. When Ben learned that the professors were down the hall searching rooms, he threw the sign into the fireplace and taking advantage of a regulation that no one might disturb a student in his devotions recited a prayer until the board had burned up.[1]

Ben Butler's interest in law as a profession he owed to Lawyer Jeremiah Mason. In one of Mason's murder cases and in a suit to break a will, the college student's imagination was set afire by "the professional acumen, the varied learning, the great and commanding insight into men's motives, and the mastery of the minds of other men, shown by a lawyer in conducting a trial of a case before a jury where facts are to be elicited, fraud and falsehood foiled, conflicting testimony and discordant facts compared and put together, and a great result worked out." [2]

When the ice broke up in the middle of May 1838, Ben went for an early swim in the frigid Kennebec and caught a cold that hung on for weeks. When on August 8, 1838, he received his diploma, he weighed only ninety-seven pounds.[3]

His mother would not hear of his settling down immediately to study, but packed him off for a voyage on a Newfoundland codfishing boat. Exercise, the dry, frozen air of the northern latitudes, and a dipper of cod liver oil every few hours added twenty-five pounds to his weight and brought him back to Lowell fresh and eager to read law.

The office of William Smith, across the hall from the Lowell Savings Institution on Merrimack Street, became Ben Butler's retreat. Here, in return for clerical chores for a lawyer who practiced chiefly in Boston, Butler enjoyed the use of the most complete law library in Lowell. With an occasional direction from Lawyer Smith, Butler studied Blackstone, Kent's *Commentaries,* and Stephens on pleading. Through Blackstone his progress was slow since he undertook to read entire most of the cases cited. He read from half past seven o'clock in the morning until noon and from one till six, and after supper from seven to ten, about twelve and a half hours a day.[4]

On July 4, 1839, the law student made a modest debut in politics at a rally of Democrats at Groton, twenty miles west of Lowell. After listening to a patriotic oration delivered in the church, seven hundred persons, led by the Nashua Brass Band and a battery of cannon, marched down the main street to a banquet pavilion, where after meat and drink they delivered a hundred toasts. Along with Isaac Hill, Franklin Pierce, George Bancroft and ninety-six others, Ben Butler, a twenty-one-year-old law student, raised his wineglass and delivered the following toast.

"The forgetfulness of the Whigs in '36 and '38 — they plunged the people into the deepest distress, *forgetting* that they might discern political truth, as men from the bottom of a pit may see stars at noonday."[5]

His opposition to the well-to-do Whigs lined him up with the minority party in New England, known as "Loco Foco" Democrats. Young Butler and his fellows were described by the Lowell *Advertiser* as "the 'bone and sinew' part of the country . . . the 'huge paws,' the stout hearts, and the clear heads . . . always to be relied upon to protect the liberties and rights of freemen."[6]

By the fall of 1839 Butler, though earning small fees for handling Lawyer Smith's real estate eviction cases, was compelled to supplement these earnings by teaching for a term in Dracut, across the river from Lowell. A strict disciplinarian, he flogged and dismissed the rowdiest boys, but he more than recovered this loss in the number of new students that were attracted to his well-behaved school.

While teaching in Dracut he formed a close friendship with Fisher Ames Hildreth, an ambitious young man of Butler's own age interested in farming, real estate, newspaper publishing, and running for political office. Fisher Hildreth lent him a small gray saddle horse which Ben rode several nights a week, after he had finished his reading. Fisher also invited Ben to his house for Thanksgiving dinner, and introduced him to his talented sister Sarah Jones Hildreth.

Sarah Hildreth was a professional actress, rosy-cheeked, intelligent, graceful, though scarcely beautiful. A daguerreotype of 1839 shows a bold forehead, almond eyes set wide apart under heavy brows, a long pointed nose, surmounting a sensitive cupid's-bow mouth and small chin. Her dark hair, parted in the middle and pulled straight over the forehead, was fluffed up over the ears in puffs from which curls fell to bare shoulders. Her dress was an off-the-shoulder style.

Sarah was twenty-three, two years older than Ben, and had been on the stage since she was sixteen. As the oldest unmarried daughter of the household, she was hostess at the Thanksgiving dinner to which Fisher Hildreth invited him. Ben found her intelligent and witty, and was completely fascinated by her. Among Ben's earliest surviving mementos is a printed invitation and admission card which enabled him to escort Miss Hildreth to the cotillion party at Merrimack House on Sunday, November 28, 1839.[7] Dr. Israel Hildreth, her father, was a Fourth of July orator and public official as well as physician. He had set aside a large room in which his children could exercise their dramatic and forensic talents, and here Sarah as a child had sharpened her wits and polished her delivery in declamation and debate with her five sisters and one brother. As might be expected in a household where females so greatly outnumbered males a frequent topic was the equality of women. Sarah Hildreth believed that women as well as men had a right to public careers. She had studied dramatics under a Mrs. Vernon, an actress at Wallack's Theater in Boston, and had made her debut at the Park Theater in New York as Mariana in *The Wife,* and the same season at the Tremont in Boston she had played Mariana, Lady Teazle and other parts.

On Thursday, September 3, 1840, Ben Butler appeared for his bar examination before Judge Warren. After he had satisfactorily answered the Judge's questions, he proceeded respectfully, to differ with the Judge's decision in a case which he had audited earlier in the day. Judge Warren heard him through, and asked him to send him his references. Butler after midnight took the lawbook with the references marked to the Judge's hotel. Butler slept little that night and the next morning had the dual pleasure of hearing Judge Warren reverse his previous decision and pronounce the magic words which admitted him to the bar.[8]

Ben was twenty-two and Sarah twenty-four. For several years the Juliet of his dreams seemed unattainable. When she left for an extended engagement in Charleston, South Carolina, Ben accompanied her as far as Boston and was with her for several hours at the American House. She refused to quit the stage until he had won his spurs in the courtroom and could earn enough money to support both of them.[9] When he told her goodbye, he was completely confident of winning her, though Sarah still would make no promise.

To get ahead in his profession became Ben's driving ambition. He worked intensely, steadily, and with an energy as tireless as that of Lowell's waterwheels. He developed the mental habit of breaking down a situation into its basic elements and studying these elements both separately and in combination. He had many strings to his bow.

To get his name before the public, the one-time rebel against attending chapel in Waterville gave a formal lecture in Boston before the Young Men's Society for Diffusing Missionary Knowledge, upon the subject of Christian Missions. Missionary enterprise he considered in relation to secular interests, and, oddly indeed in a speech before a Protestant group, he extolled the work of Catholic as well as Protestant missions. He joined the Masonic Order, of which Sarah's father was a member; and when the Lowell City Guards was formed in 1840, he enlisted as a private. His friends twitted him for parading through dusty streets on hot summer afternoons, but he ignored their taunts. Infantry drills and horseback rides were his only diversions. As he galloped over the country roads at night he recalled snatches of poetry from Byron, Moore, Pope and Scott.[10] The romantic ideas of "Maid of Athens" and "She Walks in Beauty" often merged with his picture of a glamorous young actress from Dracut, who, perhaps, at the very moment of his riding around Lowell was in Philadelphia playing her favorite role from Shakespeare.

It is the east, and Juliet is the sun!

During his first year of law practice Congress passed a bankruptcy act. Butler perceived at once that a number of bankruptcy cases would arise, and that with industry he could be as well prepared as anyone to handle them. He therefore gave the new law painstaking and exhaustive study, devoting to it all the time he had and what he could rob from sleep, in order to prepare himself in this specialty.[11]

When two other lawyers advertised that they were the *only* lawyers prepared to handle bankruptcy cases, Butler inserted a paid notice in the *Daily Advertiser:*

> Benjamin F. Butler, Attorney of the U. S. Court for the Massachusetts District, will attend its sessions at hearings in bankruptcy, for the purpose of attending on either side to the cases of those who wish to avail themselves of the provisions of this law. He is induced to publish this notice, to correct the report that only two in this city can practice under this law.[12]

Butler's bid for business brought him two of the earliest cases in this line which were tried before Judge Story in the Circuit Court in the District of Massachusetts and before Judge Harvey in the Circuit Court of New Hampshire. He won both cases.

Police court cases fell to him by the hundred. He became a specialist in criminal pleading and adhered to its rules with strictness. In the interest of his client he took advantage of slovenly practices of rival lawyers, allowing no backtracking, no amendment of the charge, no rephrasing of the indictment.

An instance of Ben Butler's sharp practice in an early case is his defense of Peter Moore, indicted for adultery with Mary Stuart, a married woman having a husband living. When Moore was called on to plead guilty or not guilty, Lawyer Butler raised a technical objection that in the draft of the indictment no offense had been stated against his client because the indictment had failed to allege "that Mary Stuart was not Moore's wife." The prosecutor explained to the Court that in a long practice he had never before heard this objection raised. Butler replied that this was a technical question of pleading, and that the length of time the fault had existed did not make it right. The Judge ruled against Butler's sharp point, saying that he "preferred to err with the ancients." [13] Butler carried the case in a writ of error to the Supreme Court of the state, where the lower court's decision was reversed in his favor.

A burglar caught in the act of stealing a key from a lock, Butler successfully defended by contending that the act was not larceny, since legally a key is an integral part of real estate and taking real estate is not larceny. The burglar went free and the legislature at its next session passed an act specifying that "the severing of portions of real estate" with a felonious intent did constitute larceny. [14]

In Butler's philosophy an expert witness for the opposition was fair game to be demolished in cross-examination. In one of his earliest homicide cases the defendant, Butler's client, was charged with striking the victim on the temple with a stone, which, according to the theory of the district attorney, had caused death. Butler, after studying the physiology of the head, confronted the prosecutor's expert medical witness with a barrage of questions about the temporal artery and having got him twisted up on "the emergence of the artery through the skull," Lawyer Butler produced a skull from his green bag. [15] There being no such opening as the doctor had described, he was, of course, unable to find it. Butler dismissed the witness and possibly saved his client's life on the technicality.

Lawyers whose professional laxness Ben Butler exposed in court and trial judges whose rulings were reversed by the Supreme Court were understandably provoked or angered by the young lawyer's sharpness. These professionally trained men could understand the technical legal issues that Butler raised. Not so the general public. Laymen, particularly literate laymen in the newspaper profession, were more likely than not to label the legal technicality as more or less absurd and the lawyer who would resort to such strained interpretations as a social nuisance, a blackguard, or a scamp and a disorganizer.

After Butler's altercation with Reporter Robinson in the *Courier* office in July of 1842, even Fisher Hildreth reproved his friend Ben Butler with a squib in the *Advertiser:*

> Somebody says "never bite your neighbor's nose off: Noses are not good to eat; besides a nose is of very little use to anyone but the owner." To which we will add, never *pull* your neighbor's nose, especially an editor's; if you do he will *blow* you in his paper.[16]

In Lowell, and throughout Middlesex County, Ben Butler's name became a household word. The zeal and vigor with which he fought his courtroom battles, together with his high percentage of favorable verdicts, brought many new cases to his docket, and with them financial independence.

In the spring of 1843 Ben Butler, considering that he had won his spurs, made a trip to Cincinnati hoping to bring Sarah Hildreth back with him. Sarah was now the leading actress at the National Theater, and was playing the title role in Thomas Noon Talfourd's play *Ion*.[17] Fragmentary and enigmatic reminiscences, scattered through their correspondence in later life, suggest that there were tense scenes between the lovers. Sarah's references to "a wild romance in which I had shared"[18] and to her other self struggling and striving, torn by conflicting passions, frantic with emotion, and Ben's reference to Sarah as a fresh-cheeked rosy girl with flowing curls,[19] and his allusion to the parting scene in Boston — "Do you remember that the first time I ever spent any considerable hours with you was at the American House Boston just previous to your voyage to Charleston? It has occurred to my thoughts more than once. I felt sad at parting from you but I thought then I should see you again although you thought not so"[20] — all would seem to indicate that Ben was the pursuer in the courtship. His emotional dependence upon her is recalled by Sarah in August of 1861: "I feel, I know, that you will never fathom all the deep emotion, the yearning sympathy that holds me to you. Besides the fond devotion of a wife, there is still the same responsibility felt by me for whatever you may do, as there was years ago when you laid your head on my lap, and prayed me to look kindly and lovingly into your face. I saw then what I have since seen in Paul, but not in the other children, peculiarities easily wrought upon, and dangerous from their very simplicity . . ." [21]

Sarah's refusal in the spring of 1843 to break off her engagements at Cincinnati's National Theater in favor of an immediate marriage severely wounded the successful young lawyer's pride. Thirteen years later when Butler had returned to Cincinnati on a political mission, the old memories welled up and he wrote Sarah: "As we were passing up the street in Cincinnati I saw a well remembered house and it called up a cloud of sweet memories till they were dashed by a shade of bitter thought of one who refused to leave it and come home with me and staid for what purpose? Ah! The man of thirteen years since but the heart of a boy was not fairly treated in that transaction. He never should have been sent to a solitary ride home; for had he had the heart and pride of a man he never again would have seen the one who caused that lonely journey!" [22]

They were married a year later on May 16, 1844, in Lowell's fashionable St. Anne's Episcopal Church, by the Reverend Theodore Edson. Though neither Ben nor Sarah was a church member, they had the highest respect for the liberal-minded Dr. Edson, whose wise counsel had once saved Ben from being expelled from school.

4

RADICAL REFORM

BUTLER had promised to allow Sarah Hildreth to return to the footlights after a year if she so desired. But by that time Sarah was safely immured in their home on Central Street.

A son Paul, namesake of Ben Butler's friend Paul R. George, arrived in June of 1845. A daughter, Blanche, followed two years later. Little Paul died before he was five and his name was given to a second boy. A third son, Ben-Israel, was named after both his father and his maternal grandfather. The second Paul fell down a feed chute in the barn, and his legs, crippled in this accident, failed to develop to normal size; yet despite his handicap he grew up a cheerful youngster with a fondness for swimming and boating. Ben-Israel with his straight body and tractable mind was early marked to fulfill the West Point ambition denied to his father.

As his law practice expanded, Ben Butler invested in real estate and Banker James G. Carney, across the hall from Butler's office, became the first of several lifelong friends who were his financial agents. W. P. Webster, one of Sarah's brothers-in-law, was another. Fisher, Sarah's brother, became Butler's chief partner.

One of the properties which Butler and Hildreth purchased was the building once occupied by the First Free Will Baptist Church. This structure was located on the most prominent spot in town, on Merrimack Street opposite Central. Its new owners remodeled it in 1846 as an officebuilding and theater. Butler set up his own office in Room No. 4, and Fisher Hildreth moved his newspaper, the *Daily Advertiser,* into the building. As Lowell had never possessed a theater, Butler had to fight for a license to present dramatic exhibitions. He won this battle at the City Hall. Some former members of the congregation, however, were scandalized by the new use made of the old auditorium, and it was easy for them to air their complaints in print. Newsmen like Robinson and Schouler of the nose-pulling episode were now using Ben Butler as a whipping boy, a form of amusement to which Butler himself had grown tolerant or callous. What exactly were Butler's motives for setting up his theater which conservative church members considered wicked? Was he antagonistic toward the church he had attended as a youth? Did he establish the theater to vindicate Sarah? The correspondence and records which Ben kept in his law office in the former church building have been destroyed. The edifice, under an evil star, had three fires in ten years. The last completely destroyed it. Ben Butler's law library was badly damaged, and the bulk of his private correspondence prior to 1856 was thus lost.

In the 1840's the city of spindles was no longer a paradise for New England country girls. Gone was the familiar sight of farm wagons bringing to Lowell recruits for the mills. New hands arrived by train and were mainly from famine-stricken Ireland. In the boardinghouses, where single rooms were now crowded to accomodate entire families, the strict moral supervision of early days declined. Mrs. Charlotte Butler by 1846 had given up her boardinghouse and returned to a farm at South Deerfield. Many Irish lived in mud-walled shanties on a crowded common known as "The Acre," and kept alive the feuds that agitated their homeland. During the fights between Corkonians and Far Downer Irish, Ben Butler was called out with the Lowell militia to restore peace. He was also hired by the city to prosecute the riot leaders. His sympathy went out to them. He boasted of his own Irish descent, and was quick to resent a disparaging remark about his Irish blood.[1]

Butler handled many cases for Irish clients and was not always able to obtain justice for them. Patrick Gillshannon, an Irish laborer hired as a trackworker, was injured while riding to work when the railroad's gravel train ran into a handcar. The court held that Gillshannon while proceeding to work was not in the employ of the railroad, had not paid for his ride, and refused to award him damages. Butler appealed, but the Supreme Court upheld the lower court.

With a growing sense that for many of the inequalities brought about by the Machine Age some political solution would have to be sought, Lawyer Butler in 1844 entered politics. With Fisher Hildreth's backing, he was chosen as a delegate to the Democratic National Convention in Baltimore that nominated Polk. His first political speech was at the Lowell City Hall on Monday, September 2, 1844, when he spoke for Polk against the Whig candidate Henry Clay. Hildreth's *Advertiser* reported the occasion:

> B. F. Butler, Esq., being loudly called for from all parts of the hall, came forward, and was greeted with a hearty round by the dense mass present. His speech was replete with all the cutting irony, wit and sarcasm, for which he is . . . conspicuous, interlarded with frequent bursts of real eloquence. He went into a scathing review of the presidential candidates of the coons; putting the "knife to the hilt" into all his old personal sores . . . His speech was, throughout, bold, effective and eloquent, and was loudly applauded.[2]

After Polk's victory Butler celebrated with a trip to Washington, where, mingling business with politics, he obtained admittance to practice before the Supreme Court of the United States.[3]

Throughout the 1840's Ben Butler won fame as a hard-scrapping lawyer, with a specialty in criminal law. The sensational nature of his cases kept his name in the press. Editors assigned special reporters to cover his trials. So crowded was his docket that he formed partnerships with other lawyers in Lowell: A. W. Parr, B. F. Dean, and W. P. Webster; and he acquired an office in Boston as junior partner of J. G. Abbott. His partner Webster was the husband of Sarah's sister Susan.

In the trial of Daniel H. Pearson for the fatal stabbing of his wife and twin daughters, Butler set up what at that time was a novel defense: a plea of insanity.[4] When the jury convicted his client, Butler took the case before the Governor and Council at the State House and at the same time applied to the Supreme Court for a writ of error. Butler's efforts failed and Pearson became his first client in years to be hanged.

The courtrooms of Middlesex County saw many a scuffle between counsel. The lawyers in the Wentworth-Parker case, when Butler defended a confessed murderer, had frequent and bitter wrangles, "all of which is quite interesting to the two thousand spectators who are always present." [5] During the trial the Lowell *Advertiser* and the Boston *Bee* took opposite sides and flayed one another for trying to create prejudice against prisoners, witnesses and counsel.

The Lowell Police Court was a hodgepodge of magistrate's court, grand jury, and criminal court combined. In one of Butler's cases in this court the hearings ran from January to March. The lawyers, reported the *Advertiser,* competed with each other in harassing witnesses and carried their quarrel into the *Vox Populi* and the *Morning Star* of Lowell, "day after day and week after week . . . garbling . . . misrepresenting testimony." [6]

Lawyer Butler, who was fighting for reform of the Police Court and disliked its presiding officer, Justice Nathan Crosby, overstepped his bounds on September 7, 1847. Crosby jailed Butler for contempt of court, in "threatening violence to the person of said Justice — by using menacing gestures and insulting attitudes toward said justice in his presence and view." [7]

After a week in jail, the chastened lawyer appeared under a writ of habeas corpus before Chief Justice Lemuel Shaw in the Supreme Court in Cambridge, and explained that he had not used the word "damn," or intended any disrespect to Judge Crosby. If, in the heat of defending his client, he had used any improper expression, he regretted it.[8]

From defending millworkers in court it was but a step to pleading for them in the City Hall. During the November campaign in 1848, Ben Butler denounced a contemplated reduction of wages of the mill operatives. In a two-hour speech before a literally jammed City Hall Butler argued that the millworkers had always received too small a share of the profits.[9] Over and above the declared dividends, ranging from 8 to 30 per cent, the corporations had had surplus funds with which to build new mills, improve old ones, purchase real estate, dig new canals. During prosperous years, the workers' pay scale had ranged from 50 cents to $2.25 per day. "Is it quite charitable . . . to cut down the wages of the operators and make them bear the evils of hard times when they are not allowed to share the blessings of the more prosperous seasons?" [10]

Butler appealed to the factory workers of Lowell to seek a remedy for their troubles in the ballot. Girls who had homes in the country he advised to go back to them, and "strive to remove the false impression (created by corporation emissaries to lure young men and women from their homes) that Lowell is an Eden; tell them to cling to their own green, native hills, if they would possess health, wealth and happiness; they are not to be found here. Let the power which legislation has given and continues to give to corporate bodies, be diminished. They are bound together in a common selfish interest, and under the sanction of the law, conspire to oppress and reduce the price of labor." [11]

Butler's audience gave him cheer after cheer. He had struck the keynote for a determined minority of reform Democrats.

Four days later, with the tenacity of his courtroom practice, he followed through with another two-hour flagellation of the textile mill owners. "If it is necessary to reduce wages, why not let the reduction fall upon the high salaries of agents and treasurers?" He urged the masses to unite "for thorough, radical reform." [12]

The corporations denounced Butler's tactics as: "A part of a game now playing by self-chosen champions of the operatives in our mills, to excite prejudices against the owners of these establishments. It is a species of wickedness, unpardonable and cruel, which deserves the strongest terms of denunciation." [13]

There being no secret ballot at the time, Butler lost to the corporations this battle over lowering wages. He now added the secret ballot to his list of radical reforms that he considered worth fighting for. Once the worker got the power to vote without being watched over by his employer, he might at the polls win other reforms.

5

TEN-HOUR DAY

EVERYWHERE Ben Butler saw opportunities for reform from procedures in the police court to currency and banking, and shorter hours for labor. But the subject nearest his reformer's heart was the ten-hour day for factory workers. The Lowell textile mills still operated on their original schedule of fourteen hours per day, with which they had started in the 1820's. At that time corporation managers had defended these long hours with the argument that Lowell's new waterpower project was experimental and expensive and no one knew whether it would work out financially. In 1850 Butler was told that similar mills in Rhode Island, Connecticut and New Hampshire worked fourteen hours and that their competition forced the Lowell corporations to hold to the same schedule. Butler used his father-in-law Dr. Hildreth's argument that such hours, month after month and year after year, eventually undermined the health of the factory worker. To this the corporation people replied that their operatives were free to leave whenever they chose. "But their needs force them to work here." "Yes, and one duty is to give the people as cheap calico as can be made." [1]

As leader of the ten-hour movement Butler lobbied in the state legislature and made speeches over the state. The legislature, however, was controlled by Whigs, who, Butler charged, were ruled by the Boston bankers who owned the Lowell Mills. Not without eloquence Butler described Lowell, the second largest city in the state, as "the beehive of Boston, to labor for her, and when the honey which we had gathered had been appropriated by Boston, it was of very little consequence whether the bees were smoked out or not." [2]

Butler's first move was to get a ten-hour plank written into the state platforms of both minority parties — the Democrats and the Free Soilers. Then he engineered a coalition of Democrats and Free Soilers to wrest control of the state from the majority-party Whigs. The agreement he arranged with the minority groups was that in counties where the two of them together held a majority they would both nominate a single "Coalition" candidate, and where the Whigs held a majority they would, by nominating separate candidates attempt to disrupt the Whig majority. If this strategy succeeded, the Democrats would get the governorship, state reform being their chief objective; and the Free Soilers, interested primarily in a national policy of limiting slavery, should have the United States Senator.

The program of reform proposed by the Coalitionists included the ten-hour day, the secret ballot, popular election of judges, a homestead exemption law, redistribution of seats in the House of Representatives, a lien law benefiting laborers and mechanics, and reduction of the poll tax.[3]

Catching the Whigs completely off guard in November 1850, the Coalitionists won the election. Democrat George S. Boutwell was seated in the Governor's chair and Freesoiler Charles Sumner was sent to the United States Senate. In the state legislature the election netted 21 Coalition State Senators against 11 Whig, and 220 Coalitionist State Representatives against 176 Whig.

In the legislative session of 1851 the Coalitionists achieved several of their objectives. A Homestead Act reserved to a bankrupt an undisturbed interest in a homestead to the value of about $500. A Secret Ballot Law was passed. Hitherto, with each voter having to voice his preference publicly, corporations could monitor their employees at the polls. The first Secret Ballot Law was an effort to eliminate their surveillance.

In practice, however, the procedure under Massachusetts' first secret ballot law did not actually conceal a workingman's vote. There were in 1851 no ballots, uniform in size, printed and distributed by the government. The secret ballot law, by its failure to provide blank forms for ballots, left to each party the printing of its own ballot sheets.

The Whigs, accordingly, made their ballot sheets extra large, so that when folded and squeezed into the half-inch square hole in the top of the ballot box they could easily be spotted by watchers from the corporations.

In November of 1851 when it appeared that Lowell's ten delegates might wield the balance of power in the House of Representatives, Ben Butler managed to get all ten of the Coalitionist candidates in Lowell committed to the passage of ten-hour legislation. "Working-men, be not deceived!" he warned; "The party that carried through the Secret Ballot, will carry the 'Ten Hour System.' " [4] Whigs and Coalitionists alike entered the battle with no holds barred.

Nine of Lowell's ten Coalitionist candidates were elected, and these, according to the usual procedure, were certified to the Mayor and Aldermen by election officials in the various wards; and the Mayor and Aldermen in turn were obligated to certify them to the legislature. An election clerk in Ward 4, however, made an obvious error in certifying a total of 8000 in place of 800 votes. Angered over the election of the Coalitionists, the Whig Mayor and Aldermen, about half of whom were overseers for corporations, used the ward clerk's mistake as an excuse to declare the Lowell election void, and ordered a special election.

From the platform in the City Hall Ben Butler denounced these "wicked" proceedings. When Lowell's Whig paper, the *Daily Courier and Journal,* named Butler "a demagogue, hypocrite, tyrant and liar," [5] Butler struck back in kind at the paper's publisher, John H. Warland. Certain blemishes on the latter's face were attributed to Warland's "illicit dalliances with the fair, frail, black-eyed Creoles whom he had met while with Gen. Scott in Mexico." [6]

During the campaign before the special election, Butler discovered that the Mayor and Aldermen had padded the rolls of qualified voters with over a hundred new names. Butler confronted them with evidence and forced them to correct the list.

A week before the election a placard on its front gate notified workers of the Hamilton Corporation that anyone who voted "the Butler ticket" on the following Monday would be discharged.

In a handbill Butler summoned workingmen to a mass meeting on Saturday before the election, to flay the corporations for their declared policy not to employ men who voted the ten-hour ticket.[7] At the meeting Butler squeezed up a crowded stair into a hall filled almost to suffocation. With a loud shout the crowd picked him up and rolled him over their heads to the speaker's stand.

Speaking of the corporation notice that voters for the ten-hour ticket would be discharged, Butler declared that they had got the cloven foot out, and should take care and keep it out. He pledged the workingmen of Lowell that, should such a thing be done, the corporations' charters would be taken away. Butler depicted in lurid colors the "base attempt at fraud" on the part of the Mayor and Aldermen of Lowell, and told how he had compelled them to expunge the bogus names from the list of voters. This announcement "brought forth stunning cheers for Butler, and demonstrations of indignation against those functionaries who had thus attempted such foul injustice upon the free people of Lowell." [8]

Until near the close of his speech Butler spoke in conversational tone.

> I know the power of these corporations, I know many of the men who have been in charge. They have made a mistake in the appeal to force. When that weapon is tried, they are weak and you are strong. They have their mills and machinery, their bricks and their mortar, and that is the extent of their power.[9]

The speaker's high-pitched voice now rang out:

> As God lives and I live, by the living Jehovah, if one man is driven from his employment by these men because of his vote, I will lead you to make Lowell what it was twenty-five years ago, a sheep-pasture and a fishing place; and I will commence by applying the torch to my own house. Let them come on.[10]

The Whig *Daily Courier and Journal* branded Ben Butler as a demagogue "willing to see the city sunk in ruins."

This notorious demagogue and political scoundrel, having swallowed three or four extra glasses of liquor, spread himself at whole length in the City Hall last night. Nature herself has set her seal upon him by giving him a face like a wrecker's light, warns all whom it may concern, to be on the lookout while in its vicinity. A man is not to be ridiculed merely for being homely — but when his homeliness is a faithful exponent of the ugliness of his heart, the matter may with propriety be alluded to. In the present instance the uncouth figure of the demagogue as he swung about, is said to have borne a striking resemblance to that of a Bornese ape, with a speech very like the chatterings of that hairy and feeble imitation of humanity. It pleases the Almighty occasionally to send such monstrosities into the world for some good purpose though the design may not at the moment be clear to our limited comprehension.[11]

This alone Ben Butler might have accepted as campaign abuse, but elsewhere in the same paper occurred for the first time in print the back-country, hearsay libel on his father, Captain John Butler, couched in the form of an epitaph of himself:

Here lies Ben Butler at last you see his miserable carcass just brought to a stand, — the father was hung as a pirate at sea, — and the son as a pirate on land.[12]

Infuriated by this smirch on his father, Butler brought suits for libel against Editor Samuel J. Varney and Publisher John H. Warland. Butler's law partner A. W. Farr, acting as District Attorney, prosecuted the cases and Judge Ebenezer Rockwood Hoar, a Whig lawyer with whom Butler had been repeatedly associated in Middlesex courtrooms both as friendly and as opposing counsel, sat as judge in the Court of Common Pleas in Cambridge. Varney was indicted on two counts: (1) The libel charged Butler "with being a notorious demagogue and a political scoundrel, with drinking three or four extra glasses of liquor, with resembling a Bornese ape, and also the publication of an epitaph, alluding to Butler's father having been hung as a pirate at sea, etc." (2) "The libel charged Butler with the design of depreciating the stock of the corporations at Lowell — that to do this he was willing to see the city sunk in ruins." [13]

The defense lawyers tried to put on the stand one Eben G. Knowlton of Manchester, New Hampshire, to testify to "a report for thirty years in the town in which Captain Butler's family resided, that he was executed for piracy, and this report had been uncontradicted during that time," but Knowlton's testimony was ruled out by the court. In a charge to the jury lasting an hour and a half Judge Hoar reminded them "that we live in a peculiarly excitable political community." [14] Varney was convicted on the first count only, and fined $50. Warland, tried later on the same charges, escaped through a legal technicality for which Butler held Judge Hoar responsible. Thus began a famous Massachusetts feud which was to outlast the two principals, and to discolor the memory of Butler for years after his death.

After his libel suits Ben Butler flourished in the role of castigator of "the hireling press," and several Boston papers pitched into him. In Washington, D.C., politicians lifted an eyebrow at the doings of Butler's Coalitionists in Massachusetts, and in the New York *Day Book,* a smart sheet sponsored by Horace Greeley, there appeared a full-length portrait of Benjamin F. Butler of Lowell:

> Benjamin was the champion of the working classes, and when they had grievances wanting redress he was their man . . . At his bidding . . . he could stop nearly every spindle in that city, and in a few hours time could have near ten thousand of both sexes marching through the streets, having caused them to strike for higher wages, or for wrongs to be righted. He usually made the corporations do justice. He was detested and feared by one party, and admired and respected for his boldness by the other and greater party.[15]

A specialist in "politics which dealt with the condition and welfare of the citizen," he perceived that the basic conflict of interest between capital and labor would have to be fought out in the political arena. The Democratic Party's interest he identified with the interest of the working classes, and the Whig Party's with corporation interests. The tug of war between capital and labor, he believed, constituted the basis for the two parties — "for labor wants all it can get, capital wants all it can get, each takes all it can." [16]

The author of the article in the New York *Day Book* credited Butler in 1852 with ability to grow as a human being, to get the rough corners rubbed off: "He has . . . a hundred times the discretion when he first set out." [17] But the *Vox Populi* of Lowell lectured Butler for his want of adroitness: "Every politician who has attained to any eminence in his profession and become at all hacknied in the rough experiences to which his calling subjects him, becomes perfectly impervious to the jibes, slanders, insinuations and innuendoes of his antagonist. He is as callous as the hide of an alligator. If he is not so, he has not learned the rudiments of his profession. He should be put to school a little longer. We allude to the libel suits which have been recently tried at Cambridge. We are decidedly of the opinion that it was ill-judged in Mr. Butler bringing matters which had arisen out of the November election in this city, into a criminal court. He is himself proverbially a hard hitter. He is just the sort of man, therefore, to bear a blow with philosophy. But unfortunately hard hitters very seldom do bear blows with philosophy." [18]

In September 1852 Ben Butler was elected president of the Granite Club at a Democratic meeting in Market Hall. The word "granite" indicated that this club was politically too hard to be intimidated by corporations. Nominated for state Representative, he staged a whirlwind campaign, speaking five nights a week as far away as Norwich, Connecticut, and Portsmouth, New Hampshire. He spent his energies backing the presidential candidacy of his fellow lawyer and friend Franklin Pierce, with the result that his own cause suffered. In the campaign the Lowell City Guards, wearing bearskin caps with red pompons, paraded, staged a military ball, and in a jamboree at American House elected Lieutenant Colonel Benjamin F. Butler to be full Colonel of the Fifth Regiment of Massachusetts Volunteer Militia.

In this election campaign Linus Child, agent of the Boott Mills, again threatened to discharge men who voted Butler's ten-hour or Democratic ticket. On the eve of the election the Whig Party proposed to give the voters the right kind of ten-hour law, a law that would "prohibit corporations from employing any person in laboring more than ten hours a day, except in cases of necessity or charity," and to ensnare voters they printed across the top of their ballot Butler's own label: "Ten Hour Men." [19]

John Van Buren, son of President Van Buren, under whom the ten-hour system had been adopted for federal employees, was imported from New York as a speaker for the Democrats. Van Buren, Butler, and J. G. Abbott spoke on the Saturday before election at Lowell's Northern Depot, a meeting place that could accommodate twice the number that any hall would hold. The applause was deafening. Three cheers were given for Ben Butler, and three for the nominees on the national ticket.[20]

In the regular election six out of ten Democratic ten-hour candidates were chosen. Four of the most prominent leaders, including Butler, went down temporarily before the forces of "Whiggery, Rum, Rum and Whiggery," but the redoubtable Ben Butler ran again in a special run-off election and this time he *won*.

In the State House in Boston the Gentleman from Lowell was watched like a firebrand in a powder magazine. William S. Robinson, the reporter whose nose Butler had pulled, was also a representative. William Schouler, in whose office the nose-pulling incident had occurred, was Clerk of the House.

Unable to make any progress toward the ten-hour legislation, the Coalition faction now being in a minority, Representative Butler threw himself into other causes. He opposed a prohibition act which would have deprived the common man of his cider. He sponsored an act to indemnify the Ursuline Convent for the destruction of its buildings by mob action nineteen years before. His lecturing was hardly calculated to endear him to Proper Bostonians. Nor were the financiers of Beacon Street better pleased by his exposure of illicit transactions by the officials of the Cochituate Bank of Boston.

In his fight against repeal of the Secret Ballot Law, Butler resorted to a filibuster which invested him, in the eyes of certain of his foes, with an aura of wickedness.

On Saturday, the Whigs decided to endure the filibuster no longer, and acting under a ruling of Speaker Bliss, they repealed the Secret Ballot Law. Butler was furious. He charged Mr. Bliss with being drunk, and he was alleged to have muttered against the Speaker — in the hearing of the assistant clerk — "Wish to God I could knife that old cuss." [21] On September 21, 1853, when the corporations themselves voluntarily reduced the number of working hours from fourteen to eleven, the compromise victory belonged to the Lowell politician, who had done so much to stir the question up.

6

POLITICAL GENERAL

BUTLER's showmanship in the courtroom and high percentage of favorable verdicts won him in the 1850's the largest criminal practice in New England. Indeed his total practice on the eve of the Civil War was estimated to be equal to that of any other four lawyers in the state. A general practitioner, he enjoyed plunging into all types of cases. The case of the SS *Storm King* carried him into admiralty law. The owners of the China Clipper *Storm King* were sued because the vessel's skipper had been so intent upon winning a race that he had neglected to supply proper food for his crew. At the end of the voyage the crew, debilitated by scurvy, had to be hoisted out of the ship in blankets. Butler represented the crewmen in a trial that lasted nineteen days. In the courtroom he exhibited a large map of the world, and read from the log of the ship, as he did so marking on the map the ship's course, showing that on four occasions, while the crew were "rotting with the scurvy," the ship was passing within a few hours' sail of islands renowned for abundant and cheap vegetables. Each night after the court session he rummaged libraries, ferreted out old sailors, and went into court every morning carrying in his green bag a mass of new material, and followed by a train of doctors and seamen to support a position shaken the day before.[1] In the course of the trial he had on the witness stand nearly every eminent physician, sea captain and shipowner in Boston. He won the verdict.

In December of 1852 President-elect Pierce with his wife and ten-year-old son were in a train wreck a few miles outside of Andover, Massachusetts. An axle broke under their car and it rolled down an embankment. Neither Pierce nor his wife was injured, but their son who had been standing at a window was killed. The Pierces did not sue for damages, since the head of the Maine Railroad Company was a personal friend, but the company was sued by another of the injured parties, and President Pierce persuaded Butler to defend the railroad as a favor to his friend. Butler made a personal study of their machining methods in the railroad's shops and won the case.

In 1858 Butler purchased a controlling interest in the Middlesex Corporation, Lowell's first woolen mill, and as part of the deal he also bought the handsome, newly built residence of the Middlesex Corporation's agent Samuel Lawrence. The mansion, located on Andover Street in the fashionable Belvidere suburb, was valued at $50,000.

The Middlesex Corporation, owing to heavy financial losses, due, Butler believed, to "the mistakes and irregularities" of its agents, was reorganized. Butler gave Richard S. Fay, Jr., son of his banker in Boston, the post of treasurer. Under the new management the profits of the firm soared. On the eve of the Civil War the company was operating three mills, with 16,640 spindles and 772 employees. As an employer Butler put into effect a ten-hour rule, but during rush seasons gave extra pay for overtime, leaving the employee to decide whether he should work beyond the normal day.[2] As a businessman Butler was content to get a project started, but he left active management to his associates, Hildreth, Fay and Carney.

At home he awoke at 6 A.M. in his rose-tinted bedroom whose frescoed walls were hung with paintings. There was usually a fresh breeze from the river blowing in the open window. From down the hall came voices of children just getting up. Although he had not gone to bed until after midnight, after Sarah had several times called to him to put out the light, he rose promptly. From the large bay window on the west side of his bedroom he looked up the Merrimack to the tumbling white-crested falls. The north-side windows overlooked his lawn and the wooded hill on the Dracut side of the river. He had a "Russian" bath installed in a corner of his bedroom, and his house was heated by steam to sixty-five degrees in the coldest weather.

Briefly he would greet the children. Blanche, his favorite, would soon be off to boarding school. A rosy-cheeked but retiring child, she needed to get away from home, and meet girls of her age from other parts of the country. There was a minute for a brief romp with Paul and Ben-Israel.[3] Then breakfast with Sarah — a breakfast of fish, beans, pie, buckwheat cakes. And afterwards, she would send him off with a flower in his lapel. His man Charles would drive him to the office or, if he were bound to Boston, to the station. He enjoyed seeing how fast he could get there and it gave him keenest pleasure to step onto a moving train just after he had purchased his paper. Catching the seven o'clock train, he would arrive in Boston at eight, put in a full day in court or in his office at 20 State Street and be back in Lowell by 7 P.M. An hour for supper, then two or three hours in his office on Merrimack Street. After this he would return home, again to pore over books and papers until midnight, when Sarah once more would call Ben to turn off the gaslight and come to bed.

In his rough-and-tumble world of law and politics, Sarah (or Sally or "My dear little Heigh-Ho!") was a being apart. She was his idol. Away from home on their eleventh anniversary, he sent her a book filled with pictures of beautiful women, and from the accompanying letter Sarah cut out and pasted on its flyleaf Ben's pleasant compliment: "No features limned within the book by the burin of the engraver appear to me half so beautiful as those which for eleven years shed so much light and joy into my life."[4] But Sarah, who had originally inspired him to push on to win his spurs in his profession, could not induce him now to slow down. On rare occasions he would take the family to the seashore, but would never remain there with them for more than two or three days. Once in a while he would go yachting with political friends. On the eve of the Civil War, after seventeen years of married life Sarah Butler felt that her busy husband never had any time to devote to his family. She begged him not to give all his time to work, even Sundays; not to feel irritated when interrupted in his work.[5] She wanted him to take time for little trips with the children, or by themselves, but as he grew older his original drive and ambition, which Sarah herself had awakened, showed no sign of lessening.

In 1855 when the "Know Nothing" governor, Henry J. Gardner, came into office on a wave of anti-foreign feeling, he ordered Colonel

Benjamin F. Butler to disband his company of Irish militia known as the "Jackson Musketeers." By way of protest Colonel Butler marched his company through the streets of Salem with "clubbed," or upside down, muskets.[6]

Governor Gardner discharged Butler from the militia and removed the state-owned muskets from Lowell to Cambridge. There were newspaper rumors that Butler would demand a court-martial to contest his removal, and when he failed to do this he was berated as "a renegade." Instead of fighting to recover his old position, he quietly set his sights upon the next rank above it. After two months of campaigning that did not reach the newspapers, the cashiered colonel was elected Brigadier General of the Third Brigade, Second Division, of the Massachusetts Militia. The offending governor was compelled to sign the new commission.

On February 21, 1857, Secretary of War Jefferson Davis appointed Butler a member of the Board of Visitors at West Point. In June, accordingly, he put on his new uniform and at the Military Academy as "the youngest general in the United States" enjoyed a handshake from General Winfield Scott, the oldest.[7]

As a politician Butler was like a talented but unrestrained organist, who pulled out all the stops and cavorted up and down the keyboard, not unable to read music, but preferring to play by ear, with the score crumpled in the wastebasket. From 1844 to 1860 he attended every national convention of the Democratic Party. Reporter Murat Halstead recalled Butler's appearance at the Cincinnati Democratic Convention that nominated James Buchanan. He was thin, dapper, slender, bald at thirty-eight, and an inveterate show-off who gained attention by his "habit of springing into his chair as quickly as a squirrel and speaking in a shrill, rasping voice."[8] J. Q. A. Griffin, a slightly envious Proper Bostonian colleague of Butler's on the Charlestown Annexation Case, thus described him as a speaker:

> His sentences are ungrammatical and disjointed. He makes awkward work when he undertakes to utter compliments. His laughs are more often appreciated by those on the back seats, rather than the front . . . He is not eloquent, he is not learned. He has not superior judg-

ment. He has no taste at all, so to speak. But he has the power to do . . . Like Caesar the Dictator, he would rather find himself the first man in a small hamlet than the second in a mighty Empire. And he spares nothing within his means that will minister to his ambition.[9]

Another observer, H. P. Jackson, rated him as bold and energetic, fond of creating a sensation. "Tameness was his horror . . . Turbulence of some sort was the breath of his nostrils." A handwriting expert described Butler as wanting to do a great deal of good but trammeled by the customs of society and too much of a stickler for little things; as a reformer he would like to "turn this world bottom side up, and see if he could by some means make a better one."[10]

Elected a state senator in 1859, but lacking the support of a strong group, he spent his time on minor concerns. He sponsored a bill to declare drunkenness a disease and not a crime. He demanded equal suffrage for native and foreign-born citizens. Taking a fling at aristocratic Harvard, which derived part of its income from the state, Senator Butler inveighed against state endowments for certain colleges and not for all. He defended the minority-group Catholics in their resistance to sectarian religious instruction in the schools. He resisted the grant of a tract of land to the Boston and Maine Railroad on the score that the government was making no comparable concession to workingmen. If the railroad could so easily obtain valuable real estate, shouted Senator Butler, then he the Senator would put in his bid for a piece of the State House lawn! He precipitated an abolitionist dispute by introducing a clause to exclude Negroes from the militia, for the logical reason that the Federal Constitution did not recognize blacks as citizens. He nursed through the legislature a judiciary bill which set up a Superior Court to replace the Court of Common Pleas and thus eliminated the position of Judge Ebenezer Rockwood Hoar, who had ruled against Butler seven years earlier in the libel suit.

A Republican governor in 1859 appointed Butler as a member of a committee to approach Congress for restitution of state funds spent in the nation's interest during the War of 1812.[11] Senator Butler thus had an opportunity for a conference with United States Senator Jefferson Davis of Mississippi in which, in addition to the refund matter, the two men canvassed the slavery question that was threatening to disrupt the country.

Butler agreed with "Hunker" Democrats that the Constitution of the United States permitted slavery, but disagreed with them when he declined to support the Fugitive Slave Law. He could not feel obliged by his party ties "to go bounding over the graves of my fathers to catch a fugitive slave." [12] In the Lincoln-Douglas debates on extension of slavery in the Territories Butler could not wholeheartedly support the Democrat, for he felt that Douglas' idea of "squatter sovereignty" could only lead to repetitions of the Pottawatomi massacre. To John Brown's scheme for promoting servile insurrection in Virginia Butler was wholly opposed. In a formal speech on John Brown in Lowell's Huntington Hall, in February 1860, Butler condemned Northern abolitionists and Southern fire-eaters alike. "The mistake is mutual," he declared. "We look at the South through the medium of the abolitionist orators — a very distorted picture. The South see us only as rampant abolitionists, ready to make a foray upon their rights and property . . . Let us fairly appreciate the difference of our position. These questions, which to us locally are of so little practical consequence as hardly to call our attention, are to them the very foundations of society — ominous of rapine, murder, and all the horrors of a servile war." [13] He advocated preserving the Union, with every part of the country respecting the institutions of every other part.

On his way to Charleston, South Carolina, in 1860 as a member of the Massachusetts delegation to the Democratic National Convention, Butler stopped briefly in Washington. In Georgetown he investigated the Convent of the Visitation as a school to which he might send his daughter Blanche, and he had a brief conference with Judge Stephen A. Douglas. Although the Massachusetts State Democratic Convention meeting at Worcester had favored Douglas for President and apparently assumed that their delegates would vote for him, they had not actually instructed them to do so. Butler, accordingly, felt free to sound out the prospective nominee and to make up his own mind as to how far he should support him.

With several other delegates, Butler now sailed on the steamer *S. R. Spaulding* to Charleston. How his ship entered the harbor he described in a letter to Sarah on April 22: "We came here after a very pleasant passage of from Wednesday at night (6 o'clock) till Friday at 10 P.M. We lay on the quarantine ground till morning, when about 8 o'clock we came up to the city and skirted along its whole length with flags flying, guns firing, and drums beating all in the finest style. Fisher and Clemence were very seasick but are all right now. George was also very sick. For myself, I ate five times a day, slept soundly, smoked incessantly, and drank sparingly. Charleston is much the same apparently that it has been for a half century . . . you will see by the enclosed prospectus (which I pray you preserve) that I have visited the school at Georgetown. I am more in favor than ever of sending Blanche there; you will agree with me when you visit for yourself, as we will do next winter. How are all at home? I long to be with you at home again with an inexpressible longing. We shall start probably a week from today and be home in four days. Love to all. Yours, Benj." [14]

As a member of the Platform Committee Butler held out for the Cincinnati Platform of 1856, which had ridden out one storm over slavery, and which, as Butler saw it, represented the maximum political concession which the North could offer. Butler's proposal, adopted by a vote of 230 to 40, split the convention. [15] South Carolina's delegation, having in vain demanded a plank favoring slavery, filed out of the convention hall.

In the subsequent balloting Butler voted seven times for Douglas. Then deciding that Douglas could not be nominated, he broke away from the other members of the Massachusetts delegation and cast his ballot fifty-seven times for Jefferson Davis, a moderate Southerner whom he regarded as a candidate most likely to heal the breach between the sections. On casting these fifty-seven ballots Butler, after springing up into his chair, always spoke shrilly and distinctly: "And the State of Massachusetts casts one vote for the Hon. Jefferson Davis of Mississippi." [16]

Butler returned north by train, convinced that sooner or later the "slave power" would make war. At the "rump" convention in Baltimore he helped to nominate Breckinridge and Lane, and in the following September was himself picked to run for Governor of Massachusetts on the "Breckinridge" ticket. His acceptance of this nomination was made with no thought of election. Democratic voters of Massachusetts had been thoroughly angered by his shifting from Douglas to Davis at Charleston. Boston heard his explanation in Faneuil Hall without enthusiasm. Lowell howled him down. The *Courier* criticized his defense as "specious and sophistical." When after Lincoln's election South Carolina and other states in the Deep South had seceded and sent commissioners to Washington to urge President Buchanan to arrange a peaceful separation of the Southern Confederacy, Ben Butler advised President Buchanan to arrest the Southern commissioners for treason and by getting the case at once before the Supreme Court to decide the issue, and he offered his services to the government as prosecutor. Buchanan declined Butler's idea.

The free-lance politician's fifty-seven votes for Jefferson Davis were forgotten now as Militia Brigadier General Benjamin F. Butler set about active preparations to place his brigade on a wartime footing. Butler went to Governor John A. Andrew, against whom he had recently run in the contest for governor, and persuaded him to place an order immediately for 2000 woolen overcoats for the Massachusetts Militia. The men had no overcoats at all, and their uniforms were of flimsy, flashy material suitable only for Fourth of July parades. Butler had the order for the overcoats placed with his own Middlesex Company. To make certain that the state would have funds for her emergency war preparations he induced his banker friend James G. Carney to offer Governor Andrew a loan of $50,000 and also to persuade other bankers to make similar loans. Certain newspapers at the time accused General Butler of a desire "to feed the moths with overcoats," and praised his shrewdness in promoting a war scare so as to get for his company a profitable contract.[17]

Then, on April 12, came the explosion at Fort Sumter.

On April 15, when Secretary of War Cameron asked Governor Andrew to send forward 1500 men for the defense of Washington,

General Butler telegraphed his friend Senator Henry Wilson in Washington, requesting him to make known the need for a Brigadier to accompany the troops. Governor Andrew yielded to this pressure and signed the requested orders.

Brigadier General Butler, in the middle of a trial when the Governor's orders came through, explained the situation to the Court and at once retired from the case. He established temporary headquarters in the State House and began sending mobilization directives over the state. Colonel E. F. Jones of the Sixth Regiment was dispatched by train on the night of the 17th, and the next day the Eighth Regiment with its new overcoats was drawn up on the State House yard for a patriotic send-off by Governor Andrew. General Butler then embarked on the cars with the troops and headed toward threatened Washington.

Ben Butler was not at all reluctant to doff his lawyer's garb for the uniform of a politician general. He was aware that Presidents in America are sometimes made on the battlefield. There can be little doubt that visions of moving Sarah into the White House danced in his ambitious head. As politician, however, he had an Achilles' heel that would be easy for enemies — North or South — to seize upon. For ten years — ever since the libel suit against Editor Warland — Ben Butler's name had appeared almost daily in the newspapers. For most of these press notices there was some factual basis, but quite frequently the stories consisted of rumors, chance remarks, surmises, wisecracks, and anecdotes fabricated out of whole cloth. What disturbed Sarah Butler — and might prove embarrassing for Ben's later career — was the fact that Ben himself had grown completely callous to these press notices. He ignored the false with the true, the bad with the good, the harmful with the innocuous. Whether or not he appreciated it, he had become a popular whipping boy whom the reporters might laud to the skies today and consign to hell tomorrow. It would, in short, be easy for such a politician general to become the chief butt of Confederate propaganda as the very incarnation of evil; and equally easy for political opponents in the North to brand him as a scapegoat.

PART TWO

The Political General

7

RELIEF OF WASHINGTON

THE Eighth Massachusetts Militia moved forward as on a picnic. Except for their steel-gray overcoats from the Middlesex Mills, which were rolled up, there was no single article of apparel to distinguish them as members of a military group. Flashy Moorish sashes of the Salem Zouaves, sou'westers of the men from Marblehead, homespun clothes of the Middlesex farmer, tough work jackets of machinists from Lowell — a jumble of peacetime garbs which were saturated with the pungent universal reek of tobacco smoke. At Springfield, where the Pittsfield company boarded the train, the president of the railroad apologized for having no sleeping car for the General and his staff. Butler sat up with the men all night in the rattling cars. Next morning while his regiment breakfasted at the Astor House, Butler and his officers ate at the Fifth Avenue Hotel.

In New York, Butler's brother, Andrew Jackson Butler, joined him as a member of his staff. Andrew, after taking a pioneer's homestead in Hannibal, Missouri, had served in the Mexican War and since then had made a small fortune in California. With his son George, Andrew had recently returned to New York. Andrew was a big, burly man, who stood six feet two barefooted, weighed 180 pounds and was known as Colonel.[1]

The gala scenes along the route, cheering at the stations, expensive picnic fare donated by hotel operators, merry joking of the men themselves were all brought up short by news from Baltimore.

The Sixth Massachusetts Militia, having departed a day earlier from Boston, had encountered a Secessionist mob in Baltimore which disputed its passage across the city. Nine of the troop train's eleven cars had already been drawn by horses across the city from the President Street Depot to the Camden Station on the south side, when a gathering mob checked the last two cars with a shower of paving stones and brickbats. The troops were forced to get out and march. Several muskets were snatched from the soldiers by the mob. In a futile attempt to quell the disorder Mayor George W. Brown placed himself at the head of the Massachusetts militia, now drawn up in a solid square and advancing with fixed bayonets. Inciting the yelling mob of 8000 to 10,000 were a number of "plug uglies" and "blood tubs" who continued to hurl bricks and rocks and to fire random shots from revolvers and muskets. A number of the militiamen suffered cuts and contusions, eight were seriously wounded, three were killed. Several Massachusetts men acting on their own fired back, killing a number of Baltimoreans. At length having scrambled through the city, they got under way for Washington. As reported by the press, "The mob completely reigned in Baltimore after the attack. All the gunshops were plundered. Other shops throughout the city were closed . . . Secession sentiments prevailed." [2] Mayor Brown of Baltimore and Governor Thomas Hicks of Maryland notified President Lincoln that no more troops could pass through Baltimore unless they fought their way.

Soon after the early news of the Baltimore affair reached Butler in Philadelphia, the telegraph went dead. If Baltimore became secessionist, Washington might be permanently cut off from its rail connections with the North, and might fall to invaders from across the Potomac. It was necessary for Butler to get his men into Washington at the earliest moment.[3]

With his route through Baltimore barred, Butler spent the last night in consultation with Captain S. F. du Pont, Commandant of the Philadelphia Navy Yard, and S. M. Felton, president of the Philadelphia, Wilmington & Baltimore Railroad, and decided to push on to Washington via Annapolis. From Perryville, on the Susquehannah across from Havre de Grace, he planned to take the railroad ferryboat down the bay to Annapolis, which was about thirty miles by railroad from the Capital. Felton gave Butler permission to seize the railroad company's ferryboat *Maryland*.

Next morning while three days' rations for his regiment were being cooked, Butler sent his brother, who was a peripatetic individual unable to sit still in time of suspense, to scour Philadelphia for pickaxes, shovels, tinware, camp kettles and provisions for use in a possible emergency. When the Seventh New York Militia, also bound for Washington, reached Philadelphia later in the day, Butler tried to persuade its commander, Colonel Marshall Lefferts, to accompany him in forcing open the route via Annapolis, but Lefferts elected to take his regiment by the sea route and up the Potomac. While Butler was completing his preparations, members of the Seventh New York took over the plush lounging spaces of the Continental Hotel. So many of its members were sportsmen and young blades from Broadway that the Seventh New York was dubbed the "Kid Glove" Regiment.

With his plebeian Eighth Massachusetts Butler embarked at 11 A.M. on the 20th, just as word came in that the Secessionists were burning bridges on both railroads north out of Baltimore. Butler detailed the officers who were to surprise and capture the ferryboat. As they rattled south Butler went through the cars inspecting rifles and explaining how the ferryboat was to be seized at Perryville. In one car he settled an altercation over whether a youth not yet of age should give up his rifle to a captain who had none. Then not having had his clothes off since leaving Boston he sat down and went to sleep. He seemed hardly to have closed his eyes when a cry of "Man overboard" awakened him. The train had stopped. He looked out of the window and saw that one of his militiamen, who proved to be a sergeant, had stripped himself of everything but his trousers and shoes and was streaking across the fields. Butler offered a $30 reward to a group of country people if they would return the fugitive and pushed on. At Perryville his men seized the *Maryland* without difficulty.

Butler shoved four cars loaded with coal onto the upper deck of the ferryboat. In the shed at the ferry slip he filled several empty whisky barrels with drinking water, embarked his 700 men and shoved off for Annapolis. The weary militia dropped to the coal-dusty deck and slept during their cruise down the bay. Exhausted by excitement, few were wakened when Butler in making the rounds of the boat trod on their tightly packed bodies.

At midnight, Butler anchored two miles off Annapolis. Lights were on in the town. Mysterious rockets shooting across the sky from the direction of Baltimore had alarmed Naval Academy officials who feared a visit from the rowdies of Baltimore.

Within a short time a boat from the Naval Academy came alongside, and Lieutenant Mathews, aide to the Superintendent, delivered to Butler a message from Governor Hicks:

State of Maryland, Executive Chamber, Annapolis, Apr. 20, 1861.

To the Commander of the Volunteer troops on board the Steamer Sir: I would most earnestly advise that you do not land your men at Annapolis. The excitement is very great, and I think it prudent that you should take your men elsewhere. I have declared to the Secretary of War advising against your landing your men here.

Very respectfully, THOS. H. HICKS, *Gov. of Md.*[4]

Butler detailed his aide Captain Peter Haggerty, a Boston lawyer, to accompany Lieutenant Mathews to see the Governor, and afterward, being skeptical as to the good faith of this dispatch from the Governor as well as to the reported state of things in the town, he sent his brother Andrew ashore in plain clothes to make a reconnaissance. Whether the Governor deemed it prudent or no, Butler had no alternative to landing his troops. Undisciplined and with no idea of the demands of military life, most of his militiamen had eaten their three day's rations before they reached Perryville, and the foul-tasting water in the whisky casks was insufficient to last through the day.

About daybreak Haggerty returned bringing Captain Blake, Superintendent of the Naval Academy. Blake told Butler that the Baltimore Secessionists could erect a battery on the heights across the Severn River and compel the surrender of the *Constitution,* and asked whether Butler's instructions would permit him to help save her.

His instructions left him plenty of latitude to save the *Constitution,* Butler punned, "whether the ship or form of government."

Captain Devereux with 150 Marblehead fishermen was detailed to lighten and careen the *Constitution,* while the ferryboat *Maryland* gave her a tow.

Old Ironsides was "aground on beef bones." She drew 19½ feet when the depth of water was 18. Her guns were lifted ashore and by afternoon the ferry transport had tugged her two miles out. Despite parching throats and empty bellies the men of the Eighth Massachusetts, whose grandfathers had built the *Constitution,* cheered her rescue.

But their cheering in the afternoon rasped to an angry roar when their own boat, hawsers straining, ran hard onto a shoal. From their first seizure of the craft, the Massachusetts militiamen had doubted the loyalty of the *Maryland's* skipper, whose glum looks they had interpreted as indicating Secessionist sympathy. Butler clapped the man in irons and put a Yankee engineer in his place.

The *Boston,* carrying Colonel Lefferts and the Seventh New York now came up the Bay to Annapolis. They had sailed around from Philadelphia by sea, intending to ascend the Potomac, but finding that Confederate batteries had closed the river approach to Washington, they had shifted course to Annapolis. More than ever it was now clear that a way must be opened through Annapolis to relieve the City of Washington.

Theodore Winthrop, clever, lighthearted globe-trotter and *Atlantic Monthly* writer, who came on the *Boston,* witnessed the efforts of Butler's men to free their grounded ferryboat.

> We could see them, half a mile off, making every effort to lighten her. The soldiers tramped forward and aft, danced on her decks, shot overboard a heavy baggage truck. We saw them start the truck for the stern with a cheer. It crashed down. One end stuck in the mud, the other fell back and rested on the boat. They went at it with axes, and presently it was clear. As the tide rose, we gave our grounded friends a lift with a hawser. No go! The *Boston* tugged in vain. We got near enough to see the whites of the Massachusetts' eyes and their unlucky faces and uniforms all grimy with their lodgings in the coal dust. They could not have been blacker if they had been breathing battle smoke and dust all day.[5]

Leaving his stranded vessel, Butler hitched a ride ashore on board the *Boston,* taking with him as many Massachusetts men as the *Boston* could squeeze on in order to lighten the *Maryland.* To Governor Hicks's protest of the night before, Butler sent word that he could not take his men elsewhere without first obtaining supplies. "I desire of your excellency an immediate reply whether I have permission of the State authorities of Maryland to land the men under my command, and of passing through the State on my way to Washington, respecting private property, and paying for what I receive, and outraging the rights of none . . . Ps. — It occurs to me that our landing on the grounds at the Naval Academy would be entirely proper and in accordance with your excellency's wishes." [6] The note requesting permission to land was not dispatched until Butler along with the Seventh New York had landed at the wharf of the Naval School, and while the New York troops stretched themselves around the parade field under the trees, Butler was asked to breakfast with the Superintendent.

Annapolis was in ferment. Of its 2000 population some had fled into the country on the appearance of the troopships; others, when the *Constitution* was hauled away from her wharf, broke through the gates and surged into the yard. Small boys pranced the streets with wooden sabres and revolvers, their faces aping the "solemn and revengeful cast of their elders." [7] Twenty-two Southern midshipmen, a professor and four officers had already resigned. Captain Blake was pushing preparations to send the loyal remnants of the Naval School north on board the *Constitution.*

At the breakfast table Butler mentioned the *Constitution* when he detected a warning in the eye of Mrs. Blake, and changed the topic of conversation to deviled hard-shelled crabs, which formed a considerable portion of his breakfast. [8] After the meal when the Superintendent and young Blake had left the room, Mrs. Blake explained that her son had Secessionist leanings, and that while she did not feel he would communicate military intelligence to the enemy, she nevertheless preferred to take no chances.

In the Superintendent's office Butler met Governor Hicks, the

Mayor and the police chief of Annapolis. Hicks informed him that while the state of Maryland would not interfere with his landing the remainder of his troops he must encamp them three or more miles outside of the city. The Mayor and the police commissioner, backing up the state official, disclosed that the city government had voted not to molest Butler but to urge him to march out of town at once. There were "bad" men in Annapolis and others might come from Baltimore and elsewhere.

Butler seemed to agree with his opponents while drawing them out.

"Since I am in need of supplies, would you furnish me if I would march?"

They shook their heads. Nor would they permit him to buy anything in Annapolis.

"Could I be furnished with means of transportation to Washington?"

Again the answer was no. There were not five horses left in the town, and the railroad company had taken up their tracks, which, being their private property, they had a right to do.

To all this Butler rejoined that without supplies he could not march, and that he could not put three or four miles between himself and his boats when the alleged reason why he should march was that in marching he should leave between himself and his boats "so very excited a mob that the city authorities were not able to control it." [9]

Butler warmed to his subject. "My troops from Massachusetts are also very much excited because of the murder of their brothers at Baltimore by a mob. In this situation I have the advantage that we can not only control our own excitement, but can also control and suppress the excitement of others. I propose to stay as long as convenient at Annapolis, and march when it is convenient. If we are attacked we will repel the attack, and there are none that we shall be more happy to see than a representation of the murderers of Baltimore whenever and wherever they visit us. While we stay in Annapolis, if the citizens choose not to have any collision with us, there must be on their part neither stray bricks, nor fugitive shots, thrown at us." [10]

From atop a mound outside the wall a harmless-looking knot of Annapolitans peered over into the Naval Academy yard at the soldiers, but the latter, excited by rumor-mongers in their group, felt that at any minute those onlookers might "unmask a battery of giant columbiads and belch blazes at us." [11] Everywhere men speculated on the chances of their arriving in Washington before the Virginians did. Men of the Seventh New York wisecracked that Jeff Davis was possibly already ensconced in the White House, "spitting in the Presidential spittoon." While the New York troops drilled at one end of the field, the midshipmen paraded in another part. At dusk the *Boston* brought ashore the remaining troops of the Eighth Massachusetts, thirsty and grimy from their stranded ferryboat. The "fine little bluejackets" of the Naval School served them biscuit and coffee piping hot from their galley, and gave up part of their dormitories to them. Recitation halls, the old fort, porches everywhere were filled with soldiers. Many slept under the stars.

Early the next morning Butler asked Colonel Lefferts to move his Seventh New York down the railroad, repairing the track and guarding it against further damage. Lefferts carried the matter for decision to all his regimental officers who advised him to await reinforcements before leaving Annapolis. Butler tried every argument short of military coercion, but Lefferts as a colonel of New York militia declined to be commanded by a brigadier of Massachusetts militia.

Although the Eighth Massachusetts was now already split up — a detachment having been sent to rescue and man the *Constitution* — Butler did not hesitate to divide it further, so imperative seemed the need quickly to open the route to Washington. He directed Lieutenant Colonel Edward W. Hinks to march two companies out along the Annapolis and Elk Ridge Railroad and hold it against all comers. Butler rode with Hinks across Annapolis to the depot.

The locomotive was locked in a shed, and the railroad agent refused to give up the key. Butler had the door forced and called for volunteer engineers and mechanics.

Among those who stepped forward was one Charles Homans, Beverly Light Guards, Company E, who took a quick look at the engine and recognized from its name plate that he himself had helped to build this locomotive. Homans and a gang of railroaders "passed their hands over the locomotive a few times," as Theodore Winthrop de-

scribes it, "and presently it was ready to whistle and wheeze and gal-
lop, as if no traitor had ever tried to steal the go and music out of it." [12]
While Hinks's men repaired the track, the locomotive with armed
sentries posted on either side of the cow-catcher chugged back and
forth along the repaired stretch to guard it.

Back at his headquarters in the Naval Academy's superintendent's
office, Butler received another note from Governor Hicks protesting his seizure of the railroad. Hicks had just summoned the legislature and objected that Butler's occupation of the road would "prevent
the Members of the Legislature from reaching the city." [13]

"You are credibly informed," Butler retorted, "that I have taken
possession of the Annapolis and Elk Ridge Railroad. It might have
escaped your notice, but at the official meeting which was had between
your Excellency and the Mayor of Annapolis and the Committee of
Government and myself, as to my landing my troops, it was ex-
pressly stated as the reason why I should not land, that my troops
could not pass the Railroad because the Company had taken up
the rails, as they were private property. It is difficult to see how it could
be that if my troops could not pass over the Railroad one way the
members of the Legislature could pass the other way." [14]

Butler's policy toward Governor Hicks was to smite him with one
hand while stroking him reassuringly with the other. When he heard
that all Annapolis was quaking with fear of a Negro uprising, Butler
offered — most indiscreetly as it turned out — the services of Massachusetts' Militia to quell any slave insurrection in Maryland.[15] And
when Governor Hicks switched his plans and called for the Maryland
Legislature to hold its meeting in Frederick, Butler let it be known
that should that body pass an ordinance of secession he would arrest
every one of them! [16]

Within a week after Butler's arrival the steamer *R. R. Cuyler* disembarked at Annapolis the 71st New York, the steamer *Kedar*
brought the Fifth New York, an all-German regiment, and the ocean
liner *Baltic* came with Colonel Elmer E. Ellsworth's flashily dressed
Fire Zouaves. Butler assigned the *R. R. Cuyler* to tow the *Constitution,* with the remaining midshipmen to New York.

There was now in Annapolis a concentration of several thousand troops, enough to hold the city against a square mile of Plug Uglies. The Seventh New York prepared for its trek to Washington in the wake of the Eighth Massachusetts. All afternoon on the 23rd the barbers' shears were at work under the trees around the parade field, close-cropping each head so as to render it difficult either for lice or an enemy to get a good grip. After midnight of the 24th they were "rattled up" and issued enough pork, beef and biscuit to last three days, and at seven-thirty were marched through Annapolis. "We deem ourselves a fine-looking set," recorded Winthrop, "although our belts are blanched with pipe-clay and our rifles shine sharp in the sun, yet the townspeople stare at us in dismal silence." [17] Four miles out of town they came upon the track repair detail. The rickety train, loaded with mess gear, howitzers and railroad tools, crept along slowly over newly repaired sections of track. The day grew sultry, breezeless, brewing thunder gusts.

The timbers of South River bridge, six miles out, had been partially sawed through, making it impossible to risk the locomotive. With the trestle temporarily strengthened by fresh timbers, the train's two flat-cars mounting howitzers were shoved across, while the locomotive was left to patrol the track in the rear. From time to time trackwalkers ahead of the flatcars would shout "Halt! a rail gone." Men would scatter out to find the rail. Even after nightfall such search continued. New York dandies and Massachusetts workmen together waded knee-deep in the wet grass of hayfields searching with their feet. Most of the rails were easy to find, and were replaced quickly. Occasionally they had been dropped into a creek. One young militiaman who dived and knotted a rope around a sunken rail so that it could be recovered, spurned a Kid Glover's offer of a twenty-dollar goldpiece as a reward, saying he had not enlisted to make money. But for Lieutenant Merrick of the Eighth Massachusetts, who lost a leg in an accident, the men of the Seventh New York raised a purse of $1000.

Because rails continued to disappear behind the trackmen, in spite of the roving, owl-eyed vigilance of the locomotive, Butler arrested the superintendent of the railroad and stationed 16-men detachments every 500 feet along the entire road bed, under orders to shoot on the spot anyone found tampering with the rails.

While repairs were going ahead, Butler requisitioned locomotives and cars from Philadelphia. Since freight boats that ordinarily would ascend the Potomac were now crowding into Annapolis, Butler laid a track from the Naval Academy dock across the town to the railroad track. No longer were the gates of the Naval Academy open to the public. Visitors were limited to those having essential business. Across the Severn River Butler placed a small battery, Fort Nonsense, with 600 men from the Sixth New York. Further up the Severn at Round Bay he located another outpost to guard the land route from Baltimore. Despite the large concentration of troops in Annapolis, rumors of a descent upon the town by Secessionists of Baltimore continued to be circulated, and sky rockets were set off by unknown parties in the countryside.

"Dear Sarah," the General wrote Mrs. Butler on the 23rd, "I have worked like a horse, slept not two hours a night, have saved the 'Old Ironsides' Frigate from the secessionists, and have landed in the Capital of Maryland against the protest of her Government. I am now about to march on Washington as I have telegraphed you. You must not hope to get regular intelligence, as the mails are stopped. I think no man has won more in ten days than I have. We will see, however. Goodbye — kiss the children for me. Butler." [18]

On the 25th Lieutenant General Winfield Scott in Washington dispatched formal orders for Butler to command the "Department of Annapolis," and directed him to keep open the rail communication between Annapolis and Washington. By authority of President Lincoln, Butler was to take all measures to defend Annapolis. Should the Maryland Legislature attempt to arm the state against the Federal Government, Butler was to adopt the most prompt and efficient countermeasures, "even if necessary to the bombardment of their cities, and, in the extremest necessity, suspension of the writ of *habeas corpus*." [19]

Butler now sent to the State House and took possession of the Great Seal of Maryland so that the legislators meeting in Frederick, even if they chose to pass an ordinance of secession, would be unable to make it legal by affixing the seal!

On April 27 General Butler sent his brother Colonel Andrew Jackson Butler over the newly opened railroad to Washington with dispatches to explain the extraordinary measures already undertaken during the three days when Annapolis had been without telegraphic connection with the Capitol.

By this date he had converted the Academy into a military base and relayed 7750 troops over the railroad to Washington. Butler would, the New York *Times* believed, hold an iron rod over the Secessionists to insure their good behavior.[20]

To guard his water route from Perryville to Annapolis, Butler placed two light guns on board the *Maryland,* and the railroad officials, with a gift of $5000 from William B. Astor, armed the steamer *Yankee* with two long 32's of the vintage of 1812. So safe was the situation that Butler sent to have his daughter Blanche brought from her convent school in Georgetown to Annapolis. "Little Bunty" had written her father: "My toes seem to be going without my consent." [21] If she could not go home the impatient Blanche feared that she might even join the Secessionists!

As commanding officer of the Department of Annapolis, Butler exercised military authority over militia colonels from other states. His commands were now decisive, mandatory, not to be caviled over. The Generals' anterooms were thronged and it was exceedingly difficult to get any passes to go anywhere, or to find out anything. "Great credit is here given to General Butler's management," wrote a New York *Times* correspondent.[22]

Carl Schurz, passing through Annapolis, found General Butler "clothed in a gorgeous militia uniform adorned with rich gold embroidery. His rotund form, his squinting eye, and the peculiar puff of his cheeks made him look a little grotesque." Schurz winced at "the tone of curt peremptoriness" with which Butler gave his instructions, but noted that he did expedite business.[23]

Sarah Butler relayed to her husband Dr. Kimball's word "that you're astonishing everybody by your executive ability . . . Brady is starting a company to be called the Butler Rifle Guards. Everybody is wild with excitement. The ladies are making soldiers' shirts and rolling up bandages. I would gladly go to you if you would not find me an encumbrance. *Always yours,* Sarah." [24]

Her note crossed in the mails a very military note from Annapolis, dated April 28:

Dear Sarah: I am ordered by the War Department to take command of this department of Maryland. A high honor never yet conferred upon a Militia Genl. who had seen no service. *We have won.* I have a very excellent house here, well furnished, a good corps of servants, and am keeping house. Shall be here some months. Harriet [Sarah's sister, Mrs. Heard] has come. I have sent for Blanche. She will be with me tonight and wait your coming. You had better come on yourself. I shall detain Harriet a day or two as housekeeper. Shut up the house and come on. Bring Gilman [the coachman]. You can send the children over to Dracut or to the salt water with Lote [Sarah's youngest sister]. Bring nothing but your table service of silver. The horses had better be turned out to pasture except Charly for the farm. Burley [the gardener] had better move in to kitchen. Bring summer clothes as weather is warm. Love to all in great haste.

Then the busy commander, remembering how little Sarah cared for peremptoriness in others, added:

If you do not like this do not execute it. I am so in the habit of giving orders lately that I write in a peremptory style. All our people are well and have behaved gloriously. (You may put this last in the newpspapers — it will relieve all men's minds.) *Yours respectfully,* B. F. Butler.[25]

After she received this appealing letter, Sarah closed the lonely house on Merrimack River and came on to Annapolis.

8

BUTLER SEIZES BALTIMORE

THE secession movement began to subside in Maryland soon after the route via Annapolis was opened. The more active Baltimore Secessionists began migrating southward through Harpers Ferry. As their numbers diminished, Baltimore's merchants raised their voices to deplore the disruption of their trade. Some Unionists drew up resolutions protesting their loyalty and Baltimore papers grumbled against the Northern press for assuming that *all* Baltimoreans were in a class with the mob leaders who had attacked the Sixth Massachusetts. Not very consistently, however, Baltimore did not arrest the mob leaders or repair the railroad bridges. Officially, as did the state generally, Baltimore held out for a neutral position in the forthcoming struggle. And as recruits for Southern armies made their way southward, emissaries from Virginia continued to press secession upon the Maryland Legislature meeting in Frederick. The state of Virginia even sent several hundred of the invaluable firearms they had captured at Harpers Ferry to enable Baltimoreans to resist the "vandal hordes from New England."

On May 3 Butler, who had been called to Washington by General Scott, arrived early and inspected his troops which had already reached the Capitol. He found them billeted in the Capitol building, the Sixth Massachusetts in the Senate Chamber, the Seventh New York in the House, and the Eighth Massachusetts in the rotunda under the unfinished dome, where they could joke about the fresh air. Colonel Lefferts had preempted the Speaker's parlor. Colonel Jones hoped that his Sixth Massachusetts Regiment might continue to serve in Butler's brigade now that they had been sworn in as United States

Volunteers. Butler persuaded the writer Theodore Winthrop to join his staff. Throughout the Capitol building soldiers were writing letters, and keeping several Congressmen busy franking their envelopes. Beards were growing. As Winthrop quipped, the days were gone when men shaved the upper lip and dressed like parsons.[1]

Since Butler could not see General Scott before eleven o'clock, he paid a brief call on his political friend Salmon P. Chase, now Secretary of the Treasury. He listened to Chase's idea of protecting Washington by seizing the railroad junction at Manassas, and agreed with him that to carry the war into the South was the best policy.[2]

At the West Point commencement in 1857, Winfield Scott had been hale and hearty at seventy-one. Now at seventy-five, despite afflictions of increasing age, he held the most ticklish administrative job in the country, that of General-in-Chief of the Federal armies. A recent carriage accident had shaken him up; he was scarcely able to walk because of gout; he tired quickly even when he rode in his carriage; he had insomnia. For twenty years he had been General-in-Chief and his mind, exact, formal, unpliant, had been set in the molds of 1812 and 1848.

General Scott was pleased with Butler's energetic handling of affairs in Annapolis and assigned him to lead a column of troops in an assault on Baltimore. Scott envisaged four columns of 3000 men each converging on Baltimore from Washington, York, Perryville and overwater from Annapolis. He planned that Butler should first put reinforcements into Fort McHenry, a few miles south of Baltimore and then lead the force from Washington. As a preliminary to this operation Scott directed Butler to occupy the Relay House, about nine miles south of Baltimore.

After lunching with Scott and Secretary of War Simon Cameron, a wealthy Pennsylvania politician, Butler issued marching orders to the Sixth Massachusetts. Although their uniforms and tents had not yet arrived, the Sixth welcomed the prospect of a shift from the Capitol into the open fields, and cheered, too, the possibility of a return visit to the toughs of Baltimore. Butler in high spirits wrote Sarah from Washington, "I am on a flying visit here to see the President and Gen-

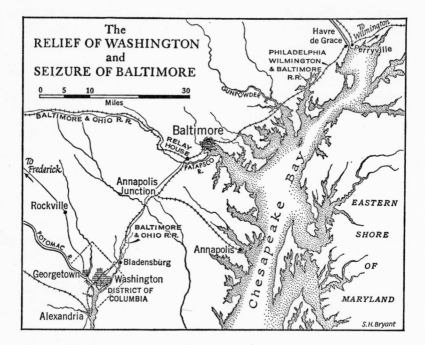

The
RELIEF OF WASHINGTON
and
SEIZURE OF BALTIMORE

0   5   10   30
Miles

S.H.Bryant

eral Scott. The old General holds up wonderfully. I have promise of some work to do. Baltimore is to be retaken, so is Gosport Navy Yard . . . I will either bring back my shield as a proud trophy to you, dearest, my own heart's home, or I come back upon it with a name which you will not be ashamed to bear and teach our children to love and reverence." [3]

Early on Sunday morning the Eighth New York and the Boston Light Artillery joined the Sixth Massachusetts at Annapolis Junction. By eleven o'clock their combined trains of thirty cars reached the Relay House. The men disembarked quietly and fanned over the surrounding hills to establish their camp.

At the Relay House the Baltimore and Ohio Railroad, after crossing the Patapsco River, left the Baltimore-Washington trunk line and stretched westward toward Frederick and Harpers Ferry. Some of Butler's men scooped out a lunette on the the bluff and mounted howitzers overlooking the stone railroad bridge, while others laid out encampments on the low hills on either side of the right-of-way. The white tents of the Eighth New York dotted one hill while opposite them the Sixth Massachusetts, still without tents, improvised shelters of tree limbs, thatched with leaves and lined with straw. "General Butler himself has a fine military presence," reported the New York *Times,* "self-possessed and full of vigor, with a hearty urbanity of manner that makes him very popular. He rides over the camp daily, mounted on a splendid animal apparently as full of fire as his manly-looking rider. The officers attached to the General's staff and to the regiments are noble looking men — strong, sinewy, and full of a determined force of character." In view of Butler's later troubles with Southern women, the newsman's concluding comment on Butler and his staff is interesting: "They are of polished manner also, and know how to treat a lady with deference, even though she be a Secessionist. They meet with many having such sentiments in this latitude." [4]

In the confusion on the first day a train from Baltimore loaded with wheat, whisky, spades, picks and shovels had been permitted to pass to Harpers Ferry. Checking for contraband freight was ticklish since the miners of Western Virginia depended upon Baltimore for supplies and any interruption of traffic flowing west might provoke retaliatory interruption of traffic flowing east — beef, pork and corn from the Ohio Valley, which was vitally needed on the seaboard.

At first Butler found the country people around the Relay House exceedingly friendly, and anxious to sell to the camp eggs, pies, cakes, coffee and tobacco. But a cloud overspread the happy panorama when the doctor reported a case of strychnine poisoning from food bought from a local vender. "Are our few insane enemies among the loyal men of Maryland prepared to wage war on us in this manner? Do they know the terrible lesson of warfare they are teaching us?" [5] Butler queried in his general order forbidding peddlers to sell to troops. Among the crowds that came out from Baltimore was a drunk who boasted that he had been one of the mob at Baltimore, and that Baltimoreans were itching for the troops to return to give them a like reception. Arrested and carried to General Butler's headquarters in the Relay House Station, he received an angry grilling and was jailed.

From agents in Baltimore Butler learned of the steam gun which the pro-Secessionist millionaire Ross Winans had built, a mobile steam engine attached to a revolving drum from which by centrifugal action shot were hurled. Winans, a septuagenarian delegate in the Maryland Legislature meeting in Frederick, was taken from a train at the Relay House and placed under arrest. Butler denied Governor Hicks's request that Winans be freed on bail, and held him incommunicado. Butler considered him "a very proper specimen of traitor to be hanged," and had no doubt that a military commission composed of officers of the Sixth Massachusetts whom Baltimoreans had mobbed would be very likely to hang him. He thought that if such a man, worth $15,000,000, were hanged for treason, it would convince the people of Maryland "that the expedition we were upon was no picnic excursion." [6]

For several days the telegraph from Washington to the Relay House was interrupted by Secessionists cutting the wires. General Scott sent Butler a grumpy message via rail: "The railroad from the junction to this place is not guarded. This surprises me. Please supply this deficiency." [7] And when it appeared that the green troops were drinking while on picket duty, the Lieutenant General modified his plan for seizing Baltimore. Each of the four columns of 3000 militia troops moving in for the grand assault should be spearheaded by several companies of the regular army; although how this latter refinement was to operate was not clear, the regulars, for the most part, being kept busy guarding Indians on the western frontier.

After a few days the reported "strychnine" case recovered from what had been simple indigestion. But on May 7 a private in Company G, Eighth New York, committed suicide by resting his chin on the muzzle of his musket and kicking the flintlock. To spare the feelings of this first casualty's relatives, Butler listed him in the Brigade Order as "accidentally killed by the discharge of a musket from which he was drawing the charge." [8]

Leaving the regiment drilling at the Relay House, exercising their artillery against abandoned cabins across the river, and rigidly inspecting all trains out of Baltimore bound for Harpers Ferry, Butler returned to Annapolis. Not only was he plagued by dysentery, he had to square away for a long fight with Governor John A. Andrew of Massachusetts.

On April 25 the abolitionist governor had scolded Butler for offering Governor Hicks the aid of Massachusetts troops to suppress a servile insurrection in case there should be one in Maryland.

Butler had been too busy to reply at once to Governor Andrew's letter. Two weeks elapsed, and the New York *Tribune* ran an article by William S. Robinson (the reporter whose nose Butler had pulled in 1842): "There is a good deal of talk here about Butler's offer . . . [of] Massachusetts troops to put down a local slave insurrection. There is no disposition to criticize incidental movements, especially with imperfect information, but General Butler gets no praise from any quarter for taking this course." [9] Butler's explanation was temperate enough: We were not at war with Maryland, and Massachusetts would not wish the horrors of Santo Domingo's servile insurrection to be visited upon "those whom we hope to reunite with us as brethren." [10] The letter so long delayed and at last written while in bed under the harassments of dysentery might have been left on the shelf a few days before mailing. But Butler was determined to repay the Governor in his own coin.

He called in reporters and gave them the Governor's letter with his own 1700-word reply of May 9. And to Governor Andrew by special messenger he sent a private explanation: "I am impelled to this because the substance of your dispatch to me has been given to the public from Boston through the columns of the *Tribune,* with strictures upon my conduct." [11]

In a letter to Sarah, who still had not reached Annapolis, and whose much looked-for letters had not arrived, the wretched husband chided: "My dear Wife: why don't you write to me? Not one word have I had from you except by Harriet. You telegraphed me that you would write. Where is the letter? The newspapers tell you every move I make, but the newspapers do not tell me of the loved ones at home . . . I am now troubled with a little touch of my old complaint." [12] Sarah arrived in Annapolis by May 13, before she had had time to receive Ben's distraught message, and by this time Ben himself, having regained his health, was back at the Relay House.

Butler's aide, Captain Peter Haggerty, having spent three days in Baltimore in civilian garb, reported that the city could be taken without any of the formalities planned by General Scott. Butler, however, knew if he broached the subject to the General-in-Chief he would be turned down. He talked instead with President Garrett of the Baltimore and Ohio Railroad, with representatives of the Association of Butchers and Provision Dealers of Baltimore and other leaders able to size up the situation. Continuing reports of Baltimore Secessionists heading south did not indicate that the rebels were preparing to hold the city. Butler decided to chance a bold stroke.

At 4 P.M. on May 13, Butler entrained a thousand men and several pieces of artillery and, to confuse enemy spies, set them first in motion westward toward Harpers Ferry. At six he reversed course and about an hour later under gathering storm clouds chugged into the Camden Station in Baltimore.

The station was practically deserted. His men leaped from their train into marching order with loaded muskets and fixed bayonets. A section of artillery followed the first two companies. Should they be fired on along the route, the entire column was to halt and burn houses in the neighborhood before proceeding.

Owing in part to the torrential rain that descended about this time, the invaders encountered no opposition. Here and there a few lights were held up to windows and noses were flattened against the panes. Butler conspicuously mounted on a white horse led his rain drenched column down Light Street to Federal Hill, upon whose summit the artillery was quickly placed to command the narrow harbor and the center of town on the opposite side. "As I looked back from my horse, while the column slowly wound up the hill, the effect of the rolling thunder and playing lightning that made for an instant the point of every bayonet a glittering torch, was gloriously magnificent." [13] Butler had his men bring up firewood from a nearby woodyard and light bonfires all over the hill. To the Commander of Fort McHenry, two miles east, Butler sent a message. "My troops are on Federal Hill, which I can hold with the aid of my artillery. If I am attacked tonight, please open upon Monument Square with your mortars. I will keep the hill fully lighted with fires during the night so that you may know where we are and not hit us." [14] A midnight report of a riot in the city kept the invaders keyed up until daybreak.

Butler took over a tavern at the top of Federal Hill as headquarters, and while his clothes were drying before a fire he wrote a proclamation to the citizens. He was prepared to enforce their state and civic laws as well as the Federal. He promised large purchases by the government and a return to normal conditions. They were to turn in all arms and munitions. They were not to drill troops without authority or ship contraband goods to the enemy.

Butler seized the presses of the pro-Secessionist Baltimore *Clipper* to publish his proclamation.

In the early morning Mayor George W. Brown with members of the City Council called at Butler's headquarters. Brown, still jittery from the mob action of the 19th, told the General that the city authorities could not check the sending of arms to the rebels, but he handed the General a list of addresses where guns and powder were hidden so that Butler could stop it.

Shortly after General Butler's proclamation reached the streets the General with half a dozen aides rode downtown to the Gilmore House for dinner, and while he was at table a company detailed from the Sixth Regiment under Captain Follansbee appeared in front of the hotel to escort him back to headquarters. "The people flocked in to see the distinguished military strangers," reported the New York *Times,* "and looked on with respect, some smiling, others looked glum, but others frequently cheering as they passed." [15]

Butler's men ferreted out caches of muskets, carbines, and "John Brown" pikes, and carted them to Federal Hill under military and police escort. The train of fifteen wagons that hauled the firearms from the Gittings warehouse on Gay Street was followed by a yelling and hooting crowd, who were kept back by the city police. A boat loaded with muskets and pikes was seized and taken across to the southern side of the harbor under the Union guns. During the day the Sixth Massachusetts, jubilant over their bloodless return to Baltimore, received a shipment of much needed coats, pants, drawers, shirts, rubber blankets and a thousand other things, "which made them all as merry as crickets." [16]

Meanwhile General Scott in a circuitous manner heard about Butler's coup in violation of his strategy. Captain D. H. Williams, an acting aide-de camp, whom Butler had sent across Baltimore to the Calvert Station with instructions to telegraph to York, Pennsylvania, for reinforcements if Butler should run into resistance, found that the telegraph to York was out of order and, exaggerating the import of the midnight rumor of riot, he himself took a special train for York where he besought Major General W. H. Keim to dispatch four or five regiments at once to aid Butler. Keim in turn telegraphed to Major General Robert Patterson at Philadelphia that Butler's need was urgent, and at the same time Colonel Andrew Porter telegraphed Patterson that the Northern Central Railroad, over which reinforcements should have to be sent from central Pennsylvania to Baltimore, was out of order. Patterson, now in haste, dispatched Brevet Major General Cadwallader by boat from Perryville to Fort McHenry, as the speediest means of reinforcing Butler at Federal Hill; and telegraphed Scott what he had done.

General Scott, knowing that Fort McHenry was already filled with troops, tried to countermand Patterson's order, and not until Scott received Patterson's detailed explanation did he learn that Butler had moved from the Relay House into Baltimore. "When I telegraphed you about sufficiency of the garrison at Fort McHenry," fairly sputtered the Lieutenant General in his return telegram to Patterson, "I did not know that General Butler had called for Pennsylvanians to reinforce him. He had occupied Baltimore without my knowledge, and was equally without authority in his call for Pennsylvania troops." [17]

At eight-thirty on Wednesday morning, May 15, Butler received Scott's rebuke: "Sir: Your hazardous occupation of Baltimore was made without my knowledge and of course without my approbation.

It is a God-send that it was without conflict of Arms. It is also reported that you sent a detachment to Frederick [a report of Butler's feint toward Harpers Ferry], but this is impossible. Not a word have I received from you as to either movement. Let me hear from you. Very respectfully, yours, Winfield Scott." [18]

Butler had expected the General-in-Chief at first to be disappointed in the failure of his scheme for taking Baltimore; but once Baltimore was *in-the-bag,* and *by a bloodless victory,* he did expect him to be pleased. Butler delayed making a reply.

Scott, riled, sent another crackling telegram: ". . . Issue no more proclamations. Why assume the authority to call for reinforcements from General Patterson? Answer my letter of last evening. Did you have [leave?] any men at Relay House? Look to their safety. Not a word received from you in several days. Patterson's reinforcements will be at Locust Point this morning early. Winfield Scott." [19] This time Scott omitted the "Very respectfully," and before Butler's detailed report of May 15 reached the War Department the testy General-in-Chief ordered Major General Cadwallader to replace Butler as commander of the Department of Annapolis. Butler was ordered to Fortress Monroe.

Butler turned over the command of the Department to Cadwallader as ordered, and proceeded to Annapolis, where he talked the problem over with Sarah before going to Washington.

In Washington only Scott seemed displeased with the turn of events. Butler received from Secretary of War Cameron the offer of a promotion to Major General, and a crowd gathered at the National Hotel to greet him. Butler made a "happy little speech" to the audience outside his hotel. "The Union must be preserved at all hazards of money, and if need be, of every life this side of the Arctic regions. If the 25,000 Northern soldiers who are here are cut off, in six weeks 50,000 will take their place, and if they die by fever, pestilence or the sword, a quarter of a million will take their place, till our army of reserve will be women, with their broomsticks, to drive every enemy into the gulf . . ." After ten minutes he sent them away. "It is impossible for me to go on speech-making: but if you will go home to your beds, and the government will let me, I will go south fighting for the Union, and you will follow me." His remarks evoked cheers, laughter and cries of "Good, go on." [20]

The next morning General Scott allowed him to stand at attention without asking him to be seated. Then he broke into angry vituperation over the great and needless risk Butler had run.

Butler waited, standing before him, until his patience was exhausted. Having decided to quit the army if necessary, he turned upon the old general and gave him as good as he sent.

He was so wrought up that back in his hotel room he threw himself on a lounge and burst into tears. [21]

From Butler's point of view his transfer from command of a department to command of a fort implied an unjust censure upon his conduct. But Cameron and Chase both urged him to accept the proffered promotion to a major-generalcy as evidence of the Government's real attitude toward him. General Scott, as Cameron pointed out, could not remain much longer as active head of the army. Butler was a prominent "War Democrat" and as such, if for no other reason, was needed in the service, lest the war begin to take on the color of a Republican Party affair.

When on the 18th he received General Scott's detailed orders to proceed to Fortress Monroe and take command, Butler wrote the Secretary of War demanding that the matter be laid before Lincoln.

Lincoln greeted Butler cordially with the hope that he would accept the position at Fortress Monroe and continue to use the same energy that he had displayed at Annapolis and Baltimore.

With Lincoln's permission, Butler returned to his hotel to consult his wife.

Sarah, knowing how unhappy he would be if he refused it, advised him to accept the new commission. In accepting it Butler assured the President that although as a Democrat he had opposed Lincoln's election, he would support the administration as long as he held his commission. "And when I find any act that I cannot support I shall bring the commission back and return it to you." [22]

"That is frank, that is fair." Lincoln broke in. "But I want to add one thing: When you see me doing anything that for the good of the country ought not to be done, come and tell me so, and why you think so, and then perhaps you won't have any chance to resign your commission." [23]

To his brother-in-law and law partner William P. Webster in Lowell Butler wrote: "You will see that I have accepted a major Gen'l. position for the war. I am to go to Virginia to prosecute the war vigorously into the heart of the enemy. God only knows what may be the result. I am in His hands. I speak with reverence. Meantime there is an end to all professional business on my part. Wind up, therefore, our affairs. Save for me what you can. I shall be ruined I know, but that can't be helped . . . Love to all, and God bless you! If anything happens, you and Fisher will take care of those I leave. Yours, Butler. P.S. I go to Fortress Monroe tomorrow." [24]

To his delight Sarah, whom he was prepared to send back to Lowell, decided to accompany him to his new post.

9

BUTLER'S FUGITIVE SLAVE LAW

WHEN Butler went to Fortress Monroe the third week in May his name had become a household word. "Under Providence," asserted Theodore Winthrop in the *Atlantic Monthly* for June of 1861, "Washington owes its safety, 1st to General Butler whose genius devised the circumvention of Baltimore and its rascal rout, and whose utter bravery executed the plan; — he is the Grand Yankee of this little period of the war." [1] B. F. King warned Butler flatteringly from Boston that he had put a keen weapon in the hands of his enemies, the aristocrats. "Your recent achievements have armed them with adulation and flattery. They who were most cunning and bitter in malignity, are now loudest in applause." [2] "You are doing a glorious work, and your name is blessed throughout the Old Commonwealth," wrote his one-time enemy William Schouler, *Courier* editor of 1842, and now Governor Andrew's Adjutant General.[3] In Baltimore, on the other hand, the incident of Butler's dining at the Gilmore House was distorted into an orgy from which Butler emerged drunk and unable to mount his horse.[4] The Norfolk *Day Book* scoffed at "the hero of Annapolis." [5]

The Philadelphia *Press* compiled items on Butler allegedly published in Southern papers:

> Benjamin F. Butler is the son of a negro barber, who, early in the century, did business on Poydras-Street in New Orleans. The son in early manhood, emigrated to Liberia, where an indisposition for labor and some talent turned his attention to the Bar, to prepare for which he repaired to Massachusetts. Having mastered his profession, he acquired a fondness for theological studies and became an active local preacher, the

course of his labors leading him to New York, where he attracted the notice of Mr. Jacob Barker, then in the Zenith of his fame as financier, and who discovering the peculiar abilities in that direction of the young mulatto, sent him to Northern New York to manage a banking institution. There he divided his time between the counting house and the court-room, the prayer-meeting and the printing office . . . and upon the election of Mr. Van Buren to the Presidency was, notwithstanding his color and his complicity in numerous swindling transactions, appointed to the position of Attorney-General. At the close of his term of office he resumed his legal practice in Massachusetts, took a command, and distinguished himself by cowardice in the Mexican War; and had an active part in support of the Buffalo Abolition Platform of 1845. The regiments he led from Massachusetts to Maryland, in April, were, with the exception of two or three drummers composed exclusively of negroes . . . Butler is also the author of Hudibras, a bitter satire on the Democratic Party.[6]

The New York *Times* reprinted the story from the *Press* and denounced Southern forgers of such slanders. A closer view, however, should have revealed to the *Times* editors that several of the alleged details actually applied to different men named Butler. The inclusions of the New York B. F. Butler, the well-known lawyer who had been attorney general under Jackson and Van Buren, and of W. O. Butler of Kentucky, a Vice-Presidential candidate in 1848, should have put the editors on guard, as should the even more conspicuous reference to Samuel Butler, seventeenth century author of the satiric poem *Hudibras,* which was certainly no satire on the Democratic Party.

The *Press* now explained that its Butler story had been "intended as a burlesque upon Southern representations of Northern men and matters, [and] was therefore jocosely ascribed to the New Orleans papers."[7] Despite the disclaimer, however, the hoax was solemnly reprinted throughout the country under such headings as "The Picayune's Pedigree of Gen. Butler." With dismay the New Orleans *Picayune,* an innocent bystander in the case, noted the widespread publicity given to the faked story and denied ever having fathered it.[8]

Nonetheless, the original hoax, rather than the corrections and disclaimers, continued to be circulated and widely credited. To many

Southerners the idea that General Butler was a Negro, the son of
"Old Ben the barber who kept a shop on Poydras Street," invested
this particular Union general with a peculiar and terrible fascination.
The imaginative P. G. T. Beauregard of New Orleans, now commenc-
ing his career as a Confederate general in Virginia, sounded this note
shortly after Butler set foot on Virginia soil at Fortress Monroe, when
he announced to the people of Virginia: "A reckless and unprincipled
tyrant has invaded your soil . . . All rules of civilized warfare are
abandoned, and they proclaim by their acts, if not on their banners,
that their war-cry is 'Beauty and booty'!" [9]

Fortress Monroe, built after 1812 to keep the British ever again
from burning Washington, is a squat masonry fort located at the tip
of the Yorktown Peninsula, between the York and the James Rivers. Its
guns in casemate and in parapet scowled across the lower Chesapeake Bay toward the Virginia Capes and the mouth of the bay. At

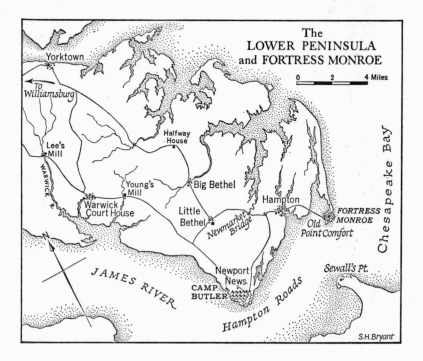

The
LOWER PENINSULA
and FORTRESS MONROE

0   2   4 Miles

Yorktown

TO
Williamsburg

Halfway
House

Lee's
Mill

WARWICK

Young's
Mill

Big Bethel

Warwick
Court House

Little
Bethel

Newmarket
Bridge

Hampton

Old
Point Comfort

FORTRESS
MONROE

Chesapeake Bay

JAMES RIVER

Newport
News

CAMP
BUTLER

Hampton Roads

Sewall's Pt.

S.H.Bryant

the outbreak of the Civil War it was commanded by Colonel Justin Dimick, an elderly West Pointer, and manned by 300 loyal regulars. As a threat to the South, Fortress Monroe sealed the entrance to Norfolk and afforded a safe landing beach for Union troops in Virginia territory from which an advance might be made up the Peninsula to Richmond. Butler hoped that the base of the Federal attack might be shifted from Washington to Fortress Monroe, from which point both Norfolk and Richmond could be menaced.

General Butler, stepping ashore from the steamer *Cataline* at 2 P.M. on May 22, was greeted by his first major general's salute and a parade of the troops in the fort. Colonel Dimick quickly showed him over the seventy-acre enclosure surrounded by the masonry slope inside the walls which caught water for the cisterns. Then they inspected the barracks, the hospital, the little chapel, the avenues lined with live oaks, the parade ground, and, in the center, set among trees and gardens of full-blown roses, the solid, broad, slate-peaked brick residence of the post commander. Sarah worked a dozen men and women a week scouring the new residence and moving in the furniture brought by boat from Annapolis.

To prepare to receive the twelve new regiments that Washington had promised him was Butler's first job. The barracks being crowded already, campsites on the mainland beyond the causeway had to be selected. To supplement the supply of rainwater Colonel Dimick had been hauling water from a spring on the mainland; Butler laid a pipe from the spring along the causeway and posted a guard at the spring. There being no mules or horses at the fort, aside from Butler's own mount and those of his staff, barrels of food and ammunition were rolled in by hand from the Wharf. Butler laid a railroad on the sand from the wharf into the fort and set men to digging an artesian well inside the fort. In a moment of geniality before Butler left Washington, General Scott had congratulated him that his new billet afforded the choicest oysters in the world. Butler now found this to be true. Indeed so many oyster shells had been tossed through the portholes of the bachelor officers' quarters in the casemates as practically to fill up some sectors of the moat. Butler had the ditch cleaned and the exposed magazines on the landward side of the fort banked with sandbags.

The writer Theodore Winthrop, now Butler's secretary, found Fortress Monroe not so neat as a grand military post should be. "But the new regime must change all this, and make this the biggest, the best equipped, and the model garrison of the country." Winthrop dined with the General and his staff and caught their spirit of brisk efficiency. "The new men and the new manners of the new army do not altogether suit the actual men and manners of the obsolete army . . . The Silver-Gray Army needs a frisky element interfused." [10]

The Third Massachusetts, as the first contingent to arrive of Butler's division of twelve regiments, were quartered inside the walls, as were Colonel Dimick's 300; but later arrivals — the Fifth, First, and Second New York — had to be billeted on the mainland. Colonel Dimick's informal agreement with the Virginia militia not to encroach on their soil if they would not deny him access to his water supply was now abandoned. Butler with his aides rode over the flat terrain between the town of Hampton and Black River to select campgrounds. Across this flat country the only roads were cart tracks, the farmhouses were miserably mean and without paint and the cattle mostly bony scalawags hardly worth foraging for. The plantation house of ex-President Tyler, from which Butler's aides jerked down the Confederate flag, was "a bare blank brick house." The fastidious Winthrop was appalled by the drab lot of the tidewater planter: "Here are men claiming to have been worth forty thousand dollars, half in biped property, half in all other kinds, and they lived in dens such as draymen would have disdained and a hodcarrier only accepted on compulsion." [11]

Campsites were allotted the New York regiments. "Each is in a wheat field, up to its eyes in dust. In order of precedence they come One, Two, and Five; in order of personal splendor of uniform they come Five, One, Two . . . The Second has done rather the most robbing of henroosts. The Fifth, Duryea's Zouaves, Lighten up the woods brilliantly with their scarlet legs and scarlet head-pieces." [12]

While Butler was riding over the back country, Major J. B. Cary, a politician of Butler's acquaintance and now a member of the Virginia Volunteers, set fire to the bridge near Hampton. Colonel Phelps with 500 troops rushed ahead to extinguish the blaze. Phelps, a lanky Vermont farmer and an ardent abolitionist, assured Cary that he had come "with no hostile purpose, but simply, by order of General Butler, to reconnoiter";[13] whereupon Cary — the war being as yet young — aided him in stamping out the fire. Afterwards from the dome of the Chesapeake Female College in Hampton, Cary looking out across the treetops saw the Union regiments pitching camp in Virginia wheat and knew "that Virginia's sacred soil had been violated."

The next day Hampton was occupied by Union troops and the fine strategic position at Newport News was seized. Newport News commanded a view of the lower James River and a few batteries placed there would interrupt water communications of the Confederates between Richmond and Norfolk and afford Butler a base for operations up the James toward Richmond.

While his force was accumulating and his military strategy assuming definite shape, Butler found himself faced with the baffling legalistic-military problem of the fugitive slave.

Three field hands belonging to Colonel Charles K. Mallory, 115th Regiment of Virginia Militia, who commanded in the lower Yorktown Peninsula, escaped to Union pickets and were brought before General Butler. The blacks said their master intended to send them to North Carolina to work on Confederate fortifications. Butler questioned the Negroes and himself having need of laborers to unscramble the quartermasters' stores on the beach, he set them to work there. He decided to send a receipt to Colonel Mallory, as was customary when seizing any other private property, but before he had done so he heard from the Confederate Colonel's agent, Major Cary.

Major Cary approaching under flag of truce requested an interview with General Butler. As the General did not wish him to be brought inside the fort, where sandbags were being piled over vulnerable magazines, he rode across the causeway to meet him, accompanied by two aides. The Confederate officer was a fellow Democrat whom Butler had last seen at the Charleston and Baltimore conventions. As they sauntered on horseback up to the head of Mill Creek and back they held their conference.

Cary asked whether Butler would release Colonel Mallory's Negroes in accordance with the Fugitive Slave Act.

"I intend to hold them," Butler replied.[14]

"Do you mean, then to set aside your constitutional obligation to return them?"

"I mean to take Virginia at her word, as declared in the ordinance of secession. I am under no constitutional obligations to a foreign country, which Virginia now claims to be."

"But you say we cannot secede," countered the Virginian, "and so you cannot consistently detain the Negroes."

"But you say you have seceded, so you cannot consistently claim them. I shall hold these negroes as contraband of war, since they are engaged in the construction of your battery and are claimed as your property. Yet, though I greatly need the labor which has providentially come to my hands, if Colonel Mallory will come into the fort and take the oath of allegiance to the United States, he shall have his negroes, and I will endeavor to hire them from him."

As the Union officers rode back to the fort Peter Haggerty questioned the legality of the General's classification of Negroes as contraband. "At any rate, Haggerty," Butler parried, "it is a good enough reason to stop the rebels' mouths with, especially as I should have held these Negroes anyway."[15]

Butler's decision to classify Negroes as contraband of war, struck the popular imagination. Abolitionists everywhere exulted, and the people of the North generally applauded this means of retaliating against Virginia's First Families for carrying their state into Secession. Virginians, crowed the New York *Times,* "will find the General a match for them in more ways than one."[16]   Theodore Winthrop jotted down a note for an *Atlantic* article: "An epigram abolished slavery in the United States . . . 'Negroes are contraband of war' . . . As General Butler takes contraband horses used in transport of munitions of war, so he takes contraband black creatures who tote the powder to the carts and flagellate the steeds . . ."[17]

Washington was both delighted and baffled. Secretary Cameron approved Butler's action. "The Department is sensible of the embarrassments which must surround Officers conducting Military operations in a State by the laws of which Slavery is sanctioned . . . refrain from surrendering to alleged masters any persons who may come within your lines . . . The question of their final disposition will be reserved for further determination." [18] General Scott, to whom Butler now wrote often and lengthily, at first growled to Andrew Jackson Butler, the General's bearer of dispatches, that he would reverse General Butler's actions: but Montgomery Blair sent word that Scott had since changed his mind.

> Dear General [wrote Blair], Your brother brought me your note. But I suppose by this time you will hardly think my opinion necessary to convince you that you were right when you declared secession niggers contraband of war. The Secessionists have used them to do all their fortifying, and I suppose nobody can doubt that this sort of work at which the Secessionists have applied themselves with immense energy is the essence of their military operations. The question is to come up in the Cabinet tomorrow, and whilst your brother says that old Scott said he intended ordering you to change your actions, the President told me this morning that he had not seen old Lundy as merry since he had known him, as he was this morning at your decision on the fugitive slave question. He called it Butler's fugitive slave law. The President seemed to think it a very important subject, however, and one requiring some thought in view of the numbers of negroes we are likely to have on hand in virtue of this new doctrine.[19]

Washington could delay before reaching its decisions. At the front, however, Butler's "fugitive slave law" commenced its inexorable operation. Not only able-bodied males — to whom the contraband decision applied — but Negro women and children, babies at the breast and decrepit ancients, streamed into the Federal camps. On May 27 Butler reported to Scott the growing acuteness of the problem:

> The escapees . . . are very numerous; and a squad has come in this morning to my pickets, bringing with them their women and children. Of course these cannot be dealt with upon the theory on which I de-

signed to treat the services of able-bodied men and women who might come within my lines, and of which I gave you a detailed account in my last despatch. I am in the utmost doubt what to do with this species of property . . . I have therefore determined to employ, as I can do very profitably, the able-bodied persons in the party, issuing proper food for the support of all . . . As a matter of property to the insurgents, it will be of very great moment the number I now have . . . Twelve of these negroes I am informed have escaped from the erection of the Batteries on Sewell's Point, which this morning fired upon my expedition as it passed by out of range.[20]

Butler appointed a Commissioner of Negro Affairs, and set up a Negro camp, which the darkies called "Freedom Fort."

Lote Hildreth, Sarah's youngest sister, who helped manage the commandant's busy household, wrote: "Negroes come in every day from the outside, and one day as many as forty came into the backyard; of all ages, from babies up to old men and women. It was a ludicrous and at the same time a sad sight to see the poor creatures, homeless, not knowing when or where they were to get their next meal . . . We called them the 'Virginia Volunteers' . . . We have new recruits daily, and our Commissary is getting to be one of the largest and most important in the fort." [21]

By the end of May, the influx of Negroes had become, in Butler's word, a "Disaster," about which he and his staff did not know whether to rejoice or weep. There was much in the situation that was tragic and much that was comic.

One day an old "church-warden looking" gentleman was admitted to see the General. He had come to request the return of one of his Negroes — "just one." Because of the military encampments around the Fort, his wife had gone to be with relatives some eleven miles away, leaving him alone on the plantation with his thirty Negroes. "I have always treated my Negroes kindly," said the old man. "I supposed they loved me. Last Sunday, I went to church. When I returned from church, and entered into my house, I called Mary to take off my coat and hang it up. But Mary did not come. And again I called Mary in a louder voice, but I received no answer. Then I went into the room to find Mary but I found her not. There was no one in the room. I went into the kitchen. There was no one in the kitchen. I went into the garden. There was no one in the garden. I went to the Negro quarters. There was no one at the Negro quarters. All my Negroes had departed, sir, while I was at the house of God. Then I went back into my house. And soon there came to me James. 'James, what has happened?'" James after finding his master some cold victuals and whisky, hitched the best horse to the cart and drove his master to his wife's home. "I met my wife, sir," continued the old man, "I embraced her, and went to bed; and, notwithstanding my troubles, I slept soundly. The next morning, *James was gone!* Then I came here, and the first thing I saw, when I got here, was James peddling cabbages to your men out of that very cart." [22]

General Butler's "contraband" decision, commented the New York *Times,* "was a happy fancy, and is very well when applied to fifty or a hundred persons; but when the number swells, as it is likely to do, to 10,000, 20,000, or 50,000, such a mass of contraband can hardly be put to a valuable use upon fortifications. But they must be taken care of." [23]

At the end of May, 1861, the New York *Times* found no military man who "concentrated upon himself a larger share of public interest and attention" than General Butler. "It is not too much to say that Gen. Butler, by his memorable movement to Annapolis; his seizure of the ship *Constitution;* official correspondence with Gov. Hicks; his occupation and repair of the road to Washington; his sudden encampment at the Relay House; his noble march to Baltimore; his posting cannon upon the hill overhanging the city; and his wise proclamation to the people of Baltimore, saved the state of Maryland from plunging into the black depths of treason, and from political and social woes unnumbered." [24] A not entirely flattering brochure on Butler which had been first published in the Charlestown, Massachusetts, *Advertiser* of September 7, 1859, was now dusted off by the Northern press: "Through life he has cut his own way, and a wide, long breadth of swath has he carried. He has wrung success from men and circumstances . . . that were reluctant to concede it to him . . ." [25] Thumbnail sketches of Butler from all quarters of New England, anecdotes of his court trials and political campaigns, any and all stories, both friendly and hostile, were eagerly sought by the hungry presses. His crossed eyes promptly gained for him South of the Potomac the nickname "Old Cock Eye."

In the South Butler's decision to classify Negroes as "contraband of war" was popular only with the Negroes. Literate whites whose property in slaves was jeopardized did not reflect that almost any Union general penetrating the agricultural South might have been compelled by circumstances to confiscate slave property, without, perhaps, offering the catch-phrase as a legalistic reason. The fact was that Butler was the first general to face the issue, and boldly to dramatize the decision. Thus he drew upon his own person the wrath of every Southerner who owned slaves.

Henceforth, whatever success Ben Butler might achieve in the military field, he could definitely count on derision and hatred from the loyal Southerner to a degree that none other of Lincoln's generals could rival.

10

ENOUGH ROPE

WHEN General Scott in anger banished Butler to Fortress Monroe, he had no intention of launching him on the highroad to military success, but meant to tie him down to local action. On the Yorktown Peninsula — the direct route to Richmond — he was permitted "to capture any batteries the enemy may have within a half-day's march of you, and which may be reached by land." [1] Butler's seizure of the fine military post of Newport News, which enabled him to control the lower James, and his handling of the contraband question so pleased General Scott that he unleashed Butler. "The restriction . . . as to capture of batteries within a half day's march by land is removed. Though more distant expeditions are not enjoined, they are yet not prohibited." [2]

Gustavus Fox, the Old Reynard of Butler's school days and now Assistant Secretary of the Navy, feared that Scott was giving Butler enough rope to hang himself. "I do trust," he cautioned Butler, "you will be fully prepared before you move. The first battle must be won. All others will be easy, and I pray you take care of this point, whatever may urge you to quicken measures. There is no impatience here, in fact all goes well, so don't trouble yourself. We will take care of your rear." [3] But in the same mail Butler received a letter from Fox's brother-in-law, Postmaster General Montgomery Blair, in effect advising him to go slow, but win a victory quickly. [4]

Despite the obvious wisdom of waiting until fully prepared, there was one compelling reason to push on at once into military action. The enlistment periods of the three-months volunteers were running out. Several of Butler's regiments would have to be returned to

Boston for demobilization early in July. Added to this was the fact that the other troops that had been promised him either were slow in arriving or had been diverted elsewhere. "It was understood when I left Washington," Butler reminded General Scott, "that the three Massachusetts regiments — two of which are at the Relay House — should be forwarded to me here, and also Cook's Light Battery, of which I have the utmost need if I am expected ever to occupy an extended camp with safety. May I ask the attention of the Commanding General to this subject, and inquire if the exigencies of the service will permit these troops to be sent to me immediately." [5]

Fresh regiments from Boston came without tents. "Why is this?" Butler asked Governor Andrew, "I have written three times upon this subject . . . It is much *more necessary* to the health of the men than the luxuries of the table so lavishly bestowed by the open hand of the Commonwealth (Heaven bless her!) upon us all." [6]

In this early stage of the war recruiting was not limited to State and National authorities. A free-lance named Washington A. Bartlett, enrolling 880 men in an organization styled "the Naval Brigade," chartered a leaky steamer and came on to Fortress Monroe, supplied with nothing but rip-roaring enthusiasm. Butler allowed them to disembark at the fort because of the foul condition of their boat, and fed them. The still hungry adventurers robbed a number of henroosts in the belief that all property of the inhabitants was subject to plunder, until Butler cracked down on them. Those who would not accept jobs in the engineer, or ordnance and quartermaster departments about the fort, he re-embarked on their leaky tub and sent home.

On June 6 Butler's force had increased to 6750 men, about equally divided between three-months volunteers who had received a maximum of two months of military training and newly recruited, three-year volunteers whose drilling had not commenced until after their arrival at Fortress Monroe. Colonel Dimick's few hundred regulars were struggling to transform these citizens into soldiers, but there was no ready means of procuring efficient officers. Regiments recruited under state auspices were commanded by militia officers, picked by state governors. Butler's ranking assistant, Brigadier General Ebenezer W. Pierce, was like Butler himself a Massachusetts lawyer and politician. Actually the fact that Pierce had at one time before the war been senior to Butler in the State Militia made Butler feel an obligation to honor him with a post of responsibility in the forthcoming military campaign.

In equipment Butler's regiments were unevenly provided. One Massachusetts regiment lacked tents, another had no kettles, a New York regiment faced hot weather with only heavy winter clothing, another had been outfitted in shoddy they could push their fingers through, so that after a few weeks in camp they were in rags. Though a few companies were armed with modern rifles, a majority in all the regiments carried old-fashioned muzzle-loading muskets like Daniel Boone's. Ammunition was at first too short to permit target practice. For some 5000 muskets Butler had only 8000 rounds of buck and ball! Butler had a few horses for his commissary, a few for his staff — he had brought nine of his own horses down from Lowell — but he had no mounted pickets to be thrown out wide to protect his outlying encampments at Hampton and Newport News.

Butler expected a Confederate attack on Newport News. Small detachments of Rebel cavalry regularly harassed working parties outside the Newport News fortifications, killing or capturing a man now and then, and panicking the raw Union troops with their war whoops.[7] Unable to scout the countryside for want of horses, Butler obtained the assistance of naval gunboats which at night stood by on either flank of Newport News ready to enfilade the sector in front of the Union earthworks in case of a Rebel assault.

Confederates from Yorktown placed a few guns at the crossroads village of Big Bethel, midway between Yorktown and Fortress Monroe, and from this outpost raided the countryside, impressing farmers into their army and seizing Negroes around the Federal camp at Hampton for work on their Yorktown–Williamsburg fortifications. Butler engaged Professor John La Mountain the balloonist to make an aerial reconnaissance to see what the enemy was about.

On Sunday June 9 Butler planned a military expedition to dislodge the Rebels from Big Bethel before they had had time to develop a stronghold. George Scott, an intelligent contraband who boasted that he could "smell a rebel furderer den he ken a skunk,"[8] brought information that naval howitzers were mounted behind earthworks near the bridge at Big Bethel.

Butler's plan was to move out several regiments on Sunday night from his advanced bases at Hampton and Newport News, to unite these in the forest and before dawn deliver a surprise attack at a Confederate picket outpost a few miles east of Big Bethel known as Little Bethel. "If we bag the Little Bethel men, push on to Big Bethel, and similarly bag them. Burn both the Bethels or blow up if brick."[9] The uncertainty in the Federal camp as to whether these churches were of frame or brick construction was indicative of their lack of familiarity with the terrain over which the forthcoming action would occur. The expedition was to carry only two small mountain howitzers and one six-pounder fieldpiece. George Scott, the scout, was to accompany the party, and make history for his race as the first Negro in the Federal forces to defend his freedom with a musket.[10]

General Pierce, to whom Butler entrusted the command of the expedition, left the fort early in the afternoon with one day's cooked rations. He had but recently arrived at Fortress Monroe and his status as senior commander of Massachusetts Militia, but without a National commission, left him in the dubious position of "first among equals" when he came to command the several colonels of New York volunteers. The green troops were spoiling for a fight; and Butler was sending them out on a comparatively simple mission to experience their baptism of fire.

Major Winthrop, Butler's military secretary and a favorite because of his nimble wit and ready pen, begged to be allowed to go. Butler reminded him that the correspondence load was very heavy. "Oh, General we will all work extra hours and make that up when we get back."[11] Butler assented, and later regretted it.

By midnight General Pierce had two regiments on the road.

The bridge over Hampton Creek having been destroyed, the troops from Camp Hamilton were ferried across in flatboats. The red-legged Zouaves under Colonel Abram Duryea, first to be ferried over, plunged about midnight through the pine and live-oak forest toward

Little Bethel. Several miles behind marched Colonel Frederick Townsend's Third New York, with their neat gray uniforms that in the dim light were scarcely distinguishable from Confederate uniforms. General Pierce, with his staff, rode at the head of Townsend's column.

Shortly after midnight as he reached the village of Little Bethel with its Negro church, Duryea flushed a group of mounted pickets of the enemy. One of these they seized, a luckless youngster caught asleep on the roadside. Duryea, about to give chase to the other pickets, was brought up short by a spasm of musket and artillery fire *in his rear*. Wheeling, he marched back to join Townsend.

Meanwhile Colonel John E. Bendix, leading the reserve force from Newport News, had arrived at a crossroads five miles west of Hampton. He knew that Duryea's column had already passed down the road toward the Bethels; but he did not know that Townsend's gray-clad column was marching in the dim blackness over the crossroads ahead of him. General Pierce and his staff on horseback two hundred yards ahead of Townsend were mistaken by Bendix for a body of enemy cavalry.

In the dark, unable to see the white identifying armbands of Townsend's men, Bendix ordered a fieldpiece to be unlimbered and loaded. Apparently this order to alert the artillery was misinterpreted by Bendix's company of German-speaking riflemen from the Seventh New York as an order to fire, for without more ado these gentry let loose a volley of rifle fire upon the dim shapes ahead and Lieutenant Greble the artillerist, possibly without orders from Bendix, fired several rounds of shrapnel that scattered the dark target shapes into the woods.

Pierce and Townsend retreated as their men took cover. At length skirmishers were sent to shout the watchword "Boston"; whereupon Colonel Bendix's force was recognized as friendly. Bendix's blunder at the crossroads cost Townsend 2 killed and 21 wounded.[12] From a farmhouse several excited shots were now fired upon the rear of Bendix's line. Bendix arrested two Secessionists and set fire to their house.

While the blaze of the burning dwelling lighted up the sky over the flat sandy forest, General Pierce sent back to Camp Hamilton for reinforcements and huddled in a council of war with his officers. Two of his staff advised giving up the mission, as the enemy, being warned, would be able to gain reinforcements from Yorktown. Against this counsel Theodore Winthrop and Peter Haggerty, Butler's aides, urged him to go on with his mission; and Pierce once more, as dawn was breaking, faced westward on the forest road toward the Bethels. Marching toward their first encounter, the men sang "The Star-Spangled Banner" and "Dixie Land." [13]

In the village of Little Bethel, which was found to be undefended, the Negro church building was burned to eliminate its possible use as an outpost by the enemy. A dry, unpainted frame structure, it flared like a torch. From a woman at a farmhouse General Pierce gathered the misinformation that Big Bethel was garrisoned by 4000 men, and this fourfold exaggeration was "vouched for" by a Negro encountered on the road. By Pierce's own advance scouts the enemy's five small fieldpieces and one Parrott rifle at Big Bethel were multiplied by three and listed as "heaviest rifled cannon." Three-foot earthworks that any horse could have walked over were reported by Pierce's big-eyed and inexperienced militia soldiers as "embankments twenty feet high." [14]

A mile farther on, within sight of Big Bethel, the Federal column halted and deployed on either side of the road. It was now ten o'clock, the thermometer nearing ninety, and the heavy clothing of some of the Northern troops was better suited to the bivouac on a cold night than a battle encounter at midday. Duryea's red-hatted and red-legged Zouaves vaulted a fence to deploy in a cornfield, their colonel on horseback leading. Townsend's regiment poured through an orchard to the left of the main road, and as they advanced toward the enemy's batteries took shelter behind a house and a barn, several hundred yards from the Confederate positions.

At Big Bethel the Confederate Colonel J. B. Magruder's fieldpieces commanded both the County Bridge and the milelong length of cleared fields that approached it. On the Hampton side of the bridge and overlooking the cornfield across which the Federals were advancing, Magruder had placed a howitzer.

Lieutenant John T. Greble of the Second U.S. Artillery moved his six-pounder fieldpiece and two twelve-pounder mountain howitzers down the open road within two hundred yards of the enemy and began a duel that lasted over two hours. He was protected from the nearest Confederate battery by a barn, now occupied by Townsend's troops. A Confederate youth who volunteered to dash across the field and set fire to the barn was shot down by sharpshooters. There was much scrambling to and fro across the cornfield from the woods on the right and back again. Lieutenant Duryea, son of the colonel, led a charge against the hill battery. The excited Confederate gunners, having jammed a priming wire in their gun, dumped it into Marsh Creek to prevent its capture, and ran. Later in the day another group of Confederates retook the hill.

On the Federal right Duryea failed in an attempt to outflank the enemy. George Scott, the contraband, held the horse for Major Theodore Winthrop while the latter led a charge, and never saw Winthrop again. The globe-trotting journalist, brandishing a borrowed sword, leaped from the top rail of a fence and was shot by a squirrel-shooting drummer boy from North Carolina. According to Southern sources he fell closer to the Confederate earthworks than any other Federal soldier came that day. Of the four companies of skirmishers who demonstrated in front of the enemy, Captain Kilpatrick's "Red Devils," with their red hats and leggings, suffered more casualties than any other group.[15] One of Colonel Townsend's companies, while executing a flank movement, became separated from the rest of their regiment by a thicket and Townsend mistaking them for a body of enemy troops ordered a retreat.

From his central command post in the rear, General Pierce, noting Townsend's retirement, at 12:20 P.M. decided to give up the attempt to take Big Bethel. Throughout the entire affair Pierce had understood nothing of the situation as a whole, but instead of attributing the failure to poor intelligence service, he ascribed it to the reluctance of the New York colonels to support a Massachusetts brigadier! Thumbnail descriptions of Pierce which the New York troops gave to newspaper correspondents depicted him as confused and unable to give any orders that his men could comprehend, crying "Boston charge!" when none could hear him, and running up and down the lines "like a crazy man, shouting to his men without any system, or apparent knowledge of what he ought to do . . ." [16]

Nor did it enhance Pierce's reputation that some front-line soldiers believed that they had been about to win at the moment when his retreat was sounded. Lieutenant Greble whose meager artillery had made the finest military display on the field was struck on the back of the head by a cannon ball just after he had begun the retreat.

During the retreat so many undisciplined Federals discarded their canteens and clothing that the area back of the battleground suggested a wholesale rout — a circumstance that the Confederates exploited in their newspaper accounts of this fiasco. A Yankee chaplain managed to rally several rescue parties and bring off some of the dead and wounded, but others fell to the enemy. In the late afternoon the Confederates, too, uncertain about the Federal plans, abandoned their position at Big Bethel and returned to their base at Yorktown. Although their force of 600 had been increased during the engagement to over 1200, they were unwilling to accept the hazard of a night encounter with a force estimated to be four times the size of their own.

The outnumbered Confederates fighting from behind cover had lost only one man killed and half a dozen wounded while the Federals paid for their maneuvering in the open field with 18 killed, 53 wounded and 5 missing. Rated with later actions of the war, Big Bethel, of course, was a mere skirmish. On June 10, 1861, however, the first Federal disaster at Bull Run was yet six weeks in the future, and Big Bethel's casualties, taken in conjunction with Bendix's error in firing on his fellow New Yorkers, Townsend's mistaking a company of his own men for the enemy, Pierce's inept conduct during the battle, and the generally amateurish conduct of the troops in throwing away their equipment, gave the affair a news value out of all proportion to its actual importance. And since the newspapers doggedly refused to drop Big Bethel until after Bull Run had occurred, the incident almost cost "citizen general" Butler his shoulder straps.

After 7 A.M., when Butler received Pierce's call for reinforcements, he at once sent from Hampton the two reserve regiments under Colonels Carr and Allen, and mounting his favorite gray stallion Butler himself raced at top speed to Newport News to alert the four regiments there to be sent forward if necessary.[17] Back in Hampton, he started forward the ambulance for the wounded and was about to proceed to the front in person when word came that the engagement at Big Bethel had been called off and that the troops were returning to camp. Butler, accordingly, remained on the ground at Hampton, dispatching boat howitzers to guard the retreat at New Market bridge and interviewing the captured Confederate picket and the prisoners whose house had been burned in retaliation for their firing on the troops. After the first weary soldiers reached Hampton about 4 P.M., Butler saw the wounded put on boats and towed around to the hospital at the fort. Before midnight on this crowded day, while yet unable to get a clear picture of events, he dictated a 1500-word preliminary report to General Scott.

In this report Butler accepted General Pierce's mistaken assurance that "the dead and wounded had all been brought off, and that the return had been conducted in good order and without haste." "I think," Butler concluded, "in the unfortunate combination of circumstances and the result which we experienced, we have gained more than we have lost. Our troops have learned to have confidence in themselves under fire. The enemy have shown that they will not meet us in the open field. Our officers have learned wherein their organization and drill are inefficient." [18]

As the first shock of arms in the area, this skirmish revealed the deficiencies of Butler's own management as the responsible general of the Department. He had leaned too heavily upon the advice of Winthrop, the war correspondent, and also upon General Pierce, Governor Andrew's political appointee. Washington, too, could share the blame for failure to supply Butler with horses for cavalry and artillery units, as Quartermaster General M. C. Meigs freely acknowledged.

Old General Scott, with more reason now to cashier Butler than he had had after the Baltimore incident, nevertheless played a craftier game of waiting to let the situation clarify . . .

For Butler and everyone else at Fortress Monroe the weeks following Big Bethel were full of heart-searching anguish, while their little corner of the world was critically scrutinized by a none-too-scrupulous and wholly uncontrolled press. The death of Lieutenant Greble — the first casualty of the war from the Philadelphia area — provoked angry comment from the Philadeophia *Inquirer;* which charged that Greble had been sacrificed "in order that Butler might be made a Major-General, without possessing the rudiments of military skill." [19] Understandably the Confederate press ignored their own force's retirement from Big Bethel after the engagement, as with distortions and amplifications they trumpeted the Federal "repulse" into every corner of the South. Everywhere Southern bonfires were lighted and bells were rung. Jefferson Davis hailed Big Bethel as a "bright augury of more important victories in the future." [20]

11

RECOVERY AFTER BIG BETHEL

BUTLER'S most imperative need, as he now saw it, was trained military officers. New England zeal and parade-field experience alone were not enough. He suggested a board to go through the entire list of officers and weed out the weaklings before they disgraced themselves and the country. He combed the records of junior officers of the Regular Army units attached to his command and sent his brother Andrew to Washington to get them appointments to more responsible positions. Let newly inducted civilian officers handle the services of supply. To officers who were alcoholics, Butler granted generous leaves of absence, in the belief that their departures would benefit the unit. For Colonel J. W. Phelps, the Vermont abolitionist and an ex-officer in the Regular Army now serving as a volunteer, Butler sought the rating of brigadier; "although some of the regular Officers will when applied to say that he is not in his right mind, the only evidence I have seen of it is a deep religious enthusiasm upon the subject of Slavery, which in my judgment does not unfit him to fight the battles of the North." [1]

Next to officers Butler needed horses. He wanted advanced pickets, mounted on horseback, he wanted artillery, he wanted cavalry. He felt that was the clearest lesson of Big Bethel. Butler sent his brother Andrew to Baltimore as a private purchaser to procure horses. Ironically, after Andrew Butler had rounded up 135 animals, the quartermasters commandeered 100 for service in Washington. Big burly Andrew, boiling mad, was for several days bedridden with bilious fever before he could get back to Fortress Monroe. Butler promptly sent Andrew's son George to Boston to induce the Massachusetts State authorities to send cavalry horses to Fortress Monroe. At the same time, with Washington's permission, he dispatched Judson Kilpatrick to New York to recruit artillerymen. New York City's Union Defense Committee had several pieces of artillery which Butler wanted, but which the Committee was reluctant to part with. Upon investigation Butler learned that Henry J. Raymond, Editor of the New York *Times,* recently entertained by Butler as a war correspondent at Fortress Monroe, had frowned upon the project. Butler sent his faithful Andrew back to Washington to work through New York Congressmen to circumvent Raymond and get the artillery.

The affair of Big Bethel attracted to Fortress Monroe an assortment of Congressmen, Cabinet members, foreign observers and inventors, and in entertaining them the General's wife played a leading role. Fireworks were displayed for guests on the Fourth of July. On the fifth the Secretary of War and Mrs. Cameron with a party of important people came down from Washington to spend the day.

Of course [Sarah explained to her sister Harriet Heard] it was my duty to play the courtier to the people who have it in their power to send troops here and everything else that is wanted! It was a mere chance that Mrs. Lincoln was not of the party. We kept the carriages and horses running, guns firing, but I might as well begin at the beginning. Fifteen guns when they landed, and after breakfast, which they had at Capt. Dyer's, they called on me, and we started at once for Newport News, seven or eight miles down the bay. Firing again when we reached the point, a review of the troops there. Boiled potatoes, new, with a pinch of salt taken from the soldiers' rations, champagne and cakes furnished by Drs. Sanborn and Martin, which they got by rushing on board the "Monticella" or sending perhaps. It was so fortunate, for the Secretary's wife can drink nothing but champagne, poor woman. She is quite advanced, and very seldom eats meat. Great shouting when we left the wharf to return to the Fortress. Went all through Dr. Kimball's hospital, a glass of wine at Col. de Russy's, back to our house to dinner. A review in the Fort, into the carriage and away to the boats, to go on board the "Minnesota," a vessel of War. Back from there and out to Hampton, two miles outside the Fort for another review. In again between eight and nine for tea, and at half past nine away they go for Washington . . . Did you ever hear of such a day's work . . . It is only persons in office who are obliged to dance attendance. I flattered myself I did it for once with a good deal of skill. And the time required it, several points have been gained and more are to be had we believe.[2]

Concessions granted one day might be reneged upon the next. A month after Big Bethel, Butler's brother Andrew after waiting all morning in Cameron's anteroom, found the Secretary "cool to the point of insolence" toward Butler's necessities. In his hurried scrawl Andrew reported that Cameron "looked over the papers *official* and *unofficial,* and very cavalierly turned one over to Gen. Scott, another to Qr. M. Gen., a third to the Surgeon Gen. & c. & c., with the remark that 'he could not attend to such matters; if he did he would have the whole war upon his shoulders' . . . I don't like the looks of things here, and my deliberate opinion is they all, *Lincoln, Cameron, & Scott,* are against you, but there is a bare possibility I may be mistaken." [3]

Enlistments of the Third and Fourth Massachusetts Regiments expired by mid-July and the First Vermont by August 1. Mustering these troops out of the service and arranging for their transportation north and the training of the new regiments which arrived to replace them occupied much of Butler's time. Because of scarcity of serviceable firearms among troops at the front, Butler retained the rifles belonging to homeward-bound troops. Every move of this sort entailed interminable correspondence with nettled State administrative officers. Sarah Butler, exhausted by midsummer social activity, returned to Lowell to get the children ready for school. She was also angry with Ben for leaning so heavily on the advice of his brother Andrew and of Andrew's son George, both of whom Sarah distrusted.

To Ben's difficulties there was now added that of the hypochondriac tone in Sarah's letters. "You know, dearest, how full of tears I was when I left you. Mile after weary mile I watched the houses, trees, and fields, and kept the tears from brimming over. When we reached the boat for Fall River the black rings round my eyes and the exhausted, hopeless face scared me into the berth, and, ceasing to struggle, let the flood swell up and take its own sorrowful course. You will not be surprised at this deep sadness which held me even up to our own gate, without one throb of pleasant expectation at sight of home and all it contains until I heard the sound of the children's voices, playing in the evergreens. They saw the carriage, and ran to us with shouts of delight. The driver stopped, and they clambered into the hack with such a noise, screaming, 'Here is mother, and we thought father was coming too! Where is he? And why did he not come?' They think you ought not to be away so long. The children hung round me all day so that I could not write a word till now. Home looks lovely, sweeter than any place I have ever seen, if we were ready to enjoy it . . . I know you are too busy to have much thought for us, but yet, sometimes *remember* . . . Think of the years long gone by, kiss me, and do not forget. Sarah." [4] And a week later her opening sentence demanded "Do not read this with your business letters, wait till you are at leisure . . . Oh, dearest, have half an hour at night, when you are alone, and let it be sacred to me, to home, and the children." [5]

"My dear Sarah," retorted Ben; "Why do you write me so much grief and despondency? Our home is not to be broken up or our lives embittered. We are as fortunate as the lot of humanity will admit . . . Meanwhile, I am not so jolly as to need so mournful letters as yours to keep me from being too jubilant . . . Shake off this hypochondria. You claim to be a woman of mind. Why not exert that mind in making yourself and me happy — not miserable. Be cheerful, cheer me. I need it enough. It never rains but it pours. Every trouble, public and private, comes pouring in at once. I hardly dare open my mail lest I should find that my house is burned or my children dead . . . Pray be cheerful, you, so that there may be one spot where I can believe there is a happy welcome for me. Very affectionately, dearest, *Your, Husband.*" [6]

Most of his public troubles at this time concerned discipline. Soldiers flagrantly disobeyed their officers and mocked them to their faces. Officers appeared before their companies reeling from drink, to damn and goddamn their men. Butler made a drive against sutlers who sold liquor to soldiers. He stove in their barrels. When he caught them hiding liquor beneath the floorboards of their shacks he packed them away on the next boat. Butler discovered that some officers had used their purchasing privilege to obtain whisky which they then peddled to their troops. Butler now banned both sale and use of liquor throughout his military department, and shipped his private stock of wine back to Lowell.[7]

Robbing henroosts and pigsties Butler was never able to stop. However, when his soldiers made off with chairs, tables and other furniture, these articles were taken from them and restored where possible to their owners.

Several companies of the Ninth New York at Newport News, whose pay accounts were snarled up and whose shoddy uniforms had not yet been replaced, announced through a committee their intention to do no more duty, and failed to turn out for inspection. Butler, going at once to Newport News, ordered all regiments into line and kept them standing at attention in the burning sun for three hours. The mutinous companies were ordered to step forward.[8] Members of their committee on grievances were arrested and imprisoned. Butler now lectured the companies on their position as soldiers, and explained why they had not yet been paid or provided with new uniforms. Then, as he reported to Scott, he "required all who intended to return to duty to obey an order which I gave them. Everyone immediately and promptly obeyed the order."[9] The next day Butler sent Andrew Butler to Washington to get a paymaster, and another messenger to Philadelphia for uniforms. If a paymaster was not sent within three days, he let it be understood, he would pay them himself from funds commandeered from the Adams Express Company.

Colonel William H. Allen of the First New York arrested several farmers who with Butler's permission were trying to harvest their crops, and ordered his troops to set fire to a wheat field. Allen's troops promptly got out of hand in violations of property and insults to the civilian population.

Butler haled Colonel Allen before a court-martial, on the theory that it would be better to shoot a colonel than to let the army degenerate into a rabble. The case dragged on for weeks. Allen's fellow colonels, who had lodged complaints against him, backed down now that the issue had been joined, so that Butler himself was left to do the prosecuting. This, however, he proceeded to do. "General Butler can do nothing that will rebound more to his honor than in wiping out this stain upon the forces under his command," wrote the New York *Times* reporter. Allen's men "have entered private houses, which had been deserted and shut up by their owners, and destroyed, from sheer wantonness, the furniture which they contained. I have heard of elegant pianos broken in pieces — boxes containing libraries broken open and books scattered about — chairs and sofas cut, pictures defaced, mirrors broken and other outrages perpetrated more worthy of savages than of soldiers drawn from the ranks of civil life. It is said that Col. Allen has done nothing to check these disgraceful excesses, — but on the contrary, he screens them from blame and encourages and even aids them in their acts of wanton destruction." [10]

For some days the confirmation of Butler's commission as major general hung fire in the Senate. The New York *Times* reported: "There is a strong impression . . . that Gen. Butler will not pass the ordeal of the Senate. Perhaps the wish is father to the thought. Whether justly or unjustly, it is nevertheless true, that the feeling here against Gen. Butler is very strong and decided." Butler's sternness toward his politically potent subordinate officers generally came under fire. "Instead of warmly taking the inexperienced officers by the hand and pointing out to them in a kind manner the path of duty, he seems to delight in crushing them out with austerity, frigidity and hardness. Woe to the luckless Captain or Lieutenant upon whom the glitter of his phosphorescent eyes — brilliant but cold — falls with displeasure." [11]

For the edification of Senators about to pass on Butler's commission, an anti-Butler newspaper correspondent signing himself "Macawber" scribbled a bit of doggerel about General Butler's eyes:

> *Two suns the world could ne'er endure*
> *Nor man thy double glance—*
> *So nature set thy right eye straight*
> *And turned thy left askance.*[12]

The anti-Butler propaganda might have defeated the ratification during the hubbub over Big Bethel. The vote on July 21, 1861, however, was close, but favorable. For once in a dreary stretch of reverses and difficulties, luck favored Butler in that so many of the senators had gone out to see the battle of Bull Run! The appalling rout of the Federal troops at Manassas instantly deflated the Big Bethel affair to the insignificant skirmish that it was.

Three days after Bull Run, however, and coincident with Butler's confirmation in the Senate, Lieutenant General Scott let fall the ax on Butler by ordering to be withdrawn to Baltimore four and a half of Butler's best regiments.

Butler received the order at 2 A.M. on the 26th by boat from Baltimore, and at first interpreted it as an emergency move due to the debacle of Bull Run. Accordingly before daybreak he issued embarkation orders and, commandeering all available vessels, he got the troops off before nightfall the same day.

His own plans for an advance on Yorktown he perforce postponed indefinitely. His company of light artillery, which he had just assembled had now to be restricted to the immediate vicinity of Fortress Monroe. Newport News, being strongly entrenched, he continued to hold; but the town of Hampton, whose fortifications were not yet completed, had to be abandoned.

The Negroes at Hampton, wards now of the United States Government, were panicked by the withdrawal of the Union troops. "To de Fort! To de Fort! De Seceshers is comin'!"[13] Blacks of all ages stampeded to Fortress Monroe, with their chickens and bundled belongings. Butler headed off some of the migrants and billeted them in the Chesapeake Female Seminary lately vacated by Colonel Duryea's Zouaves; but the ever augmented streams of frightened fugitives flowed to the very moat of the fort. In a few hours the improvised village outside the fort resembled a vast auction room through which it was difficult to keep passageways clear for military use.

On Sunday morning a column of smoke ascended over Hampton. Butler sent two fire engines from Fortress Monroe. Excited Union troops had set fire to Hampton's jail and the Odd Fellows Hall. A few miles west of Hampton Confederate scouts, advancing in high spirits after the news of Bull Run, burned the Newmarket Bridge, near the scene of Colonel Bendix's error. Scarcely had Butler's firefighters withdrawn from Hampton when Confederates under Colonel Magruder appeared and put the torch to all of Hampton's five hundred houses to prevent their use by the Federals.

Two days after his troops had been withdrawn from Fortress Monroe by General Scott, Butler learned that Bull Run had been not the real cause of the withdrawal, but rather a plausible cover for the old general's intention to hobble Butler. The troops had not been taken to Washington at all but ecamped in Baltimore.

"As soon as I begin to look like activity my troops are taken away," Butler wrote. "What ought I to do under these circumstances? I ought not to stay here and be thus abused . . . To resign when the Country needs service is unpatriotic. To hold office which Government believes me unfit for is humiliating." [14]

Without troops, what sort of military action could he undertake? In Hampton Roads Commodore Silas H. Stringham's anchored flagship *Minnesota* and other ships might afford an answer. The Confederates were fortifying various inlets down the coast. Why not descend on these *before* they were fully prepared? Naval ships operating as cavalry, their long guns as artillery, might be employed in conjunction with a small expeditionary army to land and capture enemy garrisons.

Butler himself went to Washington the first week in August. Secretary Cameron was out of town, but he indulged a free airing of grievances to Montgomery Blair, a sworn enemy of Scott. Apparently in the course of his interviews with General Scott and Lincoln Butler was able to contain his wrath. He obtained official sanction for his idea of a descent down the coast in conjunction with the Navy. Lincoln finally consented to make Phelps a brigadier general; and, when Butler raised the problem of his serious need of troops Lincoln signed an order authorizing Butler to raise 5000 troops in New England.

But the next week these concessions were followed by a climaxing blow from General-in-Chief Scott's office. Major General John E. Wool, a superannuated officer, next senior in rank below Scott himself, was now recalled from retirement and ordered to Fortress Monroe to supersede Butler as commander of the Department of Virginia.[15]

Not long before this change Butler had written an extended letter on the Government's want of policy toward the fugitive slaves which he now thought might have a connection with his being superseded. What was Butler to do with the village of a thousand blacks that had collected outside Fortress Monroe? "Are these men, women, and children slaves? Are they free? Is their condition that of men, women, and children, or of property, or is it a mixed relation? . . . When I adopted the theory of treating the able-bodied negro fit to work in the trenches as property liable to be used in aid of rebellion, and so contraband of war, that condition of things was in so far met, as I then and still believe, on a legal and constitutional basis. But now a new series of questions arise . . . [The women and children] must be considered the incumbrance rather than the auxiliary of an army, and, of course, in no possible legal relation could be treated as contraband. Are they property? If they were so, they have been left by their masters and owners, deserted, thrown away, abandoned, like the wrecked vessel upon the ocean . . . If property, do they not become the property of salvors? But we, their salvors, do not need and will not hold such property, and will assume no such ownership: has not, therefore, all proprietary relation ceased? Have they not become, thereupon, men, women and children? No longer under ownership of any kind, the fearful relics of fugitive masters, have they not by their master's acts, and the state of war, assumed the condition, which we hold to be the normal one of those made in God's image." [16] Secretary Cameron, unable to come to grips with the fundamental issue — freeing slaves who came within Union lines — because Lincoln himself was unready to face that problem as yet, sent Butler so weak and weaseling a reply to his request for a ruling that Butler now wondered whether his having been superseded by Wool might have been due to his emancipation views.

"What does it mean? Why this?" he demanded of Montgomery Blair. "I supposed when I last saw the President one week since that I had his confidence. Now I am superseded and no duty assigned me . . . As a friend, may I ask you what is the wish of the Administration? What have I done or omitted to do? Why this sudden change of policy? . . . I have witnessed the disgusting scene of a burning village when I had only 2000 men against 5000, and could not oppose it, the enemy coming down solely because they knew I had *no troops.* Is this because General Scott has got over his quarrel with Wool, or is it a move on the part of the President, or is it because my views on the Negro question are not acceptable to the Government? I suppose the last. Meanwhile I am in the dark. Please give 'more light.' " [17]

To Sarah he wrote: "You see I have been superseded by Wool. I suppose it is because of the letter about negroes; at least I shall so accept the issue. The reply of the Secretary, which you will see in the papers, is too namby pamby, and shows these people are not up to the occasion. I shall have to take issue with them. This war cannot go on without direct conflict. The negro will be free. It is inevitable. We may patch it as we please but the fact will work itself out . . ." [18]

General Wool reached Fortress Monroe on August 18. Butler, punctilious in fanfare and amenities, loaned him his fine gray horse, and the septuagenarian general wheeled about under the prickly live-oak boughs as dexterously as a soldier of forty. By the day's end Butler had reached an understanding that Wool should remain in the fort and exercise overall command while Butler should lead the troops in the field, an arrangement of which General Scott certainly had never dreamed.

"Dearest Wife . . ." Butler reported a few hours later, "I am coming home one of these days, but say nothing about it. . . . You may be assured that I am doing everything that a high-minded and true gentleman should do for the protection of his own honor and the duty he owes to his country . . . Wool is completely taken by me, I think. I so much wish to see you, and a kiss for self — and one for the children. Don't be unhappy, dearest — there is a long time before us of happiness and quiet home. I am now to go to ride, the mail closes. *Truly your husband,* Benj." [19]

Sarah, her spirits lifted by her husband's troubles, wrote, "Your desire to stand well with Gen. Wool is right. I wish I was there to help you. Do not undervalue my aid in reading quickly, and acting promptly in those places where a woman can be of service . . . To keep your commission seems to be the advice of all your friends, if you can with honor. I am cheered, delighted, that you are coming home if only for a short time. But even there be careful. I think your name would do more towards enlisting troops here than any other in the country, yet you must not stand exactly as a recruiting officer. Try to get as large and full orders as you can, whatever they are." [20]

With a dramatic suddenness unlike anything that had yet been done in the war, Major General Butler and Commodore Silas Stringham sailed south on August 26 with six naval ships and a convoy of 860 troops. The next day they turned into Hatteras Inlet, the entrance into Pamlico Sound. Two log-and-sand Confederate forts not yet completed engaged the ships in a brief and unequal duel for honor's sake and then surrendered. Butler's men took over the forts, and the Confederate prisoners, a total of 615 officers and men, were embarked for the North.

Butler's spectacular move hit the jackpot of popular acclaim in the press, and again there were serenades at his hotel in Washington, as after the seizure of Baltimore. Although he reached Washington late at night with his heartening news, his friend Assistant Navy Secretary Fox hurried him over at once to the darkened White House. Lincoln received them in his nightshirt. The news caused the boyish and demonstrative Lincoln to dance a jig with Fox, who, short and stocky, flung his arms around Lincoln's middle, while the lanky President reached over Fox's shoulders with arms that seemed long enough to touch the floor. As they flew about the Cabinet room — so Butler told it — the nightshirt was "considerably agitated," and the General rolled back on a sofa and roared with merriment.[21] Lincoln, pleased with this first taste of victory since Bull Run, was glad to grant General Butler leave of absence to visit his home in Lowell. And Butler, with the President's authorization to raise troops in New England for other ventures down the coast, proceeded northward to visit Sarah and the children and to begin work on a new assignment.

PART THREE

Administrator of New Orleans

12

LAUNCHING THE NEW ORLEANS EXPEDITION

THE slip of paper bearing Lincoln's authorization for Butler to raise 5000 troops in New England got lost in the rat-nest files of the War Department. Butler had left it with the Assistant Secretary to be shown to the Secretary when the latter returned from vacation. Although after he was superseded by Wool he wrote repeatedly to retrieve the precious document, he never set eyes on it again.[1] Riding the crest of popular applause after Hatteras, Butler appeared in Boston without his signed paper.

He found Governor John A. Andrew of Massachusetts insisting that he first produce the official authorization. Butler canceled a speech in Faneuil Hall and sped back to Washington. Secretary Cameron now let Butler write his own orders for the Secretary's signature: "Major General B. F. Butler is hereby authorized to raise, organize, arm, uniform, and equip a volunteer force for the War in the New England States, not exceeding six (6) Regiments of the Maximum Standard, of such arms, and in such proportions, and in such manner as he may judge expedient."[2] Further to expedite the matter a telegram signed by Lincoln was sent to the several New England Governors requesting them to aid General Butler.[3]

Lincoln felt, as the war dragged on and recruiting became more difficult, that it was necessary to enlist all classes in the struggle — non-abolitionist Democrats as well as Republicans, — and Butler's offer to tap a vein of Hunker Democrats, men who had not enlisted because recruiting officers in New England were abolitionist, was enthusiastically accepted by the President. Lincoln's telegram was favorably responded to by Governors Washburne of Maine, Fairbanks of Vermont, and Buckingham of Connecticut.

The Massachusetts Governor, however, had already collided with Butler over the latter's unauthorized offer to use Massachusetts troops to repress a slave uprising in Maryland. In effect Governor Andrew replied to the President that he would relinquish no jot or tittle of his control over recruiting in Massachusetts.[4]

From the start Butler and the Governor clashed over the selection of officers for the new regiments. Butler offered his recruiting agents officer ranks commensurate with the number of recruits they raised, but Governor Andrew did not always regard these men as "proper" officers to represent the State. Applying his own abolitionist yardstick, the Governor refused to appoint Jonas H. French a lieutenant colonel, because French had once broken up a John Brown meeting. And Caleb Cushing, whom Butler recommended as a brigadier general, was unacceptable because he had once denounced Governor Andrew for being a "one-eyed abolitionist."[5]

For almost a month Butler deferred his enlistment campaign in Massachusetts to allow the state's prior commitments to be filled, while in other New England states he opened offices, established camps, interviewed governors, addressed legislatures, laid plans with recruiting officers and made speeches to recruits.

Governor Buckingham of Connecticut gave Butler an Irish regiment, the Ninth Connecticut, whose rowdyism had got beyond control of the State authorities. Butler moved them to Camp Chase on the agricultural fair grounds near Lowell. There inside a high board fence they were drilled and brought under discipline. The Ninth Connecticut invented a new game to be played in Lowell. Whenever marching with wooden guns grew tiresome, some lugubrious trainee with an old-country brogue would call "Connicticut over the fince!" and a mob of cheering Irishmen would scale the fence and invade the town.[6] Factory girls spotting them would mimic "Connicticut over the fince," and flee to cover before the onrushing Irish. Presently the city council objected, and Butler stationed sentries with real guns outside the fence who put back climbers at the point of the bayonet.

To enhance his prestige Butler persuaded Secretary Cameron to create for him the Department of New England, with headquarters in

Boston. The move permitted Butler to claim an authority equal to that of the Governor, and precipitated an argument over States Rights. Henceforth whenever Butler tried to call on Governor Andrew to smooth out their troubles face-to-face, he always found him in Executive Council or out of town.[7]

At outs with the state administration, Butler set up camps at Lowell and Pittsfield. The state recruiting officer declared Butler's actions to be unauthorized and warned enlistees that they would not receive the financial benefits that state-sponsored recruits would receive. Butler assured his new regiments that he would personally guarantee to their families the same aid that was given to other Massachusetts soldiers.

The state recruiting officer, Brigadier General W. W. Bullock, sputtered when he heard that Butler was going ahead anyway. "General Butler be damned! He has no Brigade, nor any authority to raise a Brigade — didn't you see my orders in the paper?" [8] State agents lured away some of Butler's recruits. Butler sent his own officers to Fort Warren to retrieve these "deserters," and directed Colonel J. H. French at Camp Chase near Lowell to admit no one looking for soldiers, even if he came with a writ of *habeas corpus*.

The feud was carried to Washington. Governor Andrew sent copies of his correspondence with Butler to Massachusetts' Senators Wilson and Sumner. Butler made many trips to Washington to counteract Andrew's moves and to bypass the Governor in the matter of officer appointments for his Massachusetts regiments. Butler pointed out that recruiting was a national matter, and ought to be administered by a national draft. "Suppose the Governors of the states should refuse to raise any volunteers, would not the President have a right to draft men for the service of the United States?" [9]

While the feud dragged on, Butler lost the chance to lead a campaign he had projected on the eastern shore of Virginia. But his being so frequently seen in Washington on recruiting business, led to his selection in November 1861 to lead the troops in conjunction with Farragut, Porter, and the naval forces in an attack on New Orleans.

To keep secret as long as possible the precise destination of the new expedition, an advanced base was set up on Ship Island, about midway between Mobile and the mouths of the Mississippi. C. J. Harrison, Butler's agent in New York, chartered the Pacific Mail steamer *Constitution,* just off the ways and holding her trials off New York Harbor. This fine steamer was expected to carry about 2500 troops with their equipment and stores. On November 19, the Twenty-sixth Massachusetts, Colonel Jones, and the Ninth Connecticut, Colonel Cahill, paraded through Boston Common past General Butler's reviewing stand, with a full band and drum corps. The Governor, who still had not approved the appointments of their officers, took no notice of the embarkation. Along with this first contingent Butler sent his brother, Andrew, as Commissary of Subsistence. En route south the *Constitution* touched at Fortress Monroe to pick up General Phelps, who would command the advanced base at Ship Island until Butler's arrival there.

To command the Maine regiment, Butler appointed George F. Shepley, successful lawyer and Democratic wheelhorse of Portland, a handsome man with steady blue eyes, long brown hair swept boldly back from a square forehead, a neat moustache and a perky imperial.[10] To facilitate recruiting, Shepley, though no teetotaler himself, had contrived to be seen on the streets of Portland arm in arm with Neal Dow, author of Maine's prohibition law, whom Butler had also appointed as a military officer. Shepley was a good executive upon whom Butler felt he could depend. When the *Constitution* returned to Boston after her first trip to Ship Island, Shepley's Twelfth Maine and the Eastern Bay State Regiment, under a Boston Democratic lawyer, Lieutenant Colonel Jonas H. French, were embarked.

On this occasion, however, the enraged Governor Andrew wrote individually to Butler's recruits declaring them ineligible to receive state aid, and charging upon Washington he got the sailing orders of the *Constitution* held up.

General-in-Chief McClellan ordered Butler by telegraph ". . . disembark your troops from the 'Constitution' and report by telegraph the terms of the charter of that steamer." [11]

Butler stalled. "Would advise against disembarkation if possible to be prevented. Troops are now comfortable. Will begin preparations for disembarkation, but await orders?" To his aide in Washington, Major George C. Strong, Butler wired: "Get orders to disembark revoked. Save the ship for us. Get connections. Report at length by mail." [12]

Major Strong managed to nullify the order to discharge the troops at Fortress Monroe. Butler accordingly dispatched the transport, and himself went to Washington to get the officers' commissions which Governor Andrew had declined to give.

On January 11, 1862, President Lincoln appealed to Governor Andrew: "I will be greatly obliged if you will arrange somehow with General Butler to officer his two unofficered regiments." [13] Governor Andrew replied by restating his grievances and offered to provide officers "in the manner in which I have performed it . . . exercising my own discretion in all matters in the same manner." [14] Washington sided with Butler. On January 16, Adjutant General Lorenzo Thomas quietly announced the ranks and commissions of the officers of Butler's regiments, as though these commissions had been granted in the regular way! [15]

Two general officers on Butler's staff, however, were turned down by the Senate, because of Governor Andrew's opposition. They were Butler's brother Andrew and his close friend and business associate Paul R. George. When Butler began recruiting, with an Eastern Shore of Virginia expedition in view, his requirement had been only two Massachusetts regiments. When New Orleans had become the secret objective, Butler had raised three regiments in Massachusetts and had never apprised the hostile Governor of his increased need for troops or of the reason for it. Governor Andrew, in the dark, and thinking in terms of the earlier and smaller project, saw Paul R. George, Butler's Assistant Quartermaster, and Andrew Butler, Butler's Commissary of Subsistence, running up so large a bill for supplies that he broadcast a warning that "the whole course of proceeding under Major General Butler in this Commonwealth seems to have been designed and adapted simply to afford means to persons of bad character to make money unscrupulously." [16] The U.S. Senate, dis-

turbed by the Governor's loose charges, disapproved the commissions
of Paul George and Andrew Butler; although upon later investigation after the New Orleans plan had become known a Congressional
committee approved the audit of their accounts and ordered them
paid.

There was confusion in Washington. Stanton replaced Cameron,
and McClellan relieved Scott. Butler had trouble obtaining from Mc-
Clellan his own final sailing orders for New Orleans. The new
general-in-chief doubted the Navy's ability to withstand the fire of the
New Orleans forts, and hesitated to send even 15,000 men to New
Orleans when they might be needed near Washington.

"My poor, dear little Heigh-Ho!" Butler wrote to Sarah on January
21, 1862, "I have treated you very shamefully, wretchedly. Will you
ever forgive me? I have not written yet, but I have been each day in
expectancy of getting home. But the change of secretaries and
change of plans of the campaign have detained me from day to day.
Every morning I have packed my carpet bag in expectation of going
home, but each day have had to wait. I am determined not to leave
until everything is fixed to my mind. I am on the most intimate
terms with the new Secretary, who is an old political and personal
friend of mine. I breakfasted at his house by special invitation on Sunday and spent the whole morning with him . . . Why the deuce is
it that you cannot come with me? I am as weary as a man can be of
this life . . . Goodbye, dearest. I hope to see you before this does, but
if not a thousand warm embraces for Mrs. Butler, B.F.B." [17]

But three days later, instead of the desired orders, he received from
the General-in-Chief a report which branded the New Orleans expedition as not feasible. The tedious routine of interviews and arguments had to be repeated. "My dear good wife," Ben wrote the following Sunday: "Shall I never see you again? This wearisome business
drags its slow length along, day by day. I hope to start for home, but
am detained day by day. Not to speak of the minor discomforts of
being away from home without baggage or conveniences of stay, there
is a delay of public duty and public business which is intolerable. I
have been sick at heart and heartsick in all this troublesome time.

Two weeks now have I been waiting for a decision that should have been made in an hour by any person fit to be trusted with the affair at all. The Secretary, Mr. Stanton, has done all and more than I could ask of him. Intrigues, petty malice, and a jealousy have all had their share. . . . After waiting day by day till Friday, I then got a report by McClellan *against* my *expedition*. By dint of hard work and personal exertion I have got that matter overruled, but what may be done now I am in some degree uncertain. This war has been prosecuted long enough to demoralize both the men in the army and the politicians . . . Were it not for the Sec. of War I should have gone to the dogs . . . I hope to get away from the gloomy place tomorrow or Tuesday at farthest, and then for the happiest of all places, home . . . Goodbye, goodbye — Kiss Paul and Blanche for me. Love to Mother. I send none to you — you have it now. Benj." [18]

It was the 29th of January before Butler received verbal orders from McClellan to get his expedition under way for Ship Island. He directed Shepley at Fortress Monroe to embark the troops on the *Constitution* and sail. Back in Boston, Butler gathered the remaining necessary food supplies, ammunition, medical stores, fuel. Colonel Shepley departed from Hampton Roads on January 31. Two days out he overhauled the gunboat *Miami* in distress, and towed her into Hampton Roads before again proceeding south. Flag Officer David G. Farragut with his heavy warships sailed on February 3. Commander David D. Porter, to whose Mortar Flotilla the *Miami* belonged, got away on the 12th. At length on February 21 Butler embarked the last 1500 of his New England troops on the transport *Mississippi*.

As a result of the long delay, Sarah Butler decided to accompany her husband to New Orleans.

During a brief layover in Washington, Butler obtained a grant of $10,000 to be used at his discretion for purchasing information, and he dispatched a spy overland to New Orleans. At Fortress Monroe the steam tug that brought his party from Baltimore ran alongside the transport steamer *Mississippi*. A plank was extended from the top of the tug to the *Mississippi* to permit Mrs. Butler to walk safely on board. The General and his staff, scorning that arrangement, climbed aboard by rope ladders. "Such a struggle for places! Those that sailed from Boston occupied more room than could be yielded after the new arrivals," Sarah Butler wrote to her sister Harriet Heard. "Sixteen hundred people to be stowed away somewhere. Mr. Butler with the staff began giving orders, and in two or three hours it became very quiet, every one assigned his place by right of rank. Dinner served at two, plainly but very well. Condensed water, I do not like it. Mr. Butler and 'staff' go on shore to dine with Gen. Wool. It is expected we shall be off tonight, in the meantime I should be glad of a place to warm my feet." [19]

The orders from McClellan which Butler carried directed him to keep his destination secret even from his staff. "Should the Navy fail to reduce the works, you will land your forces and siege train, and endeavor to trench the works, silence their fire, and carry them by assault . . . the great object to be achieved is the capture and firm retention of New Orleans." [20]

13

NEW ORLEANS CAMPAIGN

THE transport *Mississippi* bowled southward over a smooth sea expecting at eight or ten knots to reach Ship Island in less than two weeks. In Butler's ears rang Secretary Stanton's jocular remark as they were leaving Lincoln's office, "You take New Orleans and you shall be Lieutenant-General." [1]

Flag Officer Farragut and Commander Porter, if they followed their original schedule, should be entering the Mississippi River any day now, and Butler wished to be there on time to lead the troops from the advanced base at Ship Island against the New Orleans forts. He was convinced, as he explained to Parton in 1863, "that the closing and decisive encounter would be with the Confederate army on the swamps and bayous of the Delta," and he had provided himself with materials to build small boats to navigate bayous and swamps and with scaling ladders to assault the forts. [2] One of his aides, Lieutenant Godfrey Weitzel, an engineer officer at New Orleans before the war who had shot ducks in the swamps behind Fort St. Philip, assured Butler that it was possible to land from the Gulf side and walk into Fort St. Philip unopposed. There were no guns on that side.

The *Mississippi*'s voyage was dogged by storms and bad luck. It was too rough off Hatteras Inlet to pick up General Thomas Williams. The seas roared. Boiling phosphorescent swells struck the quivering ship. Colonel Neal Dow's Maine troopers who were whalers and cod fishermen were routed from their bunks to bail water and help the civilian crew manage the ship.

The third day out of Hampton Roads the storm let up. The ship hoisted three sails and flew down the coast like a fire-breathing bird. [3]

Off Wilmington, North Carolina, just as many of her seasick troops were struggling on deck to enjoy the morning sun and the sight of land in the distance, she ran aground on Frying Pan Shoals.

Captain Fulton cast loose the port bow anchor, — the worst possible move at this moment for the ship with filled sails was driven forward against a fluke of the anchor and a hole was punched in her hull. Forward compartments began taking water. Pumps were started.

Butler had soldiers run forward to the prow and back to the stern, but the ship had struck bottom at full tide and could not be budged. The longer she sat the more the water ebbed from under her. Heavy supplies were dumped overboard to lighten her. In the afternoon her distress signal was answered by the USS *Mount Vernon,* whose skipper, Captain O. S. Glisson, himself fearful of grounding, took several hours to feel his way in with the lead and came to a stop about a mile away.

Although the Navy Captain could offer Butler little hope, since only one ship to his knowledge had ever grounded on Frying Pan Shoals and survived, the next full tide loosed the vessel's grip on the bottom and she was floated out into deep water.

Again the *Mississippi* set out for Port Royal, where Butler hoped with Navy help to patch her punctured hull. The *Mount Vernon* escorted her, and a young naval officer remained on board as pilot. Yet, as the ship crept southward, the General slept soundly, his envious wife noted.[4]

The *Mississippi* lay in Port Royal Sound from the 2nd to the 13th of March. While her troops were drilled on shore the transport was careened and her hull patched with tarred oakum, canvas, rosin, rubber and boiler iron. With most of the leak stopped, the vessel once more set out for Ship Island.

Contrary to the advice of naval officers present, Captain Fulton backed the *Mississippi* away from the wharf under her own power and rammed her rudder against a submerged shell bank. Then her tiller rope parted and she ran crazily on shore half a mile from the wharf, where she stuck until a team of naval vessels jerked her free at high tide the next day.[5]

Butler convened a board of inquiry and ousted Captain Fulton from command. From the Navy he obtained a navigator to take the transport to Ship Island.

Ship Island lay in the Gulf sixty-five miles east of New Orleans and ninety-five north of the nearest mouth of the Mississippi River. It was a seven-mile ribbon of sand, flat and narrow at its western end where a lighthouse and a rude fort were erected, wider and rising to a high sand dune on its eastern end which was covered with pine and scrub oak. Above the billowing white sand the tents of the soldiers fluttered like white caps in the Gulf breeze. Ship Island's harbor was crowded with black-hulled naval craft when Butler's transport, as though harried by some malevolent deity of the sea, proceeded again to run amuck.

Mrs. Butler recorded its caprices upon arrival at Ship Island.

It is rather funny the trouble we have with the ship. In the first place the pilot undertook to take her up to the wharf, which is, you see, but a little thing (the wharf), and by the time we were up, the wind was blowing furiously. They did not dare to fasten to it — she would have carried all away, so after holding there a while, she swept away, and in her backward movement caught a brig by the rigging, tangled it all together, knocked some wood from her bow, and held fast. Thus we anchored. The next morning made all clear and they prepared to separate, the wind still blowing. As the brig tried to draw off, it gave a lurch, came in endwise, and ran her bow clear up on to our deck. There it hung, broken and dangling, like an elephant's trunk, hoisted into our rigging. Everybody on deck was in danger, with this great thing striking in all directions, yet nobody could help laughing, and besides we expect anything now. At last, with pulling and cutting, they tore it away, and we started again on our adventures. This time we rushed madly at the "Black Prince," which was anchored a little farther on, knocked her out of her moorings and tore at her rigging. Then we plunged at another ship, the "Wild Gazelle," caught and grazed her, scattered a few splinters, and stood out into the harbor, and anchored apart from the other vessels.[6]

Butler held his troops on board for several days, both because a storm made landing them difficult and because he was not sure when he should have to take them on down to the deltas. On the third day Flag Officer Farragut returned to Ship Island for a conference. Butler was relieved to find that the heavy naval ships had not yet been dragged across the bar into the Mississippi River. His accident had not delayed the Navy as he had feared.

Butler loaned Farragut 1700 tons of coal and sent his brother Andrew to Havana for a fresh supply. "But how," asked the naval commander, "can you in the army let the navy have the coal? Your army regulations are against it, are they not?" Butler quipped, "I never read the army regulations and what is more I shan't . . . If the navy uses the coal for the benefit of the government, I, as a lawyer, know that the government will not get the pay for it out of me." [7]

The excellent relations thus established between Butler and Farragut continued throughout the New Orleans campaign.[8] Farragut turned over to the army several invaluable small craft for use as lighters, and Butler sent Lieutenant Weitzel to the mouth of the river to give the naval authorities useful information about the construction of the forts which Commander Porter's mortar schooners were preparing to bombard. Butler set carpenters to work making small boats and scaling ladders.

For transporting troops from Ship Island into the Mississippi River Butler had counted on the services of the steamer *Constitution* which had earlier brought General Phelps and General Shepley to Ship Island. To Butler's dismay, frugal General Phelps, alarmed at the vessels' costing the government $2500 a day, had sent her back to New York. Butler raked together the sailing schooners on which Captain Paul George had sent supplies and horses to Ship Island and formed trains of emergency transports to be towed by his steamers.

The failure of the Senate to approve the commissions of Butler's supply and commissary officers (Captain Paul R. George and Captain Andrew J. Butler) further complicated his situation at Ship Island. Captain George was replaced in Boston by Captain J. W. McKim, but for many months there was no replacement for Captain Butler. Andrew Butler, having sailed with Phelps and the first contingent of troops in November, was already here at Ship Island before the Senate, influenced by Governor Andrew, vetoed his commission. The redoubtable Andrew Butler had been filling two jobs, as Quartermaster and Subsistence Officer. Captain George's invoices, held up by the machinations of Governor Andrew, had not come to Ship Island with the supplies themselves, so that Andrew Butler had been without the means of checking the goods actually received against the invoices; although he had secured receipts for the stores disbursed.

Shuttling between Ship Island and the Deltas for conferences with Farragut, Butler was compelled to neglect his wife as much as ever, but Sarah saw to it that the sand was dusted from his headquarters table and that his army rations were varied.

One day a little girl of six or seven was brought to the General's headquarters on Ship Island. The small coastal vessel on which she had been traveling with her parents had foundered in a storm, and, separated from her parents, she had been rescued by a naval blockade ship. After Mrs. Butler had bathed the child and mended her clothes, the General sent her in the care of his aide Major Strong under a flag of truce to Biloxi, Mississippi. Strong delivered her to the postmaster and on returning to his boat discovered that the ebbing tide had stranded him. In this situation he was, after nightfall, challenged by a band of armed Confederates who threatened to, but did not actually, attack him. To avenge this insult to his flag of truce Butler promptly sent the Major back to Biloxi with the Irish Ninth Connecticut and a section of artillery. The now disciplined soldiers of "Connicticut over the fince" fame exacted an apology from the mayor.

New Orleans newspapers brought back by Major Strong revealed the Confederates' belief that New Orleans was impregnable against attack from below. "The Mississippi is fortified so as to be impassable for any hostile fleet or flotilla," read one New Orleans news item; "Forts Jackson and St. Philip are armed with one hundred and seventy heavy guns . . . The navigation of the river is stopped by a dam of about a quarter of a mile from the above forts. No flotilla on earth could force that dam in less than two hours." The success of the ironclad *Merrimack* against wooden ships at Hampton Roads on March 8 further inspired New Orleans with confidence in its own iron vessels that were being built. "In a day or two we shall have ready two iron-cased floating batteries . . . Each ironcased battery will mount twenty, sixty-eight-pounders, placed so as to skim the water, and striking the enemy's hull between wind and water. We have an abundant supply of incendiary shells, cupola furnaces for molten iron, congreve rockets and fireships. Between New Orleans and the forts there is a constant succession of earthworks." [9]

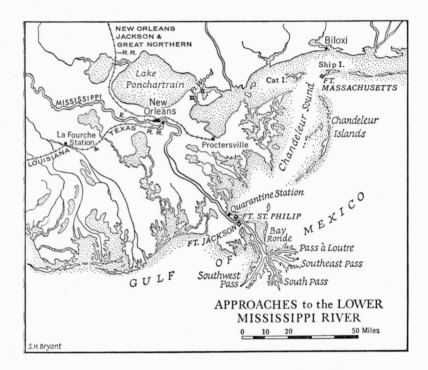

APPROACHES to the LOWER
MISSISSIPPI RIVER

0   10   20   50 Miles

S.H.Bryant

In the several trips Butler made from Ship Island to the Head of the Passes, he came to appreciate Flag Officer Farragut as a collaborator. "He is the youngest man in the fleet," Butler declared.[10] The sixty-three-year-old seadog could still climb nimbly into the rigging to have a look for himself. A modest, quiet man, he was in his forthright way quite as critical as the lawyer-general of the officials in Washington who had failed him in the matter of supplies. He had had to borrow shells, fuses, cylinder cloth from Porter's Mortar Flotilla, and coal and medical supplies from Butler. "I have been on the parish," Farragut wrote Secretary Welles on April 20. "I find myself dependent upon the Army for everything; and General Butler has been most generous — he gives me everything in his power." [11]

During the preliminary bombardment of Forts Jackson and St. Philip by the Mortar Flotilla, Butler had most of his troops on board transports in the lower river, in readiness to assault the forts if necessary. Farragut soon decided that the mortars alone were unable to reduce the forts. Mortar shells set fire to barracks and other wooden structures, but did not diminish the fire from Fort Jackson's casemate guns. On April 20, Farragut issued a general order for the fleet to pass up the river. "The forts should be run, and when a force is once above the forts to protect the troops, they should be landed at Quarantine from the Gulf side by bringing them through the bayou, and then our forces should move up the river, mutually aiding each other, as it can be done to advantage." [12] In Butler's mind the correct strategy was to capture the forts before moving on to the city.

On the 22nd Butler's reconnaissance party returned from the swampy area back of Fort St. Philip. There were still no guns mounted on the landward side of the fort, they reported. Troops might be brought from the Gulf in small boats through a tidewater channel known as Maunels Canal.

At 2 A.M. on April 24 Farragut hoisted red lanterns to the *Hartford*'s peak. His ships, with protective chain cables dangling over their sides and their vulnerable vitals protected by bags of sand and ashes, set out to run the gantlet between the forts. Butler with his staff watched from the deck of the *Saxon*, about eight hundred yards below Fort Jackson. The predawn blackness was broken by flashes from Farragut's broadsides. The guns from both forts angrily disputed the passage, while Confederate fire rafts and river steamers also pitched into the melee. From his position below the forts Butler witnessed the inferno. "Imagine all the earthquakes in the world," one of Butler's aides described it, "and all the thunder and lightning storms together, in a space of two miles, all going off at once; that would be like it." [13] Several of Farragut's rearmost ships failed to get through, and the Confederate ironclad battery, moored near Fort St. Philip, appeared through Butler's spyglass to be lively enough after the daylight came.

To Farragut, Butler dispatched a hearty note: "Allow me to congratulate you and your command upon the bold, daring, brilliant and successful passage of the Forts of your fleet this morning. A more gallant exploit it has never fallen to the lot of man to witness." [14]

Borrowing from Commander Porter the light-draft steamer *Miami,* Butler transferred to her the Twenty-sixth Massachusetts from their transport lying inside the river below the forts and sent them out into the Gulf. In the Gulf behind Fort St. Philip the troops were transshipped into thirty rowboats, in which they paddled upstream against the mill-race current of Maunels Canal into the swamps back of the fort. Butler with his men waded in hip-deep water for the last mile and a half before they reached Quarantine Station.

Here the mud-spattered troops learned that Farragut, after leaving the gunboats *Wissahickon* and *Kineo* near Quarantine, had proceeded on up to New Orleans without them. "This I deem wholly an unmilitary proceeding on his part," Butler wrote Sarah, "to run off and leave forts behind him unreduced, but such is the race for the glory of capturing New Orleans between him and Commodore Foote that thus we go." [15]

The Mississippi River, at flood stage for the past month, spilled over its banks and rushed seaward through numerous bayous like that through which Butler's troops had made their way. Of dry land in the area of the lower river there were but the two narrow strips that bordered the river. Thus it was possible for Butler at Quarantine Station, five miles above Fort St. Philip, completely to block off communications by land between Fort St. Philip and New Orleans. By ferrying a few companies of troops across the river to the western bank he cut off Fort Jackson. The garrison of the battered forts were now doomed.

Butler could not feel safe about General Phelps's troops that were still on board the wooden transports in the lower river so long as the

Confederate ironclad gunboat at anchor under St. Philip remained undestroyed. His great need now was for shallow vessels to transport these troops through the canal behind Fort St. Philip.

General Shepley at Ship Island was instructed to send to him all the small craft he could find. "Dispatch is of the first moment." [16] He then took passage on the gunboat *Wissahickon* up the river to New Orleans to confer with Farragut.

Along the seven-mile, crescent-shaped waterfront of New Orleans the blackened ruins of cotton piles on the levees attested the mounting hatred of Southerner for Yankee. As the pungent odor of smoldering cotton filled his nostrils, Butler, as a stockholder in the Merrimack textile mill in Lowell, must have experienced a wave of anger and frustration.

Farragut's warships were anchored in midstream with one broadside bearing on the city of New Orleans and the other on the village of Algiers to the west. As the *Wissahickon* passed them, the navy crews snapped to attention at the rails and cheered General Butler. The latter found the flag officer several miles above the city examining the fortifications that Confederate General Mansfield Lovell had been building to defend New Orleans from downriver attack.

New Orleans was like a tiger, whom Farragut was holding by the tail. He was delighted to see Butler, as a man who could relieve him in his embarrassing predicament. The city lay helpless under the guns of the fleet, but the mayor, fearing mob violence, declined to surrender the city or haul down its Secessionist flag.

On April 26 Farragut's seamen had raised the flag over the United States Mint. The next day, Sunday, while church services were being held throughout the fleet, four New Orleans men had rushed onto the roof of the Mint and dragged down the flag. The lookout in the *Pensacola*'s maintop shouted, "The flag is down, sir," and fired his howitzer. The 12-pound shell was thought to have killed one of the four men on the roof, but another made off with the United States flag trailing it in the dust, tearing it to bits, wearing a scrap of it as a boutonniere. New Orleans newspapers had praised one William B. Mumford as the leader of the affair.

General Butler advised Farragut to demand that the New Orleans officials themselves haul down the flag of Louisiana under threat of bombardment. Farragut, however, elected to prolong the negotiation through the few remaining days until the arrival of the Federal troops would enable him to hand over to General Butler the ticklish job of treating with civilians who refused to recognize their defeat.

Meanwhile, events at the forts reached a climax. Confederate troops inside Fort Jackson mutinied, spiked their guns and surrendered to Butler's pickets. At 2 P.M., about the time Butler in New Orleans was receiving the cheers of the fleet, the officers of Forts Jackson and St. Philip were gathering on board Commander Porter's flagship, the *Harriet Lane,* to conclude the surrender. In a military sense the Crescent City was at the mercy of the Federal arms. Butler hurried down the river early the next morning.

In the light of any future candidacy for the Presidency of the United States, Butler's failure to be present at the capitulation of the forts was a point against him. He seemed to sense this when in his official report to Stanton, he overemphasized the credit due his troops for forcing the surrender of the forts.

14

THE WOMAN ORDER

The people of New Orleans were stunned by the Federal victory. For months the Confederate Government in Richmond had insisted that their city was invulnerable to attack from the Gulf and had withdrawn many New Orleans regiments to stem the southward advance of Grant and Halleck at Shiloh and Corinth. Seven miles above the city, at Carrollton, Confederate General Mansfield Lovell had thrown up fortifications to defend New Orleans from the Federal river ironclads that were descending the Mississippi. During the bombardment of the lower forts, spectators from New Orleans had gone down the river to watch the fireworks and had been assured that the damage to the forts inflicted by naval bombardment was but trifling. They were quite unprepared, therefore, when General Lovell, hot from a horseback flight up the levee from Quarantine, broke the news that Farragut had passed the forts.

Then followed the excitement and exhaustion of the holocaust. Fifteen thousand bales of cotton blazed along New Orleans' levee.[1] Black smoke billowed up from flame-licked barrels of turpentine and tar. Warehouses were emptied by frenzied workers who hauled cotton and tobacco to the wharf to be heaped on the fires. Negroes with sledges knocked out the heads of barrels. Gutters ran molasses. Across the river the shipyards of the village of Algiers were set ablaze. Several dozen seagoing cotton ships and river steamers were set on fire. Coal was burned. Miles of cordwood, cut for steamboat fuel and tinder-dry, were ignited. Thousands of Negroes and indigent whites salvaged what sugar they could, gathering it up in aprons, pails or baskets. There was looting and mob violence. Governor Thomas

Overton Moore of Louisiana fled up the river on a steamboat and General Lovell stripped the Jackson railroad of its rolling stock to evacuate from the city as much military equipment and food as possible. Then he marched his men to Camp Moore, seventy miles north of the city, leaving Mayor John T. Monroe and the City Council to deal with the victorious Farragut.

The Mayor protested that he could not haul down the Louisiana flag, that no man in New Orleans could haul it down and live! Throughout the city the mob ruled. Several who cheered the returning flag of the Union were killed by the rabble, and paroled Confederate troops from the forts were beaten with sticks and stones. New Orleans had a large foreign population, chiefly French, Spanish and English, and Mayor Monroe requested a semi-military organization called the European Brigade to help the city officials maintain order.

Flag Officer Farragut sent ashore his chief of staff with all the marines in the fleet to haul down the Rebel flag and hoist the United States flag over the Custom House and the City Hall. While Captain Bell was executing his mission, the people were "orderly and quiet, though full of rage," but as he was returning to the ships, the Rebel ensign rolled under his arm, the masses screamed hurrahs for Beauregard and Davis and someone threw a stone which hit him in the chest.[2]

"It affords me," wrote Farragut on May 1 in reply to Butler's note of congratulation, "no little gratification that our friends who were anxiously looking on should consider that we had 'not only performed our duty,' but 'did it brilliantly' . . . The intrepidity with which you so soon followed up our success by landing your forces at the Quarantine, through mud and mire and water for miles, and which enabled us to tighten the cords around them, has also added to my obligations; and I trust that you will now occupy and hold the city without further difficulty other than those incident to a conquered city disordered by anarchy and the reign of terror which this unfortunate city has passed through."[3]

After landing the 26th Massachusetts as garrison for Forts Jackson

and St. Philip, Butler boarded the transport *Mississippi* and proceeded up the river. Mrs. Butler had come from Ship Island and was
on board.[4] The river being at flood stage like a cup spilling over its
rim, the troopships stood above the level of the land on either side,
beyond the levees. At plantations above Quarantine, Negroes jerked
off hats and aprons to wave to the soldiers of "Massa Linkum." Pickaninnies from cabins along the riverbanks yelled and jumped up
and down. Grizzled blacks on their knees invoked God's blessing
upon the invaders. Planters in broadbrim hats with their wives and
daughters in crinoline watched in silence from verandas and gardens.
When the army transport *Mississippi* at noon on May 1 tied up to the
wharf at the foot of Poydras Street, the New York *Times* correspondent on board reported: "I saw several instances of the bitter spirit of
the rabble, and even of people whom one might have taken from
their appearance to be respectable. The levee, for the whole length of
the river front of the city, was constantly crowded by a turbulent
throng and whenever a boat belonging to the fleet passed them, its
occupants were jeered and hooted at . . . This wall of human beings
stood there as enemies to bar our entry to the city." [5]

As the soldiers were disembarking, angry citizens had to be held
back at point of bayonet. Voices from the mob called out "Picayune
Butler," "You'll never see home again," "Halloo, epaulets, lend us a
picayune." [6] The picayune, Louisiana's smallest coin in colonial days,
had recently achieved minstrel-show fame in a jocular song about "the
arrival of a mythical Picayune Butler at a mythical town for mythical
purposes." [7] General Butler, in his stateroom, hearing the outcries for
"Picayune Butler," paused in the composition of his proclamation to
the citizens of New Orleans long enough to inquire if any of the bands
could play the tune. As the music was unavailable, "Yankee Doodle"
and "The Star-Spangled Banner" were played instead.

At 5 P.M. Butler began his march through the downtown section of
the city to the Custom House. Behind the rattling drum corps of the
31st Massachusetts came Butler and his staff on foot, flanked by files of
the Thirty-first. Next in order were Captain Everett's battery of
artillery, the 31st Massachusetts under Colonel O. P. Gooding, the

band of the Fourth Wisconsin, General Thomas Williams and his staff, and finally the Fourth Wisconsin under Colonel Paine. Keeping step to the music of "The Star-Spangled Banner" — a feat not easy for the General himself who had no ear for music — the Federal troops proceeded down Poydras, St. Charles, and Canal Streets to the Custom House.

Crowds on the pavements craned their necks. Here and there a throat screamed: "Where is the damned rascal?" "There he goes, God damn him!" "I see the old damned villain!" Others taunted the Federals with "Shiloh!" "Bull Run!" "Hurrah for Beauregard!" "Go home, you damned Yankees!"[8] The flag raised over the Custom House by Captain Bell was still flying, although its marine guard had been withdrawn and the building locked. Not having the keys, the troops broke open the front door and the block-long edifice was taken over by the Thirty-first Massachusetts as barracks. With troops quartered in the center of town, on its principal squares and on the levee, Butler retired to the transport for the night.

Butler hoped to be able to station inside New Orleans only a nominal force for police duty. By so doing he could send most of his troops to cooperate with the Navy in opening the Mississippi River and in seizing Mobile and Galveston. At best his forces were meager. In New Orleans, in the forts, and at Ship Island — all told — he had scarcely 12,000 effective men, and they unacclimated to this subtropical region.

In his proclamation to the citizens of New Orleans Butler emphasized the peaceful intention behind the mailed fist. There would be martial law, but only for so long as it might be necessary, since the United States forces had come "to restore order, maintain public tranquillity, and enforce peace and quiet under the laws and constitution of the United States." Secessionists were required to surrender their arms and suppress all flags except those of the United States. Full protection of person and property was held out to all who would renew the oath of allegiance. "If any soldier of the United States should so far forget his duty or his flag as to commit outrage upon any person or property, the commanding general requests his name to be instantly reported to the provost guard so that he may be punished and his wrong act redressed . . . All the inhabitants are enjoined to pursue their usual avocations. All shops and places of amusement are to be kept open in the accustomed manner, and services are to be held in the churches and religious houses, as in times of profound peace." [9]

The St. Charles Hotel, vacated by Confederate General Lovell, was taken over for Butler's headquarters, with cannon posted at each corner. Mayor John T. Monroe, summoned on May 2, made his way to the St. Charles through packed, sullen streets and was received in the high-ceilinged, ornately decorated Ladies' Parlor.

Monroe, remembering Butler as a fellow Democrat in prewar days, greeted the General as "always a friend of the South."

"Stop, sir!" Butler interrupted. "Let me set you right on that point at once. I was always a friend of Southern rights but an enemy of Southern wrongs."

The interview was interrupted by loud shouts in the streets of "hang the traitor," and an aide rushed in. "General Williams orders me to say, that he fears he may not be able to control the mob." [10]

"Give my compliments to General Williams," directed Butler, "and tell him, if he finds he cannot control the mob, to open upon them with artillery."

The Mayor was permitted to go out on the balcony and speak to the crowd, which quieted down slightly, as they buzzed with the rumor of Butler's order to Williams.

A few minutes later Lieutenant Kinsman called General Butler aside. The object of the mob's wrath was a Kentucky-born Unionist named Summers who had taken refuge on board one of Farragut's ships. Summers' mistake had been to condemn the rowdy Mumford's removal of the United States flag from the Mint building. For this he had been jailed by the Secessionist city government; but later had been permitted to escape to the fleet. The Unionist was recognized as he rode through the streets with Kinsman. The crowd, several times, forced the carriage to a stop. Each time Kinsman, flourishing his pistol, compelled the driver to get on, until they reached the hotel.

Butler ordered Kinsman to escort the man to the Custom House. "We may as well settle this question now as any other time. Take what force you require. If anyone molests or threatens you, arrest him. If a rescue is attempted, fire." [11]

Captain Edward Page's company of the Thirty-first Massachusetts formed two lines four feet apart, with two men closing the front and two the rear and in the space thus enclosed walked Kinsman and Summers. The mob churned around the marching column, but its most active agitators kept out of the soldiers' reach. Halfway to the Custom House a man leaned out of an omnibus to incite the mob. "Halt!" ordered Lieutenant Kinsman. "Bring out that man!" Two soldiers collared the miscreant and placed him between the lines, where he continued to call out and wave his arms until threatened with a bayonet.[12] The column resumed its march. A second screaming fanatic was caught, put in the line and sobered by the bayonet. From a window General Butler and Mayor Monroe watched the affair.

Butler adjourned the conference until after supper in order to bring Mrs. Butler from the ship to the hotel.

Although he had to coerce a hackman, Butler employed only two soldiers as escort. Sarah Butler relished the experience, and described it for her sister:

> And what do you think of my being among the first to enter New Orleans . . . Mr. Butler ordered the opening of the St. Charles, compelled a hackman at the point of the bayonet to drive us to the Hotel. We had no guard but an armed soldier on the box and another behind the carriage. A regiment was drawn up around the hotel and four howitzers on the corners. If we were to encounter a mob, it was decided to give them an opportunity. The band was stationed on the piazza, and they played with fiery energy all the national airs from Yankee Doodle to the Star Spangled Banner.[13]

In the evening the Mayor and Council, bringing the Honorable Pierre Soulé as spokesman, returned to the St. Charles. In one corner, the staff of the commanding general, starched and stiffened in full dress uniforms, had already assembled. In front of them sat the General. The New Orleans City Council filed in along the opposite walls. Mayor Monroe was given a chair close to the General's, while Mr. Soulé, a former United States Minister to Spain and a squat little man with shoulder-length hair and Napoleonic stance, was seated in front of the council members.

While the band on the veranda outside played patriotic songs, General Butler read the first draft of his proclamation.

"The sum and substance of the whole is this," he stated at the conclusion of the reading, "I wish to leave the municipal authority in the full exercise of its accustomed functions. I do not desire to interfere with the collection of taxes, the government of the police, the lighting and cleaning of the streets, the sanitary laws, or the administration of justice. I desire only to govern the military forces of the department, and to take cognizance only of offenses committed by or against them, representing here the United States against its enemies."

Pierre Soulé objected to occupation by Federal troops. "I know the feelings of the people so well," he warned, "that I am sure your soldiers can have no peace while they remain in our midst. Withdraw your troops, general, and leave the city government to manage its own affairs. If the troops remain, there will certainly be trouble." [14]

"I did not expect," retorted Butler, "to hear from Mr. Soulé a threat on *this* occasion . . . New Orleans *is* a conquered city. If not, why are we here? How did we get here? Have you opened your arms to bid us welcome? Are we here by your consent?" By way of justifying martial law, Butler reminded the civic committee that General Jackson and General Lovell had resorted to martial law in New Orleans to control "the insulting, irreligious, unwashed mob in your midst." "I have means of knowing more about your city than you think," admonished Butler. ". . . if a shot is fired from any house, that house will never again cover a mortal's head; and if I can discover the perpetrator of the deed, the place that now knows him shall know him no more forever. I have the power to suppress this unruly element in your midst, and I mean to use it." [15]

The Mayor now raised the question of the desperate need of food in

New Orleans and the almost complete lack of any currency except Confederate with which people might buy food. Butler agreed to admit the importation of foodstuffs from New Orleans's usual sources of supply, and modified his proclamation to permit the temporary circulation of Confederate bank notes.

The proclamation, printed by Butler's soldiers on the confiscated press of the *Daily True Delta,* was first circulated as a handbill, and within a few days the regular newspapers carried it, since not to print it was to invite suspension.

In the important matter of restoring the normal life of the city — which had been disrupted by the Federal naval blockade for about a year — the proclamation had but slight effect. Butler was forced to crack down on food profiteers by compelling them to reopen their stores and by placing a ceiling on the prices of flour and other staples. On May 3 he issued general orders guaranteeing a safe conduct to shippers bringing flour from Mobile and to ranchers from Texas who might bring cattle to New Orleans over the Opelousas Railroad, but this, too, failed to revive an adequate flow of food to the city. In an effort to check destruction of cotton on the "coastal" plantations up the river, Butler issued the controversial General Order, No. 22:

> The Commanding General of the Department, having been informed that rebellious, lying, and desperate men have represented, and are now representing to the honest planters and good people of the State of Louisiana that the United States Government, by its forces, have come here to confiscate and destroy their crops of cotton and sugar, it is hereby ordered to be made known, by publication in all the newspapers of this city, that all cargoes of cotton and sugar shall receive the safe conduct of the forces of the United States; and the boats bringing them from beyond the lines of the United States forces may be allowed to return in safety, after a reasonable delay, if their owners so desire: Provided, they bring no passengers except the owners and managers of said boat and of the property so conveyed, and no other merchandise except provisions, of which such boats are requested to bring a full supply, for the benefit of the poor of this city.[16]

Even had the Confederates desired to help Butler solve his totally unexpected problem of getting food into the occupied city, they would have found it difficult, for most of the freight boats had been burned and the few steamers that remained in Southern hands had been secreted in out-of-the-way creeks and bayous for use in their war effort. New Orleans, narrowly squeezed in between swamp and river, had no near-by suburban truck farms on which to rely, but was compelled to import all of its food from a distance. Happily Butler's agents discovered in a Confederate warehouse a quantity of beef which was seized for distribution to the poor.

After he had made a temporary arrangement whereby the Mayor and City Council would carry on their usual functions, Butler turned his attention to the bankers and the foreign consuls in the city. On the third day of the occupation the consuls called upon him in a body, and were apparently cordial and cooperative. Butler thanked them for the services of the European Brigade in maintaining public order during the interim between Farragut's arrival and Butler's. Butler exempted these men from his general requirement that all citizens turn in their arms, and requested them to continue their assistance to the police of the city.

In view of his early career as a crusader for currency reform, it was to be expected that Butler would look narrowly into the affairs of the New Orleans bankers. The latter were required to register all funds belonging to the United States Government. Where were the funds from the U.S. Mint? It was a tough problem for secret agent or bank examiner, yet Ben Butler, the lawyer, was determined to track down these funds. If the New Orleans banks had been receivers of "stolen goods," they should be made to disgorge. Under Butler's cross-examination the bankers admitted that during the panic attending General Lovell's evacuation, they had shipped twelve millions of specie out of New Orleans into Confederate-held territory.

In the hope of luring some of this money back to New Orleans, Butler offered safe conduct through military lines to operatives of the banks.[17] Learning from his agents that the Citizens Bank of Louisiana had hidden a large amount of specie in the vault of the Netherlands consul, Butler sent his officers to call on Amadié Couturié, a New Orleans liquor dealer who doubled as consul for the Netherlands. The latter histrionically pointed to the foreign flag over his establishment, invoked the aid of his fellow consuls, and finally submitted to force. Butler's men extracted from his vault not only the 800,000 Mexican dollars of which the informers had told but also the steel dies and plates of the Citizens Bank of New Orleans.

"Indeed, the claims of these Consular Gentlemen are most extravagant," Butler reported to Stanton. "Men who have lived here all their lives now claim perfect immunity from the ordinary laws of war for themselves and all property which they can cover, although they may have been in arms against the U. S. Many of these pretensions are too absurd to be for a moment entertained. Amongst other things it is claimed that the Consular Flag and Consulate have all and more than all the privileges accorded to a resident Minister Plenipotentiary and Envoy Extraordinary by the laws of Nations. Almost all property, therefore, useful to the United States which has not been burned or carried off, will be found to be held here by persons who have lived in Louisiana all their lives, and now claim to be foreigners. Every schooner and fishing smack that cannot venture out of the river raises a foreign flag. All wood for steamers for miles up the river has been burnt except isolated yards covered by such flags, and in one instance the owner refused to sell one of my boats any wood, and when the officer went to take it, hoisted the French flag over it. The Steamer wooded up, however." [18]

A few days after an amicable interview with the British consul, Butler was informed that about sixty members of the British Guard, a contingent of the European Brigade, had sent their arms and uniforms to General Beauregard. For this flagrant violation of neutrality, Butler ordered every British Guardsman who could not produce his gun and uniform to leave the city within twenty-four hours.

Consuls that refused to be neutral, disingenuous bankers, uncooperative city officials, cotton-burning merchants, street prowlers shouting for Jeff Davis and General Beauregard exasperated General Butler, absorbed his time, diverted his military forces to profitless police duty. But there was still another kind of difficulty.

On Sunday May 4, as two young Union officers seated themselves in Dr. Palmer's church a lady next to them stood up and, drawing her dress in close, left the pew. During the first weeks of the occupation, officers and soldiers could not enter a streetcar or omnibus or pass a lady on the sidewalk without encountering sneers of contempt and an ostentatious pulling in of the skirts, as if the New Orleans ladies were afraid they might be contaminated by the touch of a Federal uniform. Tiny Confederate flags were flaunted on the bosom. Upon the appearance of Federal officers in the better neighborhoods ladies on verandas turned their backs, or dashed inside their houses to pound out on the piano "The Bonnie Blue Flag" and other Secession songs. In public schools pupils were instructed by their teachers to show contempt for Union soldiers and to sing "The Bonnie Blue Flag." [19]

"I confess, that, after a day or two," wrote one of Butler's senior officers, "the sneers and contortions of countenance, the angry withholding of the dress from contact with my person, and the abrupt departure from the sidewalk to the middle of the street to avoid even passing the hated uniform, was too much for my philosophy, and gave me a sense of humiliation more painful than I can express." [20] Young officers red faced with anger begged the general somehow to suppress such insults.

In theory Butler believed in exemplary punishment but in the case of the New Orleans ladies he felt that this was hardly the thing. To arrest a lady might conceivably incite a riot. Some regulation had to be invented which was self-enforcing.

The order he finally wrote, with Sarah's approval, put the issue bluntly, and, so far as Southerners were concerned, with horrible forcefulness: [21]

> Headquarters, Department of
> the Gulf, New Orleans,
> May 15, 1862
>
> General Order No. 28
>
> As the officers and soldiers of the United States have been subject to repeated insults from the women (calling themselves ladies) of New Orleans, in return for the most scrupulous non-interference and courtesy in our part, it is ordered that hereafter when any female shall, by

word, gesture, or movement, insult or show contempt for any officer or soldier of the United States, she shall be regarded and held liable to be treated as a woman of the town plying her avocation.

By Command of Major-General Butler

George C. Strong, A.A.G., Chief of Staff

"After all, general," Major Strong remonstrated, "is it not possible that some of the troops may misunderstand the order? It would be a great scandal if only *one* man should act upon it in the wrong way." [22]

"Let us then," replied Butler, "have *one* case of aggression on our side. I shall know how to deal with that case, so that it will never be repeated. So far, all the aggression has been against us. Here we are, conquerors in a conquered city; we have respected every right, tried every means of conciliation, complied with every reasonable desire; and yet we cannot walk the streets without being outraged and spit upon by green girls. I do not fear the troops; but if aggression must be, let it not be all against *us*." [23]

Sarah Butler saw eye to eye with her husband and wrote Harriet Heard, her sister, concerning the soon-to-be-infamous Woman Order:

Never has anything been more deserved. Their insolence is beyond endurance, and must be checked. Such forbearance was never shown to a conquered town as our people have shown to this. Feeding them, and giving them protection from their mobs and ruthless assassins, respecting their property and demeaning themselves so courteously, that these women say "they did not expect the dirty, mean Yankees would behave so well," we, the Yankees, seem like the conquered and they like conquerors. To show their appreciation of such forbearance, they step out of their parlors on to the piazzas and grossly insult our officers as they pass along the streets. About a dozen ladies have called on me to express their feeling for the Union, but apparently in fear lest their coming should be known. They say the town ought to have been shelled, that leniency is not understood by this bragging, cutthroat people, and that they deny being whipped, because they have not yet suffered . . . Mr. Butler gets letters almost daily, that he will be poisoned or assassinated, and that leagues are formed, sworn to accomplish it. He fears them not, this city *will be governed,* and made to wear the *outward* forms of *decency,* however much they may struggle against it . . . I think Mr. Butler would rejoice at some demonstration from a mob that he might sweep the streets, and make these people feel that there is a power here to sustain or crush them according as they merit protection from the government or deserve punishment for their traitorous deeds.[24]

Butler's "Woman Order" was immediately effective. Insults by word, look or gesture abruptly ceased. No Union trooper overstepped the bounds of propriety, so that Butler had no occasion to clarify his intent by a spectacular example. The New York *Times,* whose first thought was that General Butler had "penned the very worst words he could have chosen," soon noted with surprise that "it has had the desired effect, and the soldiers cease to be insulted." [25]

Throughout the South, however, the Woman Order evoked a universal shout of execration. Widely circulated in Confederate newspapers was an anonymous propaganda piece signed "The Daughters of New Orleans" and entitled "An Appeal to Every Southern Soldier":

> We turn to you in mute agony! Behold our wrongs! Fathers! husbands! brothers! sons! . . . Do not leave your women to the mercy of this merciless foe! Would it not have been better for New Orleans to have been laid in ruins and we buried up beneath the mass, than that we should be subjected to these untold sufferings? [26]

Paul Hamilton Hayne urged fellow Southerners to reserve for General Butler, "this fiend of lust," a "swift cord! and felon grave!" Louisiana's Confederate Governor denounced Butler as a "panderer to lust" who invited his soldiers "to perpetration of outrages, at the mention of which the blood recoils in horror." [27]

One hot June night Butler sat up past his bedtime swatting mosquitoes and writing to an old classmate the fullest explanation he ever offered of the incident:

> . . . if the order had not been issued I would issue it tomorrow in *ipsissimis verbis.* See where we were. We had come into a city where the dirt [dirk] and pistol had ruled for ten years at least. A handful in

numbers, for there were more of those who had served as soldiers of the
Confederate ranks in plain clothes in the city than the Union had troops,
when the order was issued. The men had tried to provoke a riot, and
failed — the result of prompt arrest and stern justice. The women, more
bitter in their secession than the men, were everywhere insulting my
soldiers; deliberately spitting in their faces and upon their uniforms,
making insulting gestures and remarks, tending to provoke retort, recrimination, and return of insult, which would have ended in disgraceful
and murderous riot. What was there to be done? O, my friend, sitting
in your easy chair at home! Is a she-adder to be preferred to a he-adder
when they void their venom in your face? You say "arrest the women
and put them in the Guard House." But that is the place where we
shut up thieves and assassins and drunken soldiers, not a bower for
lovely ladies. What would have been said had I shut up Mrs. Judge
This and Mrs. Colonel That and the honorable Miss so and so; redolent
of civet and radiant with rouge, in such a place? Would their *honor*
have been particularly safe there? But these insults came from the bal-
conies of houses whence Juliet made love, and my men must have
broken open private dwellings and chased the fair, feeble, fretful and
ferocious rebels to their bedroom to have seized them. How many riots
do you think I should have had dragging screeching women through the
streets to the Guard House? If there had been any manhood in a New
Orleans mob it would have felt itself called upon to have fought then or
never. What was done? An order characterizing the acts of these
women in plain English was made which at once executed itself. "Any
woman who should by gesture, words, and looks insult my soldiers was
to be regarded and treated as a common woman plying her avocation."
How do you "regard and treat" a low woman and her remarks as she
passes you in the streets? Pass her by, do you not? You are not bound
to notice her acts or remarks. Some of your New York editors seem to
think they must hold dalliance with such a person, therefore take offense at my order. Rightly, if that construction were the correct one.
After that order, every man of my command was bound in honor not to
notice any of the acts of these women. They were no longer insulted.
They became the blandishment of which Solomon speaks in the Proverbs.
What has been the result? Since that order, no man or woman has insulted a soldier of mine in New Orleans.[28]

What he thus offered in justification was true enough, but many
Northerners felt that his wording had been in bad taste. Yet, more
than anything else he ever did, the promulgation of the Woman Order,

justly or not, established his notoriety throughout the South as the most diabolic officer in the Union army. Southern propagandists seized upon the cross-eyed and sharp-tongued politician general as the most suitable Yankee for purposes of propaganda. The sobriquets of "Brute" and "Beast," as applied to General Butler, became household words in the South. Cartoonists worked over a catalogue of epithets from Hyena to Bluebeard. Butler the Beast became raw-head-and-bloody-bones to frighten babies with.

Indeed for years after the Civil War steamships plying the lower Mississippi were furnished with chamber pots bearing the likeness of "Beast Butler."

15

MILITARY GOVERNMENT REFORMS

IN ADDITION to collecting taxes and lighting the streets, Butler expected Mayor Monroe and his City Council to assume some responsibility for relief for the many jobless parolees in the city and for taking reasonable sanitary precautions against yellow fever. If the safety of unacclimated New England troops had not demanded strict sanitary measures, the General's personal interest in yellow fever which years ago had carried off his father would have spurred him to clean up all breeding grounds of the plague.

The first week of the occupation went by, and no food came in from the surrounding country in response to Butler's offer of safe conduct. Instead Butler learned that Confederate leaders in New Orleans were blocking such shipments by circulating word that Butler intended to confiscate them. There were even indications that "rebellious, lying, and desperate" men had collected food from the limited stores within New Orleans and had smuggled it out to the Confederate army — at a time when destitute cases by the hundred were appealing to Butler for relief. During the first week the Mayor and Council did nothing about these problems.

On May 9 Butler tried prodding them. "Resolutions and inaction will not do. Active, energetic measures, fully and promptly executed, are imperatively demanded by the exigencies of the occasion. Specially, present suspension of labor furnishes ample supplies of starving men, who can be profitably employed . . . It will not do to shift the responsibility from yourselves to the Street Commissioners, from them to the contractors, and them to the sub-contractors, through all the grades of civic idleness and neglect of duty." [1]

A fundamental difference in theory of labor developed between Butler and the City Council. According to the latter, street cleaning was menial work for Negroes only. Butler's insistence that the hundreds of starving white men be given some of these laborers' jobs was looked upon as a Yankee factory operator's effort to place white labor on a par with Negro, and so to debase their scale of living.

Toward the skilled mechanics and laboring classes of New Orleans, whom he regarded as victims of the Secessionist oligarchy, Butler's attitude was as warmly sympathetic as it was hostile toward the Confederate leaders. "This hunger does not pinch the wealthy and influential," reads Butler's castigation of the South's ruling class on May 9 (in General Order No. 25), "the leaders of the rebellion, who have gotten up this war, and are now endeavoring to prosecute it without regard to the starving poor, the workingman, his wife and child. Unmindful of their suffering fellow-citizens at home, they have caused or suffered provisions to be carried out of the city for Confederate service since the occupation by the United States forces. Lafayette Square, their home of affluence, was made the depot of stores and munitions of war for the rebel armies, and not of provisions for their poor neighbors. Striking hands with the vile, the gambler, the idler, and the ruffian, they have destroyed the sugar and cotton which might have been exchanged for food for the industrious and good." [2]

The social reformer sought to drive a wedge between the workingmen and their leaders. "MEN OF LOUISIANA, WORKING MEN, PROPERTY HOLDERS, MERCHANTS AND CITIZENS OF THE UNITED STATES, of whatever nation you may have had birth, how long will you uphold these flagrant wrongs, and by inaction, suffer yourselves to be made the serfs of these leaders? The United States have sent land and naval forces here to fight and subdue rebellious armies in array against authority. We find, substantially, only fugitive masses, runaway property burners, a whiskey-drinking mob, and starving citizens with their wives and children. It is our duty to call back the first, to punish the second, root out the third, and feed and protect the last." [3]

On May 16, the day after the issuance of Butler's Woman Order, Mayor Monroe sought to shift the issue from street cleaning and the starving poor by protesting that Butler's war against women would arouse the citizens and make them uncontrollable. "Your officers and soldiers," complained the Mayor, "are permitted by the terms of this order to place any construction they please upon the conduct of our wives and daughters, and upon such construction to offer them atrocious insults . . . To give a license to officers and soldiers of your command to commit outrages such as are indicated in your order, upon defenceless women, is in my judgment a reproach to the civilization, not to say the Christianity of the age in whose name I make this protest." [4]

Butler immediately had the Mayor brought in by the Provost Marshal and told him that his protest itself was insulting and would not be tolerated, and that if he could no longer control his people, he would be relieved of his job and sent to Fort Jackson.

The Mayor explained that he only desired "to vindicate the honor of the virtuous women of the City." [5] Butler instructed him that such vindication was unnecessary because the order did not concern virtuous women, but only those who had insulted his officers and soldiers.

The Mayor affirmed that he was satisfied with this explanation and signed a written apology withdrawing his letter as being "improper in language." [6]

Later the Mayor, once more assailed by doubts, dispatched a second missive to the General, withdrawing the apology. This "weathercock business" called for a showdown. Butler laid before the Mayor and chief officials not only the Mayor's second "disrespectful" letter on the Woman Order, but the treasonable matter of the Monroe Guards as well. Six Confederate troopers of those on parole from the garrison of the forts had been caught enlisting for active duty in a Secessionist group named in honor of the Mayor the "Monroe Guards." Butler had had them hailed before a military court, which had sentenced them to be shot for violation of parole. After extracting from the Mayor a confession that he had contributed $20 from his own pocket to support these men, Butler forthwith ousted him and sent him downriver to Fort Jackson, along with his secretary and police officials.

The civil government of New Orleans now devolved upon Butler;

the duties of the mayor were assigned to General Shepley, and the office of Chief of Police to Captain Jonas H. French.

Captain French hired 500 new policemen. Loyal Union men were placed in every department of the city government. A Sanitary Commission was organized under Colonel T. B. Thorpe to put in effect General Butler's revolutionary labor reform in New Orleans and at the same time to minimize the danger of a midsummer epidemic of yellow fever. Some 2000 men under Colonel Thorpe were employed to scrape and sweep the streets, clean drainage ditches and canals, and wheel away semi-solid silt or batture from the riverbed at low water to fill depressions and swamps.

This hiring of white men for such labor constituted an economic and social revolution in New Orleans, where the belief was current that white men could not endure the subtropical sun. "It was a grotesque sight," wrote Secessionist Marion Southwood, "to see a battalion of stalwart men, with brooms and spades, sallying forth on a hot summer morning to scrape and sweep the streets, and, without doubt, the city has been more healthy since." [7]

One day Butler drove over the city in a calash with Mrs. Butler. A little way up the river lay the "basin," a broad pond for the reception of canal boats en route to Lake Pontchartrain. As they approached the basin, the stench took their breath away. The whole surface of the pond was coated with green scum, variegated with dead cats and dogs. On the banks of the pond were carcasses of mules rotting in the sun. The thermometer might have been 120°. They turned to the right and drove along the canal as far as Lake Pontchartrain, and found the entire canal in the same condition until within a few rods of the lake. [8]

On another drive Butler detected a similar plague spot in the old French market. Here he found the stall women accustomed to drop on the floor and trample the offal made in cleaning their birds, meat, and fish. This debris had been trod underfoot until it was now fourteen to eighteen inches thick.

Urged on by the commanding general, the Sanitary workers, in squads of twenty-five men each, cleaned the market down to the

original pavement, tore away shanties, filled up scum-covered pud-
dles, cleared the dead animals from the main canals, flushed and
scraped clean the open-sewer drains, cleaned the streets. The refuse
was spread over swamps and covered with clean silt from the Mississippi to create new land. Citizens of New Orleans wrote letters calling
attention to neighborhood nuisances, and even the most bitter Secessionists confessed to a left-handed admiration of Butler as "the best
scavenger we have had among us." [9]

Prominent obstructionists Butler seized and charged with treason.
The two chief leaders, Pierre Soulé and High Sheriff M. Adolphe
Mazureau, were sent to Boston for imprisonment in Fort Warren.[10]
Ministers who observed a moment of silent prayer for the Jefferson
Davis government or who held days of fasting and prayer in accord-
ance with the Confederate President's proclamations were roughly
dealt with. The church of one recalcitrant was closed and — to the
scandal of the city — turned into a school for Negro children.

When the day of execution approached for the six Monroe Guards,
Butler received numerous requests for leniency. He had no inclination
in that direction. Here were soldiers from the Rebel forts who had
surrendered, and were living in New Orleans on parole and hence
bound in honor not to take up arms against the United States Government until after they had been regularly exchanged. To forgive
these men would be to invite similar trouble with three thousand
others in their category. On May 31, accordingly, General Butler
signed their death warrant.[11]

The newspapers of New Orleans in extenuation of their fault published a copy of the capitulation of the forts to Commander David D.
Porter, of the Mortar Flotilla, showing that only the Confederate officers had been paroled, and that they in turn had been made responsible for the men. In other words the condemned men had not in
legal strictness broken their paroles since the oath had not been administered to them personally. As one of these ex-soldiers had expressed it when explaining his action to the Military Commission,
"Paroling is for officers and gentlemen. We are not gentlemen." [12]

At this embarrassing juncture two prominent Union men of New

Orleans asked that mercy be shown the prisoners. The miserable creatures had been duped by superior minds, argued J. A. Rozier and T. I. Durant, and had now learned the futility of resistance to the Government. Given this way out, General Butler was glad enough to call off the execution at the eleventh hour and commute their sentences to hard labor on the fortifications at Ship Island. It stuck in his crop, however, that the last-minute reprieve had the color of chickenheartedness in administration, against which Butler himself had often inveighed. And it caused New Orleans to believe that the execution of Mumford for desecration of the flag would never be carried through.

In Butler's mind, however, there could be no flinching in Mumford's case. The flaw in the indictment of the Monroe Guards was not present here. On April 29 Butler had written the Secretary of War: "This outrage will be punished in such a manner as in my judgment will caution both the perpetrators and abettors of the act, so that they shall fear the *stripes* if they do not reverence the stars of our banner," [13] and he enclosed for the Secretary's perusal a clipping from the New Orleans *Picayune* of that date lauding Mumford as a "patriot" whose tearing down the flag from the U.S. Mint symbolized the "unflinching determination" of New Orleans to continue in spirit to sustain the Rebel cause.

Open activity by the mob, particularly assassinations of Union men for expressing their loyalty, had been quickly checked after the occupation. On May 8 Butler reported to Stanton: "My officers and myself now walk in any part of the City when occasion calls by day or night without guard obstruction or annoyance. There is, however, here a violent, strong, and unruly mob that can only be kept under by fear," [14] and in June a New York *Times* reporter wrote enthusiastically but with a warning: "No New England village could be safer than New Orleans under the iron rule of General Butler. The streets are full of people, including a plentiful sprinkling of ladies — promenading and shopping. The stores on Canal and other principal streets are mostly open . . . prices fabulously high. Soldiers in the blue uniform of the United States, passing along the streets in squares, in companies and sometimes in regiments, remind you of the military

occupation of the city. About the 'St. Charles,' General Butler's headquarters, sentries, pretty thickly posted, pace to and fro, with fixed
bayonets . . . The city wears on the surface the air of quiet and submission, but there are hoarse mutterings below — curses deep, not
loud. Butler's policy is producing great indignation." [15]

The curses were also being reported to Butler by spies and informers
and by anonymous letters. A typical unsigned warning reads: "You
are mistaken if you suppose that the mere presence of U.S. troops has
afforded any protection to Union men. On the contrary they are closer
watched than ever. Spies are stationed at every corner where your
troops are found, to *mark* every man who even speaks to a U.S. soldier." [16] The eighty-six-year-old banker Jacob Barker informed the
General of the attempts of the Southern Independence Association to
intimidate bankers who, like himself, were pro-Unionist.

It was not the occasional street shouter for Davis and Beauregard
who forced Butler's hand in the Mumford case, but the mob that had
gone underground, the secret societies who had to be made to understand that their machinations would be rooted out and punished.

Accordingly on June 5, one day after he had reprieved the Monroe
Guards, Butler wrote Special Order No. 70:

> William B. Mumford, a citizen of New Orleans, having been con-
> victed before the military commission of treason and an overt act thereof
> in tearing down the United States flag from a public building of the
> United States, for the purpose of inciting other evil-minded persons to
> further resistance to the laws and arms of the United States, after said
> flag was placed there by Commodore Farragut, of the United States
> Navy: It is ordered that he be executed, according to the sentence of
> the said military commission, on Saturday, June seventh instant, between
> the hours of eight A.M. and twelve M., under the direction of the
> Provost Marshal of the district of New Orleans; and for so doing this
> shall be his sufficient warrant.[17]

The next morning Butler received forty or fifty anonymous letters,
in almost every language and degree of literacy, replete with sketches
of pistols, coffins, crossbones and skulls. One of Butler's agents
who the night before had attended an indignation meeting of a group

whom he characterized as "blacklegs and blackguards" was persuaded that Butler's life would be in danger if Mumford were hanged.

Butler took a contrary view. "I thought I should be in the utmost danger if I did not have him executed, for the question was now to be determined whether I commanded that city or whether the mob commanded it."[18] From this position Butler refused to be swerved. Mrs. Mumford and her three children appealed in vain. Sarah Butler, also, it is said, pleaded with her husband without effect.

Early on the seventh the crowds gathering on Esplanade Street in front of the U.S. Mint saw a gallows projecting from a window in the second story of that building, directly under the flagstaff where the treasonable act had occurred. At a quarter to ten a covered wagon halted in front of the building, and a short man with dark hair and whiskers who had been seated on a pine box coffin descended from the wagon, glanced briefly up at the scaffold and was led inside the building. In a few minutes he emerged wearing a black cassock. He walked quickly to the scaffold, and stood in the bright sunlight with thousands of eyes fixed on him. The order of execution was then read to him and he was allowed to make a brief speech to the crowd. At thirteen minutes before 11 A.M. the signal was given and the platform, loaded with iron, swung heavily down and in a few minutes the first man to be sentenced for laying violent hands on the United States flag was dead.[19]

Within the hour the crowd dispersed in orderly fashion. General Butler was judged the victor in the nerve-trying tug of war by the Northern press. "In this severe administration of justice," commented the New York *Times* editor, "General Butler has done right. His whole course of action in New Orleans indicates that he is determined to show the Southern traitors of all classes that the day of trifling with treason is past . . . His measures of severity against traitors heretofore have produced only good effects."[20]

The execution of Mumford, however, like the Woman Order, inflamed the imagination of Southerners against Butler. In Southern eyes the obscure gambler Mumford was no traitor but a martyr to the Confederate cause. Confederate President Davis instituted inquiries into the circumstances, and failing to obtain satisfactory answers after six months of waiting he issued a famous proclamation branding Benjamin F. Butler as a felon and outlaw who if captured was not to be accorded the treatment due a prisoner under civilized codes of war, but immediately and without trial was to be hanged to the nearest tree. All over the South the incident figured boldly in Confederate propaganda. Mumford's widow and children were declared to be the sacred trust of the people. Richard Yeadon, editor of the Charleston, S.C., *Courier,* offered $10,000 reward for the capture and delivery of Butler, dead or alive, to any proper Confederate authority. A woman ran the following advertisement in the Charleston *Courier:* "I propose to spin the thread to make the cord to execute the order of our noble president, Davis, when old Butler is caught, and my daughter asks that she may be allowed to adjust it around his neck." [21]

After the Mumford case Butler punished women as well as men offenders. At ten o'clock one midsummer morning, while Secessionist hopes in New Orleans were being fed by news of Federal reverses in Virginia, a young woman in white with a Confederate flag pinned on her bosom made a scene in front of the St. Charles Hotel. Arrested by a policeman with the assistance of a soldier, she appealed to the crowd for protection. The next moment the policeman was knocked down and the soldier was wounded by a shot fired from the crowd. The man who had fired the shot escaped, but the woman, along with several of her sympathizers, was brought to General Butler's headquarters. She was recognized as the wife of the gambler John La Rue, now by Butler's orders lodged as a vagrant in the Parish Prison. Butler sent her, for attempting to incite a riot, to Ship Island.[22]

The opportune arrival from Fort Jackson of the Twenty-sixth Massachusetts, which took up its encampment in Lafayette Square, was credited by the New York *Times* correspondent with having possibly checked a serious disorder of unemployed Confederate soldiers in New Orleans.

A *cause célébre* was the case of Mrs. Philip Phillips, wife of an ex-Congressman from Alabama. Because of her frenzied pro-Southern outbursts in Washington at the beginning of the war, Mrs. Phillips had been imprisoned for a time in the Old Capitol Prison and had later moved to New Orleans. Here she first claimed Butler's attention when one of her children was caught spitting on Union officers. Butler had her and her husband brought to headquarters, where they made an apology.

A few weeks later, Mrs. Phillips in her high-pitched voice laughed aloud when a Federal funeral cortege passed in front of her house. The situation was a difficult one. Lieutenant George C. DeKay, a nineteen-year-old New Yorker on General Williams' staff, had been mortally wounded by guerrillas in the fighting up the river. For a month he had lain helpless in a New Orleans hospital, cheerful, uncomplaining to the last. After his death his friends arranged with the Reverend W. T. Leacock for a funeral at Christ's Episcopal Church and provided several carriages for Unionist citizens who, it was believed, might attend.

The funeral, however, provoked a mass demonstration of anti-Unionist feeling, in the face of which the Union sympathizers dared not attend. With a number of its carriages empty, the cortege wound its way to the church "through collections of street cars, crowded with ladies wearing secession badges and passively smiling and cheerful crowds studiously collected to insult the dead." The church was "thrown open like a stable," as Lieutenant Godfrey Weitzel described it, its galleries and most conspicuous pews "occupied by a rabble and Negroes." [23] Leacock, himself a Secessionist sympathizer who held silent prayers for the Confederate Government, refused under the circumstances to conduct the service.

As the funeral cortege was passing her house, Mrs. Phillips, standing on her balcony with several friends, was observed by some Federal officers to laugh at the procession. Mrs. Phillips was arrested and taken before Butler, where, as Marion Southwood, a fellow prisoner, puts it, "While denying that her gayety had any reference whatever to the funeral ceremony, Mrs. Phillips refused to make any apologies or concessions to the vulgar tyrant," but insisted "that she was in good spirits that day." [24]

Butler in wrath sentenced her as follows:

New Orleans, June 30, 1862

Mrs. Phillips, wife of Philip Phillips, having been once imprisoned for her traitorous proclivities and acts at Washington, and released by the clemency of the government, and having been found training her children to spit upon officers of the United States at New Orleans, for which act of one of those children both her husband and herself apologized and were again forgiven, is now found on the balcony of her house during the passage of the funeral procession of Lieutenant DeKay, laughing and mocking at his remains; and, upon being inquired of by the commanding general if this fact were so, contemptuously replies, "I was in good spirits that day," *It is therefore ordered:* That she be not regarded and treated as a common woman of whom no officer or soldier is bound to take notice, but as an uncommon, bad, and dangerous woman, stirring up strife and inciting to riot. And that, therefore, she be confined at Ship Island, in the state of Mississippi, within proper limits there, till further orders; and that she be allowed one female servant and no more if she so choose. That one of the houses for hospital purposes be assigned her as quarters; and a soldier's rations each day be served out to her, with the means of cooking the same; and that no verbal or written communication be allowed with her except through this office; and that she be kept in close confinement until removed to Ship Island.[25]

On the same day a bookseller named Keller whose clerk had affixed the label "Chickahominy" to a skeleton in his shop window, "meaning and intending that the bones should be taken by the populace to be the bones of a United States soldier slain in that battle," was sentenced to ten years at hard labor on Ship Island. At this point Butler added the sardonic proviso that Fidel Keller should be "allowed to communicate with no person on the island except Mrs. Phillips, who had been sent there for a like offense."[26]

Keller, in the belief that the Mrs. Phillips referred to was a noted prostitute, now requested in writing "that that part of the sentence which refers to the communication with Mrs. Phillips be stricken out, as he does not wish to have communication with the said Mrs. Phillips."[27] Butler, possibly not aware of the nature of the prisoner's scruples, and hence from entirely different motives, struck out that part of Keller's sentence which related to Mrs. Phillips. Butler was widely denounced in the South and in Europe for his brutality toward Mrs. Phillips, " a delicate lady of the highest refinement, the mother of nine children," and the excoriations continued long after her early release on September 14.

Butler's next general order, No. 55, was designed to saddle some of the expense of poor relief upon the wealthy leaders of the rebellion. The large sum necessary could not be raised by taxation of the whole community without bearing equally, and as Butler saw it, unfairly, upon the "middling and working-men," whose voices had "never been heard at the ballot-box, unawed by threat and unmenaced by 'Thugs.'" In Butler's view, and his view was law in a city ruled by martial law, those who had fomented the rebellion and crippled New Orleans as a center of trade should be made to share the relief burden.[28]

General Order No. 55 singled out two classes: "First, those individuals and corporations who have aided the rebellion with their means; and second, those who have endeavored to destroy the commercial prosperity of the city."

Butler's investigators uncovered a list of firms and individuals who, prior to the Federal occupation, had contributed $1,250,000 to defend the city against the forces of the United States. Subscribers to that Rebel defense fund who had remained in New Orleans were now required by Butler to donate "for the relief of their destitute and starving neighbors" a sum equal to one-quarter of their contribution to the Confederate cause.

Butler also obtained a list of cotton brokers, who in October of 1861 had published in the papers a manifesto warning cotton planters not to bring their produce to New Orleans. These, too, were assessed sums ranging from $50 to $500 to be paid into the relief fund. A special office was set up under Lieutenant David C. G. Field, Financial Clerk, in the Custom House. Anyone delinquent in paying this assessment would have his property sold at public auction or be imprisoned until the amount was paid.[29]

In this manner began the auctions of furniture, clothing, portraits, silverware and jewels. Family heirlooms often brought only a pittance in the auction market. Occasionally a friend with funds might bid in a prized article, but with grass growing on the cotton wharves and little business traffic in New Orleans' carefully scraped, swept, lime-sprinkled streets, the spare cash tended to disappear. More and more New Orleans families who had stood high in the social life of the city suffered not only loss of property but the humiliation of seeing their ex-servants diaper pickaninnies in their heirloom laces. In Butler's army, too, there were hundreds of individuals who did not scruple to profit at the expense of "bitter Rebels" by collecting at ridiculously low cost this plunder from the auction rooms. To the Confederates of course General Butler became the arch symbol of tyrant and oppressor. In the wretched situation in which the New Orleans Secessionists were caught, about all they could do was to vent their hatred in private. Some snatched furtive glimpses at a painting being secretly executed of a gruesome beast engaged in robbing the grave of a Confederate soldier hero and wearing on top of its hyena body the head and face of Benjamin F. Butler.

In his striving toward social justice Butler often tempered the wind to the shorn lamb. Sometimes he eased up on the enforcement of a decree or made a contribution to a worthy case from his personal funds. On June 17, after he had banned the use of Confederate money, he was approached by a nun from the Orphan's Home of the Sisters of Mercy. General Butler gave her $5000 from his private purse and an order on the commissary for a quantity of assorted stores, with directions that the commissary bill be sent to him. He then sent the Sister to President Denegre of the Citizens' Bank with a request that he dispose of her Confederate notes to the best advantage. "This is only one of a great many instances of his benevolence," reported the New York *Herald*. "Indeed he is most Quixotic in his championship of the poor and distressed." [30]

As commanding general in a city ruled by martial law General Butler was in a position to apply a rough-and-ready solution to a problem. In mid-July, the food shortage continuing to be acute, he ordered his Chief Commissary to sell government flour and provisions to those who could afford to pay at a mark-up of 100 percent, and to distribute equal amounts of food gratuitously to those who had no money.

In punishing criminal offenses committed by his own soldiers Butler was as firm as in his dealings with the Secessionist Mumford. Colonel Holcomb of the First Louisiana reported how in a camp disturbance he had been compelled to shoot a man. Butler endorsed the letter "Shoot another." [31] Four Union soldiers were hanged for looting. A drunken officer who accidentally shot a prostitute through the thigh was cashiered. To an officer who kept a Negro girl in his quarters was given the choice of resignation or court-martial; and following his resignation he was jailed in the Parish Prison.

On July 18 a Frenchman Armand Thomas, convicted of threatening General Butler's life, was sentenced to prison by Judge Bell. Thomas' young wife called on the General sobbing convulsively and begged a pardon for her husband. Butler, who detested tears, issued an order approving Judge Bell's decision, but on the ground that he himself never heeded threats of assassination he set the man free.

16

SHOESTRING OFFENSIVE

As a concession to the steamy heat of New Orleans, the busy Commanding General of the Department of the Gulf wore a broad, open-neck collar and only on parade did he wear shoulder straps. However late he might have worked the previous night, he was at breakfast by seven in a small parlor of the St. Charles Hotel, with Mrs. Butler seated at his right, General Shepley, Military Commandant of New Orleans, at his left and about twenty guests, including Provost Marshal French, Postmaster Stafford, Provost Judge Bell, and Chief Commissary Clark. The General soon finished his breakfast, glanced at the newspaper and was off for work.[1] With a smart saluting of sentries around the hotel, he climbed into his barouche behind two bay horses which he had brought from Lowell to be driven to his headquarters in the Custom House. Here the guard at the entrance presented arms as he passed in.

The grandiose New Orleans Custom House had been fourteen years under construction and was not finished yet. Since Confederate General Beauregard as a U.S. Army engineer had had a hand in its construction, its present Yankee occupants were prepared to find fault with it as "a pretentious conglomeration of labyrinthine cellars, cock-lofts, narrow winding stairs, dark and mysterious passages." Fronting on Canal Street, it sprawled over one and a half city blocks. It was said that New York's custom house at this time could be stowed in one of its corners. The unfinished central portion of the building, a marble-floored courtyard, large as a public square, had never been roofed over and had been considerably damaged by dust and damp-ness and by the cooking fires of the Confederate troops that had been billeted in the upper and unfinished rooms. Fixed up on the outside walls of the building, "like swallows' nests on the side of a hill," were office rooms for collectors, postmaster and other officials.[2] On top of the building were eight cannon which the retiring Confederate troops had spiked. All the lead plumbing except illuminating-gas pipes had been ripped from the building to make bullets. In the armory on the ground level were stacks of worthless firearms collected from the countryside, live-oak timber for gun carriages, brass mountings, railroad scrap, rifling machinery, and the 418 brass bells contributed by Southern churches and plantation owners in response to Beauregard's plea for cannon metal. One of the church bells bore French foundry marks, "Fait par Jean Bagin, 1785." The bells Butler shipped to souvenir-hungry Boston to be sold for the United States Government. In addition to housing General Butler's headquarters, the building served as barracks for a Federal regiment, refuge for forty or fifty runaway slaves, warehouse for sequestered property and lockup for political prisoners.

Long before his arrival in the morning General Butler's anterooms were packed. A typical crowd was thus described by a New York *Times* reporter:

There were one Colonel, two Majors, a Lieutenant, and two Naval officers, a city judge, the only one who remained loyal of all the bench of this state; a prominent lawyer, two invalid soldiers, one of the heroes of Baton Rouge; several respectable looking darkies, eight women, all nursing children, which were semi-nude . . . innumerable citizens generally; two handsome sesech ladies . . . one very respectable looking priest, two nuns in a style of headdress similar to Guido's picture of "Beatrice Cenci" — pale, melancholy looking women . . . These people form lanes that reach away into the wide hall that approaches the presence, at the extremes of which you behold the victims of poverty and rebellion, crouching under the gaze of the well-fed and the comfortable — there they stand, hour after hour, appealing pitifully, with eyes and sunken cheeks, for labor and food . . . Crowded as are the rooms, there is no confusion, the swords of the numerous mounted orderlies, as they move about, rattle on their sides; but they are respectful, and try to be kind to all.[3]

In the anteroom sat Captain R. S. Davis, Acting Assistant Adjutant General, a smiling young man of thirty who worked hard and never became excited. Captain Davis gave a preliminary screening to the General's interviewers and picked from the correspondence the items that were most pressing. Military and civil matters were inextricably mixed, for the General's first military problem was to hold under firm control the City of New Orleans, the nerve center of his military department.

A New York *Herald* correspondent found it revealing to spend a morning inside General Butler's private office.

. . . The General hands over the correspondence to his ever active aids — Captain Haggerty, Lieut. Weigel and Lieut. Clarke — to be answered, and then the crowd waiting in the ante-room is permitted to filter in, one at a time. Their business is as varied as the contents of the correspondence. Bank officers, trying to obtain some modification of the General's financial policy; foreign Consuls, calling to discuss some question of international law in which they fancy themselves aggrieved, but in which they generally discover that General Butler hasn't been jumping to conclusions with his eyes shut; elegantly dressed ladies, who bring their private grievances to be settled at headquarters; officers, to report the progress of special duty, other officials to face the anger of their chief for disobedience of orders or for other improprieties; and indeed, for every manner of business — important and ludicrously trivial — that one can imagine. They pour into headquarters in a steady stream, from about ten o'clock A.M. till four P.M. The manners of the General in his interviews are as versatile as the subjects are varied. To the man who comes with an honest, straight-forward air, on business honorable to himself, the General is frank and genial; but if the visitor is a bank officer, trying to wheedle the General, or a weak, undecided Mayor, showing velvet at one moment and claws the next, General Butler receives him politely, but lays down the law, and exposes his trickery to his face with a sledge hammer force that would compare favorably with Peter Cartwright's style of driving home conviction to the breast of the most case hardened sinner.[4]

Returning to his hotel in the evening, the General ate a simple meal and retired to his room, to write his reports while being continually interrupted by officers and orderlies. "Late at night," wrote a reporter,

"I have seen the gas gleaming from his room (the door open by the necessity of getting some air in this suffocating climate), and the General buried in the labor of his extensive military correspondence."⁵ After covering Butler's headquarters for three months, a New York *Times* correspondent was convinced that General Butler, who seldom worked under fifteen hours a day, was the most industrious man in the nation, and the most relaxed person in New Orleans. "His complexion is as a child's, his hair is a bright auburn, his eye is bright, and his step is elastic."⁶

In a military way New Orleans under the Federal occupation was threatened more by its own heterogeneous and explosive social forces than it was by military enemies from without. With Farragut's fleet in the river and the Navy's blockade gunboats in the sounds, lakes and bayous that flanked New Orleans, all that General Butler had to do to protect New Orleans from a counterattack by land was to station a few hundred troops at Carrollton, seven miles above the city on the narrow strip of high ground along the river. This he promptly did in the assignment of Brigadier General J. W. Phelps with the Ninth and Twelfth Connecticut regiments and Manning's Battery of artillery. Had any real danger from enemy forces developed at this point, General Phelps' command at "Camp Parapet," as it was called, might have acquitted themselves handsomely, — they proved their fighting abilities later in other quarters — but during Butler's period in New Orleans, from May to December 1862, their position was not threatened. Phelps himself, a single-minded abolitionist, bent his energies toward freeing every black on the plantations in his vicinity and afterwards squeamishly refused to set these idle people to work repairing the levees, on the score that he was no slave driver; while his "Connecticut over the fince" regiment, battling mosquitoes, malaria and boredom, gained a reputation for chicken-thieving and frightening old ladies.

Brigadier General Thomas Williams, whom General Butler early in May had detailed to accompany Farragut upstream to open the Mississippi, was a West Pointer and a sundowner in discipline. Before Farragut's victory over the forts, Williams had drilled his men under

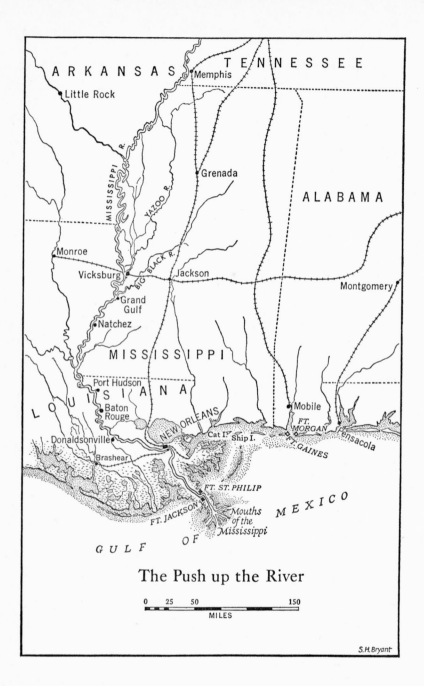

The Push up the River

0   25   50   150

MILES

S.H.Bryant

heavy packs till they dropped on the hot sands of Ship Island. "Look at those men," a reporter heard him say; "at home they are respectable, law-abiding citizens. It's the women who make them so. Here they rob hen-roosts and do things they would be ashamed to do at home. There is but one thing will take the place of their women's influence, and that is discipline." [7]

The occupation had been a week old before Butler had been able to scrape together transportation for General Williams. One boat had been captured in a back creek by a military aide. The rest had been turned over to Butler by the Navy. Onto these river transports Williams' 1400 infantry and 75 artillerymen with their four fieldpieces had crowded "more like live stock than men," without room on board to exercise or line up for inspection. "Filth and dirt, with all the authority and supervision I could exert," Williams reported, "abounded on vessels and men to a disgusting and of course most unwholesome degree." [8] Nor, owing to flooded conditions along the riverbanks, could the troops be disembarked to exercise and clean themselves on shore.

All the way from New Orleans up to Vicksburg, Butler's forces witnessed the destruction of cotton along the river ahead of them. Sometimes a planter himself set fire to his cotton piled on the riverbank. Sometimes Confederate Partisan Rangers or guerrillas dashed to the riverbank and applied the torch, threatening meanwhile to hang any Union-sympathizing plantation owner who might object. Here and there a Union officer was sent ashore in a rowboat to explain "that we were not on a cotton, or nigger, or chicken-stealing expedition," but always his breath was wasted. [9]

Throughout the back country the Confederate policy of incineration had gone forth in the clarion words of General Lovell: "One sparkling, living torch of fire in manly action for one hour upon each Cotton plantation, and the eternal seal of Southern independence is fired and fixed in the great heart of the world." [10] Town officials at Baton Rouge and Vicksburg spurned the invaders' demand that they surrender.

The city of Vicksburg, on the river slope of the Chickasaw Bluffs, overlooked a horseshoe bend in the river. For months its defenders had expected a descent down the river of the Union river ironclads under Flag Officers Foote and Davis, and had set up heavy batteries. Farragut and Williams decided not to attempt military action against Vicksburg with their present forces. Farragut's heavy naval guns could not be sufficiently elevated to reach the Rebel batteries on the heights; and Williams' handful of troops could not scale the heights along the river front or, circling around the city, take Vicksburg's batteries from the rear, because Vicksburg could be too easily reinforced from Confederate armies concentrated at nearby Jackson, Mississippi.

During their retirement down the River, Farragut and Williams were fired upon by light artillery as they were passing the village of Grand Gulf. The naval vessels promptly opened their broadsides on the town. White flags were run up ashore and the mayor hurried out to the ships to explain that Grand Gulf's three or four hundred inhabitants were entirely at the mercy of wandering bands of guerrillas who had galloped into town, fired on the Federal ships and fled.[11] General Williams sent two companies ashore to try to capture the guerrillas' artillery, but they failed and one of the officers, Lieutenant George C. DeKay, was shot in the back and paralyzed. The townspeople pleaded so earnestly that in lieu of further bombardment Farragut and Williams levied a contribution of supplies and came off with a considerable haul of cattle, pigs and poultry.[12]

At Baton Rouge, a bright little town with green esplanades on the first bluff above New Orleans, a party of "irregular cavalry" fired into a naval vessel, wounding an officer and two men. Farragut fired at the guerrillas as they spurred their mounts back through the town. The citizens appealed to Farragut and Williams to save them from pillage by guerrillas. In answer to this plea and in order to allow his uncomfortable troops to cook and clean up, General Williams landed and occupied Baton Rouge.

In his New Orleans headquarters General Butler, disappointed over the meager results of the expedition, lashed out against the guerrillas in his order of June 12 to General Williams:

> You ask me what shall be done with Guerrillas. They should be captured, tried at the drum head by Military Commission, and shot, every

man; their houses burnt, their property destroyed, and every means taken to show them that they are enemies of the human race, not soldiers but murderers and land pirates. There is only one way in which you can err toward them and that is want of prompt severity.[13]

Butler suggested to Farragut that the Mortar Flotilla now at Ship Island be brought inside the river to bombard Vicksburg's hilltop batteries with their high-angle fire, and Farragut accordingly sent Porter's forces to Vicksburg. Butler had been holding several regiments for the attack he had expected Farragut to make on Mobile, but these he now sent up the river to reinforce General Williams. To General Williams the commanding general had now given all of his troops that were not pinned down in Ship Island, at the forts, in New Orleans, at Camp Parapet and at Baton Rouge. Even so, Williams had scarcely three thousand effective men with which to assail Vicksburg. "With this force," read Butler's orders to Williams, "the general will expect you to . . . take the town or have it burned at all hazards." [14]

General Butler's fertile brain also conceived the idea of trenching across the peninsula opposite Vicksburg and diverting the river so as to enable Farragut's fleet to bypass the cannon-studded Vicksburg hills and join forces with the flotilla in the upper river. Accordingly General Williams, still with too few troops to risk either a frontal assault from the river or an attack from the rear, devoted himself to digging the proposed canal, while Porter's Mortar Flotilla bombarded Vicksburg. Some 1200 Negroes, collected from nearby plantations, were put to work cutting trees, grubbing stumps, and shoveling off the top layer of silt down to the hardpan clay. After an immense amount of manual labor had been performed, with few wheelbarrows and no horse-drawn scrapers or carts, the capricious river caved in the levee and placidly filled the trench but did not, as had been hoped, scour out a new channel. On June 28 Farragut steamed around Vicksburg's horseshoe bend with six of his seagoing ships, and three days later was joined at his anchorage above Vicksburg by Flag Officer Charles H. Davis with the upper-river fleet ironclads. While Porter's bomb vessels were lashed to trees along the east bank of the river for stability during firing, Williams had a force of 300 pickets stationed in the adjacent swamps to protect the mortar boats against surprise attack, and while Farragut was passing up the river, Williams' artillery located on the peninsula opposite Vicksburg added their gunflashes and shellbursts to the pyrotechnical display.

Farragut and Williams had now fulfilled Washington's injunction that they ascend the river and join forces with the fresh-water navy above Vicksburg. The river had hardly been "opened," however, for Vicksburg's batteries were still intact, and the season was late for seagoing warships to be so far inland where falling water increased the danger of running aground. Farragut returned to New Orleans and Williams to Baton Rouge.

On August 5 Confederate General John C. Breckinridge — the same whom Butler had supported in the Presidential race of 1860 — attempted to drive the Federals out of Baton Rouge, with 5000 men against Williams' 3000. The Confederates attacked through heavy timber and fought over the Federal campground. Breckinridge had counted on the support of naval gunfire from the Rebel ironclad *Arkansas,* but this vessel's engine had broken down a few miles north of Baton Rouge. Williams, on the contrary, had the help of three of Farragut's gunboats. On both sides the casualties were relatively heavy, about 400 each, as men debilitated by heat and malaria dragged themselves into battle. Particularly severe were the casualties among the leaders. Of the Confederate generals, Allen was killed, Clark was left on the field mortally wounded, Helm was disabled by a fall from his horse, Breckinridge lost an arm. Among the Federals Colonel George T. Roberts was killed while trying to rally his Seventh Vermont. All the leaders of the Twenty-first Indiana were put out of action. Near the close of the battle General Williams charged to the front. "Boys, your field officers are all gone," he shouted; "I will lead you." [15] Before the soldiers' answering cheers for the General had died away, Williams received a rifle ball through the heart and died instantly. After four hours of struggle both sides were too exhausted to continue fighting. The Confederates, without drinking water for half a day, retreated, and the Federals, many of whom had got out of hospital beds to fight, were too exhausted to pursue.

The transport bearing General Williams' body to New Orleans sank after collision with the gunboat *Oneida,* and some miles below the scene of the accident the corpse floating in its pine box was retrieved by naval Lieutenant Pierce Crosby. General Butler placed the body in a rosewood coffin. After funeral services in General Shepley's office in the City Hall, he sent it north on a transport. The efforts of Butler and Farragut to break open the Mississippi with their too meager forces came to an end.

In midsummer a variety of administrative problems had littered Butler's desk. With the approach of the yellow fever season came an excessive number of resignations and requests for leave. The New Orleans newspapers before Butler had clamped down on them had hailed yellow fever as an ally who, "tripping around the streets slaying his thousands and grinning as he slays," would breathe his withering breath over the unacclimated Lincolnites.[16] To this Secessionist-stimulated fear of yellow fever Butler attributed a flurry of resignations among his officers, which Butler accepted in such a way as to discourage others. A surgeon who asked to resign in order to attend to his private affairs had his application forwarded to the Secretary with the following endorsement: "A surgeon who would make his private and domestic affairs an excuse for leaving his regiment, and exposing his fellow-citizens to the want of medical attendance at this season of the year — knowing that his place could not be supplied for months — deserves to be cashiered for cowardice or neglect of duty." Another officer after nine months of service concluded that he was "incompetent." "If, in this time, he has just learned his incompetency," reads Butler's angry endorsement, "there must be something wrong in his mental or moral capacity. I believe the latter, and therefore he is dismissed the service, subject to the approval of the president. If incompetent, he has done the United States no service, but much harm, and is entitled to no pay." [17] Such endorsements were published in the New Orleans *Delta* to forestall other resignations.

On June 20 two privates of the Thirty-first Massachusetts were publicly drummed out of the service for insubordination. Sometimes petty offenders escaped with only a scolding in the controlled press, as in the case of private David Thompson, who accused a prostitute of stealing his uniform. "Ah! David, David," remonstrated the *Picayune,* "what story will you invent when you go back to moral Maine to account for your acquaintance with the false Ann Douglas? . . . Have you forgotten all the moral teachings of the past and abandoned yourself at once to the syren wiles of the tempter? Say, David, say." [18]

In New Orleans so many comely Negresses were being kept in the Custom House ostensibly for laundering that the Commanding Officer felt moved to strike a blow for old-fashioned New England morality. "Laundresses of companies are not permitted to come into the quarters of the men. They must be kept in their own quarters, and the clothing sent to them and sent for. Any officer who permits a woman, black or white, not his wife, in his quarters, or the quarters of his company, will be dismissed the service." [19]

Finding funds to pay the troops offered a problem late in June, when the funds arriving from Washington were $285,000 short of enough to pay Butler's men. "I could not let my soldiers go longer unpaid," he explained to the Secretary of the Treasury. "It was injuring the credit of the Government and breeding sickness and discontent among my men." [20] Accordingly, he seized $50,000 in gold specie from the Secessionist firm of Samuel Smith & Co. and he pledged his personal credit to borrow $50,000 more in gold from another bank. With these funds he had his paymaster pay as many men as possible. Then when the soldiers turned over their pay to the Adams Express Company for transmission to their families, Butler induced the express company to send only credit records and to return to him the cash to enable his paymasters to pay other troops. This process was repeated until all the troops had been paid. "Happily you are less oppressive in your demands on the Treasury," wrote Salmon P. Chase, "than any other of our Generals in important positions." [21]

Butler acted as his own recruiting officer. From the floating population of surrendered Confederate troops, the Irish Ninth Connecticut recruited 350 unemployed Irishmen. The First and Second Louisiana and the "Native Guard" regiment of free Negroes were mustered into the United States service. Butler's 1700 free black troops were many of them "lighter in color than Mr. Soulé." They called themselves "Butler

Guards," "Chasseurs d' Afrique" and "General Williams' Avengers." They were billeted in the Judah Touro Charity Building, and every afternoon they paraded with zest to the music of their band.[22]

Following withdrawal from Vicksburg, Butler limited his military action to the immediate neighborhood of New Orleans. As its small garrison could not defend Baton Rouge against a determined assault, Butler decided to evacuate it. In disregard of Butler's standing orders against looting, the Union soldiery had partially sacked the place. "Even officers' tents are filled with furniture from deserted houses," reported Colonel D. W. McMillan. "Disobedience of orders is the order of the day, and Negro men and women cast a dark shade over our whole camp."[23] In withdrawing his troops, Butler ordered the destruction of the city, for the same reason the Confederates under Magruder the year before had burned Hampton, Virginia: to deprive the enemy of shelter.

Throughout lower Mississippi and Louisiana bands of Confederate Partisan Rangers roamed the countryside. Major Frank H. Peck, whom Butler sent after guerrillas who were menacing Union people in lower Mississippi, reported that the people of Pearlington were "in great destitution and beset by plunderers on every side"; the inhabitants of Pass Christian "are flying daily by boat loads to escape impressment into the Confederate service. They are destitute of the necessaries of life, being dependent entirely upon the small amounts smuggled from Mobile." At Shieldsborough "outrages too gross for description have been recently perpetrated by guerrillas"; at Louisburg "All the docks and landings of this place, and at Mandeville, 2 miles distant, were burned by a party of guerrillas some two weeks since;" at Madisonville "The town was deserted, and nearly every public and private building closed."[24]

In Confederate-held territory Governor Moore of Louisiana campaigned against selling food to New Orleans. His activity fell at a moment when Northern shippers had stopped sending supplies, in the mistaken belief that the Mississippi River had been opened. Confederate Partisan Rangers harried plantations to destroy the produce of "Lincolnite desperados" and fired upon all boats seeking to trade for food stuffs. Fortunately, one of Butler's raiding parties on the west bank of the river captured a drove of 1500 cattle en route from Texas. This haul relieved the pinch of hunger in New Orleans, but at the same time stimulated Confederate cavalry general Dick Taylor to seal off Western Louisiana.

In October Butler sent Brigadier General Godfrey Weitzel with five regiments into the rich farming area to the west of New Orleans known as the Lafourche Country.[25]

Here the masters of the great sugar plantations, as reported by the Northern press, lived in "barbaric splendor," with handsome equipages, fine homes, fine furniture and multitudes of slaves. When Weitzel appeared, these planters fled. Everywhere the slaves "bressed God that Massa Linkum had come." The butternut-colored troops of the Butler Guards inspired Negroes everywhere to pack up loot for themselves and join the Yankees. Soon every private in Weitzel's army had a dozen servants, some officers had fifty. The New York *Times* reported that social chaos had come: "negroes, horses, mules, private carriages, old and new wagons, dilapidated carts, tapestry carpets, rich furniture, Sèvres china, pots and kettles — all mingled in an inextricable mass of confusion." The escaped contrabands held high carnival, feasting on chickens, turkeys, hogs and cattle. In fierce prayer meetings they invoked God's "bressing" for "Massa Linkum," destruction for the "perillas" (guerrillas) and success to the Northern Army. They begged the Almighty to punish their former taskmasters, whom they likened to frogs sitting on a log, with a big alligator (the United States Army) "goblin' up some and runnin' de res' into de bayou, bress God." [26]

Organized opposition in the Lafourche Country vanished in less than two weeks. By November Weitzel was able to report that the country was "as safe to travel now as Canal Street." [27]

17

RECONSTRUCTION

THAT Lincoln should send to New Orleans "an old Breckinridge Democrat" like Butler was a puzzle to Southerners.[1] Yet that fact made Butler appeal to Lincoln as one who might sooner persuade Southerners to return to the Union. Gustavus Fox, Assistant Secretary of the Navy, who often relayed the President's views informally to commanders in the field, wrote Butler on May 17, 1862, "The most delicate, but the most important duty is entrusted to your hands, viz: drawing back into the ark the wanderers and the deluded. This requires more brains than it does to fight." [2]

Unfortunately, several months before Butler's arrival at Ship Island, abolitionist General Phelps had muddied the waters with a manifesto declaring slavery illegal in the Gulf states. Phelps' proclamation, issued on his own initiative, was disavowed by Butler as soon as he heard of it. On May 1 Butler had tried to set Southern minds at ease on the slavery issue when he announced that all persons who should renew their allegiance to the United States "will not be disturbed in their persons or property." [3] Slaveowners, however, distrusted him from the start, and the hundreds of jubilant Negroes who flocked to the Custom House hailing Butler as a savior could not understand the language of his proclamation.

New Orleans, pinched by the blockade for a year, should be ready, Butler had thought, to return to her old allegiance and resume normal business life. During the first weeks of Butler's occupation 14,000 people in New Orleans had taken the oath of allegiance. But these were chiefly the desperately poor, the Northern born, or half-caste quadroons, who had no standing in the community which they could lose through association with the Yankee invaders. "I went to Louisiana desiring to do everything to restore it as it was," Butler told an audience in Lowell in January 1863, "to see if by any possibility I might bring the principles, the laws and institutions which govern that State into harmony with the Union; but I found there no disposition to have that done. I found the aristocracy looked upon us as their enemies; and I found that the working and middling classes looked upon us as friends." [4]

The oath taking had been slowed up by the mob, who severely beat and even killed several who had fraternized with Yankees. Butler's officers had encountered old friends among the New Orleanians who either could not speak because they were being watched or who spoke furtively and hurried on. "We are told there is strong Union feeling here but they are afraid to show it, lest, should we be driven out, they might all be murdered," Sarah Butler wrote her sister, Harriet Heard. [5]

After six weeks of the occupation Butler made his first move to draw a broad line between Unionist and Secessionist in the heterogeneous population of New Orleans. His General Order No. 41 on June 10 allowed five days in which judges, justices, sheriffs, attorneys and notaries could either take the oath of allegiance to the United States or quit their positions. Almost to a man they resigned. It was further ordered that all former citizens "asking or receiving any favor, protection, privilege, passport or any benefit of the power of the United States extended to them," must take the oath before their request would be heard. [6]

Thus encouraged, New Orleans Unionists on June 14 held their first public meeting. About 400 crowded into the City Hall to hear speeches on supporting the Federal Government. The tone of the meeting, reported the New York *Times,* was "at least hopeful"; although "the effects of the reign of terror have not yet worn away." [7] After the speeches the Unionists, led by a military band playing Yankee tunes and flying the Stars and Stripes, paraded to the St. Charles Hotel to serenade the General. Butler assured the Unionists that the presence of the National forces "meant justice to every man — high and low, rich and poor"; and that he would welcome the day when the citizens would again take their civic affairs into their own hands. His auditors listened with attention, and occasionally broke into cheers.[8]

Butler, himself under no illusions concerning the plight of the Union men in New Orleans, reported to Stanton on June 18, only four days later, "The very life and soul seems to have been crushed out of the Union men, and at this day there is not a union flag flying over a single private dwelling in New Orleans, and that, too, not from want of inclination, but from a certain undefined fear that the City will at some future time be given over to its former domestic rulers by the withdrawal of the forces of the United States, and that the knife and the pistol will do the work in avenging the Confederacy." [9]

The first instance of flag waving by a New Orleanian, as reported by the New York *Times,* was a practical joke.[10] A commotion arose in Canal Street when a Yankee soldier gave a child a toy and the Negro nursegirl did not notice until the child had waved it around and attracted an angry crowd that the toy was a miniature United States flag imprinted on a fan. On June 19 a New York *Tribune* reporter "could see no evidence that General Butler has made a shadow of progress toward reconciling to the Union those who were ever really hostile to it." [11]

So anxious were the Federals to stimulate loyalist morale that they were sometimes gulled by Confederate sympathizers. Arrangements were craftily made for two Union ladies to present a silk flag to the Thirteenth Connecticut, known as "Butler's Pet Lambs" because they were billeted in the Custom House. Its commander Colonel Henry W. Birge scheduled the ceremony for the Fourth of July as a climax to a parade. General Butler in full uniform "with chapeau and feathers" and mounted on a roan stallion took the review.[12] With ceremony several aides helped the young ladies to alight from their carriage and unfurl the flag which was now presented to Colonel Birge, as a token of the love the Union ladies of New Orleans had for their native land. The regiment presented arms. The drum corps sounded ruffles. The band played "The Star-Spangled Banner." General Butler with General Shepley at his elbow paid his respects to the young ladies.

A few days later a mortified officer from the Thirteenth Connecticut entered Butler's office. "General, we have been sold. They were Negroes."

One day a destitute "perfectly white" and well educated "mulatto" girl appealed to General Butler to be given one of her secessionist father's houses. After investigation Butler learned that she had been educated in New York City and at seventeen had been taken by her father to a Metropolitan hotel and kept as his mistress. The girl had escaped to New Orleans, whither her father, a prominent judge in New Orleans, had followed her. When she had refused to live with him, he had had her publicly whipped and married to a slave. She had afterward resumed the unnatural relation and had had a child. The father had fled from the city at the time of the Federal occupation, leaving her without support. Butler released confiscated property for the woman's use. There followed in New Orleans such a universal transferring of property as no city had ever seen before.[13] Property was given away or sold for next to nothing to persons who had taken the oath.

Five days before the September 23 deadline Butler issued an order forbidding these fictitious transfers. The next four days were busy days in oath taking.[14] "It is a singular fact," reported the New York *Times* correspondent on September 19, "that most of those who have been the noisiest in denouncing the Government, I now find the most clamorous to get in 'and take a swear.' It may be said that this oath taking jest is, in the majority of cases, heartless and selfish — that it has been done to save property, or to escape worse evils — but let the motive be what it may, the moment every resident of this city is identified alike with that act, there begins a new era in New Orleans; social and political life is changed, the distinction between the rebel and the loyalist is broken down, and a community of interest at once springs up."[15]

W. N. Mercer, one of the wealthiest planters in Mississippi and a resident of New Orleans who had neither aided the Confederate States nor taken the oath of allegiance, wrote to ask whether Butler intended to include him among the enemies of the United States? Butler replied: "In my judgment there can be no such thing as neutrality by a citizen of the United States in this contest for the life of the Government. . . . The line is to be distinctly and broadly drawn. Every citizen must find himself on the one side or the other." [16]

Dr. W. T. Leacock, the rector of Christ's Episcopal Church who had refused to read the funeral service for Lieutenant DeKay, accused Butler of breaking down public morals. "General Butler, 'you are eating up God's people as it were bread.' You have possessed them with such fear, that they are rushing, innocent and weak women, most unwarrantably, guiltless and timid men, most ingloriously, are rushing to their destruction, through fear of being deprived of their substance or of their personal liberty . . . Thousands have perjured themselves — thousands are rushing to perjure themselves in the sight of Almighty God, by bringing themselves under oath to do what they intend not to do . . . May God give you grace to see your error." [17]

Butler summoned Dr. Leacock to an interview. "Well, General," asked the minister, "are you going to shut up the churches?" "No, sir, I am more likely to shut up the ministers." [18] Dr. Leacock and five other Episcopalian clergy who as conscientious objectors registered themselves as enemies were transported to New York City.

Butler's policy toward pro-Secessionist citizens of New Orleans won him the hatred of Rebels everywhere. Southern presses teemed with the epithets "Tyrant," "Beast" and "Bluebeard." But the North in general approved Butler's adroitness in facing down the "stubborn and almost satanic" spirit of rebellion. "Of all the civil and military officers that Mr. Lincoln has sent forth to deal with treason," commented the New York *Times,* "none has manifested the wisdom, firmness and skill of General Butler. The history of his administration at New Orleans will always be regarded as one of the most extraordinary and singularly interesting chapters in the annals of our war." [19]

While Butler was forcing the citizens of New Orleans to declare their allegiance, and introducing new ideas concerning the labor of white men in the South, he was also, as by the suction of a maelstrom, being drawn closer and closer to the central issue of reconstruction — Negro slavery.

There were many uprooted Negroes in New Orleans when the Federals arrived, slaves whose masters were in the Confederate armies. These floaters sought to attach themselves to the Union barracks, which they regarded with awe as the very gateway to freedom. Other fugitives escaped from plantations; some with fresh buckshot in their legs, some wearing iron yokes or anklets. Butler's first policy was to surrender slaves to loyal masters, provided they had not been mistreated. As Washington, fearing to alienate the border states, was not yet ready to promulgate a uniform policy on slavery, Butler in distant New Orleans was compelled to muddle along as best he could. Unhappily for this policy, at Camp Parapet seven miles north of New Orleans, Butler had a fanatic abolitionist subordinate who was determined to promote emancipation whatever the policy of the Lincoln government might be.

Brigadier General J. W. Phelps led a simple and austere life. When other Union officers in New Orleans were quartered in the mansions of absent Secessionists, General Phelps considered his army tent sufficient. If professed Unionists seeking him out to demand the return of runaway slaves found his midsummer quarters crowded and unbearably hot, the General would be the better pleased, for they would not stay long. Phelps listened to their pleas, but faithful to his principles, never surrendered a black man who had come to him for refuge.

Although this was the procedure Butler himself had followed at Fortress Monroe, Butler did not wish a duplication of Fortress Monroe's mushroomed settlement of Negroes to encumber Camp Parapet. Accordingly, Butler early suggested to General Phelps that if he could use the services of fugitive Negroes he should do so, but that he ought not to harbor them as vagrants. Phelps, however, idealistic and deaf to reason, never turned a Negro away and never assigned one a job.

To get the levee repaired Butler had to send Captain Edward Page of the Thirty-first Massachusetts to oversee the Negro laborers and to Captain Page, General Phelps grudgingly loaned eighty contrabands. Page reported to Butler that soldiers from Camp Parapet were insulting planters and enticing their Negroes away from the plantations. "If on any of the Plantations here a negro is punished when he most deserves it," Page reported to Butler, "the fact becoming known at General Phelps' Camp a party of soldiers are sent immediately to liberate them, and with orders to bring them to Camp. A Negro convicted of barn-burning . . . was . . . taken to Camp. Yesterday an outbuilding on Mrs. Fendeair's Plantation was broken open by these soldiers, and three negroes, confined there over night, taken out and carried to the Camp . . . The soldiers also broke into the house and stole therefrom silver spoons, dresses, and other articles." Polycarpe Fortier, a planter with seven Negroes lost to General Phelps, complained to General Butler that discipline was cracking among his remaining blacks: "Our negroes, heretofore quiet, now feeling under no restraint commit burglary and depredations, and then seek a refuge in camp where they are received and protected." [20]

After May 23, when Butler directed Phelps to exclude all unemployed persons from his lines, Phelps carried out the order by allowing the blacks to build a settlement like Fortress Monroe's "Freedom Fort" just beyond the Union trenches. Here as their numbers doubled they supplemented the rations that Phelps's soldiers continued to give them with what they could forage from nearby farms.

"The question now pressing me is the state of negro property here and the condition of the negroes as men," Butler reported to Secretary Stanton on May 25. "It has a gravity as regards both white and black appalling as the mind follows out the logical necessities of different lines of action. Ethnological in its proportions and demands for investigation, it requires active administrative operations immediately upon the individual in his daily life, his social, political and religious status as a human being, while some of the larger deductions of political economy are to be at once worked out by any given course of conduct." In Louisiana the proportion of slave property was much higher than in Virginia, where whites as well as blacks did manual labor. In some Louisiana districts Negroes outnumbered whites ten to one. "They till the soil, raise the sugar, corn, and cotton; load and unload the ships; they perform every domestic office, and are permeated through every branch of industry and peaceful calling." The problem of manumission was complicated by the fact that very many of the slave owners —

planters, farmers, mechanics and small traders — "have been passive rather than active in the rebellion . . . In the destruction of cotton and sugar, even, which has so largely been effected, the owners and producers have not been the destroyers but in many cases the resistants of destruction." Since Butler had been left to develop his own policy on the Negro question, he had concluded to send all Negroes for whom he had no employment outside the lines where they could be subject to the ordinary laws of the community. But what further should he do? He could not confiscate the slaves of loyal owners without violating property rights which theoretically at least had been guaranteed to them. Nor could he consistently seize slave property of Rebels without also sequestering all other kinds of property. Should he receive only the first Negroes who had arrived and deny refuge to later comers? *"It is a physical impossibility for me to take all.* I cannot feed the white men within my lines. Women and children are actually starving in spite of all that I can do . . . What would be the state of things if I allowed all the slaves from the plantations to quit their employment and come within the lines is not to be conceived by the imagination." [21]

Early in June the home of planter Babilliard La Blanche, twelve miles north of New Orleans on the west bank, was searched for arms by General Phelps's men, who also, it seems, told the Negroes that they would be free if they would come to Fort Parapet. Under a leader named Jack, the La Blanche Negroes crowded into a small boat which from overloading was in danger of swamping. Babilliard La Blanche now told his Negroes that if they were determined to go he would hire them a large boat to put them safely across the river, and that they might also have their furniture. When the bedraggled troop of men, women and children arrived at the settlement on the edge of Fort Parapet, the slave leader Jack La Blanche explained to General Phelps that their master had told them: "The Yankees are king here now, and you must go to your king for food and shelter." [22]

General Phelps seizing upon the incident as an excellent argument in favor of manumission of slaves, wrote General Butler an abolitionist homily on the matter. Butler interrogated La Blanche's neighbors, and sent the record of his investigation to Stanton with the hope that the case might serve to clarify Federal policy:

> Gen. Phelps, I believe, intends making this a test case for the Policy of the Government. I wish it might be so, for the difference of our action upon this subject is a source of trouble. I respect his honest sincerity of opinion, but I am a soldier bound to carry out the wishes of my Government so long as I hold its commission, and I understand that policy to be the one I am pursuing, so I do not feel at liberty to pursue any other. If the policy of the Government is nearly that I sketched in my report upon the subject, and that I have ordered in this department, then the services of General Phelps are worse than useless here. If the views set forth in his report are to obtain, then he is invaluable, for his whole soul is in it, and he is a good soldier of large experience, and no braver man lives. I beg to leave the whole question with the President, with perhaps the needless assurance that his wishes shall be loyally followed.[23]

In Washington the Federal Government's approach to the Negro question was dilatory. Butler in mid-July sent General Shepley and a Unionist lawyer named Roselius to Washington to ask for clarification of policy.

Without coming to grips with the central issue, President Lincoln through the Secretary of War, on July 22, issued to department commanders a directive authorizing them "to employ as laborers . . . so many persons of African descent as can be advantageously used for military or naval purposes, giving them reasonable wages for their labor."[24] This Butler had been doing for over a year without authorization. By failure to decide on a Negro policy Washington in effect condoned Phelps's practices.

"The Government have sustained Phelps about the Negroes," Butler wrote to Sarah, who had gone to Lowell to escape the heat of midsummer, "and we shall have a negro insurrection here I fancy. If something is not done soon, God help us all."[25]

General Phelps, witnessing a daily increase of Negroes near his camp and receiving no answer from Washington, felt that silence gave consent, and proceeded to formulate his own policy, which was to start drilling able-bodied blacks to become soldiers. "The African," contended Phelps, "should be permitted to offer his block for the temple of freedom." [26] Butler heard informally of Phelps's drilling the Negroes with sticks in place of guns, and was prepared when he received Phelps's formal request of July 30 for arms and equipment for three regiments of Africans. Phelps already had three hundred Negroes organized in five companies. To side-track his subordinate from a course of action not officially sanctioned by Washington, Butler now ordered Phelps to employ his contrabands in cutting down the trees between Camp Parapet and Lake Pontchartrain.

General Phelps, unwilling "to become the mere slave driver which you propose," submitted his resignation, effective immediately.[27] Butler as tactfully as he could, declined to accept the resignation, yet ordered him to desist from forming any Negro military organization, as contrary to Government policy, and along with the official order he sent a "private and confidential" note in an effort to ease the mounting tension between himself and Phelps. The now utterly unrealistic Phelps, however, from his hot and crowded tent on August 2 begged Butler to forward his resignation to Washington.

"Phelps has gone crazy," Butler wrote to Sarah. "He is organizing the negroes into regiments and wants me to arm them." "He is as mad as a March Hare on the 'nigger question.' " [28]

In mid-August after Butler called for the surrender of all their arms by the citizens of New Orleans, thousands of old muskets, dueling pistols, bowie knives, and sword canes were turned in. But so many weapons were dredged from the canals that the suspicious lawyer-general offered rewards for information on concealed weapons. In his search for weapons he made full use of Negro informers, who were admitted to his headquarters at any time of day or night. In this way he obtained, he is said to have boasted, "a spy in every house, behind every rebel's chair as he sat at table." [29]

Butler's conversion to the cause of emancipation was of gradual development and was tied in with his growing awareness of the depths of Secessionist sentiment. In mid-August — after the battle of Baton Rouge and the soak-the-rich Order No. 55 for relief of the destitute — Butler, in advance of permission from Washington, began arming and drilling Negroes for military use.

True, the Lowell politician general had an ideal setup for the experiment. Washington had sent him no reinforcements, and New Orleans was being daily bombarded by threats of Rebel invasion. While he was engaged in confiscating weapons belonging to citizens of New Orleans, Butler had been waited upon by the leaders of a free-Negro military organization which the Rebel Governor Moore of Louisiana had sanctioned before the fall of New Orleans. These half-castes frankly admitted that they were interested in obtaining civil rights equal to the white man's, and therefore wished to fight for the Union cause. Butler, armed with the Confederate precedent, and the fact that these Negroes were legally free men, mustered them into the service of the United States. Butler's action preceded the President's preliminary proclamation of emancipation by exactly one month, and marked Butler's own departure as a party man from the ranks of the Democrats.

On September 24, George S. Denison, a Treasury Department investigator in New Orleans, reported to the abolitionist Secretary of the Treasury Salmon P. Chase that Butler "is satisfied that Slavery must be abolished, and he will do his part at such time as he thinks proper."

More and more, as General Butler saw it, the war around New Orleans was taking on the character of a crusade for the civil rights of the Negro and for the humanitarian and economic rights of the poor white man. The special streetcars set apart for Negroes and identified by black stars painted on their sides were eliminated in New Orleans by a court decision which gave well-behaved Negroes the right to ride in the same cars with white men. On October 25 a Negro regiment participated in the parade that launched General Weitzel's campaign in the Lafourche District. And the same evening 300 white laborers on the canals marched to Butler's headquarters to thank the General for the opportunity he had given them to earn livings for their families. "It was an interesting sight," reported the New York *Times* correspondent, "to see these strong, rough men, clothed in their plain, substantial garb, illuminated by brilliant gaslight, standing beside the General and his Staff, they in turn contrasting strongly in their blue uniforms and shoulder straps." [30]

In a brief speech thanking the workers Butler said that he would try before he left this city to elevate labor to its proper sphere. He had always fought the battles of the poor man against the rich in his far distant home in the North and he hoped that the time was not far distant in New Orleans when an honest day's work would get an honest day's wage.

The planters around New Orleans were caught in a squeeze that inevitably added to Butler's problem. Rebel guerrillas would destroy rather than allow the produce of the farms to reach New Orleans. And the Federals themselves, while attempting to persuade slaves to remain on Unionist plantations, were also freeing them by judicial process. After Lincoln's preliminary announcement of emancipation in September of 1862, more and more planters gave up the struggle and sent their slaves to the Yankee camps. These by general order Butler declared to be free. Poor white families by stealth crossed the lake into New Orleans in search of food. Butler's relief rolls grew to 32,000 whites and 10,000 Negroes.

With many plantations abandoned, Butler cast about for an emergency method of salvaging the crops. His brother Andrew Jackson Butler pointed the way for a possible solution when he purchased from a Unionist planter whose Negroes had vanished his standing crop of cane and hired Negro labor to harvest and make the sugar. Denison, the Treasury agent, after a visit to this plantation a few miles below the city, wrote to Chase: "I say he deserves credit, as being the first man bold and enterprising enough to undertake the raising of a large crop of sugar by free labor — which a little while ago, was slave labor — in opposition to the Southern idea, long established that Sugar and Cotton can be successfully raised only by compulsory labor." [31] Several other Union traders with General Butler's sanction followed Andrew Butler's lead; but the problem was too great to be handled by private individuals imported from New England.

The scheme General Butler evolved for emergency working of the plantations was to offer the Negroes a contract and induce Unionist and nonhostile planters to manage their own holdings, while the Army took over the operation of abandoned and confiscated properties. The suggested contract which Butler drafted called for wages of

$10 a month for a 10-hour day and a 26-day month. Negroes might be punished by solitary confinement on bread and water, but not by whipping. And they were to be reassured that if they would remain on the plantations their chances for general emancipation would be just as good as those of Negroes who flocked to the overcrowded Federal camps. Since few owners were willing to negotiate on these terms, the task for the Army became extensive.

Butler's "free labor" experiment worked best in the waterlogged parishes south of New Orleans which were cut off from ready communication with the Southern mainland, and after Weitzel's expedition the experiment was extended throughout the Lafourche District. The first barrel of sugar to be produced by free black labor in Louisiana was earmarked as a present for President Lincoln. On one plantation it was estimated that the same Negroes working for wages made one and a half hogsheads more sugar in a day than under the old system.

In mid-November Butler took a party of sightseers down the river to see the sugar cooking on one of the "free labor" plantations. The party of twenty included the French Admiral Reynaud, Admiral Farragut and Mrs. Butler. Sarah wrote her sister:

> We dined at the plantation, — fortunately, a very excellent dinner. No lady but myself, yet it was not in the least embarrassing. I declined to go at first, but Mr. Butler insisted, and I found it quite delightful. I wish you could see the splendid roses the younger gentlemen gathered for me. The dinner was partly provided by our servants. The plantation is owned by an old bachelor, who would have found it difficult to provide for such a party if we had not carried the material with us. Plantation life would never please me. A strip of land bordering the river, running back a mile to an impassable swamp. Houses three-quarters of a mile apart, more or less. The land a dead level, lower than the river. The negroes a miserable, ragged, degraded-looking people, far behind the city negro.[32]

Secretary Chase carried Butler's letter detailing his experiment to the White House, and Lincoln wrote Butler at once: "I was much interested by the information . . . that some of the planters were making arrangements with their negroes to pay them wages. Please write to me to what extent, so far as you know, this is being done." [33]

Butler reported to the President the most recent developments. In the Lafourche District, where army officers, civilian speculators, and Negroes had got out of hand in seizing movable property and where fugitive plantation owners were attempting to get their plantations transferred to "loyal" agents, Butler had issued a general order sequestering the entire district. To insure the planting of crops for the next year, Butler planned to employ his third Negro regiment in preserving the necessary cane stock, seed corn and potatoes.

It cannot be supposed that this great change in a social and political system can be made without shock, and I am only surprised that possibility opens up to me that it can be made at all. Certain it is I speak the almost universal sentiment and opinion of my officers that Slavery is doomed. I have no doubt of it, and with every prejudice and early teaching against the result to which my mind had been irresistibly brought by my experience here, I am now convinced:

1st. That labor can be done in this State by Whites more economically than by Blacks and Slaves;

2nd. That Black labor can be as well governed, used, and made as profitable in a state of freedom as in slavery;

3rd. That while it would have been better could this emancipation of the slaves be gradual, yet it is quite feasible even under this great change as a governmental proposition to organize, control, and work the negro with profit and safety to the white, but this can be best done when under military supervision. Of which, allow me to say, I do not desire the charge.[34]

In December Butler, having completed the separation of Unionists and Secessionists by a progressive series of registrations, felt free to conduct an election of Members of Congress from the two Congressional districts which his army occupied. Although the Unionism of many takers of the oath was of the most fishy kind, the majority of the citizens of New Orleans were now nominally within the Union camp. Of the fewer than 4000 conscientious souls who had finally registered as enemies, the majority were women ineligible to vote, and the men were a well marked minority unlikely to create election-day disturbance.

Ex-Congressman Bouligny, a Union man in whose candidacy Lincoln was interested, failed of election because he had run for Justice of the Peace under the Secessionists. The two who were elected to Congress were pro-Union and longtime residents of New Orleans. B. F. Flanders, a New Englander and a Dartmouth graduate who had lived for twenty-five years in New Orleans as a railroad official and had been driven out of the state upon the advent of Secession, was elected from the First District; and Michael Hahn, of German extraction and a lifelong resident of New Orleans, was elected from the Second District.

As if to set the seal of permanence upon his labors toward political reconstruction in New Orleans, General Butler caused stone chiselers to get busy on the pedestal of two of New Orleans' public statues. On the base of the monument to Henry Clay he had the workmen carve from one of the famous Kentuckian's speeches the motto: "If I could be instrumental in eradicating this deep stain, slavery, from the character of our country, I would not exchange the proud distinction which I should enjoy, for the honor of all the triumphs ever decreed to the most successful conqueror." And on the granite pedestal of the equestrian statue of Andrew Jackson in the square opposite the Old Cathedral, Butler ordered that there should be deeply incised and covered with gold the words: "The Union must and shall be preserved." [35]

18

COMMERCE, CONSULS AND THE RECALL

PROBLEMS of commerce had thrust themselves upon Butler as soon as he had set foot on Ship Island. Since his transports had to anchor out, and men and stores had to be put ashore in small boats or lighters, he needed all such craft he could lay hands on. Suitable for a lighter was a small schooner he requisitioned from the Navy which had been captured while attempting to run cotton through the blockade. What should he do with the approximately $5000 worth of cotton on board this vessel? On shore at Ship Island he found the quartermaster's civilian laborers almost in a state of mutiny from want of pay, and not a dollar of government funds on the Island.[1] What should he do for money? Following the law, he should have sent the $5000 worth of prize cotton to his Army quartermaster in Boston and waited several months until the funds arrived from the Treasury Department. Butler, disregarding rules, put the captured cotton on board the transport *Black Prince,* which was otherwise returning empty to Boston, consigned the cotton to his own personal broker, Richard S. Fay, Jr., in Boston, and by giving a draft on his private banker he borrowed from the Ship Island sutler about $4000 with which he paid the Government's debts to the laborers.

In New Orleans, with hunger already pinching the needy and a food supply for less than thirty days, Butler issued safe-conduct orders to steamers to go to Mobile and up the Mississippi River to bring flour and produce, and he authorized the Opelousas Railroad to bring cattle, sugar and cotton from Texas. To stimulate trade General Butler personally borrowed $60,000 from Jacob Barker. With these funds he bought sugar, tar and turpentine — cotton for the most part having been destroyed — and loaded it on government transports, instead of ballast, to be sent North. These operations were managed for him by his brother, Colonel Andrew Jackson Butler.

Butler looked upon such trading as an emergency measure, justified by exceptional circumstances, and he stood ready to turn over any profit to the Government. "Nobody can be better aware than myself that I have no right to buy this property with the money of the U.S., even if I had any of it which I have not," Butler reported to Stanton on May 16. "But I have bought it with my own money and upon my individual credit. The articles are Sugar, rosin and turpentine. I have sent these as ballast in the several transport ships, which otherwise would have been sent to Ship Island for sand. These articles will be worth more in New York and Boston than I pay for them here through my agents. If the Government chooses to take them and reimburse me for them, I am content. If not, I am quite content to keep them and pay the Government a reasonable freight. Whatever may be done, the Government will save by the transaction. I only desire that neither motives nor action shall be misunderstood." [2] Butler also informed his friend Fox in the Navy Department that he had shipped some naval stores to his broker R. S. Fay in Boston: "I think that I should allow the Government to take it and reimburse me, and if your department chooses so to do, I have no objection . . . If you do take it, please send some money at once to Fay, so that my drafts can be paid from the proceeds." [3]

On May 12 President Lincoln, following Butler's recommendation, lifted the blockade at New Orleans, and for the next six weeks Washington officials chewed their fingernails over what to do about General Butler's private trading operations. Meanwhile in Boston an assistant quartermaster tied up the consignment of cotton from Ship Island that had been sent on board the *Black Prince*. Fay, the agent, was not permitted to sell the goods. Banker Carney refused to accept the merchandise in lieu of cash. Butler's draft to the sutler went to protest. Finally Fisher Hildreth, Paul R. George and a merchant named Read of Lowell together raised $60,000 to meet Butler's draft upon Carney for the New Orleans purchases. Fay went to Washington to consult Quartermaster General M. C. Meigs, and that official in mid-June ruled as follows: "General Butler's action in this matter has evidently been wise and patriotic. He has incurred much responsibility, and ought to be protected. At the same time, as a public officer, he ought not to be involved in private trade and profits arising out of his official power and position. I recommend that Mr. Fay be authorized to sell at public auction the cotton, sugar, and naval stores shipped by General Butler, to pay out of the proceeds all drafts and expenses drawn against it, and to deposit the net proceeds, after deducting such expenses, to the credit of the Secretary of the Treasury to be disposed of as may hereafter be determined. Such sum as may be the correct freight charge should be placed to the credit of the U.S. Assistant Quartermaster at Boston, to reimburse in part the cost of the transports upon which the goods are shipped North." [4]

Stanton cautioned Butler: "The matter of your shipments to Mr. Fay was submitted to this Department, and, in the desire to afford you every aid and facility for re-establishing trade and commerce in New Orleans, an arrangement was made by the Quartermaster General which was entirely satisfactory to Mr. Fay. Such operations, however, should not be engaged in without an absolute and overwhelming necessity." [5]

Of all shipments out of New Orleans made prior to June 1, when the blockade was lifted, the profit was $17,550.16 and this was held by Fay until the Government could decide what to do with it. Fay reported to Butler in mid-July that these shipments had caused "a great deal of discussion . . . in view of the jealousy with which the blockade is regarded by foreign powers . . . Although I am very sorry the profit on these operations does not accrue to you, I think Gen. Meigs' view a just one, and it will be far better to be able to silence the many remarks current here about the business from which your reputation would have suffered if uncontradicted." [6]

From June on General Butler took no direct personal part in trading in New Orleans. The money he had originally turned over to Andrew Jackson Butler multiplied under the latter's shrewd manipulations. About once a month the General received a statement of accounts from R. S. Fay. There were several accounts kept by Fay for General Butler. The account marked "Sales" held the $17,550.16, profit on the goods shipped before June 1, in which operations Fay had acted as agent both for the government and for Butler. This account remained frozen throughout the remainder of Butler's tenure at New Orleans. In another account Fay entered income from the General's rental properties and the frequent dividends declared by the Middlesex Corporation. A third account in the General's name was kept for income from the operations at New Orleans after June 1 that were carried on by Colonel Andrew Butler. Into this third account, from which only the General could draw, the Colonel had instructed Fay to transfer from time to time "any considerable sum" from his, Andrew Butler's own personal account.[7] The General frequently drew on Account Number Three for poor relief, for the bombed-out Sisters of Charity at Donaldsonville, or for transfers back to Andrew Butler.

Sarah Butler, who credited "blustering and overbearing" Andrew Jackson Butler with causing many of her husband's troubles, was afraid people would think the General was speculating because of Andrew's being engaged in it. Her inability to convince her husband of the danger from Andrew seems to have been in part responsible for her almost hypochondriac condition when she went home to Lowell for the summer and early fall.

In Lowell, after two months of rest with the children, Sarah relayed to Ben the word that his friend Paul R. George was also opposed to Andrew Butler's trading. George had said that no matter what was done to advance the General politically, there would always be Andrew, "a spectacle for public comment ready to topple you down as fast as others could build; that you did not see it, and if you did you were reckless about it."[8]

In New Orleans, meanwhile, Treasury Agent Denison was reporting to Chase unfavorably upon the situation: "Col. Butler . . . is here for the sole purpose of making money, and it is stated by secessionists — and by some Union men — that he has made half a million dollars, or more . . . It leads to the belief that the General himself is interested with him . . . I do not believe the General is interested in his speculations." [9] Two weeks later Denison was less certain: "While all admire his [General Butler's] great ability . . . many soldiers and citizens — Union and Secessionists — think he is interested in the speculations of his brother (Colonel Butler) and others. Sometimes circumstances look very suspicious, but if I happen to hear his explanation of the same circumstances, suspicion almost entirely disappears. I have never been able to discover any good proof that General Butler has improperly done, or permitted, anything for his own pecuniary advantage. He is such a *smart* man, that it would, in any case, be difficult to discover what he wished to conceal." [10] On October 10 Denison reported to Chase the current rumor that Colonel Butler "by various practices has made between one and two million dollars since the capture of the city . . . There are eight or nine river boats here, all seized and now in the hands of the military authorities. Colonel Butler has used these boats as he pleased for carrying up and bringing down freight. I had no control over them, and could not know what was transpiring, for the military authorities controlled them . . . Of late, frequently, one or two infantry companies would accompany a boat taking up cargo and bringing back produce. This service was unpopular with officers and men, who enlisted for the benefit of the country and not of speculators." [11] Every speculator, moreover, who was in competition with Andrew Butler at New Orleans was a potential talebearer to Washington.

Secretary Chase in some alarm warned Butler, "So many and seemingly such well-founded charges against your brother, Colonel Butler, have reached me and other members of the administration, as well as the President, that I feel bound to say to you that in my judgment you owe it to yourself not to be responsible, even by toleration, for what he does. Many do not scruple to express their conviction that you and some other of your officers are concerned in his speculations . . . It is said that Colonel Butler's gains amount to between one and two millions of dollars." [12]

Thus alerted to the danger of a trading scandal that could smirch his fame and damage his political chances in the future, General Butler asked his brother to wind up his business as quickly as he could and leave New Orleans.

> My brother [General Butler explained in a letter of November 14 to Chase] has been indeed engaged in commercial adventure in New Orleans, and has been successful. I know and cannot be mistaken that he has been no more successful than many others. I believe that every transaction has been legitimate mercantile operations. I have aided him in no way officially. On the contrary, I have avoided it, and have aided him far less than I have strangers, so far as all matters of official action were concerned. I have aided him to capital and credit by the use of my name at the North, and drawing on my bankers where I had some means before this war, but very little now. I have aided him in no other way. I believe this is a legitimate course toward a brother. I have not heard, nor do I believe, that he has done anything which in any way interferes with the Army of the Gulf or with the department. Certain it is that he has supplied the army with nothing or bought anything from it that was not sold at public auction. That his acts have been misrepresented is most true, and in nothing more than in the extent of his transactions, — you say you have heard his profits were *two* millions!! Why he shew me his balance sheet the 1st of October, and his entire transactions were only rising of *eight hundred thousand* dollars, a large portion of which was in buying sugar here at nearly the same price it sold for in New York, sometimes higher, and depending upon the difference of exchange 12 or 15 percent for his profits. How much he has been able to gain you will conjecture. I have not asked him, nor do I believe he knows . . . I have determined, however, that no appearance of evil shall exist to rob me of the fair earnings of a devotion of life and fortune to the service of my country. I have therefore asked Colonel Butler to close up his business and go away from New Orleans, so as to leave me entirely untrammeled to deal with the infernal brood of slandering speculators who have maligned me because I will not allow them to plunder the Government.[13]

Early in December after Butler's tightening of regulations had stopped trade across Lake Pontchartrain, the skipper of the schooner *L. L. Davis* attempted to maneuver around the law by obtaining from Acting Collector Denison a clearance for Matamoras, Mexico. Farragut's blockaders, however, in the belief that Matamoras stood in no great need of a cargo of salt, kept watch on the *L. L. Davis,* and found that after heading down the lake a little way she changed course and ran her cargo to Pontchatoula, a well-known Confederate depot for blockade runners. Farragut complained to Butler that "This and similar things . . . bring discredit upon the whole of us, for it is said publicly that it could not be done without the connivance of the authorities." [14]

In a meeting in Butler's office suspicion was pointed at Andrew. A man named Wyer of New Orleans, who worked for Colonel Butler, had loaded the salt on the *L. L. Davis* and it was he who had requested the clearance for Matamoras. Denison had granted the clearance against his better judgment and was convinced, though he had no proof, that Colonel Butler was the owner of the cargo. "General Butler assured me he will immediately investigate the matter thoroughly," reported Denison to Chase, "& if Col. Butler, or those associated with him are interested in the operation, he & they shall instantly leave the Department of the Gulf. He manifested great indignation which I cannot believe feigned, judging from his appearance." [15]

But any investigation which might have proved the case for or against Andrew Butler was soon elbowed aside when General Butler himself was relieved of his command of the Department of the Gulf.

At the commencement of the occupation Butler had assumed that the consuls and other foreign residents were neutral as far as the domestic quarrel between Federals and Confederates was concerned. Then a week later he learned that thirty-seven members of the British Guard had donated their guns and uniforms to Confederate General Beauregard. Butler confined two of their leaders in Fort Jackson and ordered the rest to leave New Orleans within twenty-four hours, on the theory that Beauregard should be able to use the men as well as the uniforms. Eventually Lord Lyons, the British Minister in Washington, interceded with Secretary Seward, who admitted the justice of Butler's actions but released the two Britishers from Fort Jackson.

Beating the bushes to locate steamboats, Butler early in the occupation had captured the Confederate blockade-runner *Fox* in Bayou Lafourche. Even more interesting to the lawyer-general than the *Fox*'s cargo of contraband rifles, powder, lead, quicksilver, acids, chloroform and morphine were her papers. These letters to consuls, invoices, letters of advice, bills of lading, bills of exchange gave Butler irrefragable evidence that the Spanish firm of Avendano Brothers had been shipping cotton out through the Federal blockade and bringing back munitions and other contraband for the Confederates. Since the Confederate Government permitted cotton to be shipped out only on condition that a portion of its value be returned in munitions, it was clear that the foreign-owned mercantile houses of New Orleans were operating as arsenals of secession. These *"quasi"* foreign houses "tempted by the immense profits . . . have done everything they could to sustain the war and to inflame the passions of the people against the United States," Butler reported to Stanton.[16] Avendano Brothers were required to pay a fine of $9600, the amount of a captured bill of exchange, which represented a part of their profits from a single voyage of the *Fox*.[17] As rapidly as he could assemble the evidence, Butler levied similar fines against other foreign firms who were aiding Secession.

Butler's agents tracking down Federal silver from the U.S. Mint, learned that Amadié Couturié, a professional liquor dealer and spare-time Consul of the Netherlands, had early in April rented a disused bank vault at 109 Canal Street and had received for safekeeping under the Netherlands flag some $800,000 belonging to the Citizens Bank of New Orleans. On the bank's ledgers this money had been applied to a debt they had owed to the Dutch firm of Hope & Company but which was not yet due. In Butler's opinion the consul's caching the money and "conniving" with Secessionist bankers in premature payment of the debt was a subterfuge not to be tolerated.

A squad of soldiers was dispatched to the Consulate on the afternoon of May 10 to seize the reported kegs of silver. Couturié protested against violation of his consular office, claiming to have only private property in his vault. Captain Shipley forcibly took the keys from the right pocket of the consul's pantaloons, and opening the vault discovered 160 kegs of specie, $16,000 in bonds of the cities of Mobile and

New Orleans, a tin box containing the consul's exequatur and office records, and a number of plates and dies belonging to the Citizens Bank, all of which were carted under guard to the U.S. Mint for safekeeping.

To Couturié's protest General Butler retorted:

> The nature of the property found concealed beneath your consular flag, the specie, dies, and plates of the Citizens Bank of New Orleans, under a claim that it was your private property, which claim is now admitted to be groundless, shows you have merited, so far as I can judge, the treatment you have received, even if a little rough. Having prostituted your flag to a base purpose, you would not hope to have it respected so debased.[18]

All the other New Orleans consuls joined formally to protest the "indignity and severe ill usage" to the person of the Consul of the Netherlands.

General Butler's quarrels with the consuls created more than a flutter in the State Department in Washington. Secretary Seward, just convalescing from the migraine of the *Trent* affair, had no wish to offer Europe another cause for intervention in our Civil War. When the Couturié case reached his ears he promptly persuaded President Lincoln to create the new office of "Military Governor of Louisiana" to be given to General Shepley — a move, which as he interpreted it to Joest van Limburg, Minister of the Netherlands, would relieve Butler of his responsibilities toward the consuls. At the same time Seward appointed Reverdy Johnson as a special commissioner of the State Department to go to New Orleans to investigate the matters in dispute between General Butler and the consuls. Seward explained to Stanton "that the utmost delicacy is required in transactions with consuls and with foreigners, so as to avoid not only just cause of complaint, but groundless irritation in a critical conjuncture." [19]

Reverdy Johnson had been one of the Maryland legislators whom Butler had brushed aside when he arrested the millionaire Ross Winans and was one of those hostile persons who had spread the canard that Butler had been drunk in Baltimore in the spring of 1861. George C.

Strong, Butler's aide in Washington, when he heard of the appointment, foresaw a fight. "Who was it," he exclaimed, "that named that damned . . . Reverdy Johnson as Vice-regent of the Offended Majesty of the Netherlands?"[20] Stanton wrote Butler that "Mr. Seward desires me to say to you that he has been informed, since sending Mr. Johnson as Agent to visit New Orleans, that he might not be acceptable to you on account of something that occurred at Baltimore during your command there. That he (Mr. S.) was altogether unconscious of your having any reason of complaint against Mr. Johnson, who was appointed because he was well known abroad, familiarly acquainted with the diplomatic representatives at Washington and therefore supposed to be more acceptable to them than would be any other person. Mr. Seward is also quite sure that Mr. Johnson has the kindest feelings toward yourself, and will perform his duties in a manner entirely satisfactory to you. In this belief I entirely concur, and hope that your relations with Mr. Johnson will be cordial, and that you will be well pleased with the result of his mission."[21]

Commissioner Johnson presented his credentials to General Butler on July 10. Secessionists who had surmised that Johnson's business was to arrest the General were disappointed to find him welcomed with every courtesy. Johnson was given a pleasant office in the Custom House, and one of the General's "most competent and showy" orderlies to guard his door and act as messenger. Mr. Johnson at once got in touch with the consuls, inquiring as to their grievances. The rumor circulating that Reverdy Johnson owned slaves in Maryland, New Orleanians flocked to him as to "one of us." Soon his office became a "bureau of complaints and grievances" where anyone who found fault with General Butler might receive a hearing.

Commissioner Johnson, correctly interpreting Secretary Seward's desire that he pour oil on the waters of consular discontent, looked into the Couturié case and others that General Butler presented to him from the narrowest legal point of view. Instead of investigating, as Butler had hoped, and uncovering the facts and motives behind the "paper" case, Johnson accepted in almost every instance the consular view or that of the financially interested foreign merchants whose unneutral conduct had drawn from the General a fine or a threat of imprisonment. Johnson restored the 160 kegs of silver to the Netherlands Consul, together with the municipal bonds of New Orleans and Mobile, — everything except the dies and plates of the Citizens Bank which obviously had not belonged to him. To the French Consul Comte Méjan, Johnson returned the $405,000 of specie belonging to the Bank of New Orleans which Butler had impounded. The 3205 hogsheads of sugar, probably owned by Secessionists but lodged in the warehouse of Covas and Negroponte under the protection of the Greek consul, were released to the foreign firm.

The fine Butler had exacted from the British firm S. H. Kennedy & Co. for having run the blockade and supplied the Confederates with arms and munitions was remitted by Johnson. Butler contended that the foreign merchant who aided the Confederates was personally responsible to the commanding general, ruling by martial law in a conquered city. Johnson held that the person of the merchant was immune, that only his goods and the ship were to be forfeited when captured. It had been illegal, Johnson claimed, for Butler to force S. H. Kennedy & Co. to pay for the bill of exchange itself.

In his single show of temper during Johnson's three weeks in New Orleans Butler dissented from the rose-water decision in the Kennedy case. "It says, in substance: 'Violate the laws of the United States as well as you can; send abroad all the produce of the Confederate States you can, to be converted into arms for the rebellion; you only take the risk of losing *in transitu,* and as the profits are fourfold, you can afford to do so.' " [22] To this, Johnson, "as one lawyer to another," replied by denouncing the "fitful, unregulated unrestrained promptings of military power" that had entered into General Butler's decisions. Of the thirteen cases submitted to him, Johnson reversed Butler's action in eleven. [23]

To Butler's exasperation the $405,000 which Johnson had released to the French consul later found its way into the pockets of a French concern in Havana as payment for supplying clothing to the Confederate army. To Stanton Butler reported on October 21 that Commissioner Johnson's actions had done more "to strengthen the hand of secession" than any other occurrence since Butler had come to New Orleans. "This Commission, I say, emboldened these new complaints of my action by mercantile pirates and marauders, who supplied arms to traitors . . . They should have been *hanged,* they were only fined." [24]

That many foreign nationals in Louisiana were actively pro-Secessionist was evident from the large number who had entered the Confederate army. Before Butler's time, the Prussian consul Reichard, head of Reichard & Company, had recruited a body of Germans in New Orleans and led them to Richmond to fight for the Confederacy. He left behind him as acting consul for Prussia one Kruttschmidt, who was a brother-in-law of Judah P. Benjamin in Jefferson Davis' cabinet. A son of the French consul in Baton Rouge was taken prisoner by Butler's forces in the battle of August 5. The Spanish warship *Blasco de Garay,* lying in the river at New Orleans, constituted itself a haven for criminals as well as political refugees. "The decks of the *Blasco de Garay,*" Butler reported on October 13, "were literally covered with passengers selected with so little discrimination that my detective officers found on board, as a passenger, an escaped convict of the Penitentiary, who was in full flight from a most brutal murder, with his booty robbed from his victim with him." [25] The British warship *Rinaldo* was particularly offensive to Federal police. "When the evening comes, and the levee is crowded with our citizens," reported the New York *Times,* "the officers of this piratical craft amuse themselves and insult our ships and the people ashore by playing the 'Bonnie Blue Flag,' the supposed national air of the rebel states. There is also occasionally flying somewhere in the rigging a bit of bunting, made as nearly like the Confederate rag as possible. It is also understood, that when ladies visit this vessel, they are generally selected for their sesesh proclivities, and that President Lincoln and General Butler come in for all sorts of vulgar abuse." [26]

Every move Butler made was objected to and made the subject of tedious and sometimes heated correspondence. The oath to separate the loyal Unionists from the Secessionists was opposed as tending to force neutral foreigners, if they wished to retain their property, "to descend to the level of spies and denunciators for the benefit of the United States." [27]

The Spanish consul Callejon was angered by Butler's handling of a quarantine case. The *Cardenas,* with a cargo of fruit and passengers from Havana, when that port was infected with yellow fever, had brushed past the Quarantine Station below New Orleans to elude the customs officer. Butler, enraged at this open violation of his precautions to keep yellow fever out of the city, ordered the vessel with her perishable cargo back down to Quarantine to remain until the Medical Officer gave her a clean bill of health. Meanwhile the American steamer *Roanoke* from New York, which had touched at Havana the day after the *Cardenas* sailed, was allowed to come on to New Orleans. The Spanish consul, crying discrimination, refused to give a clean bill of health to the *Roanoke* on her return trip via Havana unless Butler would release the *Cardenas* from Quarantine. Butler threatened to banish Consul Callejon to Cuba if he did not give precisely the same bill of health to the *Roanoke* as he would have done had the *Cardenas* case not arisen.

As a whimsical witness of the New Orleans comedy observed, "if General Butler rides up the streets, the consuls are sure to come in a body, and protest that he did not ride down. If he smokes a pipe in the morning a deputation calls on him in the evening to know why he did not smoke a cigar. If he drinks coffee, they will send some rude messenger with a note asking in the name of some tottering dynasty why he did not drink tea." [28]

A curious sidelight on the situation in New Orleans was the abuse heaped upon Butler abroad. Butler's Woman Order, "a capital tub to catch such a whale as John Bull," created a sensation in Parliament. "Infamous!" cried Palmerston. "Repugnant to decency, civilization and humanity!" shouted Gregory. Pro-Southern Englishmen agreed that here was "an outrage, so wicked, so inexcusable, and so useless" that all should protest.[29] The New York *Times,* itself critical of the Woman Order before its effects had become apparent, rushed to Butler's defense: "Now this is really too good. These amiable British Bunsbys seem to forget that New Orleans is not a part of the mighty demesne of Her British Majesty, and that to be poking their noses into our affairs is an intolerable nuisance . . . Since that order, no man or woman has insulted a soldier or officer of the Union forces in New Orleans. But even if it had been otherwise, are we to brook this intermeddling in matters which are merely questions of municipal police? . . . Let them free their minds of cant, and remember with Hudibras, that —

> *Those who in quarrels interpose,*
> *Will often wipe a bloody nose."* [30]

In Paris the New York *Times* correspondent who signed himself "Malakoff" noted early in June that General Butler was gaining a worldwide reputation, "not exactly the kind to be desired." [31]

Long after it had become certain that Butler's soldiery were not going to turn New Orleans into a shambles of sex crimes the European press continued to denounce the Woman Order as "odious," and its author as "a brute." The Paris correspondent of the New York *Times* had never seen in one year's time as many columns of abuse published against one man. "Nineteen-twentieths of this is coined in London and Liverpool, and it is to be hoped that General Butler, considering the source from whence it comes, will not take it too seriously to heart." [32]

To explain the foreigners' animus one must seek some cause deeper than solicitude over outrages which did not occur. There was a pecuniary basis. Foreigners thwarted in their profitable undercover commercial ventures found it easier to vent their feelings about imaginary sex crimes than about the very real wounds to their own pocketbooks.

As for Seward's creation of the post of Military Governor for General Shepley to relieve General Butler of the responsibility of dealing with the consuls, that device never worked. Butler's first move after Shepley's new orders arrived was to send Shepley to Washington to present to the authorities there the crucial issue of the Negro question. In Washington no doubt Seward attempted to indoctrinate Shepley. But Seward, a curious, weaseling individual with a sense of the comic (he once introduced Butler's aide, Lieutenant Kinsman, to a dinner table of foreign ministers as "General Butler's agent who picked the Consul's pocket!") might conceivably have failed to make clear to Shepley what his real desires were. Certain it is that after Shepley's return to New Orleans it was Butler's firm hand and not Shepley's that continued to control all business with the foreign consuls.

Rumors that Butler would be replaced as Commander of the Army of the Gulf first came to New Orleans in September through Confederate sources and were vehemently denied in Washington. Orders for General Nathaniel P. Banks to relieve him were signed in Washington on the 9th of November. Not all the Cabinet knew this, for Chase on the 14th assured Butler that "Gen. Banks goes to New Orleans, not, as I understood, to supersede you; but to conduct an expedition to Texas while you are engaged nearer your present Headquarters." [33]

For the next month rumors of Butler's recall from New Orleans were circulated in Washington and New York. Checking reactions toward these rumors, Butler's friend and political alter ego, Paul R. George, found the response of the man-in-the-street encouraging: " 'By God, if they remove Butler I hope the country will sink.' 'They dare not do it': 'Butler is the only live General we have got.' 'Butler is the right man in the right place'; 'Butler has the ring of a good General'; 'Butler is the only Genl. that has done anything.' " Secretary Chase asked George, "Why will Genl. Butler allow his friends to be so loaded, so embarrassed with his commercial connections?" William Lloyd Garrison complained "there is hell to pay among the merchants. The talk is awful and it has had its effect." Colonel E. F. Jones of the Twenty-sixth Massachusetts suggested that Banks was intriguing in Washington to get Butler's place. Said Seward when Butler's friend confronted him, "I am afraid of the consular affairs; if Butler is changed he will have an important command." "I find no fact afloat to your prejudice," George concluded his report to Butler. "Still, my dear Genl., the atmosphere is rife with change, with intrigue, with passion, with avarice, coupled with ambition, and you are aimed at among its victims." [34]

Butler felt that only the difficult preliminary spadework had been accomplished at New Orleans, and that all was ready now, so soon as reinforcing troops arrived, to move ahead to complete the primary military task. Furthermore, he was ambitious to carry out these operations himself. On November 29, rumors persisting that General Banks was coming to New Orleans, Butler wrote directly to President Lincoln:

> My dear Sir: I take the liberty of addressing you, not as Chief Magistrate and Commander in Chief, but as a friend and a kind and just man. I think I have a right to give you the exact state of facts personally to myself. I see by the papers that General Banks is about to be sent into this Department with troops upon an independent expedition and command. This seems to imply a want of confidence in the Commander of this Department, perhaps deserved, but still painful to me . . . If it is because of my disqualification for the service, in which I have as long an experience as any General in the United States Army now in the service (being Senior in rank), I pray you say so, and so far from being even aggrieved, I will return to my home, consoled by the reflection that I have at least done my duty as far as endeavor and application [go] . . . Pray do me the favor to reflect that I am not asking for the command of any other person, but simply that, unless the Government service require it, my own, which I have a right to say has not been the least successful of the War, shall not be taken from me in such manner as to leave me all the burden without any of the result.[35]

To insure that this important missive reach the President, Butler sent it to his friend Salmon P. Chase who handed it to Lincoln on December 14. Lincoln read Butler's letter through, "and, as he did so," reported Chase, "acknowledged fully the capacity for service you have exhibited, and the past services you have actually performed. Beyond this he said nothing, except that he had written you some days since."[36]

In New Orleans on this same Sunday morning, December 14, Butler received word that General Banks and his troops had passed Quarantine on their way up to the city. Accordingly he detailed members of his staff to arrange for carriages, escort, saluting battery, and quarters in the St. Charles Hotel for General Banks and his staff. In the evening General Banks drove to General Butler's residence and informally presented his orders.

The astonished Butler now learned for the first time that he was being recalled. Banks's orders read:

> By direction of the President of the United States, Major-General N. P. Banks is assigned to the command of the Department of the Gulf, including the state of Texas.[37]

The command of the Department of the Gulf was formally shifted, and Butler remained a week to indoctrinate his successor.

In answer to an anonymous letter threatening assassination if he should appear in public, Butler on the eve of his departure made his only appearance in a New Orleans theater. The comedy *Honeymoon* was being played at the Varieties Theater. The moment that General and Mrs. Butler appeared in their box, the actors stopped the play and the whole house burst into applause. "It was impossible," wrote the New York *Times* correspondent, "to attribute such a vehement reception to any 'dead-head' arrangement, and I give the fact for what it is worth." [38]

A farewell address to "Citizens of New Orleans" was published as the General took leave of the city. "I shall speak with no bitterness, because I am not conscious of a single personal animosity. Commanding the Army of the Gulf, I found you captured, but not surrendered; conquered, but not orderly; relieved from the presence of an army [General Lovell's], but incapable of taking care of yourselves. I restored order, punished crime, opened commerce, brought provisions to your starving people, reformed your currency, and gave you quiet protection, such as you have not enjoyed for many years." As it progresses the speech is slanted more toward a Northern audience. "The enemies of my country, unrepentant and implacable, I have treated with merited severity. I hold that rebellion is treason, and that treason, persisted in, is death, and any punishment short of that due a traitor gives so much clear gain to him from the clemency of the government." If the punishments he had inflicted seemed harsh, they had not been so severe as the actions of the French in Algiers or the British in India:

"Your sons might have been blown from the mouths of cannon, like the Sepoys of Delhi . . . But I have not so conducted. On the contrary, the worst punishment inflicted except for criminal acts punishable by every law, has been banishment with labor to a barren island, where I encamped my own soldiers before marching here. It is true, I have levied upon the wealthy rebels and paid out nearly half a million of dollars to feed forty thousand of the starving poor of all nations assembled here, made so by this war. I saw that this Rebellion was a war of the aristocrats against the middling men, of the rich against the poor; a war of the land-owner against the laborer; that it was a struggle for the retention of power in the hands of the few against the many; and I found no conclusion to it, save in the subjugation of the few and the disenthrallment of the many. I therefore felt no hesitation in taking the substance of the wealthy, who had caused the war, to feed the innocent poor, who had suffered by the war. And I shall now leave you with the proud consciousness that I carry with me the blessings of the humble and loyal, under the roof of the cottage and in the cabin of the slave, and so am quite content to incur the sneers of the salon, or the curses of the rich." [39]

Toward the close of his address Butler as a politician publicly bolted from his old political group the Hunker, or pro-slavery, Democrats, and assumed a role in the forefront of the abolitionists themselves. "I have found you trembling at the terrors of servile insurrection. All danger of this I have prevented by so treating the slave that he had no cause to rebel. I found the dungeon, the chain, and the lash your only means of enforcing obedience in your servants. I leave them peaceful, laborious, controlled by the laws of kindness and justice . . . There is but one thing that at this hour stands between you and your government — and that is slavery. The institution, cursed by God, which has taken its last refuge here, in His providence will be rooted out as the tares from the wheat, although the wheat be torn up with it. I have given much thought to this subject. I came among you, by teachings, by habit of mind, by political position, by social affinity, inclined to sustain your domestic laws, if by possibility they might be with safety to the Union. Months of experience and of observation have forced the conviction that the existence of slavery is incompatible with the safety either of yourselves or of the union. As the system has gradually grown to its present huge dimensions, it were best if it could be gradually removed; but it is better, far better, that it should be taken out at once, than that it should longer vitiate the social, political, and family relations of your country . . . Such are the views forced upon me by experience." [40]

General and Mrs. Butler left their residence at the corner of St. Charles and Julia Streets and proceeded to the wharf to board the transport *Spaulding*. "An immense throng of people, principally from the poorer and laboring class of the community, crowded the levee to witness the departure," wrote the Boston *Journal's* correspondent; "I could not repress the conviction that General Butler, with all his harshness and severity toward the rich and rebellious, had won the love and esteem of the downtrodden and suffering masses in this city." [41]

19

POLITICS BEHIND THE LINES

DURING his voyage north, while Butler in anger and bitterness puzzled over the pros and cons of his recall, both Lincoln and Davis issued proclamations in which Butler's fortunes were involved.

At long last Lincoln dropped his earlier policy of concession to the border states and proclaimed the Federal policy to emancipate the Negro. The decision was clear-cut. If Butler had been recalled because of his expressions on the subject of slavery, that objection no longer held and, as Butler saw it, he should be at once returned to his old post in New Orleans to wipe out any implication that his services there had been disapproved.

In retaliation against the Federals for freeing the slaves, Jefferson Davis announced to the world his intention to treat all white officers of Negro troops not as soldiers engaged in honorable warfare but as criminals guilty of inciting the blacks to insurrection. Such officers when captured were to be reserved for execution. This drastic new Confederate policy relative to prisoners of war was announced, in effect, in the fine print of a propaganda blast of which General Butler was the chief subject. The Confederate President, having elicited from Washington no satisfactory explanation of the execution of William B. Mumford, assumed that the Federal Government had sanctioned the conduct of Butler.

Now, therefore, I, Jefferson Davis, President of the Confederate States of America, and in their name, do pronounce and declare the said Benjamin F. Butler to be a felon, deserving of capital punishment. I do order that he shall no longer be considered or treated simply as a public enemy of the Confederate States of America, but as an outlaw and common enemy of mankind, and that, in the event of his capture, the officer in command of the capturing force do cause him to be immediately executed by hanging.[1]

To justify his drastic policy on prisoners of war Davis had seized upon Butler as a scapegoat. For the moment at least this most unoriginal of Davis' moves added to Butler's prestige as the only Union officer to receive such distinction. New York hailed him as a "rebel tamer."

A telegram informing him that he was being considered for "a peculiar and important service" urged him to come to the White House immediately upon debarking in New York.[2] In Washington after Lincoln had greeted him, Butler asked why he had been recalled from New Orleans. Lincoln replied that he was not at liberty to tell him, but that he might ask Stanton.[3]

Said Stanton: "The reason was one which does not imply, on the part of the Government, any want of confidence in your honor as a man or in your ability as a commander."

"Well," said Butler, "you have told me what I was *not* recalled for. I now ask you to tell me what I *was* recalled for."

"You and I," laughed Stanton, "are both lawyers, and it is of no use your filing a bill of discovery upon *me,* for I shan't tell you." [4]

The New York *Times* surmised that he had been recalled "through foreign influence, backed up by semi-Secessionists of the Reverdy Johnson school," but that possibility Butler was unable to track down.[5] Seward gave Butler a hearty dinner but no answer to his question.

Chagrined, Butler decided not to accept any other assignment than a return to New Orleans. He turned down Lincoln's offer of a command in the Mississippi above Vicksburg, with power to enlist Negro troops. Hearing Butler's counterproposal that he be returned to New Orleans, Lincoln paced back and forth the length of his study, then turned toward his visitor with an appeal, "But I cannot recall Banks." [6]

Lincoln persuaded Butler to keep his commission, and sent him home to Lowell for a vacation.

Northern newspapers speculated about where he would be sent

next. Their guesses ranged from Secretary of War to disciplining Charleston. Said the New York *Times* concerning this last conjecture, "Gen. Butler, of all men in the nation, seems best calculated to administer the needed discipline . . . He appreciates . . . the exact frame of mind of a captured rebel city, and the various ingenious modes of escaping the just inflictions of penalty for treason. No veteran pedagogue ever understood the tricks of truant schoolboys better." [7]

In Philadelphia, where a crowd gathered outside his hotel, Butler replied to Davis' proscription of himself as an outlaw. The execution of William B. Mumford, he said, still commended itself to his judgment. "Feeling the utter unworthiness of the man that treason had attempted to exalt into a patriot, I was inclined to spare him. But that was not permitted. The thugs, rowdies and gamblers assembled before the execution, and resolved that he should not be hung. It became a question whether they ruled New Orleans or the Commanding General of the United States . . . Owing to the uncourteous terms in which the so-called Confederate Government demanded an explanation, no report could be made. By offensive language that Government shut up all possible communication on our part. Then it was assumed that some wrong was done, and the Proclamation, which you have all doubtless seen, was issued in consequence." [8]

In New York's Fifth Avenue Hotel a stream of callers, headed by General Scott, greeted "the hero of New Orleans." Ladies especially were curious to see the author of the Woman Order.

To a New York audience Butler explained his switchover in politics from Hunker Democrat to Republican-Abolitionist. He had gone out to New Orleans as a Democrat "of the hunkerest sort," and had changed his views on slavery as a result of sights he had seen every day in New Orleans.

In this war the entire property of the South was against us, because almost the entire property of the South was bound up in that institution . . . The South had $163,000,000 in all other kinds of property. And this was the cause why the merchants of New Orleans had not remained loyal. They found themselves ruined — all their property being loaned upon planters' notes and mortgages upon plantations and slaves, all of which property is now reasonably worthless.[9]

At first he had not believed that slavery was the cause of the rebellion, but attributed it to Davis, Slidell and others . . . When Butler saw the utter demoralization of the people, resulting from slavery, it struck him that it was an institution which should be thrust out of the Union. He had on reading Mrs. Stowe's book — *Uncle Tom's Cabin* — believed it to be an overdrawn, highly wrought picture of Southern life, but he had seen with his own eyes, and heard with his own ears, many things which went beyond her book as much as her book went beyond an ordinary school girl's novel.

In Lowell's Huntington Hall among other topics Butler took up the issue of civil rights for Negroes. His former opinions, he explained, had changed. He now wanted the Negro free, and with as little political dislocation as possible.

Boston on Tuesday, January 13, gave him a parade, with brass bands, National Guards, and both houses of the Legislature — Governor Andrew alone absenting himself. Butler arrived at noon on a special train and was drawn in a barouche by four white horses, escorted by generals and by the mayors of Lowell and Boston. En route to Faneuil Hall, the politician-general heard salute guns on the Common and shouts of crowds. In the hall flag-draped panels proclaimed Butler's victories: "Annapolis," "Baltimore" and "New Orleans." When the General entered, two thousand ladies in the galleries waved their handkerchiefs.[10]

In the enthusiasm of the moment, Mayor Lincoln, erring in mathematics by $40,000, introduced the speaker as a man for whose head the Rebels had offered $50,000. Butler presented to the Mayor the Confederate flag once flown over the City Hall at New Orleans.

To his Boston audience — many of whom were merchants — Butler proposed "the introduction of free labor at the South, whereby labor would become honorable, and by which more abundant crops of cotton could be raised with profit at less cost than by slave labor." To the value of all cotton exported to Europe the Government might add a tax of 100 per cent to amortize the war debt. In this way those nations which had prolonged the war by aiding the Confederate States would "be obliged to pay a proportion of the debt." [11]

In mid-February, following a second summons to Washington which failed to land him a suitable job, General Butler was given a reception in the now loyal city of Baltimore. The hall of the Maryland Institute was jam-packed. Thirty-four ladies in white and carrying flags sat on the platform and sang patriotic songs. Butler voiced his determination to stand by the Government. Another year, he believed, would see the Confederacy annihilated. Should foreign nations intervene, "We'll put down treason at home and foreigners, too . . . The Giant of the Western World has scarcely begun to put forth his strength." [12]

In Washington the House of Representatives adopted a resolution praising Butler's "able, energetic, and humane administration of the Department of the Gulf." [13] The Legislature of Massachusetts followed suit, and Governor John A. Andrew affixed his signature to a document officially lauding his quondam enemy. An infant born in Boston to a soldier who had served under Butler was christened "Benjamin Butler Loring."

At Cooper Institute in New York City, abolitionist orator Wendell Phillips hailed Butler as "almost the only General in our service who acts upon the principle that we are right and the traitors are all wrong." "Why is General Butler here? Who can tell? Abraham Lincoln cannot . . . The best General in the service, the man that held the third city of the empire in his right hand like a lamb, that man goes home to the Capitol, saying that he cannot find a man in the Cabinet who will take the responsibility of saying that he advised his recall, or tell him the reason why he was recalled." [14] There were loud cries of "Shame," and renewed cheering for Butler.

J. W. Shafer, one of Butler's aides who was now in Washington taking soundings for his chief, reported: "The present plan no doubt is to send you back to New Orleans, but there is a strong party desirous of putting you in the War Department. I prevailed on the Republican members from Illinois to call in a body on Mr. Lincoln and warn him of the dangers of continuing Stanton and Halleck in their present positions . . . Cameron says that you must be put where you can make yourself strong with the people, that you are the only man for next President." [15]

James Parton, a popular biographer who regarded Butler as in line for the White House, interrupted his work on a life of Franklin in order to write a history of General Butler's administration in New Orleans. "This I would do," he wrote in broaching the subject to Butler, "for the vindication of the country as well as to do honor to one who, in this most difficult of all wars, has shown a capacity equal to the occasion. The work which I propose ought not to be done without your sanction, and cannot be well done without your cooperation . . . I shall require of you: *1st,* one or two long conversations; *2nd,* occasional short interviews or notes; *3rd,* some introductions to your friends, here and in New Orleans; *4th,* perhaps, copies of a few unpublished papers . . . Perhaps I should inform you in addition that I am a slavery loathing democrat, and that you are *my* candidate for President." [16]

Butler, pleased with the chance to place his controversial administration of the chief Southern City before the public, made available to Parton his letter and order books and all other correspondence. "One thing I beg shall be understood between us," wrote Butler, ". . . that you shall report it in precisely the manner you may choose — without the slightest sense of obligation 'aught to extenuate' because of the source from which you derive the materials of your work, and farther, that no sense of delicacy of position in relation to myself shall interfere with the closest investigation of every act alleged to have been done or permitted by me. I will only ask that upon all matters I may have the privilege of presenting to your mind the documentary and other evidence of the fact." [17]

Parton made several trips to Lowell to interview the General in his Belvidere home. He was charmed by the General's versatility and his desire to conceal nothing. During the seven-month-period of intensive writing the biographer had only once to remind Butler of his promise not to interfere with the production of the book. When the last chapters of *General Butler in New Orleans* went to the printers, the impatient subject of the book asked to see the "first form proofs," and Parton tactfully reminded him of their agreement.[18]

One suggestion the General could not resist making. Parton had engaged Thomas Nast to do an engraving for use as a frontispiece. The result was a rather stiff and forbidding full-face pose of General Butler in dress uniform with sword, seated and leaning awkwardly against a table on the veranda of the St. Charles Hotel, with a sprinkling of furtive-looking aides and orderlies in the background. Butler protested that he "never took much pride in public appearance, but such a cut-throat as that will keep people from buying the book." [19] Self-conscious as ever about his crossed eye, Butler suggested in place of the Nast effort an engraving of a profile view of a plaster bust recently executed by E. A. Brackett. Parton compromised by including both pictures in the book.

On January 23, 1863, Lincoln wrote Stanton that he thought General Butler should go to New Orleans again. "He is unwilling to go unless he is restored to the command of the department. He should start by the 1st of February, and should take some force with him. The whole must be so managed as to not wrong or wound the feelings of General Banks. His [Banks's] original wish was to go to Texas; and it must be arranged for him to do this now with a substantial force; and yet he must not go to the endangering the opening of the Mississippi. I hope this may be done by the time General Butler shall arrive there; but whether or not, I think we cannot longer dispense with General Butler's service." [20]

Lincoln now telegraphed for Butler, had him to dinner at the White House, and tried once again, though without success, to persuade him to undertake a mission to the Mississippi River country as the President's agent. Finally on February 24 Stanton drafted an order placing Butler in command at New Orleans and Banks at Port Hudson with the curious stipulation that Butler should proceed to New Orleans *via the upper river*. In other words, he was not to arrive in New Orleans until after Grant and Banks had taken Vicksburg and Port Hudson. Stanton authorized Chase to tell Butler these special provisions might possibly be stricken out. "It does seem to me," urged Chase, "that *without* the first of the modifications you ought to resume your post at once." [21]

Butler replied that he regarded the President's offer to return him to New Orleans as "a most complete personal vindication," that he would go there if ordered, but that he did not now want that command. The enlistments of Banks's 90-day troops would soon expire and inevitably the Commanding General of the Department must become "a magnified transportation agent."

> Let something be done or let me see that something can be done except pitiful intrigues by which I am removed from command, and the arrow shall not leave the bow with a swifter flight than I into the service . . . The whole matter may be summed up in a word, — *I see no service to the country to come out of the proposed command* unless troops can be given to finish the work on the Mississippi and in the Gulf.[22]

"The only general yet who has dared hang a traitor," he symbolized for many people a forthrightness in carrying on the war which Lincoln's Administration lacked, yet Butler was careful never to place himself in opposition to the President.[23] The Springfield *Republican,* a critic of Butler from the early dogfights of Massachusetts politics, discovered a new dignity in Butler's manner on the platform. "We have had no such demonstration in honor of one man since the war broke out," observed the *Republican.* "There is a fine presence about General Butler for which many were unprepared. We looked for stiff vertebrae and strong disquisition, but a repressed power and gentlemanliness of treatment came somewhat unawares. Up and down the platform he strode; upright and downright as his logic, but touched with *dignity* and thrilled with conviction." [24]

In his most ambitious address, in the hall of the Academy of Music in New York City on April 2, 1863, Butler plunged headlong into the touchy problem of reconstruction, and the ideas he presented at this time were to become the basis of the Radical Republican program after the war. The auditorium of the Academy of Music was crowded. "The boxes, dress circle and balcony fairly blazed with the beauty and fashion of the City, while the deep aisles of the parquet and the more remote recesses of the amphitheatre were relieved from the sombre colors of male attire by the waving of plumes, the ruddy ribbons, and the glittering jewels of New York's fairest ladies." [25] Mrs. Butler, Mrs. General Banks, and Mrs. General Frémont were in boxes, and upon the stage were General Wool, General C. M. Clay and other notables.

At seven-thirty when General Butler was conducted upon the stage, the whole interior of the Academy was alive with waving hats, bouquets and handkerchiefs.

Butler, in black broadcloth, stepped forward to discuss the constitutional results of the rebellion.

"I am not for the Union as it was. [Great cheering, "Good! Good!"] I have the honor to say as a Democrat, and an Andrew Jackson Democrat, I am not for the Union to be again as it was. Understand me, I was for the Union as it was, because I saw, or thought I saw, the troubles in the future which have burst upon us; but having undergone those troubles, having spent all this blood and this treasure, I do not mean to go back again and be cheek by jowl, as I was before, with South Carolina, if I can help it. [Cheers, "You're right!"] I will take care that when she comes in again she come in better behaved; that she shall no longer be the firebrand of the Union . . . The old house was good enough for me, but the South pulled the 'L' down, and I propose, when we build it up, to build it up with all the modern improvements. [Prolonged laughter and applause.] Another one of the logical sequences, it seems to me, that follow inexorably, and [are] not to be shunned, from the proposition that we are dealing with alien enemies, is What is our duty with regard to the confiscation of their property? I would take it and give it to the loyal man, who was loyal from the heart, at the South, enough to make him as well [off] as he was before, and I would take the balance of it and distribute it among the volunteer soldiers who have gone forth in the service of their country; and so far as I know them, if we should settle South Carolina with them, in the course of a few years I should be quite willing to receive her back into the Union. [Renewed applause.]" [26]

Butler's "Music Hall" speech evoked abuse from both the Confederate and the Northern Copperhead press. The Richmond *Examiner* turned a vituperative phrase: "After outraging the sensibilities of civilized humanity . . . he returns, reeking with crime, to his own people, and they receive him with acclamations of joy . . . the beastliest, bloodiest poltroon and pickpocket the world ever saw." [27]

Representative S. S. ("Sunset") Cox of Ohio, a leading Copperhead, scolded Butler for hauling himself on board the abolition band wagon, and the anti-administration New York *World,* possibly aiming at Lincoln, smote Butler as "a man whom all the waters of Massachusetts Bay cannot wash back into decency." [28]

During the interval when Butler was without assignment, Simon Cameron counseled him to remain in uniform. "Remember, the next President will be a military chieftain." [29] Other friends actively pulled wires to further Butler's political fortunes. Paul R. George sent a New York City delegation to Washington to press Butler for Secretary of War. Hildreth suggested that Butler run for Governor if the Cabinet post failed to materialize. In Washington Henry Wilson and other Senators began remarking over their cups that "if nothing happened" Ben Butler would be "a formidable candidate for the next Presidency." [30] Frantic calls came for Butler to speak in Ohio to counteract the mounting influence of Vallandigham's Copperheads. Colonel T. B. Thorpe, Butler's sanitary chief in New Orleans, wrote, "Your friends are moving in New York and elsewhere quietly but effectually to bring your name out for President." James Parton arranged for Butler a meeting with Horace Greeley: "I told him nothing of the object in view," wrote Butler's biographer coyly, "and how *you* will manage to do it I cannot conceive. The chastest virgin may have desires — may be tormented with desires, but she will not confess them even to herself. However, you know mankind, and will know how to shape your course." [31] A committee with a member from each of Missouri's nine Congressional districts called on Lincoln to ask him to remove General Scofield and send General Butler to St. Louis.

Butler was flattered but considered these political rumblings in his favor as premature. On March 4, 1863, he wrote a feminine well-wisher: "Whenever the subject of the Presidency has been mentioned to me I have invariably treated it as a joke or an exaggerated compliment from an over-enthusiastic admirer, and have generally replied to it that 'I thought I had never done anything bad enough to deserve to suffer such punishment as that.' But in all seriousness, — in the strain you are good enough to write — what should I want of the Presidency were it within my reach? I am not without ambition, and I trust a laudable one, but I am forty-four years old — have a constitution that with fair play should last till seventy. To my taste and judgment it has always seemed that after filling the highest office there was nothing left for a man but the graceful retirement of quiet old age. My wife would hardly agree to that proposition for me six years hence as "an old man." Fifteen or twenty years hence were I worthy it might form the crown of a life well spent in the service of the country, if so the life should be, and eminence attainable, but not now, not now! You will see that I have written in simple frankness — and discussed the subject with gravity as one might do were one in danger; but I assure you that I have been through with the croop, whooping cough, and measles, and all other dangers incident to children." He enclosed a "valentine" received in the same mail with his correspondent's letter to convince her that "there are differences of opinion upon the demerits of Yours most truly." [32]

In his numerous trips to Washington the unemployed general made political contacts with the henchmen of both Seward and Chase. The latter sent him — through an intermediary named B. F. Camp — a bid to join forces with the Secretary of the Treasury in the next election. The overture was put in writing by J. D. Sanborn, a Treasury agent, in a letter dated from Baltimore on October 5, 1863:

My dear Gen. At the urgent request of B.F.C[amp], I am induced again [to] state that he very much wishes to meet you about the matter in my postscript from N.Y. some 8 or 10 days since. He retd from Washington yesterday after having a long Confab & leaving with the promise, (so he states) that he would see you, relative to the Combination of the Secty. & yourself. I infer from what he avers, that the Secty. is very anxious to get your assistance in the Coming political Contest & if that he cannot Convince you that he can win, he is perfectly willing to go in for you, in preferance [sic] to any other person, & will throw the influence of the Dept. in your favor. Now this is a very important question & I am not prepared to say what I might think. — Even if asked. B.F.C. is fearful that you will get into wrong hands, as he has already heard of your Dinner at Delmonico's in Company with Mr. Weed, & probably that is troubling Mr. C[hase]. If you are disposed to see C[am]p he is now stopping at Barnum's but will Jump at the chance to meet you at any point . . . I expect to be in every Tuesday & hope to hear from you at the Astor Ho[use]. Yrs. Ever, J.D.S. [anborn].[33]

Butler did not rise to this bait and on November 3, the resignation of General Burnside causing a shift of commanders, Butler was ordered to replace General Foster as commander of the Eighteenth Army Corps with headquarters in his old billet at Fortress Monroe. After ten months of "eating unearned bread," he accepted the appointment with enthusiasm and zest. It presented, to all appearances, a magnificent chance to win that military distinction which his canny friend Cameron foresaw as prerequisite for political success in the postwar years.

PART FOUR

The Richmond Campaign

20

THE VIRGINIA FRONT

THE Department of Virginia and North Carolina, of which Butler took command on November 11, 1863, comprised a few score square miles of tidewater shoreline and several thousand square miles of water. It included the Peninsula from Fortress Monroe up through Yorktown and Williamsburg, the city of Norfolk with the damaged Navy yard, Cape Hatteras islands, and a number of marsh-flanked hamlets on the mainland around Pamlico and Albemarle sounds. Butler, taking with him his wife and daughter on a tour of his aqueous command, visited Beaufort, New Bern, Little Washington, Plymouth, and the unique Negro settlement project at Roanoke Island. The encampment for Negro families was marked for expansion as political and military necessities pressed upon Butler the recruitment of Negro troops.

Such recruitment, owing in part to anti-Butler influences in the Capital, soon proved absolutely essential, since in number of troops Butler was but little better off than he had been in New Orleans. With an "on paper" aggregate of 40,873 officers and men, he was able to count only 23,054 actually physically present, and these were widely scattered: 836 at Fortress Monroe; 8494 at Portsmouth under Brigadier General George W. Getty; 3921 at Yorktown under Brigadier General Charles A. Heckman; and in North Carolina under Brigadier General John J. Peck were 7079 men distributed in garrisons at New Bern, Beaufort, and smaller villages on Pamlico and Albemarle sounds.

What was he to do for troops? Butler's request for permission to draw in the garrisons of strategically valueless outposts on the sounds to strengthen his attack force at Yorktown was ignored by the War

Department. Instead of troops Washington sent him four additional brigadier generals, and might have sent more had not Butler protested that he had not troops enough for the generals he already had. Of necessity he was driven into the forefront as a recruiter of Negro troops, and this at the same time that his political friends were backing him as a future candidate for the presidency.

To enlarge the area for Negro recruitment, Butler obtained the addition to his department of Accomac and Northampton counties on the Eastern Shore of Virginia; and the War Department at the same time tossed in St. Mary's County, Maryland, between the Potomac and Patuxent rivers. St. Mary's County, with only a slight potential as a source of black warriors, contained the Confederate prisoner-of-war camp at Point Lookout. It would almost appear that in involving Butler in the immensely complex business of prisoner exchange, the War Department was willing to hobble him with administrative detail in order to curtail his military ventures. General H. W. ("Old Brains") Halleck, as Chief of Staff in the War Department, had inherited General Scott's prejudices against Butler as a politician-general. "It seems but little better than murder," wrote Halleck to General W. T. Sherman, "to give important commands to such men as Banks, Butler, McClernand, Sigel, and Lew. Wallace, and yet it seems impossible to prevent it." [1]

Butler's new staff organization was quickly assembled. Six of its original members — Lieutenant George A. Kensel, Major Robert S. Davis, Lieutenant Colonel J. Burnham Kinsman, Major Joseph M. Bell, Major Peter Haggerty, Captain Haswell C. Clarke — had served with him at New Orleans. Captain Alfred F. Puffer had been a correspondent at New Orleans for the New York *Herald* and was the anonymous author of the Butler-praising article "Our General," which had appeared in the July 1863 issue of the *Atlantic*. Colonel J. Wilson Shaffer, a Western newspaperman and politician, who had adopted Butler as his favorite candidate for the Presidency and had devoted most of the past year to pushing that project, was rewarded with the post of Chief of Staff. Shaffer became a sort of roving liaison officer to present to officials in New York, Baltimore and Washington the military problems of Butler's command — a post in which he continued his political machinations.

To navigate over his tidewater department Butler refused to rely on chartered boats or naval craft obtained by negotiation as during his first duty at Fortress Monroe. This time he organized his own Marine Brigade of lightly armed steamers which could transport troops, Negro families, prisoners, dispatches and commissary stores. Brigadier General Charles K. Graham, a volunteer soldier who had had experience in the Navy, was appointed commander of the Marine Brigade.

Graham was sent with two steamers of the Marine Brigade to destroy Confederate shipping at Wilmington, North Carolina. Butler's plan, as he detailed it for Admiral S. P. Lee, in charge of the naval blockade off Wilmington, was for the army steamer *Brewster* in the guise of a blockade-runner to sail past the Confederate forts into the river below Wilmington, thence to ascend the river and destroy Confederate blockade-runners at the docks of Wilmington.

Off Wilmington, Graham learned that the Confederates had a chain across the river and that blockade-runners were not allowed to pass it until permission had been received from Wilmington. Graham returned to Norfolk.

During the winter of 1863-64 Butler pushed the enlistment of Negro soldiers, and sent out numerous Negro-collecting raids into the no man's land beyond his fortified lines. "The recruitment of colored troops has become the settled purpose of the Government," reads his general order of December 5, 1863.[2] It was the duty of every officer and soldier to aid in this recruiting, irrespective of personal predilection. In fairness to Negro enlistees, he ordered commanding officers to bring entire families within his lines, affording them transportation, aid, protection and encouragement.

An Office of Negro Affairs was created, with Lieutenant Colonel J. Burnham Kinsman as Superintendent, to handle the problems of this wholesale influx. Lazy Negroes were not to be coerced by local officials, but were to be sent to command headquarters where they would be required to work on fortifications. Officers and soldiers were forbidden to exploit Negroes "for private use" or to employ them unnecessarily on Sunday. "And no negro shall be impressed into military service of the United States except by a draft which shall equally apply to the white and colored citizen." [3]

Butler authorized quartermasters to withhold $3 a month of the Negro soldier's pay of $10 until his uniform was paid for and he decreed that noncommissioned Negro officers, whose case was not specified in the law, should have "the same addition to their pay as other non-commissioned officers." Butler recommended that Congress pay colored private soldiers on the same scale as white. "The colored man fills an equal space in ranks while he lives, and an equal grave when he falls." [4]

From Point Lookout, Williamsburg, Norfolk and Portsmouth the raiding parties fanned out among the plantations. Confiscated teams of horses, mules and oxen hauled the Negroes to the several camps, together with their furniture and livestock. Freedmen's Village beyond the moat at Fortress Monroe doubled and trebled in size. Shriveled old crones lined the beach with pie and cake stalls. Grizzled farmhands shuffled along the wharves looking for jobs. E. A. Pollard, a Richmond newspaperman who was Butler's prisoner when the population tide at Freedmen's Village was at the full, testifies that the crowded barracoons were "reeking with squalor, and with clusters of naked bodies of little black negroes hanging in the windows." [5]

The value of Negroes as soldiers was so uncertain that Butler had difficulty procuring qualified white officers to command his colored battalions. Most officers of colored troops had had too little military experience to obtain comparable ranks among white troops. Sometimes they took to drink and had to be cashiered.

The most ambitious of Butler's raids was also an experiment to test Negro troops. It was an expedition lasting thirty days from Norfolk down the line of the Dismal Swamp Canal into North Carolina. Remote from any important Confederate military center, this swamp and farming country contained a sprinkling of guerrilla encampments, made up chiefly of soldiers who from sickness or desertion had become separated from the Confederate Army. On this raid Butler sent 1800 colored troops, backed up at a distance by two companies of white cavalry and a battery of artillery. Two steamers of Butler's Marine Brigade accompanied them down the canal while a naval gunboat showed the flag in Albemarle Sound.

As leader of the expedition Butler chose Brigadier General Edward A. Wild, an abolitionist medical doctor of Brookline, Massachusetts, who had lost an arm at Gettysburg. Wild's supply boats got lost in the Dismal Swamp and obliged him to live on the country for several days. All contrabands along the route were invited to fall in, and parties of Negro troops searched the homes of planters to release slaves who had been locked up. Teams were impressed and household furniture was taken. "In this way," wrote a New York *Times* reporter, "the train was hourly extended, until by night it was half a mile in length. The inhabitants being almost exclusively 'Secesh' the colored boys were allowed to forage at will along the road. Returning to South Mills, Gen. Wild sent his train of contrabands, numbering 75 wagons, under guard to Portsmouth." [6]

At night the Negro soldiers tore apart buildings to get planks for shelters. "All about were strewn timbers, boards, joists, shingles, and the miscellaneous debris of the buildings torn down among which, under shelter of every imaginable device, the sable soldiers were stretched upon beds of corn-stalks, while a hundred blazing fires threw their glare upon the sleeping figures, and lighted up the green cedar swamp around." [7]

General Wild found Elizabeth City deserted, its stores closed and streets grown over with grass. The doors of its bank gaped open, the town having been looted by guerrilla forces upon the approach of the Federal Negro troops.

The dwelling of a Dr. McIntosh with its farmyard and outbuildings became a temporary camp for the raiders and their booty of several hundred contrabands.

The garden fences were speedily demolished, and fires sprang up in all directions under the trees, while a large fire of fence rails was burning in the road. A hundred horses were tied to every available post and tree; a maze of carts, with their loads of contrabands, inclosed the stables and extended out into an adjoining corn field; officers were riding to and fro; squads of men were marching hither and thither, detailed on various duties; the doors of the outbuildings had been forced open and they were occupied for every imaginable purpose. In the Doctor's office a Lieutenant-Colonel and a Captain had taken up their quarters, and saddles, bridles, blankets, swords, pistols were mingled with pill boxes and bottles of physic. The neighboring kitchen was filled with women and children from our contraband train. The creaking pump-handle was unceasingly worked — horses were neighing and kicking — servants were bringing armsful of fodder from the barn. Here were soldiers plucking the feathers from poultry of which they had despoiled the secesh on the march, there a group was listening to the details of the fight with the "grillas," while near by three or four happy darkies were singing over their boiling camp kettle.[8]

To destroy the encampments of guerrillas General Wild sent working parties through the swamps. Colonel Alonzo G. Draper's Negro troops engaged some two hundred guerrillas who had been lying in wait for them and after an exchange of rifle fire charged with bayonets, driving the guerrillas into the swamp, killing and wounding 13, and themselves losing 11. Guerrilla encampments in swamps were usually accessible only by a single file over a pathway of felled tree trunks laid end to end. Before applying the torch to such camps Wild's troops salvaged new Enfield rifles, ammunition, drums, and clothing of butternut-colored homespun.

A country store in Pasquotank County, North Carolina, was the scene of the drumhead court-martial and execution of a luckless guerrilla captured in a camp near Elizabeth City. Daniel Bright, straggler from a Georgia regiment, was convicted of "carrying on robbery and pillage in the peaceable counties of Camden and Pasquotank."[9] Negro soldiers with lowered bayonets escorted him to the front of the store where a noose was swung from a projecting beam, and forced him to mount a cider barrel. The one-armed General Wild himself pulled out the wedge from under the barrel to hang the man.

In summarizing the results of his month-long campaign, Wild reported nine boatloads of Negroes and their effects sent to Roanoke Island, two to Norfolk, and four long wagon trains dispatched overland to Norfolk. About 2500 Negroes were brought in. "We burned 4 guerrilla camps — over a dozen homesteads, 2 distilleries, took a number of prisoners, including 6 Confederate soldiers, provided with furloughs." [10] Wild's losses in action had been 7 killed, 9 wounded and 2 taken prisoner.

Although Wild's expedition brought to General Butler's desk several vexing problems — Confederate retaliation for the hanging of Daniel Bright, petition-bearing delegations of Union sympathizers from the invaded area, and the military discipline case of a white officer who had sought by force to "rescue" a young white woman held as hostage by colored troops — Butler was more than pleased with the conduct of his Negro troops.

Butler's use of colored troops won the applause of abolitionist Senator Henry Wilson of Massachusetts who wrote: "God bless you for what you have done and are doing for the cause of a wronged and despised race. In this work of freeing and elevating the African race in our country, you are writing your name in letters of living light." [11] The New York *World* reporter who condemned Butler's "negro Janizaries" as "worthless to their owners, worthless to our government, and good for nothing in every aspect," [12] was ordered out of Butler's Department "under pain of being put at hard, but honest, labor." [13]

On January 1, 1864, the first anniversary of the Negro's freedom, four regiments of colored troops celebrated with a parade in Norfolk. Butler supplied a military band from Fortress Monroe and himself reviewed them in the public square. With due ceremony a flag made by the Union women of the town of Washington, North Carolina, was presented to the Second North Carolina Colored Regiment.

Negro troops, Butler found, were "from their habits of obedience and discipline . . . more apt to depend upon their officers than white soldiers." [14] Some unsatisfactory officers whom Butler dismissed appealed to Washington for reinstatement. When Lincoln revoked Butler's order dismissing Lieutenant Colonel A. D. Martin, of the First U.S. Colored, for drunkenness, Butler protested by telegraph: "Order reinstating Lt. Col. Martin dismissed for a public exhibition of drunkenness has been received. He is a drunkard and utterly unfit for an officer. I think the President must have been deceived by misrepresentation into making the order. I have had officers habitually drunk in the streets of Norfolk and to reinstate Lt. Col. Martin will be utterly subversive of discipline. May I ask suspension of the order until I can confer with the President?"[15] Lincoln honored Butler's protest, but now the discharged officer persuaded the Reverend Henry Ward Beecher and Senator Henry Wilson to bring pressure on Butler. To Beecher, Butler conceded, "If Lt. Col. Martin will enlist in the Army of the United States, and serve three months, and at the end of that time bring a certificate from his officer that he has not touched intoxicating liquors, I will commend him to be reinstated or for appointment in another regiment."[16] But to his friend Senator Wilson, Butler rasped, "Drunken officers are the curse of our colored soldiers, and I will reform it in this Dept. if I can in spite of Henry Ward Beecher or the devil."[17]

The President also intervened to save from death men sentenced for desertion or murder. To preserve discipline in his ranks Butler court-martialed 203 deserters, chiefly substitutes and old-offender bounty-jumpers. Lincoln's blanket order suspended all executions. Even Private William Boyle, of Troop H, 1st New York Mounted Rifles, convicted of murdering a lieutenant, had his execution deferred to the detriment of Butler's projected raid on Richmond.

Butler studied maps of the area around Richmond and interviewed neutral foreigners and Northerners coming through his lines. He needed a spy in Richmond.

On December 14, 1863, he questioned a German physician, Dr. G. Gavinzel, who was leaving the Confederate States to take an inheritance in France. Gavinzel volunteered his opinion that a force of 3000 men would be sufficient to wrest Richmond temporarily from the Home Guards whenever General Lee was absent upon an invasion of the North. And he gave Butler the name of a Frenchwoman, Miss Elizabeth L. Van Lieu, an established resident of Richmond, who, he thought, might be willing to serve as a spy.

Jefferson Davis' Negro gardener, who escaped through the lines, volunteered information about the daily routine in the "Confederate White House," and through agents in Philadelphia Butler made contact with a young Unionist in Richmond, Burnham Wardwell, whose job delivering ice enabled him to move unnoticed around the city. Through the iceman Butler sent a bogus message to Miss Van Lieu, which, if captured, might be read by anyone. After Miss Van Lieu had applied acid and heat according to directions relayed through Wardwell, the following real message appeared: "My dear Miss: The doctor who came through and spoke to me of the bouquet said that you will be willing to aid the Union cause by furnishing me with information if I would devise a means. You can write through Flag of Truce, directed to James Ap. Jones, Norfolk, the letter being written as this is, and with the means furnished by the messenger who brings this. I cannot refrain from saying to you, although personally unknown, how much I am rejoiced to hear of the strong feeling for the Union which exists in your own breast and among some of the ladies of Richmond. I have the honor to be, Very respectfully Your obedient servant Benjamin F. Butler." [18] Elizabeth Van Lieu became his secret agent in Richmond and Butler plied her with queries about the Federal prisoners in Libby and Belle Isle, and the Confederate forces in Richmond.

Toward the end of January Miss Van Lieu's message written in invisible ink apprized him of the Confederates' intention to remove the Federal prisoners to Georgia. To forestall this, and possibly rescue the prisoners, Butler launched a quick raid. Butler's strategy was to have General Meade draw Lee out of Richmond by an attack on the Rappahannock. Then while Lee disappeared out the front door, Butler's raiders would enter Richmond through the back door.

Halleck, at first reluctant to assist, suggested that Butler apply to Meade, then reconsidered and himself sent a directive ordering such cooperation. Meade being on leave of absence at the time, Butler applied to Meade's second in command, Major General John Sedgwick, who refused, not yet having Halleck's directive.

Butler decided to move against Richmond with or without the cooperating demonstration against Lee on the Rappahannock. On

Friday, February 5, 1864, Butler wrote to Stanton enclosing the last letter he had received from Miss Van Lieu and the minutes of his interrogation of the agent who had brought her letter. "There are now in Lee's army or about Richmond thirty thousand men. I can get no cooperation from Sedgwick . . . The roads have been good up to today. You will see that the prisoners are to be sent away to Georgia. Now is the time to strike. On Sunday I shall make a dash with six thousand men, all I have that can possibly be spared. If we win, I will pay the cost; if we fail, it will be at least an attempt to do our duty and rescue our friends." While he was writing he received a dispatch from General Sedgwick saying he would launch a demonstration on Sunday, unless the weather made it impossible. Butler wired back to Sedgwick: "Can you not make it tomorrow (Saturday) without regard to weather? I hope to strike the point Sunday morning at six (6) o'clock." [19]

On Saturday morning at ten, while General Sedgwick's guns opened up along the Rappahannock, Butler's men set out on the highway to Richmond. Brigadier General Isaac J. Wistar, their leader, had committed to memory every mudhole and stump in the road. Reports from all sources indicated that there were no Confederates along the way except a few pickets and a small guard to protect the telegraph station at Bottom's Bridge over the Chickahominy. This latter position, only ten or twelve miles from Richmond, Wistar hoped to seize before daybreak Sunday by surprise cavalry assault, and he would try to cut the wires before Richmond could be warned. Wistar's 4000 infantry, half of them colored, with six days' cooked rations marched to a lively beating of drums. If his 2200 cavalry could get past Bottom's Bridge *undetected,* he stood a chance of overpowering the Richmond Home Guards, liberating the Union prisoners, and possibly even seizing Jefferson Davis himself before Lee's army could return from its engagement on the Rappahannock.

Wistar reached Bottom's Bridge on schedule at 2:30 A.M. Sunday only to find that the Confederates had been forewarned. They had removed the planks of the bridge, set up artillery to rake the causeway leading to it, and constructed earthworks to cover all the fords above and below the bridge. From various persons in the area Wistar learned the Confederates had begun to reinforce the position just sixteen hours ahead of his arrival and that Confederate troops were still coming in over the York River Railroad. At 11 A.M. Wistar ordered his force to retire, the main object — surprise — having failed.

At his Fortress Monroe headquarters Butler received the Monday morning Richmond *Examiner* by flag of truce at about the same time the first report from Wistar came in, and was mortified to read in the Confederate newspaper the following sentence: "Some days ago a report was obtained by the authorities here from a Yankee deserter, that the enemy was contemplating a raid, in considerable force, on Richmond. The report obtained consistency from a number of circumstances, & impressed the authorities to such a degree that a disposition of forces was made to anticipate the supposed designs of the enemy." [20]

Butler, tracing the leak to convicted murderer William Boyle who had escaped from the guardhouse, telegraphed the details to Lincoln, as evidence of how "your clemency has been misplaced." [21]

In March Lieutenant General Grant came east to assume command as General-in-Chief of the Union armies and personally direct the war in Virginia. On April 1 Grant appeared at Fortress Monroe to confer with Butler as to the spring campaign against Richmond. It was the first time that Butler had met the determined, matter-of-fact fighter from the West, whom Butler's henchmen had already reported as devoid of political ambitions. Grant quickly made clear his desire to coordinate the fighting on all fronts and to subordinate all other fronts to the one in Virginia, and asked Butler to state his views of the situation as he now saw it from Fortress Monroe.

Butler unfolded his charts of the area south and east of Richmond and directed Grant's attention to the V formed at the junction of the James and Appomattox rivers known as Bermuda Hundred. "In their windings the two rivers approach each other," Butler pointed out, "within two miles and a half, at a point on the James about eight miles in direct line from Richmond, and on the Appomattox about the same distance from Petersburg . . . A line drawn across from point to point includes within the rivers a peninsula of more than thirty square miles." [22] Throw a trench across its narrow neck and the whole peninsula becomes a triangular fortification within easy striking distance of Richmond, accessible on two sides by water and large enough to accommodate any number of troops. Since Richmond was most extensively fortified on the north, Butler recommended that Grant throw his entire attack force into an advanced base at Bermuda Hundred and from here attack Richmond.

"But," said Grant, "bringing my troops to the James by water will uncover Washington, and Lee may attack there." [23]

Butler argued that troops could be shifted to Washington by water more rapidly than Lee's men could march the distance overland. Grant, certain that the Government would not permit him to uncover the Capital, determined instead to give Butler an army for offense and to attack simultaneously from the north and the south of Richmond. Butler was permitted to draw in his scattered forces that could be spared from garrison duty and organize them as the 18th Corps under Major General W. F. Smith. From South Carolina the 10,000 men of the 10th Corps under Major General Q. A. Gillmore were assigned by Grant to Butler. While General Meade operated from his present base, Butler was to seize the town of City Point at the mouth of the Appomattox and the strategic V-shaped Bermuda Hundred area, to fortify this advanced base and to direct his attack against Richmond as his objective point. Grant hoped that the two prongs of his attack might meet on the James River to the west of Richmond, and that Lee, besieged in the Confederate Capital and cut off from supplies, might be forced to surrender.

Butler was elated now over the opportunity of a spring campaign with adequate forces.

Scarcely had these plans been mapped, however, before a political henchman of Salmon P. Chase appeared at Fortress Monroe to ask Butler to seek the Vice-Presidential nomination on a ticket with the Secretary of the Treasury.

"Say to Mr. Chase that I have no desire to be Vice-President," replied Butler. "I am but forty-five years old; I am in command of a fine army; the closing campaign of the war is about beginning, and

I hope to be able to do some further service for the country, and I should not, at my time of life, wish to be Vice-President if I had no other position. Assure him that my determination in this regard has no connection with himself personally. I will not be a candidate for any elective office whatever until this war is over." [24]

Three weeks later, and only a few days before the spring campaign was launched, Simon Cameron — who had recently expressed to Butler his opinion that the politician must win his postwar political laurels on the wartime battlefield — offered Butler the Vice-Presidential billing on Lincoln's ticket.

"Mr. Hamlin is no longer to be a candidate for Vice-President," explained Cameron, "and as he is from New England, the President thinks that his place should be filled by someone from that section; and aside from reasons of personal friendship which would make it pleasant to have you with him, he believes that being the first prominent Democrat who volunteered for the war, your candidature would add strength to the ticket, expecially with the war Democrats, and he hopes that you will allow your friends to cooperate with his to place you in that position." [25]

Butler asked Cameron to thank the President for the compliment, although he must decline. "Tell him," said Butler laughing, "with the prospects of the campaign, I would not quit the field to be Vice-President, even with himself as President, unless he will give me bond with sureties, in the full sum of his four years' salary, that he will die or resign within three months after his inauguration. Ask him what he thinks I have done to deserve the punishment . . . of being made to sit as presiding officer over the Senate, to listen for four years to debates more or less stupid, in which I can take no part or say a word, nor even be allowed to vote upon any subject which concerns the welfare of the country, except when my enemies might think my vote would injure me in the estimation of the people, and therefore, by some parliamentary trick make a tie on such question, so I should be compelled to vote. No, my friend; tell the President I will do everything I can to aid in his election if nominated, and that I hope he will be . . ." [26]

21

BERMUDA HUNDRED

WITH only four short weeks to prepare for his invasion up the James River in conjunction with Grant's attack from the Potomac front, Butler hurriedly disposed his forces. General William F. ("Baldy") Smith was placed at the head of the 18th Corps, with white infantry at Yorktown, Negro infantry at Hampton and Negro cavalry at Williamsburg. A body of white cavalry under General August V. Kautz was poised to the south of Norfolk in readiness to sweep along the southern boundary of Virginia to cut rails leading south from Richmond and Petersburg. Reports of ironclad rams being built at Richmond led Butler to enlist the aid of naval monitors under Admiral S. P. Lee, ahead of whose force the light craft of General Graham's Marine Brigade were scheduled to sweep the river for torpedoes. Several schooners were loaded with stones to block if necessary the channel above the Bermuda Hundred triangle.

On April 28 Butler received Grant's final instructions: "Start your forces the night of the 4th, so as to be as far up James River as you can get by daylight of the morning of the 5th, and push from that time with all your might for the accomplishment of the object before you." [1] Butler's immediate objective was to seize the Bermuda Hundred triangle between the Appomattox and James rivers. After establishment of an advanced base here, he was to attempt, according to Grant's strategy, to push on up the south bank of the James past Richmond, and join forces with the Army of the Potomac under General Meade.

Several of the 10th Corps regiments which Grant had ordered up from the Georgia coast to join Butler arrived before the end of April, ahead of their commander General Quincy A. Gillmore. Not until

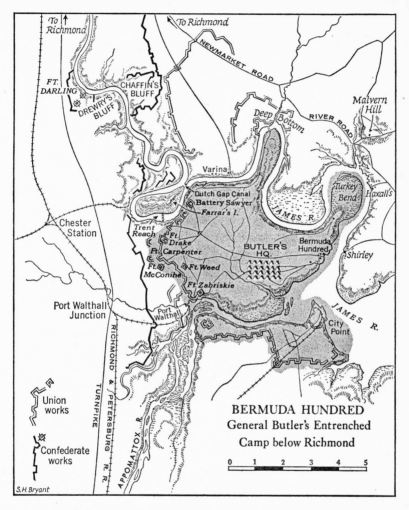

To Richmond

To Richmond

NEWMARKET ROAD

FT. DARLING

CHAFFIN'S BLUFF

DREWRY'S BLUFF

Deep Bottom

RIVER ROAD

Malvern Hill

Varina

Dutch Gap Canal

Battery Sawyer

Farrar's I.

Turkey Bend

Haxall's

JAMES R.

Chester Station

Trent Reach

Ft. Drake

Ft. Carpenter

BUTLER'S HQ

Bermuda Hundred

Shirley

Ft. Weed

McConiha

Ft. Zabriskie

Port Walthall Junction

Port Walthall

JAMES R.

City Point

RICHMOND & PETERSBURG R.R.

TURNPIKE

APPOMATTOX R.

Union works

Confederate works

BERMUDA HUNDRED
General Butler's Entrenched
Camp below Richmond

0   1   2   3   4   5

S.H.Bryant

May 3, however, did General Gillmore himself and the transports bearing the remainder of his 10th Corps arrive in the crowded anchorage
in Hampton Roads. It was now, to Butler's annoyance, too late for
him to confer with Gillmore and his staff before the invasion began.

Another exasperating matter at this moment was Secretary of
State Seward's approval for French warships to ascend the James

River and remove French purchases of tobacco from Richmond. To clear those ships from his path Butler was compelled to deal brusquely with the French consuls at Norfolk as he had had to do at New Orleans.

Early Wednesday afternoon, May 4, Butler feinted with transports up York River to deceive the enemy. Then promptly at 8 P.M. the various elements in his invasion force got under way toward Richmond. General Kautz led his white cavalry westward from Norfolk to cut railroads south of Richmond. Colonel Robert West with 1700 colored cavalry rode up the York Peninsula road to cross the Chickahominy, threaten Richmond and then join Butler at Bermuda Hundred. The direct thrust up the James was spearheaded by three steamers of the Marine Brigade; then came Admiral Lee's monitors and gunboats; and in the rear the transports. General Butler boarded his speedy new headquarters steamer *Grayhound* at midnight, and circled among the transports like a sheep dog marshaling his flock.

To Butler, General Gillmore seemed unnecessarily slow in embarking those of his regiments that had arrived early. "Having waited for your army corps from Port Royal," Butler snapped in a telegram to Gillmore, "I am not a little surprised at waiting for you here. Push everything forward." [2] At midnight Gillmore from Yorktown retorted: "The miserable conveniences for embarking troops have been a cause of great delay." [3]

Crowded paddleboats churned the water. Pontoon trains and canal barges were tugged by the swifter transports, while the wedge-shaped monitors with their awkward turrets amidships were towed by gunboats. "The swift *Grayhound*," wrote a reporter on board, "flits among the slow moving craft and slackens her speed an instant as she comes abreast each vessel, allowing Gen. Butler from the hurricane deck to order them to advance with all the celerity possible. 'Give her all the steam you can, Captain,' shouts the General, with upraised cap." As the blue-coat soldiers recognized the commanding general they broke into cheers.[4]

To seize Wilson's Wharf, thirty-five miles below Richmond, a regiment of General Wild's Negro soldiers was put ashore. Seven miles farther upstream another Negro regiment was landed to occupy Fort Powhatan. The stalwart blacks ran up the bluffs, and soon were swinging their axes with a will. At 3 P.M. on May 5 the first of Butler's troops debarked at City Point. Again, the honor of being first ashore was given to colored troops. The *Grayhound* reached City Point in time to see the Negroes "streaming up the steep bluffs like ants toward an ant-hill." [5]

To Butler's distress at the time, Admiral Lee anchored his gunboats below City Point, leaving the pontoon wharves at Bermuda Hundred unguarded against ironclad rams from above. Troops poured ashore unmolested, however, and supplies grew in toppling pyramids dotting without pattern the village of City Point and the shore line of the strategic Bermuda Hundred triangle. A Confederate signal station was seized at City Point. A white-shirted contraband on a horse made a mad freedom-dash down to the Federal lines. By nightfall Friday, May 6, the last of General Gillmore's troops were on shore. The enemy's surprise had been complete. An expedition straight up the James River to within a dozen miles of Richmond had met no opposition. In City Point and Bermuda Hundred, Butler confidently believed he held the key of Richmond.[6]

While Butler's men fell to digging a 5-mile trench across the narrow neck of the Bermuda Hundred peninsula between the James and the Appomattox rivers, Admiral Lee in the shallower gunboats dragged for torpedoes up the Richmond side of the peninsula in the area known as Trent's Reach. During these operations a Federal gunboat was sunk by a Confederate battery on the bank opposite Bermuda Hundred. Another, grazing a torpedo, was crushed and blown high in the air like crumpled paper. An escort blazed away at the Confederates.

On Saturday, May 7, while some of his troops were entrenching, others were sent to uproot the railroad between Petersburg and Richmond. It was as essential, Butler believed, to get his advanced base well fortified as it was to cripple the enemy's transportation system. General R. E. Lee's reinforcements from the south might be utilized against Butler; or Lee himself, who at this time seemed to have won a stalemate against Grant in the costly Battle of the Wilderness, might turn against Butler.

New York *Times* correspondent Winser who rode on horseback with Butler along the defense line found the weather "insufferably hot," the atmosphere "sultry . . . dense with dust raised by hundreds of cartwheels and thousands of horses." Butler's army, he noted, "are enthusiastic and will go onward with eagerness at his bidding. I believe they have great faith in his leadership . . . The cheering was hearty enough to make these Virginia woods ring again . . . the gallant old Massachusetts soldier." [7]

The first attempt against the railroad, which was led by General Heckman, ran into Confederate guns already in position on the embankments and further trainloads of troops rushing in from both Petersburg and Richmond. Butler, disappointed by the slowness of General Gillmore, detached three brigades from the latter's troops and placed them under General Smith. With these accessions Smith struck and broke the railroad. From his wife Butler received a note clamoring for information and begging to be allowed to come up to City Point to look after his health. Ben replied curtly that the fighting was pretty severe and that she had better go to New York. "Buy me a dozen Handkerchiefs. Thanks for your letter." [8]

His 1700 Negro cavalry, which he desperately needed now to explore the situation toward Richmond in advance of the infantry, had found Bottom's Bridge destroyed and in attempting to ford the Chickahominy had slipped into deep water and lost their bundles of hay. Instead of driving on ahead they had returned to Williamsburg to obtain more forage! From his attack forces Butler had felt compelled to detach men to guard his communications down the James River at Wilson's Wharf and Fort Powhatan. Then in addition to the large garrison which was pinned down at City Point to defend his supply base Butler had found it necessary to fortify for several miles the bluffs along the eastern bank of the Appomattox which overlooked and commanded his triangular fortress. Butler appealed to Stanton for an additional 10,000 men from the pool of reserves at Washington, only to learn that Grant had already used up these troops.

After three days of digging across the neck of Bermuda Hundred, Butler was ensconced inside a "Gibraltar of defense." His fortified line lay parallel to and about two miles distant from the Richmond-to-Petersburg turnpike and beyond the latter a short distance lay the Confederates' railroad. From Bermuda Hundred it was nine miles south to Petersburg, with two unfordable streams, Swift Creek and the Appomattox River, intervening.[9] Richmond, twelve miles in the opposite direction, was covered by strong fortifications at Drewry's Bluff and by the moat of James River itself.

On May 12 Butler sent all his offensive force — nearly 30,000 men — toward Richmond, while General Kautz made a cavalry sortie to tear up the Danville Railroad southwest of Richmond. Gillmore and Smith moved northward on either side of the turnpike through a rainstorm that lasted three days and turned the dusty countryside into quagmire. Slogging through clayey mud, they wrested from the Confederates the outer defenses of Drewry's Bluff, about two and one half miles beyond Bermuda Hundred.

Confederate General Beauregard with approximately the same number of troops as the invader massed his forces heavily against Butler's right wing commanded by General Smith. At dawn on the 16th Beauregard attacked under cover of a fog so dense that Smith could not see a horseman fifteen yards away. In the fog the Negro cavalry vedettes on Smith's right were forced back in tangled undergrowth along the bank of the James. Smith himself remained on the turnpike while confusion struck the brigades of Generals Heckman and Weitzel, to the right of the turnpike. General Heckman called to his men to answer the Rebel yells with Union cheers, but in the fog he and his men were shortly overrun and captured. General Weitzel's orderly got among the Rebels and called out that he had been captured. Weitzel himself placed his pistol to the head of the Confederate victor and made him give up his rifle to the orderly who in turn proceeded to march him as prisoner to the Union rear. General Butler, as the New York *Times* reported, "was out in the thick of the tempest of rifle shells."[10]

To the left of the turnpike hundreds of Confederate attackers stumbled in the fog over General Gillmore's telegraph lines that had been strung on tree stumps and were peppered by Union rifles.

Later in the day when it had become clear that General Heckman had been captured and that enemy troops were advancing against him from Petersburg, General Butler ordered his entire force to retire into Bermuda Hundred behind his fortifications.

There was something atavistic and medieval about Butler's calm withdrawal from the muddy battlefield into his moat-encircled stronghold of Bermuda Hundred. "The troops having been on incessant duty for five days, three of which were in rainstorm, I retired at leisure within my own lines," he reported to Stanton.[11]

It was so fantastic that Stanton did not take it in. Nor did Grant, or anyone else who was aware of the dogged, hard-driving, manslaughtering tactics that Grant was now employing in his wilderness campaign.

Butler's fatigued soldiers refreshed themselves in complete safety while the wounded were moved to hospitals at Fortress Monroe on transports.

And while Butler's men were recuperating, that "inconsiderate little Creole," General Beauregard, hustled his men in quite close to Butler's fortified line and duplicated it with entrenchments of his own which enabled him temporarily to contain Butler inside the latter's strategic triangle.

A week of stalemate followed during which Butler repeatedly tested Beauregard's entrenchments while strengthening his own. The fortified points that guarded his supply route along the James were now several times attacked by small bodies of Confederates, but the Negro garrisons repelled these assaults. Raiding across the trenches, Butler's men seized prisoners and deserters from so many different Confederate brigades as to indicate that they were pinning down the whole of Beauregard's army in their front.

For General Grant, however, on the bloody battlefields north of Richmond, Butler's situation was very difficult to appraise. Rumors reached the General-in-Chief of disagreements between Butler and his corps commanders, and the Confederate press claimed that Beauregard's trenches across the neck of Bermuda Hundred had sealed Butler in.

Since two weeks of head-on assault against Lee's entrenchments had cost Grant around 20,000 men, the rumors from Bermuda Hundred were especially disturbing. On May 21 Grant wrote Halleck: "I fear there is some difficulty with the forces at City Point which prevents their effective use. The fault may be with the commander, and it may be with his subordinates. General Smith, whilst a very able officer, is obstinate and is likely to condemn whatever is not suggested by himself. Either those forces should be so occupied as to detain a force nearly equal to their own, or the garrison in the intrenchments at City Point should be reduced to a minimum and the remainder ordered here. I wish you would send a competent officer there to inspect and report by telegraph what is being done, and what in. his judgment it is advisable to do." [12]

Halleck sent Quartermaster General Montgomery C. Meigs and Brigadier General John G. Barnard, Chief Engineer, to Bermuda Hundred.

Before these inspectors got there Grant again telegraphed to Halleck: "The force under General Butler is not detaining 10,000 men in Richmond, and is not even keeping the roads south of the city cut. Under these circumstances I think it advisable to have all of it here except enough to keep a foothold, at City Point. If they could all be brought at once to Rappahannock or West Point (at the head of the York River) by water, that would be the best way to bring them . . . Send Smith in command." [13]

Halleck withheld action until he could hear from Meigs and Barnard and the next day, when it appeared that Lee was falling back on Richmond, Grant ordered that Smith be held in readiness to move but to await further orders.

Meanwhile Meigs and Barnard — "a sort of smelling committee" as Butler dubbed them — reached Butler's headquarters just after Butler's forces had captured the Confederate General W. S. Walker. Butler showed them the list of prisoners captured within the past four days from ten brigades. General Walker's bullet-pierced memorandum book indicated that his brigade alone numbered 4100 men. The inspectors seemed to be pleased with what they found. "General Butler's position," they reported, "is strong; can be defended, when works are complete, with 10,000 men, leaving 20,000 free to operate. We think it already strong, and think if General Grant is engaged in decisive operations that General Butler should not remain on the defensive. We think that this force should not be diminished, and that a skillful use of it will aid General Grant more than the numbers which might be drawn from here. Supplies of all kinds are abundant; the troops in good spirits. General Weitzel has just been made chief engineer to General Butler, and advises and cooperates heartily." [14]

The next day after interviewing the corps commanders, Meigs and Barnard recommended one of two courses of action: "What in our opinion ought to be done is either, *first,* to place an officer of military experience and knowledge in command of these two corps, thus making them a unit for field operations, and then assume the offensive; or, *second,* to withdraw 20,000 men to be used elsewhere. General Butler is a man of rare and great ability, but he has not experience and training to enable him to direct and control movements in battle . . . General Butler is satisfied with the ability and aid of General William F. Smith. He does not appear to be satisfied with General Gillmore. General Butler evidently desires to retain command in the field. If his desires must be gratified, withdraw Gillmore, place Smith in command of both corps under the supreme command of General Butler . . . Success would be more certain were Smith in command untrammeled, and General Butler remanded to the administrative duties of the department in which he has shown such rare and great ability." [15]

After the investigators had departed for Washington, Butler wrote Sarah, "I believe they have gone away satisfied." That the General-in-Chief should have thought of drawing upon the Army of the James for reinforcements Butler interpreted as "the worst sign I have seen of the movements of Grant." Sarah, nonetheless, was advised, "Don't fret yourself over the situation, as all will go well." Along with the letter he sent a bouquet of roses from a deserted garden at

City Point. "They will be withered before you get them, but the gift is in the heart of the giver." [16]

According to Grant's instructions Butler concentrated Baldy Smith's 17,000 men at City Point in readiness to embark to join Grant, but also in a fine position, so Butler thought, to launch a quick thrust along the eastern bank of the Appomattox into Petersburg, and this latter thrust Butler had ordered Smith to make when, on the same day, Lee having made a stand between the North Anna and South Anna rivers, Grant ordered that Smith's men be sent to him by water to the head of the York River, thence by overland march. Grant's decision was reached at noon on May 25, probably before the report of Meigs and Barnard had reached him.

There was no minimizing the fact that this withdrawal of his troops blasted Butler's hope for military success in the field. The *Times* reporter marveled at Butler's ability to hold a poker face. "He showed no ill feeling at being deprived of the greater part of his command, but cheerfully and actively cooperated with Gen. Smith in getting matters into shape for an early movement." [17] To Sarah, Butler wrote: "Grant has sent for all my troops to move over on the other line and help him. This is a sign of weakness I did not look for, and to my mind augurs worse for our cause than anything I have seen." [18] The histrionic Sarah, who resented the war because it separated her from Ben, and in whose mind the present problem was reduced to the simple dimension of jealousy on the part of the West Point clique replied with a sizzling note of comfort: "Dearest: I can write to you now, for you are in trouble. — a few words from me may be welcome. So, they have shorn you utterly at last! Never heed it. You will yet go beyond them. In their wish to kill they will o'erleap the mark, and stumble to their own downfall. I shall be very glad to see you here." [19] The mail carrier could wait no longer, but she wrote again later in the day. "If you can escape sharpshooters, political intriguers, and the poisonous malignity, oh fie, well, if you do, you bear a charmed life." [20]

The withdrawal of Smith's corps aroused opposition to Butler in certain newspapers. One news leak from his own headquarters Butler traced to a chaplain on Gillmore's staff who was promptly squelched. Butler broke his usual rule and wrote the editor of the New York *Evening Post* to set straight the "false impression" that had been given of General Gillmore as well as of himself; but there was nothing that Butler or anyone else could do to stamp out the wildfire rumor that General Butler's seizure of Bermuda Hundred had been a fizzle. Beauregard's claim that he had Butler penned up in Bermuda Hundred seemed to have been confirmed by Grant's withdrawal of Butler's troops. The frustrated Butler suffered an attack of dysentery. Sarah sent him pickled oysters, fresh bread and coffee and after the drenching rains of the first days of June she herself visited him at the front.

Ten days after Grant withdrew Baldy Smith, he decided not only to return Smith to Butler but to follow himself with the Army of the Potomac and concentrate all his forces on the City Point base. After the loss of several thousand of his men, Smith was sent back on the same transports that had brought him around to the York River. While the Army of the Potomac slogged on foot from the bloody battlefield of Cold Harbor to the James River opposite City Point, Grant ordered Smith's men, going ahead on the speedy transports, to launch a surprise attack on Petersburg before Grant arrived. This, ironically enough, was the same move which Butler himself had planned and been compelled to countermand on the eve of Smith's withdrawal.

As one last throw of the dice, before Grant's arrival south of the James should deprive him of independence as a general in the field, Butler on June 9 stripped his Bermuda Hundred defense lines and threw 3500 men against Petersburg. Although Petersburg's defender Confederate General Wise had only one brigade of 2400, plus a number of old men and boys of the home guards, the Union attack miscarried. General Gillmore's men lost so much time floundering in a swamp immediately behind their own lines that they arrived late before the Confederates' defenses. Then they retired without making an attack and never having made contact as planned with General Kautz's cavalry, while the latter, after Gillmore's retirement, entered and captured prisoners in the outskirts of Petersburg. The "acute wounds of hopes blasted when so much was expected" [21] now caused Butler to remove Gillmore from his command and to order him to Fortress Monroe to await a court of inquiry.

General Grant himself, arriving at City Point on June 14, assured Butler that his forces would not be amalgamated with the Army of the Potomac, but would continue to operate as a separate army, under Butler. Grant approved the selection of Brigadier General Alfred H. Terry to replace Gillmore. Henceforth, under Grant's eye Butler enjoyed no real independence as a commander in the field. Although he was always tactful in his dealings with Butler, Grant frequently delivered orders on the field direct to Butler's corps commanders, as was his custom with Meade's army.

As a commander of troops in the field Butler gained a reputation for inadequacy which has followed him down through history. At Annapolis and Baltimore he had won by strategy, by the quick move that took the enemy by surprise and avoided bloodshed. His droll seizure of the State Seal of Maryland might not indeed have prevented Maryland from seceding had a secession movement matured; but after his surprise push into Baltimore it would have been suicide for Baltimore businessmen to rebel in the face of the cannon on Federal Hill. General Scott's banishment of Butler to Fortress Monroe had been due to pique or prejudice. It is true that at Big Bethel in the summer of 1861 with an untrained handful of civilians in uniform Butler ought never to have risked an engagement of any sort. But he loved to gamble when the stakes were small. The Battle of Big Bethel, despite the vast publicity it attracted, was a mere skirmish. At New Orleans Butler's army by smallness of numbers had been pinned down to chores of occupation and was inadequate for operating effectively in the field. Never able to shake off the reputation of Big Bethel, upon his return to Fortress Monroe in November of 1863 he was again pinned down by lack of troops. Only when Grant came east in the spring of 1864 did Butler at last get a chance for service in the field. Clearly he was the Ulysses, rather than the Ajax, type of general. Instead of swapping of pawn for pawn, he preferred the "Trojan horse" technique, the clever ruse, to trick, to outsmart, the feint up the

York River followed by the surprise advance up the James. Had he not abhorred the costly frontal attack, of which Grant was master, he might have hung on with Ajax grip to his foothold on Drewry's Bluff and in time have worn down Beauregard's army by the same sort of costly exchange as that being made by Grant at the Wilderness, Spottsylvania and Cold Harbor. To Butler it seemed the part of wisdom to retire into his advanced fortress and recoup his resources for another surprise. Oppose brawn with brain. "If you can win these battles by stratagem rather than rivers of blood it would surely be better," wrote Sarah echoing her husband's ideas. And whether Butler's method might have been effective against General Lee in the final campaign against Richmond, was not actually tested. Never at any time except the period of less than three weeks after the opening of the spring campaign did Butler have sufficient troops to carry on offensive action. During that brief time he had had to seize and fortify his advanced base, establish and protect his lines of supply and launch his attacks. At Bermuda Hundred he was not at all "bottled up" in the sense the newspapers and later historians charged. He frequently moved in and out through the sidewalls of the Bermuda Hundred "bottle" over the same pontoon bridge that General Grant's forces used on June 15 when they crossed from the north side of the James to City Point.

Grant, taking up his headquarters at City Point, caused five granite-laden schooners and scows to be sunk across the James to protect the City Point base from Confederate ironclads. Butler, as Grant's ranking subordinate at his Bermuda Hundred headquarters, directed the shifting about of forces during the first crucial week after Grant's arrival.

In Grant's new gambit Butler's forces were split three ways. Two thousand men under Brigadier General R. S. Foster were sent via pontoon bridge to establish a front at Deep Bottom north of the James; 7000 under Brigadier General A. H. Terry manned the Bermuda Hundred line; and Baldy Smith with 15,000 was posted to the south side of the Appomattox.

The Bermuda Hundred area, for two weeks without rain, sweltered in 100° heat and its roads were milled to powder. "Heat! Dust!!

Flies!" exclaimed the New York *Times* reporter. "Suffocating heat! blinding dust! torturing flies! . . . the dust rising from the dry and incessantly traveled roads in dense clouds that obscure the wagons whose wheels plough it through, and hide the horses whose hoofs sink into its almost fathomless depths. The flies swarming amazingly, provoking men to profanity, irritating horses to madness." [22]

On hot and humid July 21 Baldy Smith's troops, which had been ordered by Butler to march at daylight to new positions south of the Appomattox, got a late start and were only slogging past Butler's headquarters by nine o'clock, when the temperature had begun to climb. Butler considered himself a friend of Smith, but it was unfortunate that on this particular day he felt moved to jog him a bit. Slowness in executing orders, as Butler saw it, was the chief deficiency in his command. Gillmore had been ousted chiefly for tardiness; and on several occasions since Grant's arrival Butler had felt that his subordinates hesitated to obey him unless he specified that the orders had emanated from Grant.

> Major General Smith:
> To so meritorious and able an officer as yourself, and to one toward whom the sincerest personal friendship and the highest respect concur, in my mind, I am and ever shall be unwilling to utter a word of complaint. Yet I think duty requires that I should call your attention to the fact that your column, which was ordered to move at daylight in the cool of the morning, is just now passing my headquarters in the heat of the day for a ten-mile march. The great fault of all our movements is dilatoriness, and if this is the fault of your division commanders let them be very severely reproved therefor. I have found it necessary to relieve one general for this, among other causes, where it took place in a movement of vital importance, and in justice to him you will hardly expect me to pass in silence a like fault where of less moment.[23]

At 4:30 P.M. General Smith, dusty, battle weary, extremely sensitive to the heat and smarting under what he considered an undeserved rebuke, reported in anger:

> General. I have the honor to acknowledge the receipt of your extraordinary note of 9 A.M. In giving your rank and experience all the

respect which is their due, I must call your attention to the fact that a reprimand can only come from the sentence of a court-martial, and I shall accept nothing as such. You will also pardon me for observing that I have for some years been engaged in moving troops, and I think in experience of that kind, at least, I am your superior. Your accusation of dilatoriness on my part this morning, or at any other time since I have been under your orders, is not founded on fact, and your threat of relieving me does not frighten me in the least. Your obedient servant, Wm. F. Smith, Major-General.[24]

At five-thirty Butler wrote Smith an official, and at 5:45 an unofficial, letter disclaiming any threat or accusation. "When a friend writes you a note is it not best to read it twice before you answer it unkindly? . . . Read the note again and see if you cannot wish the reply was not sent." [25] He returned Smith's reply, hoping that Smith would see fit to destroy it, but the latter, bitter and unappeased, that same night sent the correspondence to Grant, with a request to be relieved from duty in Butler's Department.

President Lincoln now visited the front, and General Grant, aside from mentioning to Assistant Secretary of War Charles A. Dana the problem of Smith's difficulty with Butler, let the matter ride. Smith's subsequent request for sick leave prompted the Lieutenant General on July 1 to write Halleck on "the necessity" of sending General Butler to another field of duty:

Whilst I have no difficulty with General Butler, finding him always clear in his conception of orders and prompt to obey, yet there is a want of knowledge how to execute and particularly a prejudice against him as a commander that operates against his usefulness. I have feared that it might become necessary to separate him and General Smith. The latter is really one of the most efficient officers in the service, readiest in expedients and most skillful in the management of troops in action. I would dislike removing him from his present command unless it was to increase it, but, as I say, may have it to do yet if General Butler remains. As an administrative officer General Butler has no superior. In taking charge of a department where there are no great battles to be fought, but a dissatisfied element to control, no one can manage it better than he. If a command could be cut out such as Mr. Dana proposed, namely,

Kentucky, Illinois, and Indiana, or if the Departments of Missouri, Kansas, and the States of Illinois and Indiana, could be merged together and General Butler put over it, I believe the good of the service would be subserved. I regret the necessity of asking for a change in commanders here, but General Butler not being a soldier by education or experience, is in the hands of his subordinates in the execution of all operations military. I would feel strengthened with Smith, Franklin, or J. J. Reynolds commanding the right wing of this army. At the same time, as I have here stated, General Butler has always been prompt in his obedience to orders from me and clear in his understanding of them. I would not, therefore, be willing to recommend his retirement. I send this by mail for consideration, but will telegraph if I think it absolutely necessary to make a change.[26]

Halleck replied to Grant: "It was foreseen from the first that you would eventually find it necessary to relieve General B. on account of his total unfitness to command in the field, and his generally troublesome character. What shall be done with him has, therefore, already been, as I am informed, a matter of consultation." Halleck suggested that Butler be remanded to Fortress Monroe with authority restricted to administrative matters behind the lines. "As General B. claims to rank me," Halleck concluded, "I shall give him no orders wherever he may go without the special direction of yourself or the Secretary of War." [27] Thus, what to do, if anything, was left to Grant.

Grant proposed that General A. A. Humphreys assist General Smith, so that the latter would not have to expose himself in the hot sun, and together with General Butler he rode over to Smith's headquarters, but did not succeed in patching up the quarrel. Smith sent an account of this interview to Senator Solomon Foot:

About the very last of June or the first of July, Generals Grant and Butler came to my headquarters and shortly after their arrival General Grant turned to General Butler, and said: "That drink of whiskey I took has done me good," and then directly afterwards asked me for a drink. My servant opened a bottle for him and he drank of it, when the bottle was corked up and put away. I was aware at this time that General Grant had within six months pledged himself to drink nothing intoxicating, but did not feel it would better matters to decline to give it upon his request in General Butler's presence. After the lapse of an hour or less the general asked me for another drink, which he took. Shortly after his voice showed plainly that the liquor had affected him and after a little time he left. I went to see him upon his horse, and as I returned to my tent, I said to a staff officer of mine, who had witnessed his departure: "General Grant has gone away drunk; General Butler has seen it and will never fail to use the weapon which has been put into his hands.[28]

Whether or not he could mount his horse steadily, Grant was able accurately to appraise Smith's prejudice against Butler. The two would have to be separated.. On July 6 Grant again telegraphed Halleck, "Please obtain an order assigning the troops of the Department of Virginia and North Carolina serving in the field to the command of Maj. Gen. W. F. Smith, and order Major General Butler, commanding department to his headquarters, Fortress Monroe." [29]

After this message had been put on the wire, Grant learned that within the last few weeks General Smith had turned antagonistic to the use of Negro troops, a circumstance which minimized his usefulness as commander of an army so largely made up of Negroes as Butler's was. Butler had held up Smith's recent reports on this topic to allow for investigation and for corrective measures to be taken and this, too, had become a source of annoyance between Smith and Butler, since the latter had always cheered the Negro and magnified his military successes. During the last several weeks Butler had sought to placate Smith by quietly exchanging white soldiers in Bermuda Hundred for Negroes and instituting further drills for the latter.

On July 9 Smith went north on a ten-day leave. On this same day Butler received from Colonel J. W. Shaffer, his chief of staff and liaison man now in Washington, an unofficial copy of the War Department's General Order No. 225 which placed Smith in command of the troops at the front and specified: "Maj. Gen. B. F. Butler will command the remainder of the troops in that department, having his headquarters at Fort Monroe." [30]

Butler went at once to City Point to confront Grant with this new order. Charles Dana, in Grant's office when Butler arrived, heard Butler ask: "General Grant, did you issue this order?" And it seemed to Dana that the Lieutenant General's hesitant reply, "No, not in that form," suggested that Butler had in some measure "cowed" Grant.[31] Dana left the room at this point. "Immediately after breakfast I went to Gen. Grant," Butler within a few hours wrote to Sarah, "as I had seen him the night before and was treated by him with the utmost cordiality, and had a confidential conference. I could not tell why this order should come out and he not have mentioned it then. He received me with cordial greeting. As soon as possible after the usual compliments, and the staff had retired, I showed him the order, and told him I did not understand it. He says, 'Oh — I did not mean you should have seen that order. It was a mistake. I suppressed all the copies that were transmitted through me. How did you get this?' 'Some friend in the War Department, fearing perhaps I should not see it, forwarded me one direct,' I said. 'Well,' said he, 'I don't want this at all. I want Smith to report to you — you have the full command. I was going to add the 19th corps (predominantly colored troops) to your department, and I shall when it comes here from Washington.' "[32]

Privately to his wife Butler surmised that the attempt to oust him had been "the work of Halleck upon the application of Smith," and he was well pleased to have come out of the affair not only with a whole skin but with an accession of the 19th Corps to his command. To Sarah he confided his belief that Grant "has vindicated me and my military operations."[33] On July 19, when General Smith returned from leave, Grant relieved Smith of command of the 18th Corps and directed him to proceed to New York City and await further orders. In announcing this news to Sarah, Butler vented his feelings in a scrap of doggerel:

> *He digged a pit, he digged it deep,*
> *He digged it for his brother;*
> *But he fell in and was drowned therein,*
> *And died instead of t'other.*[34]

With younger subordinates Butler got on well in the months following the imbroglios with Gillmore and Smith. As commander of Grant's right wing, Butler held four miles of entrenchments south of the Appomattox, the five-mile front across Bermuda Hundred and a front of varying extent on the north side of the James. Grant's strategy was to alternate attacks from the opposite ends of his long line. Butler's Negro troops stood up well in the fighting north of the James; although they were more excitable than white soldiers, more difficult to hold in formation after the first shock of battle.

Under Grant's immediate supervision, Butler continued his efforts to outsmart the enemy. His observation towers, Signal Lookout and Crow's Nest, at either end of the Bermuda Hundred entrenchments, gave distant views behind the Confederate lines and often enabled Butler to supply valuable data to Grant. He mounted a thirteen-inch mortar and a long-range Parrott rifle on freight cars and ran them up the City Point railroad to bombard Petersburg. Still hoping to utilize the enormous striking power of naval guns, Butler dug across the narrow neck of land known as Dutch Gap a canal to give the Navy's monitors access into the upper James, a move which was stopped just short of completion by protests from the naval commander himself, who feared that Confederate rams from Richmond might elude the Union ships and get through to the fat prizes at Grant's supply base. Using kites Butler disseminated across the enemy lines propaganda leaflets such as copies of the President's amnesty proclamation. Skilled in the art of cross-examination, he extracted useful information from newly captured prisoners.

22

PRISONERS AND THE EXCHANGE

As THE war progressed the problem of dealing with prisoners of war, at first so humane and reasonable, came to be complicated by misunderstandings and war fever. The Confederate garrisons in the New Orleans forts, for example, had been simply paroled, i.e., placed on their honor not to participate further in the war until after they had been formally exchanged, and several thousand of these parolees had peacefully roamed the streets of New Orleans during Butler's occupation of the city. In July of 1862 a cartel arrangement was made to release all prisoners, paroling any excess above the actual number of officers and men exchanged. The cartel operated for a year under commissioners of exchange in Richmond and Washington. Then, various commanders in the field experimented on their own with retaliation for outrages. Enlistment of Negroes by the Federals raised new problems. Jefferson Davis' proclamation outlawing General Butler announced that Negro troops and their officers could not expect to be treated as prisoners of war. From here on, prisoner exchange was effected only after tedious negotiations.

When Butler was assigned to Fortress Monroe in November 1863 there were in Southern hands about 13,000 Union prisoners, and in Northern some 30,000 to 40,000 Confederates.[1] General E. A. Hitchcock, the United States Commissioner of Exchange in Washington, and Judge Robert Ould, the Confederate States Commissioner of Exchange in Richmond, were locked in dispute over alleged Southern violation of procedure in releasing the Vicksburg parolees to active duty. Newspapers North and South were featuring atrocity stories about the treatment of prisoners by the enemy.

Although at first the prisoner exchange was outside of Butler's province it was through his geographical area that intelligence from the enemy capital usually found its way north. On November 17, Butler telegraphed Stanton: "I am informed and believe that the Rebels will give us a man for every man we send them, up to the number they hold. Shall I put them in question, — or interfere about it any way?"[2] Stanton replied that the whole subject was under the direction of General Hitchcock. The exchange was being blocked, Stanton asserted, by the Confederates' refusal to exchange Negroes and officers in command of Negro troops.

Reports of desperate conditions in Richmond's Libby Prison and Belle Isle compound induced Butler to plan military raids to release the Federal prisoners, but meanwhile he was unwilling to abandon the idea of a negotiated exchange. He wrote at length to Stanton pointing out that Confederate Commissioner Ould's published correspondence indicated that he would exchange man for man, and suggesting that "we exchange man for man, officer for officer, until the Rebels stop — if then every prisoner they hold has been exchanged, then the question of color does not arise and our men will have been relieved from starvation up to that number. But if the colored prisoners and their officers shall not be produced by the Rebels for exchange, we shall have [an excess of] 10,000 of their men upon which to work both retaliation and reprisal to the fullest extent, to wring from the Rebels justice to the colored soldiers."[3]

The report that smallpox had broken out among Federal prisoners in Richmond caused Butler to send to the Confederate authorities by flag of truce sufficient vaccine for 6000 persons. "Being uncertain how far I can interfere as a matter of official duty," wrote Butler to Commissioner Ould, "I beg of you to consider this note either official or unofficial as may best serve the purpose of alleviating the distresses of these unfortunate men."[4] Stanton, whose permission Butler had not waited for, later approved his action; and Commissioner Ould wrote Butler a note that was shockingly friendly in tone for a Confederate official in high office to assume toward a Federal officer who was under President Davis' ban of outlawry.[5]

Butler now sent his chief of staff Colonel Shaffer to Washington to urge the Secretary to let him try to break the log jam on prisoner exchange. Stanton, pressed also by Butler's friends in Congress, authorized Butler to act as special agent of exchange.

Butler personally inspected the thirty-acre prisoner-of-war compound at Point Lookout and questioned a representative group of prisoners. After an examination of their teeth and gums for evidence of scurvy, he added onions and cider vinegar to their diet. To prevent spoilage of the camp's supply of potatoes, which hitherto had always been first hauled to Washington and transshipped back to Point Lookout, Butler arranged to have the potatoes in the future put off the steamers at Point Lookout.

On Christmas day of 1863, without preliminary negotiation, Butler sent 505 prisoners to City Point to be offered in exchange. His gamble was that with the prisoners within sight of home, the Confederate authorities could not refuse to exchange for them. Butler addressed to Colonel Ould a notification of his own appointment as special agent of exchange, and a detailed report of his finding at Point Lookout, "in order that you may be able to satisfy the friends of the prisoners who may be disturbed by the unfounded reports of ill treatment and cruelty suffered by the prisoners at Point Lookout, in like manner as our people are excited by what I hope are like groundless stories of ill usage and starvation suffered by our soldiers in your hands." [6]

His bold assumption of the role of official agent of exchange offered Jefferson Davis a chance to nullify the proclamation of outlawry. Indeed, Judge Ould's friendly acceptance of the vaccine indicated that the year-old ban of outlawry might now be quietly forgotten. And so it might, had not the Beast-of-New-Orleans legend taken so firm a hold upon the Southern imagination.

After a stormy session of the Confederate Cabinet in Richmond, Ould was directed to return an equivalent for the Christmas Day prisoners, but to have no official dealings with "Beast" Butler himself.

Ould, accordingly, while surrendering 520 prisoners in exchange for 505, as an earnest of good intentions, informed Butler's agent that partial deliveries of prisoners were unacceptable, that the Confederate policy was to "deliver all our prisoners now in captivity, the excess on either side to be on parole."[7] Ould, ostentatiously ignoring Butler, wrote Hitchcock: "Although we do not pretend to prescribe what agents your Government shall employ in connection with the cartel, yet when one who has been proclaimed to be so obnoxious as General Butler is selected, self-respect requires that the Confederate authorities should refuse to treat with him or establish such relations with him as properly pertain to an agent of exchange. The proclamation of President Davis forbids that General Butler should be admitted to the protection of the Confederate Government, and he cannot therefore be received under a flag of truce. Accordingly, I am directed by the Confederate authorities to inform you that Maj. Gen. B. F. Butler will not be recognized by them as an agent of exchange."[8]

Butler proposed to Stanton "the sternest retaliation." "When I was sending medicines to prevent the spread of a loathsome disease among their citizens I was not so 'obnoxious' to Jefferson Davis but that the medicine was received, and the usual official courtesies passed between his agent and myself. But when a pretext was sought for to prevent a fair and honorable exchange of prisoners of war, then a cowardly proclamation, issued after I was relieved from command to his knowledge, which has lain dormant a year, is brought forward."[9]

President Lincoln, "unwilling to concede to the rebels the right to dictate what agents this government should employ in its public business,"[10] declined to issue any order on the subject. Thus for some weeks the exchange was blocked; while the New York *World* and other anti-administration papers berated the government for making the Union prisoner in Richmond a victim to the "prurient and vulgar ambition" of General Butler "and his superiors."[11]

Meanwhile the resourceful Butler sought to proselyte the Confederate prisoners for the Union cause. On December 27 he inquired of Stanton, "Is there any objection to my enlisting as many prisoners as may desire to do so after they know they can be exchanged either in the regular or volunteer force of the United States or that of any State?"[12]

The prospect of returning "repentant rebels" to the Union fold caused Lincoln to send his private secretary, John Hay, down to Point Lookout with an "oath book" containing the forms to be filled out by such prisoners as wished to take the oath of allegiance. General Butler met Hay at City Point, and accompanied him back to Washington, taking Sarah and Blanche along for the trip.

"In the dusk of the evening Gen. Butler came clattering into the room where Marston & I were sitting, followed by a couple of aides," Hay wrote in his diary. "We had some hasty talk about business. He told me how he was administering the oath at Norfolk; how popular it was growing; children cried for it." Hay's talent in turning a phrase found a fit subject in the "excessively pretty daughter, tall statuesque & fair and named by a happy prophesy of the blonde beauty of her maturity, Blanche." [13] During the trip up the Bay, after the ladies had retired, the General filled the ear of the young man who had the ear of the President with criticisms of McClellan's Peninsula Campaign and suggestions of the Bermuda Hundred strategy which later under General-in-Chief Grant he was himself to carry out. In the small hours the General's restless imagination cavorted over many fields. "Butler had some odd stories about physical sympathies," recorded Hay, in his diary; "he talked also about the Hebrew jurisprudence & showed a singular acquaintance with Biblical studies: his occasional references to anatomy & physiology evidently surprised the surgeon (Dr. McCormick) to whom he respectfully deferred from time to time. He talked until it grew late . . . He gave me some very dramatic incidents of his recent action in Fortress Monroe smoking out adventurers & confidence men, testing his detectives and matters of that sort. He makes more business in that sleepy little Department than anyone would have dreamed was in it." [14]

After conferences with Lincoln, Stanton and Hitchcock, Butler began quietly recruiting troops from among the Confederate prisoners of war. Three regiments of "Galvanized Yanks" were raised who, under Butler's friend and Massachusetts neighbor, Colonel Charles A. R. Dimon, were employed during the war to patrol the Western frontier against the Indians.

Out of this situation there was quite naturally sprouted a new crop of "Beast" Butler legends. "The Yankees have practiced a deliberate torture," reported the Richmond *Examiner,* "to extort from our men the renunciation of their allegiance, and on the other hand have plied them with the most artful of temptations. The men are brought almost to the point of starvation; imperfectly clothed and ragged, they are exposed to the cold . . . they are persuaded that there is no hope of their release by Richmond authorities; and when their misery stares them in the face, the Yankee recruiting agent comes around, exhibiting to the unhappy wretch the fine clothes, which he can have by a word, and tempting him with all sorts of indulgences and bribes." [15]

In January of 1864 the Confederate General George E. Pickett called Butler's hand on retaliation by hanging a colored Union soldier in retaliation for General E. A. Wild's execution of the guerrilla Daniel Bright in Pasquotank County, North Carolina. The situation was complicated by a Confederate mistake in identifying their victim as "Private Samuel Jones of Company B. Fifth Ohio Regiment," an error which gave rise to the canard that a prisoner in Richmond had been chosen by lot and rushed to the scene of Bright's execution to meet his own doom. As it turned out, the victim proved to be Samuel Jordan, Company D, Fifth U.S. Colored Troops, one of Wild's regiments known colloquially as the "Fifth Ohio." Jordan had been captured by the Confederates, and General Wild to insure his proper treatment as a prisoner had seized and held two white women of the neighborhood. Wild had announced publicly that he would mete out to these hostages the same treatment the Rebels gave to the captured Union Negro. Butler who had no intention of executing Wild's threat, first permitted the husbands of the women, W. J. Munden and Pender Weeks, to ransom their wives by placing themselves in Butler's custody in their stead. Then on the technicality that General Pickett had made no distinction on the basis of color in his execution of Jordan, Butler revoked General Wild's order for execution of the hostages. To the Confederate commander of the state force of North Carolina Butler announced his future policy to be:

First, then, I do not mean to conduct the war like a fishwoman in Billingsgate, by calling hard names, such as "brute," "beast," etc.

Second, I do not mean to carry it on by any futile proclamations of outlawry against any officer or soldier duly authorized and commissioned for doing his duty.

Third, I do not mean to carry it on by threatening when I am beaten to take to the woods and organize guerrilla forces . . .

I do mean to carry on this war according to the rules of civilized warfare as between alien enemies.[16]

In February and March Butler again sent several boatloads of prisoners to City Point for exchange, and the Confederates returned not man for man as the Federals had hoped, but something like 4 for 5, and this unsatisfactory situation served to check further exchange until late in March, when Butler received a letter from Ould addressed formally to himself as "U.S. Agent of Exchange," notifying him that Ould had come to the mouth of the James River to request a conference. Butler invited Ould to come ashore at Fortress Monroe where they could confer in comfort, the weather being stormy.

Ould informed Butler that since Butler's recent raids on Richmond most of the prisoners had been removed to Americus, Georgia. In the future Ould wished the Federals to accept returned prisoners at Fort Pulaski on the Savannah River. Butler agreed to accept returned prisoners at Fort Pulaski, and in the negotiation over treatment of Negroes was able to exact the concession that "free persons of color" who had been enlisted from the Northern states would be treated as prisoners of war; although Ould was adamant on the subject of ex-slaves, who according to Confederate law were to be restored to their former owners.

Flushed with success at having so nearly opened up the log jam, Butler felt certain that he could now negotiate a settlement of all issues except the Negro issue and even on that he believed he could bring the Rebels to heel by retaliation. But at this point General Grant with different ideas stepped into the picture.

The day after Ould's departure General Grant arrived at Fortress Monroe, and gave Butler the most emphatic oral directions *not to exchange another able-bodied man until further orders from him.*[17] Grant believed that the difference in physical condition of the Union and Confederate prisoners gave the Confederates an advantage and for

purely military reasons blocked all further exchanges. Butler persuaded Grant to allow him to exchange sick and wounded and to
continue negotiations in such a way as to cause the Confederates themselves to break off the exchange. He believed that the Southerners
would never consent to treat their ex-slaves as prisoners of war, and
he proposed to Stanton that the whole negotiation could be ensnarled
on that issue.

The exchange remained in deadlock until midsummer, when, after
Farragut's victory at Mobile Bay, and with Sherman pounding the
gates of Atlanta, Commissioner Ould on August 10 agreed to exchange man for man as Butler had offered eight months earlier.

Since Grant now continued to oppose releasing any prisoners, Butler informed Commissioner Ould that no decision had been reached;
whereupon Ould published in the Richmond *Examiner* a report on
the exchange throwing the blame for failure upon an inconsistent enemy who refused to accept their own stipulated conditions. Butler
the "outlaw" again became the raw-head-and-bloody-bones of Confederate propagandists.

Butler's Bermuda Hundred headquarters in the field, a small frame
farmer's dwelling with a huge fireplace and a lean-to cookshack
made of logs, became a sort of courtroom, and himself a prosecuting
attorney. In Butler's eye it was not so much Robert Ould as it was the
leaders of the Confederacy who were defendants, and the jury was the
people of the North who soon would be reading his "brief" in the columns of the New York *Times*. In his 3000-word letter to Ould, Butler
singled out as the one point of difference the demand that ex-slaves be
treated as prisoners of war and trenchantly drove home his argument.
The captor of the slave, Butler pointed out, had the recognized right
to dispose of captured property, and this right the United States had
exercised in emancipating the ex-slave. Thus freed, the ex-slave who
put on the Federal army uniform was entitled to the same protection
as any other Federal soldier. "I take it no one would doubt the right
of the United States to a drove of Confederate mules, or a herd of
Confederate cattle, which should wander or rush across the Confederate lines into the lines of the U.S. Army. So, it seems to me, treating

the negro as property merely, if that piece of property passes the Confederate lines and comes into the lines of the United States, that property is as much lost to its owner in the Confederate States, as would be the mule or ox . . . Do the Confederate authorities claim the right to reduce to a state of slavery freemen, prisoners of war, captured by them?" [18]

In view of Grant's prohibition of exchange, which could scarcely be announced publicly, Butler's task was to dissemble, to affect a desire for a settlement, while at the same time rendering agreement impossible.

The pro-administration New York *Times* thought that nothing could be "more lucid than Gen. Butler's statement of the case";[19] the hostile *World* abused Butler for "fighting it down people's throats";[20] while the Richmond *Examiner* denounced Butler's refusal to exchange as "a brutal, cruel fraud." [21]

Butler's maneuver produced the secretly desired effect. The cartel was now definitely out for the remainder of the war and for purposes of Federal propaganda the blame was placed upon the South.

Butler's role in the prisoner exchange, which in the nature of the case could not be revealed to the public, served to mystify some Northerners like the *World* editors, and confirmed Southerners in their view that the Beast of New Orleans was a devil incarnate. Confederate abuse flourished throughout the negotiations. In Richmond, businessmen and schoolchildren contributed to a relief fund for Mrs. Mumford, widow of the man whom The Beast had "murdered" in New Orleans, and whenever Southerners recalled the Woman Order it was to flaunt anew the propaganda fiction of Butler's handing over ladies of New Orleans to the lusts of Union troops.

The part Butler played as a "cruel attorney" extracting information from prisoners further enhanced the notoriety throughout the South of Lincoln's scapegoat general. "We appeal to you for protection, sir," some prisoners besought General A. H. Terry when the latter informed them that they were to be interrogated by General Butler.[22] An exchanged prisoner from Fortress Monroe related to the Richmond *Daily Examiner* the "tortures" he had suffered under Butler's interrogation. On a number of successive days he had been brought before Butler and questioned. When he had refused to answer he had been abused with such epithets as "damned infamous scoundrel" and remanded to jail on bread and water.[23]

On morning in June, Butler permitted a New York *Times* reporter to witness his grilling of prisoners. As each man was called inside Butler's tent he was seated on a campstool opposite the General, who sat on a carpet-bottomed chair with his feet up on a stool; while at a side table Lieutenant Davenport, Butler's private secretary, took down the replies in shorthand: "Gen. Butler's fame as a lawyer is too well known to need mention; but if I had never heard of it," reported H. J. Winser, "I should, after yesterday, have classed him among those rare persons who cause the truth to flow freely from the most unwilling. Those peculiar glances of his, which appear to flash their fire into the concealed depths of the mind of the witness, assuring him that he is read through and through, compel the utterance of the facts, in spite of all determination to the contrary. There is no browbeating, no loud intonation, but questions were quietly put and forced home to the understanding of the dullest witness, by a penetrating look establishing between them, as it seemed, a magnetic chain over which the truth has free passage." [24]

Edward A. Pollard, a prisoner and a Richmond newspaperman whom Butler wished to exchange for a New York *Tribune* reporter held by the Confederates, was released from close confinement and brought to Butler's field headquarters. After sending in his name on a scrap of paper, Pollard waited several hours. "At last an orderly called my name; and with a sudden effort I strung up my nerves for an interview with the main Raw-Head-and-Bloody-Bones of the War . . . Imagine my surprise when General Butler rose, saying very pleasantly, 'Take a seat, Mr. P.,' and then offering me a fragrant Havana, asking me 'if I would not take what he could recommend as a very good cigar!' I excused myself from smoking on the ground of 'nerves.'" The Confederate journalist noted that while General Butler's large head and bust suggested "a bulky and unwieldy figure," this was not actually the case; "on the contrary he has a compact fig-

ure and a French quickness in his movements; he is short and well put
up. His head is peaked with a forehead that slants rapidly but just
over the eyes shows a remarkable development of what phrenologists
call 'the organs of perception.' He has small muddy, cruel eyes; and
there is a smothered glower in them, curtained in one of them by a
drooping lid, which is very unpleasant. The other is by no means slug-
gish. He talks with a perpetual motion of his features, and has the
Johnsonian puff in his conversation. When he essays to be pleasant he
smiles; but as he performs this operation on one side of the mouth,
and shows by it some bad projecting teeth, the effect is not reassuring."
Their conference was interrupted by official business. When Pollard
was again summoned, he continues, "I found a table neatly laid for
dinner with silver service and snow white napkins garnishing two
plates. 'Mr. P.,' said the General, 'you will get no dinner unless you
take some with me.'" During a meal consisting of soup, roast beef
and potatoes, apple sauce, apple pie, cheese, almonds and English wal-
nuts Pollard was forced to acknowledge Butler's graciousness as a host.
After the Negro orderlies had tiptoed out, General Butler lit his Havana and launched into "a long and entertaining talk." Butler told a
funny story of how he had once frightened a man belonging to the
Virginia Reserves by calling him a spy. "I must confess his laughter
was a little contagious as he gave the details of the interview." [25]

In the fall of 1864, learning that the Confederates were employing
110 Negro prisoners for work on the fortifications in his front, Butler
took the affidavits of three of the recaptured prisoners and sent them
to Commissioner Ould with the announcement that he had ordered
a like number of officers and soldiers captured by the Federals, prefer-
ably of the Virginia Reserves, to be put to digging in the canal
at Dutch Gap until this practice was stopped.

Included in the retaliation group were two superannuated employees of the Treasury Department in Richmond named Henly and
McCrae. Shortage of manpower had forced these old gentlemen into
the Confederate picket lines, and one night upon being relieved at
their advanced station they had become confused as to directions and
wandered across the Union lines, where they were held as deserters.

The pair when brought before General Butler begged him not to regard them as deserters because of their mistake, but to give them the same treatment as other prisoners of war. Because of the clothing shortage in Richmond, Mr. Henly was dressed in a threadbare black swallowtail coat and stovepipe hat, with a blanket about his thin shoulders, while Major McCrae wore his cast-off regimentals, and stood with head bent and features shaded by his little gray cap. Each of the old men sought with desperate gallantry to persuade the other that the stupidity which had brought this misfortune upon them was his and not the other's. "General Butler," reported the New York *Times,* "assured these poor old soldiers that they should be treated as prisoners of war, and in the morning they were sent off with a number of their fellow-patriots to the prison camp, Point Lookout." [26] From thence they were returned with a hundred others under a Negro guard to dig in Dutch Gap Canal. On reaching Dutch Gap, "Mr. McCrae addressed his fellow captives, stating that the retaliation was just, as of his own knowledge, he could say that negro soldiers had been used by the Confederate authorities in the manner complained of." [27]

Within a week General Robert E. Lee himself notified General Butler that he had ordered the defenders of Richmond to withdraw the Negro prisoners from the trenches and return them to prison as prisoners of war; and Butler at once removed the retaliation group from Dutch Gap.

In General Butler, as the Philadelphia *Inquirer* summed up Butler's experiment in retaliation, the Confederates found "a man not afraid to take the responsibility of acting promptly, energetick [sic] and decisively. Although they style him 'the Beast' they have learned by this time that he is not to be trifled with . . . The 'Beast' generally manages to get the best of Jeff Davis." [28]

23

MILITARY VS. CIVIL GOVERNMENT

W H E N Butler arrived in Virginia in November of 1863, loyalist civil
governments had already been "reconstructed" for governing the city
of Norfolk and the eastern outskirts of the state of Virginia which lay
behind the Union lines. These governments, begotten in a moment
when it seemed that Richmond and the rest of rebellious Virginia
might soon be won back by Union arms, were mere frameworks as
yet. There were a mayor and chief administrative officials, but no
adequate departments to provide street lights, sanitation, fire preven-
tion, police protection and poor relief. A loyal Governor and a legislature elected by a handful of professedly loyal citizens were ensconced
in a "State House" in Alexandria, Virginia, but their power was as yet
nominal. Owing to the complexities of his task as commander of an
important military department, Butler did not immediately become
aware of the existence of these governing bodies — not until Norfolk's
serious relief problem was dumped into his lap and the State Governor, Francis H. Pierpont, offered to grant commissions for officers for
the troops Butler was raising in Virginia. Always sensitive to the
humanitarian appeal, Butler promptly investigated the civil government in Norfolk. As for Governor Pierpont's offer to appoint his
officers, that courtesy Butler, with recollections of his tilt with Governor Andrew, firmly rejected.

Butler's detectives reported that Norfolk seethed with Secessionist
activity. There was open swearing against the United States Government in Johnson's Saloon. Ladies were smuggling letters through the
Federal lines. Confederate spies were all over the place and the townspeople were sheltering Confederate soldiers home on leave. Norfolk's

streets had not been lighted for months. Because the fire department had gone to pieces, a fire of suspected incendiary origin had burned several city blocks a few days before Butler arrived. Winter coming on and business depressed, the port of Norfolk still being closed and under military control, hundreds of people applied to Butler for relief.

Butler summoned the mayor of Norfolk, and, so that official thought, "indecently catechized" him for an hour on the affairs of the civil government.[1] The city of Norfolk was collecting enough money in taxes to pay the salaries of its officers and that was all. Butler ordered the embarrassed mayor to submit to him a complete financial report. When he learned that the City of Portsmouth, adjacent to Norfolk, was under a separate administration, he interrogated its mayor by mail: "Hundreds of your people are calling for aid to relieve them from cold and hunger. Until I can ascertain what the city is doing for them, without subjecting me to imposition and wrong, I can organize no system for their relief."[2]

The situation at Norfolk was comparable to that at New Orleans. As the Federal Government, heedless of Butler's experience in New Orleans in conducting relief work in a conquered territory, still allocated no funds for this purpose, Butler moved ahead with his own device of licensing trade to procure funds for relief and public services. To expedite confiscation of property owned by Rebels, Butler required all former citizens asking any favor or privilege of the government to take the oath of allegiance.[3] All transfers of real property by nonloyal citizens were declared illegal.

As in New Orleans, Butler found that bankers had smuggled out funds to aid the Confederacy. For refusing to explain why they had sent certain funds to Richmond, George M. Bain and W. H. W. Hodges, officials of a Portsmouth savings bank, were sent as prisoners to the army post at Fort Hatteras until they should be willing to answer the questions put to them. Rumors were circulated that these elderly bankers were being held in solitary on bread and water, and that Hodges had a 24-pound ball chained to his leg, and Confederate officials were so exercised over the rumors of maltreatment of the bankers that Commissioner Ould brought the matter up in his conference with Butler at Fortress Monroe and was privately assured that Bain and Hodges were being humanely treated, and never had been in irons.

Butler's provost marshals in Norfolk and Portsmouth took over the trials of all cases, from disorderly conduct to murder. After first obtaining permission from Washington, Butler engaged a Lowell engineer to repair the works of the Norfolk Gas Company and got the streets lighted. The ever-increasing population of Negroes Butler settled on abandoned farms around Norfolk. The cleaning of streets he turned over to convict labor, under a "live Yankee" from Massachusetts, who dressed his charges in black and gray uniforms with scarlet caps, and during the spring and summer carted out of the city thousands of loads of filth per week, a chore which Butler believed materially lessened the danger from yellow fever. A vigorous check-up by his detectives marked Butler's campaign against smuggling liquor into Norfolk and selling it to soldiers. Liquor licenses that had been granted by the civilian government were revoked by the commanding general and larger fees were required of the twelve dealers who alone were licensed under the new dispensation.

Butler's "usurpations" of the functions of the civilian government were denounced in the loyal legislature in Alexandria. In January of 1864 Governor Pierpont complained to President Lincoln that Butler's orders "tend to the oppression of the people." Pierpont asked that the President (1) stop the General's interference with the banks, (2) nullify his order that civic officers report to him the amounts of their salaries, (3) stop taxing trade, and (4) restrain provost courts from handling civil causes. "There is no sort of use for a Military Government in Norfolk or Portsmouth." [4]

Lincoln, recognizing the difficulties of the loyal Governor's position, and at the same time being unwilling to shackle General Butler, caused Stanton to relay to Butler a copy of Pierpont's protest. Butler's report to Lincoln of February 23 summarized the situation: "I found the streets, wharves, and squares of Norfolk in a most filthy, ruinous, and disordered state, so much so that life and limb are not safe upon them to the wayfarer, and in the coming summer, pestilence must ensue like the yellow fever of '53 unless large expenditures are made in cleansing and purifying them. I found the fire department entirely disorganized and its material out of repairs and useless. The city was unlighted for months, and the Gas Company being largely disloyal had refused to put their works in operation, so that it was impossible to properly guard or police it . . . I have already lighted the city . . . and am employing my convicts who are sentenced to hard labor in cleansing the streets and repairing them." [5] His dealings with the banks Butler explained as necessary to obtain funds to feed the poor.

Following this indecisive Round One of the tilt between military and civilian government, Butler forged ahead to enforce respect for law as administered by the black and white troops in his department. Churches were opened "to all officers and soldiers, white and colored." [6] Ministers who failed to take the oath of allegiance were forbidden to conduct religious services. Abandoned pulpits were filled by Union army chaplains.

Like his Woman Order, Butler's rough handling of ministers at Norfolk outraged Southern sensibilities. His policy toward the churches, groaned the Richmond *Sentinel,* "is the quintessence of a brutal and God-defying tyranny . . . How long — Oh, God, how long?" [7]

The Reverend George D. Armstrong before the war had written a widely circulated justification of slavery based on quotations from the Bible. Butler, accordingly, had his eye on the minister as a sort of bell-wether to the people of Norfolk. Mr. Armstrong took the oath, apparently, as did many people, to avoid confiscation of his property. As he emerged from the Provost Marshal's office in company with his father-in-law Charles Reid, who had also at the same time taken the repugnant oath, Reid expressed a desire "to spit in the face of the Northern Yankees." Armstrong now told around Portsmouth what Reid had said, as if to encourage others to take the oath in the same spirit.

Butler summoned him for an interview.

GENERAL: I have read a report, Mr. Armstrong, of an examination of yourself by my Aide-de-camp, Captain Edgar, in regard to the question of your loyalty. Now I need not say to a man as experienced as yourself that taking the Oath of Allegiance is only a *manifestation* of Loyalty. That as a man might join your Church and *still* be a very bad man after so doing, so a man might take the Oath of Allegiance and still be a very disloyal man.

ARMSTRONG: If you will allow me to make a statement to you I will do so, or I will answer such questions as you please.

GENERAL: Make your own statement, Sir.

ARMSTRONG: The view which I took of the oath was this. I believe the military Commander has a right to demand of the citizens at any time that they shall take a parole. I regarded Norfolk as for the present a conquered city . . . I took the oath with the honest intention of keeping it so far as my *actions* were concerned. *My feelings of course I cannot control* . . .

GENERAL: Now, Sir, what is the name of that Gentleman who had taken the oath, and while coming out of the Custom House with you, made the remark that he "would like to spit upon the Northern Yankees"?

ARMSTRONG: Mr. Charles Reid . . .

GENERAL: Where is Mr. Reid?

ARMSTRONG: He is in Norfolk.

GENERAL (to aide): Telegraph to Weldon [Provost Marshal of Norfolk] to arrest Chas. Reid and send him here. He lives on Main Street. (To Armstrong) He stated that, as he came out from taking the Oath?

ARMSTRONG: Yes, Sir.

GENERAL: With the Oath fresh on his lips, and the words hardly dry in his mouth, he said he "wanted to spit in the face of the Northern Yankees."

ARMSTRONG: Well, General, he *took it with the same view as I did*.

GENERAL: I agree to that, Sir.

ARMSTRONG: I meant to say —

GENERAL: Stop, Sir. I don't like to be insulted. You said, Sir, that damned infernal Secessionist wanted to spit in the faces of loyal men of this Union, and that you took the oath with the same view as he did, or rather he took it with the same view that you did. I have treated you, Sir, during this interview with propriety and courtesy up to this moment, and yet you, Sir, have told me, in order to clear this vile wretch, who shall be punished as he deserves, that you took the Oath to *my Government with the same view as he did* . . . Now, Sir, while you did preach a very virulent sermon upon "The Victory of Manassas," which I have read, at the recommendation of the Confederate Congress, have you ever since preached in your pulpit a sermon favorable to the Union cause, or one which would be likely to please the loyal and displease the disloyal?

ARMSTRONG: No sir, I never have . . .

GENERAL: I don't see, Sir, what good the Oath has been to you.

ARMSTRONG: I thought the Oath was an Oath of Amnesty.

GENERAL: You took the Oath, Sir, for the purpose of having the United States protect you, while you should by your conduct, and your life aid and comfort the Rebels. It is an Oath of Amnesty to those who take it in truth and come back repentant to the United States. You are a Presbyterian. A man comes to you. You are about to take him into communion. You say to him, "You have heretofore been a wicked man?" He says, "Yes, Sir." You ask him if he has experienced a change of heart. He says, "No Sir." You ask, "Are your sympathies with us or the Devil?" He says, "The Devil." You ask, "Which would you like to have prevail in this world, God or the Devil?" He says, "The Devil." You ask, "Where are your friends?" He says, "With the Devil." Then you ask him, "Do you think you can join the Church with your present feelings?" He replies, "I think I can to get the bread and wine at the altar." Think of it, Sir, anywhere else and as a man of Christian profession saying nothing of Christian practise, I call upon you to think of it. Sworn to be loyal and true to the United States, here you are with your sympathies against them. You, Sir, are a perjured man in the sight of God. It is an Oath of Amnesty to those who truly repent, precisely as Christ shed His blood for those who repent, but not for those who would crucify Him afresh. For you, Sir, it was an Oath of Amnesty. I should be just as wrong in receiving you, Sir, as a loyal man as you would be in receiving such a man as I have described into your church. (To an aide) Make an order that this man be committed to the Guard House in close confinement, there to remain until he can be conveyed to Fort Hatteras, there to be kept in solitary confinement until further orders, and send a copy of this examination to the official in command there.

ARMSTRONG: I am an old man, Sir. Won't you allow me to go home and get some clothes?

GENERAL: No, Sir. You may send for what you want and if they are proper for you to have you can have them. I wish the President of the United States were here to hear what his Oath of Amnesty is called by you, you unrepentant, wicked Rebel.[8]

In January of 1864 two Norfolk merchants who had taken the oath in order to continue in business began prompting Governor Pierpont on ways and means of getting rid of General Butler. They were Francis Zantzinger and J. T. Daniels of the firm of Zantzinger and Co. Zantzinger the senior partner was a member of the loyal legislature at Alexandria and a brother-in-law of Admiral Farragut's wife. Butler's agents, making a routine check on the amount of liquor the firm had on hand, found in a shed behind the store fifty-three barrels of whiskey that had not been declared. These barrels were hidden under a pile of hay and across the head of each barrel had been stenciled the label "cider vinegar." [9] Zantzinger and Daniels were tried in the Provost Court, and because they refused to open their books or offer any reasonable explanation, their undeclared liquor was confiscated and sold to a dealer from Massachusetts whom Butler had licensed.

Governor Pierpont, gathering information about Norfolk from second-hand sources in Alexandria and Washington, undertook now to defend his "loyal" retainers in a pamphlet which blasted Butler for his abuses of military power. J. K. Herbert, a Washington acquaintance, relayed to Butler a conversation he had had with Pierpont in a tavern:

> Whilst waiting for the ale, several items were talked over by us, but finally Gov. Pierpont said that he thought Norfolk was the greatest place for villany in the whole United States. "Well, Gov., who is the patron saint of the enterprize?" I asked. "Oh, Gen. Butler," he said; "he has transported the forty thieves from Boston." He told of a firm in Norfolk . . . who were called upon by your officer to know how much liquor they had on hand — as to the cellar they said "about fifteen barrels," as to the shed they said "go and see." And that on examination it was found that there were in the shed about forty bbls. marked "Cider Vinegar," and he said that it had been brought down from Richmond *before* the war broke out. He said that the liquor was all seized . . . and *sold at public auction* for over fifteen thousand dollars. He also said that in a few days after a Boston firm came in there and opened shop with a stock of about forty thousand dollars. He said you had no right to tax men in any shape whom the President had concluded to protect under his Am[nesty] Proc[lamation].[10]

While Pierpont's sixty-page pamphlet was in the press, the War Department heard of it and requested the Governor not to print it. Pierpont agreed to withhold it; but not until after review copies had gone out to several newspapers. After a partisan statement of the Zantzinger case and several others, Pierpont charged Butler with granting a monopoly of the liquor business in Norfolk to a "few men from Boston and Lowell." [11]

Accepting Pierpont's challenge, Butler set his detectives to work on the Zantzinger case, and in the course of that most crowded day, May 4th, when he launched his amphibious invasion of Bermuda Hundred, Butler wrote a tart letter to John M. Dunn, Tax Assessor of the civilian government at Norfolk, to explain what his own policy was. Butler could not resist the lawyer's jibe that if the *"soi disant* Governor of Virginia" could not run his government except upon revenue from the sale of liquor, his government "had better get itself out of existence." [12]

The facts on Zantzinger and Co. were completely unearthed. On October 28, 1863, Zantzinger in person had purchased seventy-five barrels of liquor from Jn. Scrymser and Co., 124 Front Street, New York. Since his permit called for vinegar he had labeled the barrels "cider vinegar." At the same time he purchased 1000 sacks of salt, when his permit allowed only 550. These articles with other merchandise were shipped on board the schooner *L. B. Cowperthwaite,* Captain Henry Rogers. The liquor was unloaded in Norfolk on November 7, 1863, and the fifty-three barrels were cached in the Zantzinger Company's shed. To the vessel's skipper, Captain Rogers, was paid a bribe of $1000 and to Lieutenant Hartley W. Sewell of the U.S. Revenue Service, $750. In the military court Rogers was fined $2000 and imprisoned for sixteen months while Sewell was cashiered from the Revenue Service and sentenced to prison for ten years. Butler had Zantzinger and Daniels brought to his headquarters in the field where he exacted their confessions and ordered them confined at hard labor in the trenches at Bermuda Hundred.[13] After three days they signed a letter of confession to Governor Pierpont and Butler released them.

Since Pierpont, confronted with this confession, stubbornly refused to retract his false charges against Butler, the latter took steps to liquidate Pierpont's civilian government in Norfolk. In a municipal election in June the "loyal" oath-taking citizens were called on to decide whether civil government should continue during the military occupation. Those who favored continuing it numbered 16, only a few more than the total of candidates actually running for office in that government — while 330 voted against it.

Butler accordingly issued a general order that the civilian government of Norfolk must cease, that any of its officials attempting to exercise their functions should be "stayed and quieted." [14]

For a month everything remained calm. Then public notice was served that Circuit Court Judge Edward K. Snead proposed to hold a session of his court in Norfolk, in defiance of Butler's decree abolishing the municipal government.

Butler dispatched a boat to Norfolk ordering the Provost Marshal to request Judge Snead to visit him at the front.[15] In the resultant interview Butler learned that Judge Snead was planning to open his court in defiance of what he regarded as an illegal order, his object being to raise a test case, which the President of the United States should have to decide. He had been assured by Attorney General Bates that General Butler had no right to set aside the loyal civil government in Norfolk, and had been counseled by Bates to open his court in defiance of the military.

Charmed with the frankness of the man, and sniffing a manipulation in Washington of which Snead was possibly only an agent, Butler lodged Snead in the guardhouse at the front "to be treated with tenderness and care." [16] To his wife Ben Butler confided, "They have laid a trap for me at Washington, to see if I cannot be caught on the Civil Government at Norfolk . . . I have arrested him, and shall hold him in spite of the Government's Attorney General. So you see we go. I will go home on the question before I will yield." [17]

Butler now laid the issue before President Lincoln. "It is not for the Comdg. General to use words of epithet upon the conduct of the Attorney General," wrote Butler. "If the learned Attorney General has a fancy for intermeddling with the affairs of disloyal people in a state, it might be suggested that Missouri opens a fine field for the exercise of his talents in that direction." [18]

On August 9, 1864, President Lincoln drafted the following reply to General Butler:

. . . your paper of the —— about Norfolk matters is received, as also was your other on the same general subject, dated I believe some time in

February last. This subject has caused considerable trouble, forcing me to give a good deal of time and reflection to it. I regret that crimination and recrimination are mingled in it. I surely need not assure you that I have no doubt of your loyalty and devoted patriotism; and I must tell you that I have no less confidence in those of Governor Peirpont [sic] and the Attorney General. The former . . . [is as] earnest, honest, and efficient to the extent of his means, as any other loyal governor . . . and the insignificance of the parts which are outside of the rebel lines and consequently within his reach, certainly gives a somewhat farcical air to his dominion; and I suppose he, as well as I, has considered that it could be useful for little else than as a nucleus to add to. The Attorney General only needs to be known to be relieved from all question of loyalty and thorough devotion to the National cause . . . Coming to the question itself, the military occupancy of Norfolk is a necessity with us. If you, as a department commander, find the cleansing of the city necessary to prevent assassinations and incendiarism among your men and stores; wharfage necessary to land and ship men and supplies; a large pauperism, badly conducted, at a needlessly large expense to the Government, and find also that these things, or any of them are not reasonably well attended to by the civil Government, you rightfully may and must take them into your own hands. But you should do so on your own avowed judgment of military necessity, and not seem to admit that there is no such necessity, by taking a vote of the people on the question. Nothing justifies the suspending of the civil by the military authority but military necessity, and of the existence of that necessity the military commander and not a popular vote, is to decide. And whatever is not within such necessity should be left undisturbed. In your paper of February you fairly notified me that you contemplated taking a popular vote; and if fault there be, it was my fault that I did not object to it then, which I probably should have done had I studied the subject as closely as I have since done. I now think I would better place whatever you feel is necessary to be done on this distinct ground of military necessity, openly discarding all reliance for what you do on any election . . .[19]

Lincoln did not finish the writing of this important letter to Butler of August 9. The Norfolk storm quieted down, and perhaps the President, as his irate Attorney General put it, "slurred it over in silence" so as not to offer General Butler cause again to "raise a hubbub about it."[20] After a brief detention Snead gave his parole not to hold court in opposition to the military and was released.

In midsummer while Butler was wrestling with tedious and repetitious siege operations in Virginia, he was afflicted by domestic grief in his personal household. Harriet Heard, Sarah's closest companion and Butler's favorite sister-in-law, had to be taken to Lowell in August 1864, having fallen victim to breast cancer, Sarah accompanying her.

Ben's letters to Sarah during this period were written in bed, the last thing at night or the first thing in the morning. They were shorter than Sarah's and sometimes were freighted with military problems:

Dearest:
 . . . I fear I cannot get away at present. Yesterday morning we crossed James River again and attacked the enemy at Deep Bottom . . . You cannot tell how homesick your descriptions of the place make me . . . I will try and come home if I can. Be sure of that. Meanwhile, write me a good long letter every day, and don't make me quite miserable by seeing you unhappy. Love to Blanche and the boys. Ask them if they would like to go up to the White Mountains.[21]

My dearest little wife:
 I have got your letter discribing the picnic. You do not know how homesick you make me feel . . . Poor Harriet! it seems so sad, and so good a woman, too, to be so afflicted. My very heart bleeds for her. Do all you can to make her happy . . .[22]

My dear Sarah:
 I got two letters from you last night. The mails are irregular. The proposition you make about becoming a member of the church is a most serious one. I do not wish to throw a single thought in the way as an obstacle. Mr. Edson's requirements may be few, but are the requirements of the church so? Can you say the *Creed* (*I believe*) with a full and firm faith? It is much to say. Can you believe the dogmas of the Church? That your life and thoughts are pure enough for the church or any where else I have never a doubt. The point is, do you believe in the "Holy Ghost, the Holy Catholic Church, the remission of sins," as taught by the church? If you do, and I do not say one word against your so believing, not even expressing a doubt, then be a member of the church — but not with any expectation of finding any more contentment in it than now unless you become a devotee, and that is a species of mania. This has been tried in all ages of the world and failed. The reasoning mind without faith desires something further, beyond, more

certain and convincing. The very doubts engendered by the connection with the church will become painful. If I *could* believe, I would become a member of the church, but alas! I haven't faith. You may have . . . *Yours truly,*

Benj. F. Butler[23]

My dearest wife:

We have made one demonstration north of the James . . . . Don't believe the silly newspaper stories about my sickness. I was with a headache caused by being all day out in the sun, on Sunday, and forthwith I am sick by the newspapers. I wish I could be reasonably sick, so as to get home.

Your husband and lover,

Benj.[24]

My Dearest Love:

What a pettish, mocking, sarcastic little thing it is? Railing at all the world, abusing the doctors, flying about, jumping out of its skin, and then boasting how "calm and smooth" it is going to be! How it would like to have me by to torment me good every way! I know the nature of the little creature thoroughly . . . I am in reasonably good health and hope to get to you soon for a flying visit . . . All the relation of things to each other may change . . . but there is one thing that cannot change and that is your unchanging, deep love for me, and my appreciation, reverence, and love of you, my own dearest wife.

Benj.[25]

A lull in activity at the front gave Butler a chance at the end of August to go to New York to probate the will of his brother Andrew, who had died in May; and then to make a hurried visit to Lowell the first days in September.

His visit home was not a very satisfactory trip, because a number of War Democrats seized this moment to badger him to run independently for President. For three years Butler had asserted that he would accept no political job until after the war, in the belief that the only road to the Presidency lay through Richmond or some other military victory. He was, however, in September of 1864 so discouraged over the military outlook that he listened to his tempters, and cut short his visit home in order to have more time with these political schemers in New York; although nothing came from the meetings. In mid-October Sarah brought Harriet and the children back to Fortress Monroe, since her sister would not be undergoing an operation.

Throughout 1864, though devoting his best energy to the military campaign below Richmond, Butler could not refrain in odd moments from a little quiet stirring of the political pot. His chief of staff, Colonel J. W. Shaffer, often in Washington on military business, kept in touch with Butler's friends in Congress. Thaddeus Stevens and Ben Wade, who became close political associates of Butler after the war, had been impressed by Butler's New York Music Hall speech on Reconstruction, and were reported as favoring Butler for President in 1864 if he could get the nomination. Several New York editors apparently considered him a good bet for 1864 provided he could take Richmond before the convention met: Raymond of the *Times,* Greeley of the *Tribune* and Bryant of the *Evening Post.* J. K. Herbert and George Opdyke were the center of a group of Butler supporters.[26] These adherents apparently expected the War Democrats to call a separate convention to nominate Butler, and after that failed to materialize they hoped to capture a cabinet post — either Seward's or Stanton's — for their favorite.

On November 1, 1864, Butler was summoned to Washington and given orders to take 5000 troops to New York City as a precaution against election-day disturbances. New York politicians and businessmen, recalling the draft riots of the year before, had appealed to the Government for adequate protection. There had been rumors that Richmond, in the last desperate throes of its struggle, would send fanatic Southern patriots into the chief Northern cities to incite riots and set fires on a wholesale scale. Recent raids by Secessionists across the Canadian frontier lent color to the rumors. Every day Northern papers carried stories of suspicious characters congregating on the northern border. As rumor had it, 15,000 Rebel zealots were in New York City alone preparing an election-day holocaust.

General Butler did not land his soldiers on Manhattan, but ringed the island around with troops on ferryboats ready on the instant to rush to any troubled area. In his headquarters in the Hoffman House he maintained telegraphic communication with each police station and precinct of the city.

The mere presence of Butler set off a certain amount of verbal fireworks. "No more appropriate term than 'writhing' can be applied to the actions of the Copperheads under the galling infliction of the presence of a man like Gen. Butler," reported the *Times*, "proverbial for his nerve, energy and fearlessness. They start the wildest rumors in regard to the General's orders, personal appearance and doings. If he asks a personal friend to call and see him, it is magnified into the arrest of half a dozen Copperheads. An hour's life gives the rumor strength and the number is increased to twenty, and your informant will give all the names and the color of the horses attached to the hacks which conveyed the victims to Fort Lafayette." [27]

An abnormally dull election day passed. "Well," sighed a disappointed editor, "Gen. Butler has been in active command of the city and State of New York for forty-eight hours. So far as we have heard, he has not yet erected a single gallows or hung anybody; he has crucified nobody; he has impaled nobody on a poker, or bastinadoed nobody. He has sent nobody to Fort Lafayette, and put nobody in chains or irons. He has suppressed no newspapers, and insulted no women." [28]

From the Secretary of War Butler obtained leave to remain over in New York a few days, to look after personal affairs, settlement of the estate of Andrew Jackson Butler, and a lawsuit against himself which had grown out of New Orleans charges. This delay in his return to the front enabled his New York friends to stage a reception and a political banquet for their prospective candidate for the Presidency.

On the afternoon of November 14, just before the reception at the Fifth Avenue Hotel, Butler received as a present from a jewelry company a pair of silver spurs, which he wore with his full-dress regalia at the reception. Guests crowded in early. At eight o'clock the band struck up "Hail to the Chief," and Butler was escorted in by the committee. Mrs. Butler entered on the arm of General Prosper M. Wetmore and Miss Blanche Butler was accompanied by ex-Mayor George Opdyke. "The General, who was in full uniform, received his numerous visitors with much urbanity and affability, bearing the terrible dislocating handshaking to which he was subjected with great fortitude." [29]

After Congressman James Wadsworth had assured General Butler of the company's desire to hear from him on the subject of the election and the future, the General, irrepressible, proposed amnesty to Southerners and pointed a way toward reconstruction.

> "War must come to an end, but how? . . . A war of this kind is to be prosecuted for the purpose of breaking down the power of those opposed to the Government, and bringing them into the fold of the Government, under the supremacy of the laws . . . Now is a good time for us to hold out to the deluded men of the South the olive branch of peace, and say to them, 'Come back, come back now. This is the last time of asking. Come back and leave the feeding upon the husks, and come with us to the fat of the land, and let by-gones be by-gones if by-gones are by-gones, and our country will live in peace hereafter.' [Loud applause.] . . . Let us not permit the rebel after he has fought as long as he can then, if he chooses, to come back. Let us state some time, perhaps the 8th of January . . . for all to lay down their arms and submit to the laws; and when that hour is passed, and every man who shall reject the proffered amity of a great and powerful nation speaking in love, in charity, in kindness, in hope of peace and quiet, forever to its rebel sons, — I say then let us meet him or them with sharp, quick, decisive war, which shall bring the Rebellion to an end forever, by the extinguishment of such men wherever they be found . . . But take counsel from the Roman method of carrying on war and say to our young men: 'Look to the fair fields of the Sunny South; they have refused our amity and offers of peace; they have turned away the day of grace; go down there in arms in support of the government, extinguish the rebellion, and you shall have what you conquer in fair division of the lands to each man in pay for his military service. We will open new land offices wherever our army marched, dividing the lands in the rebel States among our soldiers to be theirs and their heirs forever.' " [30]

Following the reception and Butler's address the men of the party retired to the hotel's dining room for a banquet and toasts. General Wetmore raised his glass significantly "to 1868." The Reverend Henry Ward Beecher, mounting a chair so as to be heard, declaimed:

"When we have tried honest, prudent, considerate Abraham [laughter], and he is tired and we need another man, if we cannot do better, I do trust there is no citizen present who would decline to act for a little while as President of the United States. The time may come when we need genius of executiveness (Reconstruction) and power of administration. [Cries "Butler, Butler"; "Yes, sir, he's the man."] If there is a man in the United States who has genius for administration I think that man is Butler. [Loud cheers: "Good, good": "Bravo."] I beg you to understand distinctly that I do not nominate him. ["Yes, Yes." Cheers. "Butler."] It will be proved in good time that the New York *Herald* nominated him. [Loud cheers.]" [31]

The New York *Herald,* ever hostile toward Butler, professed to be shocked at the spectacle of General Butler, "disguised in the plumage of war" yet appearing as "the dove, returning from the subsiding waters of the deluge and bearing in his mouth the olive branch of peace." [32]

This demonstration at the swank Fifth Avenue Hotel could not but strike a sour note with the newly victorious administration in Washington. When Butler, following his return to the front, renewed his feud with Governor Pierpont by ordering a military-sponsored election in the Western Shore counties of Virginia, President Lincoln on December 21, 1864, exhumed from his files the old letter of August 9 which he had not sent and dispatched it to Butler with a brief covering note:

> On the 9th of August last I began to write you a letter, the enclosed being a copy of so much as I then wrote. So far as it goes, it embraces the views I then entertained, and still entertain. A little relaxation of complaints made to me on the subject, occurring about that time, the letter was not finished and not sent. I now learn, correctly I suppose, that you have ordered an election similar to the one mentioned, to take place on the Eastern Shore of Virginia. Let this be suspended, at least, until conference with me, and obtaining my approval.[33]

But Butler did not receive this note from Lincoln on the controversy over military vs. civil government until after his own last act in the war.

24

FINALE AT FORT FISHER

AFTER Farragut's victory at Mobile Bay in August 1864, Wilmington, North Carolina, stood out as the one remaining objective of the Federal blockade. Choke off this last port of entry for supplies from the outside world and the Confederacy would soon be starved into submission. Although sealing the port was primarily the Navy's work, General Butler had early given it his attention. Wilmington fell within his Military Department of Virginia and North Carolina. The General had considered a scheme for running into the Cape Fear River a vessel of his Marine Brigade, and had sent Brigadier General Graham to Cape Fear to consult with Admiral S. P. Lee about the project. Were it found feasible, Graham was to dash through the blockade fleet and past Fort Fisher disguised as a blockade-runner, being chased the while by Lee's blockaders to give an air of realism to the hoax. Should he get inside the Cape Fear River, Graham was to ascend to the city of Wilmington and destroy Confederate shipping at its docks. The cautious Admiral Lee, however, had vetoed Butler's scheme, information having come in that the Confederates were stopping all boats at a chain barrier in the lower river.

In September, soon after Butler's return from Lowell, General Grant disclosed to him a plan for combined military and naval operations against Fort Fisher.[1] Grant asked Butler to send General Weitzel to make a reconnaissance of Fort Fisher, and in late September detailed General Weitzel as commander of the Army's contingent; but because of the heavy concentration of naval ships at Norfolk and the loose talk which advertised the forthcoming assault, Grant postponed the expedition.[2]

Godfrey Weitzel, who had led Butler's expedition into Lafourche,

Louisiana, was an intelligent, likable young man, and Butler had promoted him rapidly. But Weitzel at twenty-nine though a fledgling
major general of volunteers was only a captain in the Engineer Corps
of the Regular Army and was acutely conscious of his youth and lack
of experience. When Grant picked him as commander of the Fort
Fisher expedition, Weitzel wrote informally to Butler: "Now, this is all
very flattering and satisfactory to me and my friends. But I often, very
often (I tell you frankly) mistrust my own abilities. I think you are
over-rating me . . . I want first to feel satisfied that I am capable for
the position. I will take any one you think I am fit for, in spite of private feelings or the opinions of friends and relatives . . . But I don't
wish to be shoved ahead too fast." [3] This confession of mistrust and
uncertainty on Weitzel's part entered into Butler's decision to accompany the junior commander on the expedition.

Then, too, a feature of the Wilmington affair which especially
piqued Butler's interest was the opportunity to launch a spectacular
experiment. Why not, Butler reasoned, attempt first to neutralize Fort
Fisher by the explosion of a shipload of gunpowder? This done, the
Navy might enter the river while the fort's garrison was stunned by
the explosion, and the cost in lives lost might be held to a minimum.
A recent explosion of an ammunition barge at City Point had blown
up a pine wharf and a supply shed about a third of a mile long.[4] Hands
and feet and scalps of the victims had fallen as a ghastly rain about
the town. In September, Butler also read an account of an English
magazine explosion at Erith on the Thames which had leveled nearby
houses and broken window glass in London twenty miles off.

On his way through Washington to New York City at the time of
the Presidential election, Butler suggested his idea of a gunpowder
explosion to President Lincoln and Gustavus Fox, the Assistant Secretary of the Navy. If a ship loaded with 300 tons of powder could be
run close in under Fort Fisher and its cargo exploded all at the same
instant, Butler believed, the fort's garrison might be so far paralyzed
as to enable a landing party to seize the fort. Fox consulted various
army and navy ordnance experts but refused to accept their opinions
that the explosion of powder in an unconfined space would be like

firing feathers from muskets. Admiral Porter, whose own "crackpot" ideas of dummy battleships and siege mortars mounted on schooners had on occasion turned out well, matched Fox's enthusiasm for the project.

When Butler returned from New York in mid-November, Grant went for a week's visit with his family at Burlington, New Jersey, and during this week, while Butler as Senior Officer Present was exercising the supreme command in Virginia, the final agreement was made that the Navy should prepare an obsolete vessel to form the shell of a ship-torpedo and that its 300-ton powder charge would be furnished half by the Navy and half by the Army.

General Butler entertained Admiral Porter at dinner and an exhibition of fireworks at the Dutch Gap Canal, and Admiral and Mrs. Porter entertained General and Mrs. Butler with a ball on board the flagship, where the *entente cordiale* between the two parties was completed by the falling in love of the Admiral's aide Tom Selfridge and Miss Ellen Shepley, daughter of Butler's friend, the military commandant of Norfolk.[5]

Butler explained to Weitzel "that the rebels had frequently used torpedoes against us, and that we were going to use one against them larger than any they had ever used." He showed Weitzel a folio volume containing the adverse opinions of experts in Washington and then assured the younger man that he was himself going down with this expedition. "I am going to take you with two divisions down there, and see that this powder-boat is exploded properly."[6] Butler meant to make no secret of his intentions to accompany the expedition; but during the planning phrase of the preparation neither Grant nor Porter understood that Butler expected to go in person.

Grant, no Trojan horse type of strategist, frowned on the "gunpowder plot" as he phrased it, and directed that Butler increase by 300 or 400 percent the number of picks, axes and shovels to be taken on the expedition. He did not specifically direct Weitzel to enter upon a protracted siege, for he hoped it would be a quick move, a game of prisoners' base with the Federals slipping into Fort Fisher while most of the Confederate garrison were away fighting Sherman.

However, since the Navy was already dismasting and hollowing out the shell of the USS *Louisiana,* Grant did not veto the project. But early in December the Confederate concentration against Sherman led him to order Butler "to notify Admiral Porter and get off without any delay, with or without your powder boat." [7]

Butler telegraphed Porter: "When can you be ready with our little expedition? Captain Edson, ordnance officer at Fortress Monroe, will put ordnance stores at your disposal. Time is valuable from the news we get." [8] Porter replied: "We are ready for the one hundred and fifty (150) tons of powder. Will you give directions to have it bagged ready to go on board?" [9]

Preparations of the powder boat consumed several more days, during which tensions developed that shortly ended the era of good feeling. Several times Butler boarded Porter's flagship and the Admiral occasionally appeared at Butler's quarters. James Alden, captain of the *Brooklyn,* heard the Admiral say "that the General was very polite," and to the unsophisticated Alden these remarks augured "the best *entente cordiale* between them." [10] Porter's more critical fleet captain, K. R. Breese, however, told Weitzel that he thought General Butler too secretive about his plans: "I don't think the admiral knows what the general wants to do. I think the admiral feels a little sore that the general does not ask him anything, or tell him what he wants." [11] Admiral Porter later testified before the Joint Committee on the Conduct of the War that General Butler "never told me what his plans were . . . General Butler did come on board my vessel one night in Hampton Roads, with General Weitzel and Colonel Comstock, and asked me if I had a map of Cape Fear River, and I said I had. They asked my opinion of what I thought was the best way to go to work. They made no remarks whatsoever, but went into a far part of the cabin and consulted together. After they got through their conversation, they got up, bade me 'good evening,' and went off. That was the only consultation I ever had with them." [12]

On December 8 Butler embarked 6500 troops at Bermuda Hundred and stopped by City Point on his way down the river to let Grant know that he was off. "Then was the first that I ever dreamed of his going with the expedition," Grant testified later. "He knew that it was not intended that he should go. But all my orders and instructions were sent through him as commander of the department from which the troops intended for the expedition were taken, and also as commander of the department in which they were to operate." [13]

The departure from Hampton Roads was held up another three days by a storm, and during this interval the Admiral was allowed to surmise for himself the General's intention to go along. On December 10, Porter, growing angrier by the minute, wrote to Fox, "Butler has just put his troops on board the transports in all the rain and storm, and is now in a great hurry to get off. I believe the troops are all negroes, and I believe Butler is going himself to look on or direct — he had better leave it to Weitzel." [14] Fox showed this letter in Washington, and the faithful Sarah, who had Lady Macbeth's zest for signs and portents, wrote her husband that Fox had exhibited this missive so that "if anything adverse chanced, the Navy might be blameless . . . You know how Porter behaved at N. Orleans. He is the same man still." [15]

The storm letting up, Porter informed Butler that he would sail on the 13th. Since the slow and heavy monitors and the powder boat all had to be towed, the Admiral wanted to start thirty-six hours ahead of the speedier transports. The Admiral's wishes were followed, although Porter didn't think they were, and Butler didn't explain his plans ahead of time. At 3 P.M. on the 13th the army transports sailed out of Hampton Roads. Porter saw them leave; but he did not see that they turned north in Chesapeake Bay and ran up to show themselves in the Potomac, *in order to deceive enemy scouts on the Northern Neck*. During the following night, without lights, they retraced their course, and trailed the naval ships south from the Virginia Capes on the schedule that Porter had suggested.

Porter, deceived by Butler's fake departure, expected to find the army transports arrived ahead of him at his advanced base in Beaufort, North Carolina, but not finding them there he proceeded to load ammunition on the monitors and pack the last sixty tons of powder into the ship torpedo. During three days of waiting, his ordnance experts shifted many tons of bagged powder in an effort to assure as completely as possible instantaneous combustion of the entire mass.

Butler, meanwhile, having mistakenly understood through want of proper staff coordination, that he was to rendezvous with the fleet twenty-five miles to the east of Fort Fisher, arrived in that position on the evening of the 15th and there remained for three days before the naval forces of the expedition arrived from Beaufort on the night of the 18th.[16] These were days of "the finest possible weather and the smoothest sea," or so it seemed to the impatient general whose water and fuel were now running low. On the 16th, Admiral Porter not having arrived, Butler left his transports under low steam about twenty-five miles off Masonboro Inlet, some twenty miles north of the fort, and steamed down among the blockade vessels. To the horror of the blockaders, he ran close enough to the fort, with his colors flying, to count the several hulks of blockade-runners that had been wrecked in the channel and to run his eye over the mile-long notched horizon of Fort Fisher. Sandbags piled high over bombproof shelters between gun emplacements created this sawtooth silhouette. "I waited that day, which was very fine, and waited also the next day," Butler testified later. "The sea was so smooth that I lowered my gig and took a row for pleasure. There was not wind enough to fill the sail of a yawl boat that was let down." [17]

On the 16th he received a note from the Admiral advising that he hoped to explode the powder boat on the 18th and that during the explosion it would be well to have the transports about twenty-five miles away with fires drawn.

At 8 P.M. Porter's flagship the *Malvern* arrived at the rendezvous and the Admiral sent his fleet captain with a written notification that he had sent in the powder boat to be exploded, observing at the same time, "The weather looks threatening . . . the barometer is high yet, though the weather does not please me." [18] If Butler wished to land his troops at Masonboro Inlet, the Admiral offered naval landing craft to help get them ashore.

Butler emphatically did not want the powder boat exploded at this time. With a storm approaching, he felt uncertain of his ability to land his men and supplies. He preferred the explosion during calm weather, and at the dark of the moon, so that the ship torpedo could be taken in very close to the shore. And he had now waited so long for the Navy that his transports required water and fuel. He sent Weitzel and Comstock to the *Malvern* to present these considerations to Admiral Porter. His messengers shortly returned with word that the Admiral agreed with him and would dispatch a tug to delay the powder-boat experiment. And at the Admiral's suggestion Butler sent the transport fleet to Beaufort, in which safe anchorage they took on coal and water while storms lashed the coast for the next four days. Porter's fleet, meanwhile, including the top-heavy powder boat and the none-too-seaworthy monitors, rode out the foul weather at anchor in their open-sea rendezvous.

Not a little disturbed by the situation, while at Beaufort on the 20th, Ben wrote to Sarah: "Dearest Wife: I got your note last night off Wilmington. I am now here coaling. We have waited and lost three days, Friday, Saturday and Sunday, of as fine weather as ever was. The Admiral did not get here till Sunday night. We got here Thursday. He stopped at Beaufort." [19]

On Friday, December 23, Butler sent his aide Captain Clarke to Admiral Porter to say that he would finish coaling and be ready to commence the attack on Sunday morning, by which time he thought the sea would be smooth. Porter, on the other hand, thought that landing conditions would be right the next day, Saturday, and the weather being uncertain, he sent word to General Butler that he proposed to explode the powder vessel at 1 A.M. on Saturday. He believed that Butler would have plenty of time to arrive shortly after the explosion. Clarke left the Admiral at 1 P.M. and arrived after dark off Beaufort, seventy miles away, where because of rough weather he did not get inside to deliver his message until after daylight the next morning. By this time the powder boat had already been exploded.

Butler was furious. There welled up inside of him all the old bitterness of New Orleans, where "Mortar Fleet" Porter had received the surrender of the New Orleans forts without allowing General Butler the courtesy of being present at the ceremony! As Butler now

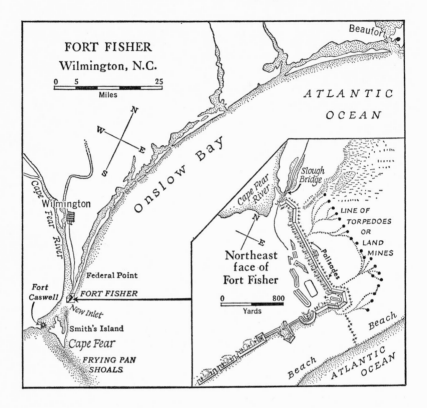

made all haste to get steam up on his transports and hurry them down to the rendezvous, he was plagued with the thought that Porter had deliberately cut him out of the proceedings. "My theory is that with these views of his the admiral supposed he would blow the fort all to pieces, and be able to land with his marines and take possession of it, so that he could say to General Butler when he got to Fort Fisher with his transports, 'Here general, this is Admiral Porter's fort, taken by him, "his work!" won't you take it and take care of it?' " [20]

Butler could hear the thunder of the Navy's bombardment of Fort Fisher for several hours before he arrived on the scene at 4 P.M. on Saturday, December 24th. Close in, within a mile of the shore, were the monitors, ugly, utilitarian, metal cheeseboxes on rafts, anchored in position, accepting the intermittent bursts of anger from the fort, in order to deliver their own missiles with precision. Beyond the monitors the wooden ships cruised on great arcs. From a distance at sea one could detect no change in the appearance of Fort Fisher. Butler sent Weitzel on board the flagship *Malvern* to make arrangements with the admiral for gunboats to cover the landing on the morrow, and for the loan of ships' boats to assist Butler's Marine Brigade in putting the troops on shore.

Butler's plan was to land a reconnaissance party, then an assault force. If everything went satisfactorily, he would land the rest of his men and supplies and entrench them. He had studied Grant's order as carefully as he would a legal document. "The object of the expedition," Grant had written on December 6, "will be gained by effecting a landing on the mainland between Cape Fear River and the Atlantic north of the north entrance to the river. Should such landing be effected whilst the enemy still hold Fort Fisher and the batteries guarding the entrance to the river, then the troops should entrench themselves, and by cooperating with the navy effect the reduction and capture of those places." [21] As Butler understood it, "effecting a landing" meant putting the entire force ashore with sufficient supplies to maintain them.

On Christmas morning a detail of naval gunboats shelled two enemy batteries protected by sandbanks a few miles north of Fort Fisher, and at noon Commander Oliver S. Glisson reported to the General that the beach was clear. Glisson was the blockade officer who had hauled Butler's transport off Frying Pan Shoals nearly three years ago when Butler was en route to New Orleans, and Porter's detailing of the tactful Glisson to aid Butler with the landing was evidence of his desire to promote amicable relations; although, like the general, he was openly suspicious of his teammate in the sister service.

The transport fleet followed Butler's "flagship," the *Ben Deford,* in within eight hundred yards of the beach and began disembarking. The troops, laden with knapsacks, muskets and forty rounds of ammunition, dropped into the boats and were rowed ashore by the seamen. The first troops hit the beach about 2 P.M. As soon as the landing was well started Butler in the gunboat *Chamberlain* ran down to a point within five hundred yards of Fort Fisher. Across the flat and almost treeless peninsula, he could see ships in the Cape Fear River beyond Fort Fisher. The Confederates in the two sandbank batteries (Flag Pond and Half Moon) surrendered without resistance. The sailors who rowed the landing boats ran up the beach and received the surrender of 65 prisoners from Flag Pond Hill Battery and Butler's troops bagged 218 at Half Moon Battery.

The reconnaissance party pushed down to the fort. One man peering through the sally port saw some of the fort's gunners huddled under bombproof traverses, another slid through a gap in the log palisade and seized a Confederate flag that had been cut off by naval fire. A Confederate courier was shot about half a mile from the fort and his dispatches and his mule were captured.

General Weitzel came off from shore and reported to General Butler that the fort, "as a defensive work, was not injured at all, except that one gun about midway of the land face was dismounted." [22] He had counted sixteen guns in proper position and apparently not injured. "The grass slopes of the traverses and of the parapet did not appear broken in the least . . . I did not see a single opening in the row of palisades that was in front of the ditch; it seemed to me perfectly intact." [23] Weitzel advised strongly against attempting to assault the fort, and Butler called to Colonel Comstock, Grant's engineer officer detailed to the expedition, "Jump into a boat with General Weitzel, pull ashore, and examine with General Weitzel, and report to me if an assault is feasible." [24] The two got ashore through a tumbling surf.

The weather roughening, General Graham, in charge of the Marine Brigade's landing craft, reported to Butler: "General, you have got either to provide for these troops tonight on shore some way, or get them off; because it is getting so rough that we cannot land much longer." [25]

In mid-afternoon the Admiral's flagship for the first time since its departure from Hampton Roads approached the General's headquarters boat and there was a brief exchange through speaking trumpets, of which two versions were given to the Committee on the Conduct of the War. Porter's account: ". . . finding that the men were not got on shore fast enough, I ran down in my flagship, and ran astern of General Butler's flagship, and asked him how he was getting on. He said, 'Very well.' I said, 'Do you want any more force?' I could not understand exactly what his reply was; but he seemed to think he had enough." [26] Butler's version: "I will state here that just before I started in on the reconnaissance Admiral Porter, with his flagship, sailed by mine, and with his speaking trumpet hailed me in these words: 'How do you do, general?' I answered, 'Very well, I thank you.' 'How many troops are you going to land?' 'All I can'; the navy having agreed to furnish me with the means of landing. Said the admiral, 'There is not a rebel within five miles of the fort. You have nothing to do but to land and take possession of it.' I had a different opinion, and avowed it. I said to those around me, 'I think there is a man on shore, by the name of Weitzel, who will find that out if it is so.' " [27]

The 218 prisoners captured by the Army at Half Moon Battery were from Confederate General Robert F. Hoke's brigade and had been moved from Petersburg after Butler left Virginia. They were the remainder of a regiment which could not be crowded into Fort Fisher's bomb proofs and had been sent up the beach out of the way of the naval fire. What damage had been inflicted by Saturday's bombardment? Two men killed, and one gun on the land face dismounted. To Butler's question about the powder vessel's explosion, Major Reese replied he had not known what it was, but supposed a boat had blown up; that "it jumped him and his men, who were lying on the ground, about like popcorn." [28]

It was now late afternoon, and growing dark, with another storm threatening. Already the landings were becoming difficult. If the men could be got ashore their supplies would be ruined in tumbling through the surf. In a blow the ships would have put to sea and would be unable to support the troops on the beach, who, moreover, might be shot up by Confederate naval vessels lying inside the river. That the powder boat had effected no damage at all Butler attributed to mismanagement on the part of the Navy. The latter's fatal delay at Beaufort, in Butler's opinion, had given the Confederates time to shift to

Wilmington and Fort Fisher the same troops that had been facing Butler in Virginia. With these facts in mind, Butler called off the landings and ordered the men back on the transports. By midnight the reembarkation had to be suspended because of dangerous surf. Of the 2100 to 2300 men who had been put on shore some 700 were left on the beach that night.

The next morning the transports rolled in swells so large that it was almost impossible for the soldiers to stand.[29] Having made arrangements for gunboat protection and removal of the men left on the beach, Butler sent word to Admiral Porter that, in his judgment, "nothing but the operations of a siege, which did not come within my instructions, would reduce the fort . . . I shall therefore sail for Hampton Roads as soon as the transport fleet can be got in order. My engineers and officers report Fort Fisher to me as substantially uninjured as a defensive work." [30] At eleven o'clock he sailed with his transports for Hampton Roads.

Butler dispatched a preliminary report to Grant, stopped overnight at Fortress Monroe, and returned early the next morning to City Point.

Grant, when around Butler, appeared to accept Butler's view that blame rested with the Navy for the delay at Beaufort during good weather and for the failure of Porter to run past the fort into the Cape Fear River, as Farragut had run through at New Orleans and Mobile Bay. The immediate publication of Porter's irate, anti-Butler dispatches, however, set off in the press a fresh stream of abuse against Butler.

That Lincoln was about ready to let the axe fall upon his scapegoat general was hinted in a report from James W. White, a political friend who about this time was attempting to persuade Lincoln to appoint Butler as Secretary of War. The President, wrote White, "was very noncommittal, or rather reticent as to his purposes; but very friendly personally in his mention of you, although I could discern that an idea had taken possession of him that he would no longer be *master* if you were in the Cabinet; and he, at one time, laughed in a manner that seemed to say 'that he saw how it would be, and knew a little too much to be caught in that way.' " [31]

On January 2, Butler was ordered by Grant to prepare an expedition "to report to Maj. Gen. W. T. Sherman at Savannah, Georgia." The troops were to be the same who had gone to Wilmington, plus one other brigade, sufficient to bring the total to 8000.[32] They were to be accompanied by a siege train, and the command of the expedition was assigned to Brevet Major General A. H. Terry.

The faithful Parton, infuriated by press tirades, wrote Butler a heartening note. "The malign bluster of that incomparable ass who commanded the fleet has harmed no one but himself. One of the Harper Brothers made this remark on the day of the publication of his report: 'To withdraw the troops without making an assault was a much braver action than to have ordered an assault.'" [33]

Unknown to Butler, meanwhile, Grant wrote Secretary of War Stanton on January 4 a request that General Butler be removed from his command. "In my absence, General Butler necessarily commands, and there is a lack of confidence felt in his military ability, making him an unsafe commander for a large army. His administration of the affairs of his Department is also objectionable." [34] Since no immediate action was taken on his request, Grant on January 6 telegraphed to President Lincoln: "I wrote a letter to the Secretary of War, which was mailed yesterday . . . I telegraph you asking that prompt action may be taken in the matter." [35]

At twelve o'clock noon on January 8, 1865, Grant's special messenger delivered at Butler's headquarters twenty miles above City Point a sealed envelope.[36]

> War Department, Adjutant General's
> Office, Washington
> January 7th, 1865

General Order, No. 1

    I. By direction of the President of the United States, Major General Benjamin F. Butler is relieved from the command of the Department of North Carolina and Virginia. Lieut. Gen. Grant will designate an officer to take this command temporarily.

    II. Maj. Gen. Butler on being relieved, will repair to Lowell, Mass., and report by letter to the Adjutant General of the Army.

> By order of the Secretary of War
> W. A. NICHOLS, Asst. Adjt. Gen'l.[37]

The labeling of the new expedition "for Sherman at Savannah" had been a ruse on the part of Grant to conceal momentarily from Butler and from the public the fact that the Fort Fisher troops now under General Terry were returning to Fort Fisher. In the second expedition the fort was assaulted by 9000 men, including seamen and marines; there were no delays due to powder boats and misunderstanding of plans; the naval bombardment was more thorough; the cooperation entirely sincere from the commanders down through the rank and file.

Any bright visions of winning the White House through success on the battlefield were extinguished for Butler by the brilliant achievement of the second expedition to Fort Fisher. Butler, who had delayed his return to Lowell, was in Washington testifying before the Joint Committee on the Conduct of the War when news of the great victory reached Washington to blast and sear his fame as a military man.[38]

PART FIVE

The Reformer

25

THE LEGEND OF THE SPOONS

As ADMINISTRATOR under military law of New Orleans and Norfolk, General Butler realized that he lived and worked "under the focus of a microscope, magnifying and distorting every action of mine a million times."[1] He preserved therefore with scrupulous care every scrap of written record. Even threats and libels were placed on file. There would be a day, Butler felt, when some "bitter rebel" whose property had been confiscated, some copperhead who felt that Butler had split the Democratic Party at Charleston, or some newsmonger whom Butler had banished from his Department would try to "get a rap at Old Cock-eye." And when that moment arrived Butler proposed to be able to take care of himself.

In his public relations, however, no prominent man of his day was so careless of the effect of his words or acts on the popular mind. In the Woman Order, for instance, he had intended no evil and had expected the public to judge the order by its results.

With plenty of clerks to copy and preserve his papers, General Butler was always ready, and even anxious, to "defy investigation." He held an exaggerated notion of the effectiveness of public investigations. He believed in the ability of the public, by mere reason and evidence, to erase from mind old prejudices based on error engrafted over months or years. What he failed to realize was that a picturesque popular belief, however fallacious, might outlive any number of investigations by Congressional committees, courts of inquiry, or civilian commissions.

After General Butler left New Orleans in December of 1862 there was circulated the canard that he had run off with the spoons of the St. Charles Hotel.[2] The hotel was an impersonal victim, a collective

symbol of the numerous property losses inflicted under the Federal
Confiscation Act upon a wide assortment of absent Rebels and Confederate sympathizers who refused to take the oath. The legend quickly
spread over the South that Butler had grown personally wealthy by
mulcting the people of New Orleans of their valuables. Inevitably the
Confederate proclamation of outlawry gained credence throughout the
South for all stories that abused "the Beast." The spoons tale immediately captured the Southern imagination, and in time it came to be whis-
pered in the North. After General Butler's recall from New Orleans
and again following the ill-fated Fort Fisher expedition the spoons
rumors burst openly in Congress.

The legend that General Butler was a thief rested primarily on four
New Orleans confiscation cases: the case of Alexander Brother's plate
and furniture; Adolphe Villeneuve's silver forks and spoons; Samuel
Smith & Company's $50,000 in gold; and the silverware and trophy
swords from the estate of the Confederate General David E. Twiggs.

Alexander Brother was one of the many New Orleans officials who
had been responsible for the destruction of public property at the
time the city was captured, and his furniture and silver plate were
seized under the Confiscation Act. Brother bribed a professed Unionist
to procure for him a pass and went to St. Louis. His story reached the
Senate via Senator Garrett Davis of Kentucky, and was widely circulated in the press. Senator Henry Wilson from Butler's state replied
to his colleague by an expression of confidence in the rightness of Butler's official action. At this time Butler pressed for a public investigation, but Davis and Wilson preferred to drop the matter after it had
been privately explained to the former. Butler then let the matter drop,
assuming that it would be futile for him to attempt to "answer newspaper paragraphs and slanders." [3] Meanwhile the corrosive little char-
acter-assassinating paragraphs in the press continued, and other cases,
like ghosts, arose.

In August 1862, Mrs. S. G. Ferguson obtained a pass from General
Butler's headquarters in New Orleans to join her family near Baton
Rouge.[4] Her pass stipulated that she carry with her her own wearing
apparel only. Federal officers making a routine search of her carriage
found in addition to clothing two bundles of New Orleans and New

York newspapers and a package of silverware and spoons. One of her packs of papers was addressed to a Mr. John Gillis at Woodside, Louisiana.

Mrs. Ferguson was brought back to headquarters and charged with smuggling. She was carrying the silverware, she explained, as a favor to Mr. M. Gillis, a resident of New Orleans. She was held a few days in the Custom House until Mr. M. Gillis was located and was then released, at which time the silver was not returned to her. Mr. M. Gillis failed to satisfy the authorities and was sent to Ship Island for imprisonment.

In December, General Butler having been relieved by General Banks, one Adolphe Villeneuve stepped forward as claimant of the Ferguson-Gillis silver. Villeneuve produced a bill of sale, dated 31 December 1860, which itemized the silver:

> 10 large silver tablespoons
> 8 large silver forks
> 10 large breakfast tablespoons
> 10 large breakfast table forks[5]

Villeneuve, claiming French citizenship, explained in a letter to General Butler that he had had no use for the silverware and had wished to lend it to John Gillis of Woodside, Louisiana, whose wife needed it. "The truth is, General, that Mrs. Ferguson, not knowing in her womanly simplicity the real meaning or indeed even the existence of the restriction stated on her pass, and not conceiving, moreover, that the innocent contents of those three bundles could even be considered as articles contraband of war, had not even an idea that she was thus contravening the provisions of the iron code which is here called Martial Law." [6]

Villeneuve's excuse for not coming forward earlier to claim his silverware was that he himself had had some difficulty with the authorities who had sought to eject him from his home and that he had been waiting for "a regular process in due form to be instituted against Mrs. Ferguson and Mr. M. Gillis, in order that I might myself intervene in the dispute and claim my property." [7]

Butler, remembering Mrs. Ferguson as "a strong-minded, high-cheek-boned, and rather brazen-faced Scotch woman, who had every other attribute that might belong to a woman rather than simplicity," [8] declined to reopen the case, particularly since he had already turned everything over to General Banks.

Three days later Villeneuve importuned General Banks to return his silver before General Butler and his officers left the department, their presence as witnesses being necessary. General Banks disregarded his plea.

After Butler's departure from New Orleans, Villeneuve appealed to General Shepley, military governor of Louisiana, who called on Colonel Stafford for a report. Stafford minuted on the back of Shepley's letter that the silverware had been turned over to Mr. D. C. G. Field, General Butler's financial agent, who had now departed with General Butler.

The intrepid Villeneuve, now fully convinced of General Butler's villainy toward himself, appealed to the French consul in New Orleans, and Count Méjan shunted the case to the French minister in Washington. The latter appealed to the Secretary of State, who in turn tossed it into the hopper at the War Department. The story of the "stolen spoons" had been circulating for some twelve months when Stanton in December 1863 endorsed Seward's letter and forwarded it to General Banks at New Orleans, "for investigation and report." [9]

From Banks it went to the Provost Marshal General who inquired of Chief Quartermaster Samuel B. Holabird, who in turn asked Assistant Quartermaster John W. McClure, who endorsed that silver belonging to Adolphe Villeneuve "was never in my possession." [10] Back through the chain of command to Washington went the "spoons" documents, the legend being freshly repeated at each turn of the merry-go-round.

On February 11, 1864, the War Department at long last relayed it to General Butler at Fortress Monroe. This was Butler's first attempt to dispose of any of the "spoons" cases. In a report to Stanton on March 12, 1864, he noted that there were two issues involved in the Villeneuve papers: (1) the validity of Villeneuve's claim that his silverware should be returned and (2) the report of General Banks and his officers that the silver was not left in New Orleans when they took over the command. [11]

The natural order of the consideration of these subjects will be to take the last first, because, if the property cannot be found, and if, as is alleged in the report of that officer, it still remained in the hands of my financial agent, I am responsible for it; and therefore should be under great inducement to make a case against M. Villeneuve in order not to be called to an account for the property. But if the property is still in the hands of the present Commander of the Dept. of the Gulf, then I shall stand as a disinterested witness on behalf of the United States, and the facts and circumstances that I report will be entitled to the credit due to such a witness.

I have more than a common interest in the first branch of this inquiry, because this is not the first time I have been called upon, as well in public prints as by official papers, to account for the articles of property of great value which were left by me for the benefit of the United States [with those] who were sent by the War Department of the United States to relieve me in the command of the Dept. of the Gulf. A notable instance of this sort of accusation was an attack made in the Senate of the United States by Senator Davis of Kentucky, alleging that I had retained for my own use, and embezzled for my own benefit, the silverplate of Alexander Brother, a rebel of La. And again in this case, this plate of M. Villeneuve, which John W. McClure, Capt. and Asst. Quartermaster, has endorsed upon the report was never in his possession, was in fact on or about the 21st of December, 1862, turned over to him by my Financial Agent, David C. G. Field, Esq., and McClure's receipt as Quartermaster taken therefor by order of Gen. Banks, which receipt I now have; so that if McClure has not accounted to the proper officer for that plate, it is because he has embezzled the same and I desire and respectfully but earnestly demand that the matter may be investigated by the proper officers.[12]

Butler sent his report to the Assistant Adjutant General, requesting as a personal favor that he bring it to the notice of Secretary Stanton. "I have suffered so much and so often from the denials of the receipt of articles by the officers who succeeded me and mine in the Department of the Gulf, which have left me open to unjust accusations, that I have strong feelings on the subject, and at least wish to be fully justified in the minds of my immediate superiors." He also desired as a personal request of the Secretary permission "to publish this report in my own vindication." [13]

To clear up the thievery charge, Butler engaged one of Sarah's brothers-in-law, J. M. G. Parker, now postmaster in New Orleans, by quiet detective work to discover whether the Villeneuve silver was "doing duty on General Banks's table." [14] He also sent Field to New Orleans to interview McClure in person and jog his memory.

Field had a satisfactory interview and reported by letter on April 29, 1864. "I have seen McClure, who now says that the Villeneuve silver 'has been in his possession,' and that he sold it and accounted for it in his 'abstract.' He says that he made his endorsement owing to its having been marked 'Gillis' instead of 'Villeneuve.' " [15]

Stanton, meanwhile, although he approved as "entirely satisfactory" the report of Butler's financial agent, still withheld from Butler permission to publish his report. The coveted investigation, accordingly, was out for the present — and another ghost arose.

About the time Butler arrived in New Orleans one Samuel Smith, a banker, secretly bricked in the space between his safe and the outside wall of his building and hid therein $59,855 in gold and silver. Butler's ferrets, examining all the banks of New Orleans in an effort to locate the bullion which the Confederates had removed from the U.S. Mint, found evidence that Samuel Smith & Co. must have in their possession the sum of $50,000 in gold. Of this Smith when questioned by Butler denied any knowledge. As he was known to have been a member of the Confederate Home Guards and "a bitter, active and unrelenting Rebel," his word was not accepted. His seized books, "erased for the occasion," contained curious references on one page to $50,000 of "lead" and on the next page to $50,000 of "tin." [16] Butler, feeling certain that Smith was lying, ordered him to be imprisoned in Fort Jackson. Smith now disclosed the hiding place of his bullion, and two kegs, each containing $25,000 in gold, were seized, along with $9855 in silver.

Butler's investigating commission decided that the silver ($9855) should be returned to the banker, but that the two kegs of gold ($50,000), in their opinion not properly accounted for, should be held as possibly liable for confiscation by the Government, and that the case should be submitted to the Treasury Department. Butler sent the minutes of the investigation to the Treasury Department, returned to Smith his $9855 in silver, and retained the $50,000 in gold.

He would have sent the $50,000 to the Treasury immediately had not an emergency developed which he explained to Secretary Chase on July 2, 1862.[17] Owing to an error in the quartermaster department, two paymasters had come down to New Orleans with $285,000 too little money to pay the troops. Butler used the $50,000 over and over again to pay his men, borrowing it repeatedly from Adams & Co. as rapidly as the men turned it in to them on allotments to be sent home. Months later the Treasury refunded to General Butler the $50,000, and he found himself holding "hot" money, for which apparently neither the War Department nor the Treasury was anxious to assume responsibility.

On February 11, 1863, when he settled his New Orleans accounts at the War Department, he explained to Stanton "that as a lawyer I supposed I might be held personally liable for the sum, and that if he would give me an Order to pay over the money to the War Office, in such form as to release me from responsibility, if hereafter called upon by Smith & Co., I should be glad to pay the money over."[18] Stanton doubted whether this could be done, and suggested that the money lie in Butler's hands until the Department was called upon for it, and that a proper memorandum should be put on file, so that Smith & Co.'s rights, if any, should be preserved. Butler, accordingly, filed a memorandum with the War Department, and kept the $50,000 pending future disposition of the case.

During the next year Samuel Smith took the oath of allegiance, moved to New York City, and engaged two lawyers, of whom one was Reverdy Johnson, the hostile investigator of New Orleans consular cases, and the other, Edwards Pierrepont, a younger lawyer.

Pierrepont suggested that Butler "pass over" the money to either the War Department or the Treasury and "leave me to such remedy there as the Government may think fit."[19] Butler explained Stanton's wish that the money remain in his hands until the Department was called upon for it, and offered to turn in the money as suggested, if only the War Department would direct him to do so and relieve him from personal responsibility.

Unfortunately Pierrepont could not persuade Stanton to execute the required order and release. The story that General Butler had in his possession $50,000 taken from a New Orleans banker gained wider and wider circulation. S. H. Gay of the New York *Tribune* in October 1864 offered to publish Butler's side of the story but the General, forbidden to publish while in uniform, had to forego this opportunity.

He now suggested that Pierrepont apply to President Lincoln for the order and release. "I took the money . . . from at the time rebellious citizens of the Confederate States, by their own oath of allegiance to that supposed government. I used it as a military officer for the service of my army. It was repaid me, and is now held by me as an officer of the Government to be paid on its order or by its permission. What I would or would not do were it left to my judgment is not the question. I should make myself, I think, personally responsible were I to attempt to act without direction. You will do me a favor if you will get the order for payment. If such is the determination of the Government, they have all the papers before them, and have the power and right to determine the question. It is the only thing that gives me any uneasiness in case of my death. But that must be borne like everything else that comes in the course of duty." [20]

On October 25, 1864, Pierrepont, failing again to obtain the order and release, brought suit against General Butler in the Court of Common Pleas in New York City.[21] Butler acknowledged the summons. Since he was shortly going to New York anyway, to preserve order during the Presidential election, he could hardly proceed there incognito. He engaged a New York lawyer to defend him and get the case transferred to the United States Circuit Court.

Butler hoped that bringing the suit would force the Government to take action. In any case the courtroom would constitute a forum for airing the truth. Once again Butler wrote a lengthy survey of the Smith case for Secretary Stanton. He asked that the War Department assume the cost of defending the suit, or else strike the whole matter off his accounts so that he could assume the responsibility to settle or defend. He hoped that the United States would defend the case and retain the money. "As this suit has been made the ground of public assault upon my integrity as an officer through the newspapers, and as my silence enforced upon the subject by the regulations of the service may lead even good men to misconstructions and doubt of the propriety of my action in the premises, I respectfully ask leave to publish this official note to the War Department in my justification, which as you are aware under the regulations without permission I could not do." [22]

Stanton, being ill at this time, was not shown Butler's communication for several weeks. Then he granted permission for him to publish the letter, but instead of taking over the defense of the suit or releasing Butler from responsibility, Stanton referred this legal conundrum to the Judge Advocate General. The latter, not acquainted with the case, proceeded to misunderstand Butler as applying for indemnity! The Judge Advocate General's decision, approved by Stanton, was therefore, that Butler should await the outcome of the suit!

As he was leaving for Fort Fisher, Butler sent copies of his correspondence with Lawyer Pierrepont to his friend in the Senate, Henry Wilson, and to his own lawyer, John K. Hackett. "If in the Providence of God I shall fall," he wrote to Wilson, "please see to it that justice is done to my memory for the sake of my children. If I live (and I have no fear but I shall) I can take care of myself." [23]

The question of when and how to publish the facts about the Smith case was solved shortly after Butler's return from Fort Fisher by Representative James Brooks, of New York. Brooks accepted the "spoons" legend as fact and was mortified that the New Orleans "rebel tamer" should have been sent to Brooks's native New York City during the Presidential election. In the heat of debate on January 6, 1865, Representative Brooks declared: "I am bound to say that an effort was made by the Federal Government, during the pendency of the late Presidential election to control the City of New York by sending there a bold robber, in the person of a Major General of the United States." [24] Some papers printed it "bold" robber, some "gold," but either to Butler was anathema.

He sent a copy of the quotation to the Speaker of the House, asking an investigation by a committee of the House. He desired, he wrote the Speaker, "to have put in issue every official act of my public life which can in any way be supposed to affect my official integrity or personal honor." [25] And he sent another copy of Brooks's remarks to Mr.

Brooks himself. General Butler's aide, Captain H. C. Clarke, delivered
the message to Congressman Brooks while he was at breakfast:

Washington, Jany. 20th, 1865

James Brooks, *Member of House of Representatives*

Sir: I find in the Daily Globe, of the 7th instant, a report of your
remarks in the House of Representatives on the 6th instant, an extract
of which is appended.

I have the honor to inquire whether your remarks are here correctly
reported, except perhaps the misprint of *bold* for *gold,* as the remarks
were quoted in other papers, and also whether there were any modifications, explanations, or limitations made by you other than appear in this
report.

The gentleman who hands you this will await, or call for an answer
at any time or place you may designate.

Very respectfully, Benj. F. Butler, *Maj. Gen'l* [26]

To Mr. Brooks this communication read like a challenge to a duel.
He told Captain Clarke that he could not give him an immediate answer, and when, later in the day, he read the letter in the House he
branded it as an invasion of Congressional privilege for having been
delivered by a military man "in full panoply."

Representative George S. Boutwell, of General Butler's home district,
arose to a question of order that the letter did not violate the congressman's rights.

Speaker Colfax ruled that the language of the note was not necessarily a challenge to a duel and thus was not infringement of privilege. "It
seemed to the chair not improper that a person who had been charged
here as a gold robber should inquire if this charge was correctly reported, and whether there was not some explanation or qualification of
it." [27]

Cries arose all over the House for Mr. Brooks to state his reasons for
calling General Butler a "gold robber," and for this purpose the rules
were suspended, by an overwhelming vote, despite Thad Stevens' objection that the whole business was only "to gratify the filthiest garbage
from foul stomachs, cast up by malignant hate." [28] Mr. Brooks sketched

in outline the case of Samuel Smith & Co. Vs. Benjamin F. Butler, now pending in New York City, in which the plaintiff alleged that the defendant while in New Orleans had stolen from Smith's vault $50,000 in gold, which he now had in his personal possession.

General Butler turned over the complete correspondence in the case to Representative Boutwell, and rode with him in the carriage the morning of January 24, sorting the papers as they mounted Capitol Hill.

The floor and galleries of the House were crowded with Senators and other visitors. After the clerk had read the documents in the case, Boutwell asked Brooks to reaffirm or retract his statements of the day before. The unhappy Brooks took refuge in counter charges and generalities — "If Smith & Co. concealed their gold, they but paid a proper tribute to the character of Butler when they supposed they would be plundered by him . . ." Brooks was now verbally cudgeled by Thad Stevens for neither admitting his error nor sticking to the point. "The gentleman who used every epithet of slander with a most foul tongue, against an absent man in the service of his country, who calls a Major General a 'gold robber' and 'cotton speculator,' and as 'dealing in contraband articles with the enemies of his country,' talks about language learned in Newgate, Cripplesgate, and Billingsgate. In all the gates there is a gate which the gentleman will enter and which I shall try to avoid. [Laughter] . . . There is not a candid and honest man in this House who would dare to say the evidence is not a complete vindication from all the charges of the gentleman from New York." [29]

So far as it was possible to shut it off, the abuse of Butler as a result of the Smith case was now checked. The case itself, however, dragged on for many months and finally was settled out of court by Butler's paying the money over to Smith & Co., the Government's rights having been tacitly waived by its failure to take action.

The case of Rowena Florence Vs. Benjamin F. Butler was instituted in the Superior Court of New York in 1869, for the return of General Twiggs's trophy swords and silver plate to his niece Miss Florence.

In June of 1862 in New Orleans General Butler confiscated for the

Government the personal property of Confederate General David E. Twiggs, whose house Butler himself occupied. One day a mulatto, former coachman to General Twiggs, informed the General that he had in his possession three swords and a box of silverware belonging to General Twiggs, which had been left with him by Twiggs's niece. Butler caused the swords and silverware to be dug up from their hiding place in the colored man's back yard and sequestered with the rest of Twiggs's property.

Miss Florence now appeared before the General with a paper written by her uncle to support her claim: "I leave my swords to Miss Rowena Florence, and box of silver. New Orleans, April 25, 1862. David E. Twiggs." [30] This General Butler refused to accept as a deed of gift, since the writer had been so obviously in flight ahead of Farragut's fleet.

No special confiscation papers were made out to cover the Twiggs silver, as it was simply returned to its wonted place on the sideboard in the Twiggs dining room, and used as a part of the furnishings of the residence. And when Butler left New Orleans he took from Banks's quartermaster no special receipt for the silver, but "a receipt for the house and everything that was in it." [31]

To President Lincoln Butler sent the swords, mementos of Twiggs's distinguished service with the U.S. Army in the Mexican War. Butler ventured to suggest to the President that the sword once awarded to Twiggs be presented again by Congress to some loyal officer.

President Lincoln on December 16, 1862, placed the swords at the disposal of Congress with the recommendation that they consider awarding one of them to General Butler. Accordingly, Senator Henry Wilson, on January 7, 1863, introduced a joint resolution that the "sword voted by Congress on the second March, 1847, . . . be presented to Major General Benjamin F. Butler, as a reward for his distinguished military services during the present campaign." [32] The resolution, read and passed to a second reading, was then pigeonholed in Committee, because at this time Senator Garrett Davis was trumpeting his accusations about the spoons.

The swords of General Twiggs remained in a corner in the White

House for several years until General Butler, in paying a call on President Johnson, saw them, and had them removed to the Treasury Building. There they remained throughout the trial of Rowena Florence Vs. Benjamin F. Butler in 1869. Miss Florence's claim for the Twiggs silverware was more difficult to refute because no special receipt had been taken to cover it when Butler left New Orleans, it having been listed merely as a part of the furnishings in the Twiggs house. Butler engaged a detective, one C. Black, to make a private investigation in New Orleans. Black found that the mulatto coachman, the informer in the case, had died in 1868. He located an aged Negro woman who had known about the plate and might be able to describe it, but she had been bedridden for three months and was not approachable on April 14, 1870, when Black sent in his report.[33] The best guess as to what had happened to the Twiggs plate is that it was sold, as were many lots of government-seized silverware, for metal. D. C. G. Fields while searching for the Villeneuve silver in 1864, was told by McClure at that time that the Twiggs plate had been sold for "pure silver." And in 1887 one John Highland, who had supplied fuel to government offices in New Orleans during the war, wrote Butler the following account: "One day I went to the office of Captain McClure, which was on Camp Street opposite Lafayette Square, and known as the Jackson Rail Road Depot Office . . . Captain McClure called on me to place on the scales a lot of silverware which formerly belonged to General Twiggs . . . He opened the vault that stood in the corner of the office, and took therefrom the silverware so often spoken about. I placed it on the scales, the Captain taking the weight, which was to the best of my recollection 16 pounds (or sixteen pounds 5 ounces), but it was either one or the other. I saw Captain McClure put the silver back in the vault." Highland volunteered further that he had once been knocked down in New Orleans for maintaining the honesty of General Butler. "The bigger the lie them days the more it was appreciated by some parties."[34]

The case of Rowena Florence Vs. Benjamin F. Butler was adjudicated in the latter's favor. Miss Florence's claim for the silverware was denied, and the swords remained in the Treasury Building until the late 1870's when Butler was instrumental in having the Secretary of the

Treasury deliver them to General Twiggs's daughter, Mrs. Marion Twiggs Myers.

A war veteran so prominent as General Butler, especially one who entered politics in the turbulent, postwar years, could scarcely hope to scotch the spoons legend despite the clean bill of health vouchsafed him in the courtrooms. Cartoonists played with the idea in every conceivable way, even making faces out of spoons that bore no mean resemblance to General Butler himself. The spoon became a favorite piece of stage equipment for politicians opposed to him. A fly-by-night New York City editor named Pomeroy gained notoriety as the author of a campaign document labeled "A Spoony Biography," and as an advertisement he stood up outside of his printing shop a wooden figure faintly reminiscent of the General which grasped like a spear an enormous wooden spoon.

Spoon stories about General Butler entered into the folklore of the country.

In the end Butler, who could resist anything but humor, was himself compelled to laugh at these yarns and even to contribute to their whimsical progress. Once while the General was making a political speech some pranksters lowered a spoon on a string from the rafters overhead. As the spoon descended it caught the speaker midway in a gesture of emphasis. Butler froze instantly, disengaged the spoon, and remarked, "That was one I didn't get!" [35]

26

RETURN TO THE LAW

"THOSE who think Gen. Butler's fortune was derived solely from the plunder of Louisiana and Virginia, should look into the [Middlesex] Company's books, and learn their mistake," wrote Charles Cowley in his *Illustrated History of Lowell* (Boston, 1868).[1] The cotton mills of Butler's home town suffered during the war from shortages of raw material. But the Middlesex Company manufactured woolen goods and was not handicapped by cotton shortages. At the wartime peak its 16,400 spindles and 262 looms enabled Middlesex to declare a dividend every few months. For the year ending May 1, 1863, for example, their dividends ran to 51 percent. In this prosperous company General Butler owned 115 shares worth $317 per share, and with Fisher Hildreth a half interest in a block of 17 shares. The treasurer of the company, Richard S. Fay, Jr., reported that Butler's balance on the company's books for the year 1863 was $101,367.29.

During the twenty-five years since he commenced practicing law he had accumulated over $100,000 in real estate near Lowell, including the Belvidere homestead, valued at $50,000. To his real estate holdings he added in the years immediately following the war a summer home near Gloucester, built upon a fine 47-acre tract overlooking Ipswich Bay. This home, called "Bay View," was listed for tax purposes at $15,000. At Fortress Monroe during the war he purchased several confiscated farms and turned them over as cooperative ventures to a dozen Negro families. Then in the months following his recall after Fort Fisher, through Fisher Hildreth, Butler took a $20,000 mortgage on the buildings of the defunct Chesapeake Female Seminary at Hampton, and through another brother-in-law, William P. Webster, he made other speculative purchases in the Norfolk area.[2]

General Butler's fortune gained through his prewar law practice and business investments ran easily in excess of a quarter of a million dollars by the close of the Civil War.

On March 14, 1865, in a moment of pique against West Point generals, Butler offered $5000 to the Academy at Andover subject to the condition that they grant "a scholarship for my black boy, the son of a soldier that I am to educate for West Point so that we may have at least one competent colored officer to two hundred thousand colored soldiers." [3]   When his alma mater, Waterville College, approached him for a gift — at an unfortunate moment when the "spoons" charges were being agitated — Butler declined to contribute, but on September 7, 1865, he quietly made out to them a check for $1000. On May 11, 1866, he gave $1000 toward the purchase of St. Anne's parsonage. [4]

As a businessman he enjoyed taking a chance. In the summer of 1863, after New Orleans, he spent a month in a tent on the beach at Gloucester resting with his family. His eye caught a promising outcrop of granite, and the result was the formation of the Cape Ann Granite Company. His election to Congress in 1866 he owed in part to his owning property in Gloucester, which district he at first represented. The Cape Ann Granite Company might have prospered under other directors, but Congressman Butler had a quicker eye than most men for discovering places where granite would be useful — for instance in Government offices in Washington. And in the 1870's, after Ben and Sarah decided to build their quarter-million-dollar home in Washington on the corner of B Street and South Capitol, in full view of the east portico of the Capitol, the material used was Cape Ann granite.

During the last months of the war General Butler asked his friend Gustavus Fox why all the flags used by the Navy and Army were made of imported materials. Fox told him that bunting had never been manufactured in this country. Butler presented the technical problem to D. W. C. Farrington, a Lowell manufacturer, got a bill through Congress, which Lincoln signed on March 3, 1865, to guarantee a market for the domestic product, and presently the U.S. Bunting Co. was at work with twelve looms turning out the first bunting of American manufacture for the Army, the Navy and Government buildings. [5]

As a manufacturer he furrowed his brows over high freight rates, with the result that the Pentuket Navigation Company was formed to tug coal barges up the Merrimack River in competition with the "monopolistic" Boston and Lowell Railroad. Butler persuaded Congress to clear the riverbed, and in the fall of 1872 the first scow loaded with coal was brought up the river. "General Butler, commanding in person, was perched on a camp stool on top of the pilot house leisurely smoking his cigar, and directing the cannon-firing as the several villages were passed." [6]

Business ventures spawned from his fertile brain were not all successful. The 200,000 acres of timberland in southwest Virginia, upon which General Butler hoped to establish settlers and to open up coal mines, never earned a penny. The best acres were seized by squatters, who hauled off the timber and defied prosecution. Eventually after the General's death the land was sold for taxes.

The Lower California Corporation, formed by Benjamin F. Butler, August Belmont and others, obtained from the Mexican government a grant of 46,800 square miles of its western peninsula. The amateur empire builders proposed to colonize this territory and develop mines, shipping and pearl fisheries. When they came to survey their plat, however, the abashed corporation officials discovered that the Mexicans had so drawn the boundaries around their grant of mesquite-covered hills as to exclude the only two useful strips of coastline in the territory. [7]

In southeastern Colorado Butler took a gamble on several hundred thousand acres of grazing land which brought him more headaches in litigation to clear its title than the land was worth during his lifetime. Butler often fought his natural tendency to speculate in mining stock, but in the case of Mountain Mining Company, a North Carolina gold mining company organized to exploit a chemist's process for desulphurization of metals, the wings of the Icarian general were clipped to the tune of $19,000. [8]

As an industrialist Ben Butler was able to put in practice some of his ideas as a social reformer. In the Middlesex mills, he dropped the hours from the prevailing eleven and one half to ten hours per day. This might have operated in his favor politically, had it not been for the fact that he did not arbitrarily enforce the ten-hour day. During the rush seasons, any operative who wished to work longer than Butler's standard ten hours was permitted to do so, for additional pay. Thus in the oratory of the platform his political opponents often found it convenient to misunderstand Butler's arrangement and accused the "millionaire industrialist" of being an inconsistent social reformer.

In his postwar career as a lawyer, General Butler maintained offices in Boston, New York, and Washington. In cases for individuals his retainer now commonly ran from $100 to $500, and for corporations $1000 to $5000, depending on the amount of money involved. In addition to retainer his client was presented a bill in which all expenses were itemized at the following rates: time in preparation in office $100 per day, time in lower courtroom $150 per day, time in Supreme Court $250 per day, with actual costs of transportation, stenographers, and printing. Deterred by high fees, few clients now came to him to have their cases started. "In later years," he noted in his autobiography, "I have been applied to most frequently to take charge of cases that have been substantially lost by proceedings had in them before they came to me, cases that in many instances could have been won if they had been properly taken in hand earlier. In other words I am called in largely in desperate cases. But I have made it the rule of my life never to refuse to assist in trying cases, however desperate, if I believe there is any chance to win." [9]

An earnest pleader, his effectiveness was sometimes enhanced by his finding an angle of his client's case that was highly personal to himself. The important Milligan habeas corpus case was an example. Lambdin P. Milligan of Indiana had been arrested in his home state in the fall of 1864 and tried by a military commission for treasonably conspiring to aid the Confederate cavalry raider Morgan. Milligan had been sentenced to death and his sentence had been approved by the President. Later the President had commuted his sentence to life imprisonment. Milligan's lawyers, after the fall of Richmond, brought a writ of habeas corpus asking that he be relieved of his imprisonment. Butler, who at President Johnson's request remained in uniform until November 1865, in order that he might assume the role of prosecutor should Jefferson Davis be brought to trial, was assigned to assist Attorney General Speed in the Milligan case.[10]

The case called in question the nature of military power as distinct from civil — the precise difficulties Butler himself had encountered at New Orleans and Norfolk — and Butler did not shrink from using the Supreme Court as a forum in which to justify his own wartime actions.

A grave danger to the Government, Butler pointed out, was "Miss Nancyism" or "imbecility of administration." Failure to exercise the strong arm of martial law in a time of crisis, he argued, might constitute a crime against the state. General Hovey had faced such a crisis in dealing with Milligan. Butler had faced it in the Mumford case in New Orleans. As viewed by the civil law, Mumford's offense had been the petty theft of a piece of bunting. As viewed by martial law, "the tearing down of the flag at New Orleans, was the greatest crime which could be committed in the face of a conquering army." Mumford's act would have justified Farragut in bombing the city. The execution of Mumford had put a stop to lawlessness in occupied New Orleans. The stern law martial had been enforced against his own troops as well as against hostile civilians, as in the case of Clary and the five other Union soldiers in uniform, who with forged passes to search homes for arms had proceeded to commit a series of burglaries. These criminal Union soldiers, as well as the Secessionist civilian Mumford, had been dealt swift execution under the law martial.[11]

Butler lost the case when the Supreme Court freed Milligan, on the score that Indiana, where his offense had occurred, had not been a war area, and therefore martial law there was unconstitutional. But the case had afforded the lawyer-general the personal satisfaction of defending his own regime in New Orleans.

The Farragut Prize Cases brought Lawyer Butler one of his largest fees ($75,000) and stirred up a flood of war memories. In the spring of 1867 Rear Admiral Theodorus Bailey, who had been Farragut's second in command, asked Butler if anything might be done about naval prize money for the battle at New Orleans.

All the ships that Farragut had taken at New Orleans and the vessels which Butler's troops had shortly rounded up in bayous and creeks, Butler assured the Admiral, were properly naval prizes, regardless of the technicality that they had not been sent north to be condemned. The Secretary of the Navy, Butler believed, should have filed "a proper proceeding . . . in behalf of the captors." Since Secretary Gideon Welles had not done so, "the law provides that . . . anybody else may do so." [12] Butler contended that the rightful prize money should now be paid from the United States Treasury.

Farragut was anxious to obtain the rewards for himself and his men, but hesitated in his capacity as Admiral of the Navy to bring suit against the Government. Calling the next morning at the Fifth Avenue Hotel and finding Butler out, Farragut sent a note accepting Butler's offer. To this Butler replied, "I will do all I can to aid yourself and the men who ran that terrible fire. If put on my personal oath, however, I will swear that Porter did nothing to aid in the capture of a single boat, but ran away from the Ram Louisiana. The question of fees will never arise between us unless they are allowed by the court from the prize money. It will be needful for you to make a written power of attorney to the Judge [Charles L. Woodbury] and myself to act for you in and about the adjustments of all claims in relation to the capture and the destruction of the Confederate vessels in the Mississippi River, but that you can do while in Boston. With best regards to Mrs. Farragut. Say to her that you must come up to Lowell before you sail." [13]

A complicated series of cases, extending over eight years, ensued. Farragut died in 1870, five years before any of the approximately $1,500,000 of prize money was distributed. Butler was the lawyer for Admirals Farragut and Bailey. Admiral Porter, Farragut's successor as Admiral of the Navy, quite understandably elected to have his interests represented by other counsel. The Navy Department and the Treasury Department both sent in lawyers against Butler. "I fought those cases," wrote Butler to Representative W. McAdoo on 12 February 1884, "against all those counsel and a rascally and drunken judge or two in the District Court for 4 or 5 years. I at last got the Navy Department to submit the matter to a reference as to prize money, and got an adjudication before that reference which the Treasury Department took to the Supreme Court where the government was beaten, and the amount of prize money was ordered by the court to be paid out of the Treasury in accordance with the law." [14]

In an era when lawyers were beginning to specialize Ben Butler continued to practice in all branches of law. In 1875 his 58-page brief obtained a patent for Thomas A. Edison for certain improvements in telegraphic equipment. He acted as counsel for Francis D. Moulton in a suit against Henry Ward Beecher that grew out of the latter's spectacular trial for adultery. The Boston Water Company case brought him a $5000 retainer. He fought the Brooklyn Street Railway case, and hundreds of others. "I will not take less than a $2,000 retainer about a $60,000 matter to a corporation," he wrote his good friend and fellow lawyer William E. Chandler, when the latter made the blunder of suggesting that Butler's charges in the Washington Market House case were excessive. "I thought you knew me well enough," rasped Ben Butler, "to know that my yea was yea and my nay nay, and I told you this before. More than this, you are a pretty member of the Bar striving to cut down a lawyer's fees in this way. Aren't you ashamed of yourself?" [15]

His most celebrated criminal trial was the Oliver-Cameron extortion case tried before Judge David K. Cartter in the Supreme Court of the District of Columbia. In this case Ben Butler befriended Simon Cameron, the Pennsylvania millionaire and the politician who in 1864 had conveyed to Butler Lincoln's offer of second place on his ticket. Mrs. Mary Oliver, a Treasury Department employee, a small gray-eyed woman of about forty, with florid complexion and a taste for stylish clothes, brought suit against the seventy-eight-year-old Cameron for breach of promise. In this case both Cameron's son, J. D. Cameron, and Butler, his counsel, hired detectives to shadow the woman and attempt to learn what letters she might have. The prominence of the accused, as well as the position of his son as Secretary of War under Grant, gave the case an extraordinary interest for the press. Mrs. Oliver, a lecturer on "Phrenology and the Affinities," who when out of funds traveled in the caboose of freight trains, claimed that in an affair with Senator Simon Cameron in March 1875 in New Orleans the former cabinet officer and minister to Russia had promised to marry her. After she had procured an abortion, Cameron obtained for her a job in the Treasury Department and paid her $1000 to get rid of her, but with this money in hand she had brought suit for an additional $5000. Bizarre characters, Pinkerton detectives, lobbyists wishing to curry favor with the younger Secretary Cameron paraded across the witness stand and into the headlines.

In defending his friend before the jury Ben Butler pointed out that the woman's testimony lacked probability. For two years the press had "subsisted on vulgar jokes about Mr. Cameron on account of this case," and Butler did not propose to humiliate the old man by bringing him to Washington to testify. Those who believed Mrs. Oliver's story would not credit Cameron's account on his oath, and Butler did not want him "to be sneered and grinned at." In his summation to the jury Lawyer Butler "grew pathetic, and his eyes actually filled with tears." [16] The jury, out for two and a half hours, returned a verdict for Mr. Cameron.

Butler's eccentricities gave rise to a spate of anecdotes of the courtroom. "Mr. Butler, are you trying to show your contempt for this court?" asked a judge. "No, your honor," retorted Butler, "I'm trying to conceal it." [17] A war veteran who had spent six weeks in futile application at the Pension Office was advised by a Negro waiter at his boardinghouse to see Ben Butler. "His heart's as big as his head, an' he's got the name of putting himself out to oblige a poor man." Butler from his inner office overheard the veteran's fumbling explanations to a secretary and called out in his rasping, buzz-saw voice, "Don't let that man go till I see him." [18] Butler took him in his carriage to the Pension Office and obtained the pension.

The National Home for Disabled Volunteer Soldiers was established in 1865 and General Butler served for fifteen years as president of its Board of Managers and as Treasurer. Branches of the home were set up at Augusta, Maine; Dayton, Ohio; and Hampton, Virginia. With the Board of Managers Butler visited the branch institutions once a year, and he had a clerk in his Washington law office on the corner of I Street and 15th, N.E., to manage the correspondence that came to him as the central national headquarters. The clerk, B. D. Whitney, a superannuated retainer of the General's, was able to answer routine letters and interview applicants for admission to the home, but he assumed no responsibility however trivial. This labor all fell on Butler himself. Although no business relating to the Home was too negligible to absorb his attention, he dispatched it quickly. His letters, personal, political, and National Home, often as many as thirty-five or forty per day, were curt and to the point. "I found him over his papers working," wrote a caller to his office, "in his huge ravenous fashion, like one gorging himself." [19]

Butler gradually moved the branch homes out from temporary quarters in the cities into the suburbs. Too many citizens considered it a patriotic duty toward one-legged or one-armed veterans to treat them at the corner saloon. With the passing of time the business of the homes snowballed. Increasing numbers of veterans applied for admission. Butler's labors included the purchase of supplies of all sorts, handling of personnel problems and adding to the buildings and grounds of various establishments. He once inquired into a number of voluntary departures from the homes and discovered that a business concern was hiring disabled veterans to grind hand organs on the streets for charity, a condition which Butler publicized in his annual report, to warn the public against such imposition. To enable the inmates of the Home at Augusta, Maine, to devote the long winter months to useful work, Butler set them up a small shoe factory in which to manufacture shoes for the other branches of the Home. In Hampton, Virginia, since it obviously suited the purpose, Butler sold for development as a new branch of the Soldiers' Home his own Chesapeake Female Seminary property. The move was fraught with danger in the political arena, as Butler no doubt recognized that it would be. A similar problem was Butler's method of handling the Home's finances. Since the income of the various branches, as at first established, was derived from military fines, funds due to soldiers deceased without heirs, etc., it had not been greatly in excess of the small initial needs of the institution. Butler's system for handling it was to turn it over to his personal banker as he did accounts for his clients. The bookkeeping of banker James J.

Carney of Lowell was of a rough-and-ready type which he alone could understand. It had sufficed in the past. But there was political danger ahead for Butler when the records of the funds of the Home could not be exhibited without at the same time exposing the private business not only of Butler himself but of all his clients for whom he held sums in trust.

With offices in three cities Butler spent much of his life on the train and away from home. Sarah usually traveled but twice a year — to Washington in the fall, and back to Lowell in the spring. Ben, although he spent his days and most of his nights working, liked to hear Sarah's sleepy voice calling to him to "turn down the gas" or "close the door" before he came to bed. Away from Sarah, he was "lonesome as an owl." After Christmas with the family in Lowell he might make a dash to Washington for his second appearance in the Supreme Court in less than a month. On New Year's Day in 1867 he wrote Sarah, "I got here just in time to save my case, the holidays giving me time for preparation. The result is that I have worked every hour when left alone two nights until 2 o'clock and today I have not left my room or changed my dressing gown and denied myself to all calls and made none. At half-past one o'clock I have finished the brief and now write to you. The brief will be a printed book of c. 100 pages." [20]

The enterprising businessman, lawyer and politician eventually became so busy that he dictated even Sarah's letters to his secretary, Mr. Clancy, and this was too much for her. "Now, with a very good opinion of Mr. Clancy," Sarah fired back at him, "I have no desire to enter into correspondence with him. Nor can there be much but commonplaces where the letters are read, and filed by clerks. You have become so much of a public man that private interests, or rather home interests must necessarily decline." [21]

In 1870 Paul and Benny were sent to Heidelberg, Germany, to live with their aunt and uncle Sue and William P. Webster, the latter having been appointed Consul. During the summer, on June 20, to the deep disappointment of Paul and Benny, who were unable to attend the wedding, their beautiful sister Blanche was married to General Adelbert Ames, who had served under General Butler in Virginia and was now a U.S. Senator from Mississippi.

With her daughter married, and her husband thoroughly tied up in his work, Sarah in the winter of 1870–71 took a five-month trip to Europe to see the boys. Four weeks after her departure her husband confessed, "I am very lonely although very busy; but the time when business is over is the lonely hour." [22] Two weeks later: "You have been away 51 days now and it seems months. Call it what you will, use, habit, wont, association, friendship, love, twenty-seven years of intimacy cannot be broken off without wrenching the heart . . . I am writing this past midnight, I do not feel like going to bed. I shall not as I used to do at once go to sleep. I shall dream and start and then turn again. But why annoy you with all this! You have enough disquiets and troubles without mine which cannot be remedied at present." [23] The following week he noted that Blanche's husband had made two creditable speeches in the Senate and that he himself remained a perennial whipping boy of partisan politics. "I have had one of those periodical attacks made upon me which begins every Congress in the hope to crush me but I have thrown off my assailants and come back upon them standing better now than ever before the country. It was a furious contest while it lasted but in such contests I feel my own strength." [24]

27

THE RADICAL CONGRESSMAN:
THE IMPEACHMENT TRIAL

AFTER the Fifth Avenue Hotel banquet, in November 1864, when Henry Ward Beecher proposed Ben Butler for President, Sarah Butler decided that she wished to live in Washington. The excitement of life in the Capital, she hoped, would prove a distraction during her sister Harriet's protracted illness. Specifically, she wanted her husband to become Secretary of War.[1]

"So the dear little puss wants to be Mrs. Secretary of War, does she? Sly little puss! Why does she not cry for a piece of the moon? She shall have it, so she shall!"[2] But Fort Fisher closed the door on any appointment in Lincoln's cabinet. After his "banishment" to Lowell, Butler redoubled his efforts, working through such Radical friends in Congress as Benjamin F. Wade, William E. Chandler, and D. W. Gooch. "What I want," he wrote Wade, "is a quiet movement, which shall justify the President in doing that which will relieve him of having treated me unjustly."[3]

Butler himself made several trips to Washington to promote his cause, and on the fateful night of April 14 he took the train for home just as Lincoln set out for Ford's Theater. The news of the assassination turned him back in New York. To an immense crowd of weeping men and women gathered in the park in front of Manhattan's City Hall Butler gave a moving oration which voiced the feelings of the masses, their sudden worship of the martyred President, their stunned and bitter anger toward the perpetrators of the crime.

Prejudiced against Southern leaders by wartime experience in New Orleans and Norfolk, as well as by postwar "nuisance" trials that Southerners were bringing against himself, Ben Butler sided naturally with the Radical Republicans. He shared their belief that Southern leaders must be brought to heel by vigorous application of the "conquered province" theory. Andrew Johnson's leniency toward rebellion leaders Butler regarded as weak-kneed administration.

Offsetting his bitterness against the Confederacy's ruling class was a very genuine desire to aid the little people of the South — the ex-slave and the poor white. For Southern leaders substitute Beacon Hill aristocrats of Boston who owned the Lowell mills and exacted their pound of flesh in terms of low pay and long hours, for freedmen and poor whites substitute mill operatives, whose cause Butler had long championed, and one can begin to visualize the situation as Ben Butler the reformer saw it. Economically and politically the poor whites had been gripped by fetters but slightly different from those of the slave. Throughout the war Butler had clung to the widely held Yankee notion that the poor white was pro-Unionist. And now in the postwar era his desire was to enfranchise the Negro and the poor white.

September of 1866 found Ben Butler parading with the Massachusetts delegation to a liberal convention in Philadelphia. It was a strange potpourri of Radical Republicans, Southern Unionists, and Negrophiles. The chief aim of the meeting was to protest against the Johnson administration's policy on Reconstruction. Recent riots in New Orleans they interpreted as the efforts of old guard Southern aristocrats to fasten a political yoke on the common people. The convention hall was bedecked with such mottoes as "Rebel Reconstruction — Its first act the assassination of President Lincoln. Its latest, the massacre of New Orleans"; "Treason is not an error to be forgiven; it is a crime to be punished, and must be made odious. We will fight it out on this line forever"; "Treason defeated in battle shall not rule by the ballot." On the platform in front of a full-length portrait of Lincoln, General Butler as representative of the North posed with John Minor Botts, a "repentant" Southerner. The gesture, evidently intended to symbolize the reunion of North and South, was reported by the New York *Herald* to have been "quite affecting . . . if cheers was any indication of the feeling." [4]

Butler selected civil rights as the cornerstone of his Congressional career. On the issue of civil rights he stood in the vanguard of the Radical Republicans. "We spurn the dogma that this is a white-faced man's

Government," he told the delegates in Tremont Temple in Boston. "We are now to look to the heart for the color, not the face. We insist that it is the loyal man's Government whether he be white or black." [5]

Since in 1866 he could not make the Congressional race from his home district of Lowell without contesting the seat of his friend George S. Boutwell, who had recently defended Butler against the "gold robber" charge, he ran for Congress from the Essex District, where he owned seaside property. He ignored the local politicians' charge that he was an interloper, and, breaking a still more important rule of the political game in his first contest for election to Congress, he expended his oratory upon out-of-state audiences.

With a talent for the spectacular, Butler made his own "swing around the circle" in the wake of President Johnson offering rebuttal to the President's speeches on Reconstruction. In Cincinnati he spoke from the same balcony that had been Johnson's rostrum a few hours earlier. Johnson had asked, "What constitutional proviso have I violated? What does General Butler say?" Butler answered that Johnson was trying to subordinate Congress. To Johnson's "slur" that this was only a "rump Congress," Butler retorted that the Congress had been elected by the same people who had elected Johnson. "Now if this Congress is only a rump Congress, does it not follow by the most inexorable logic that you are but a rump of a President? [Shouts, laughter and cheers.]" The President, Butler charged, had violated the Senate's power of advising and confirming appointments. Had not Johnson said "that any man who does not support his policy shall be removed, or, to use his chaste and dignified language, 'kicked out'? [Cheers.] Is that in all honesty and fairness of judgment, a proper use of the appointing power? [Cries of "No, no; never."] . . . He will find that the people of this country know how to deal with a usurping President, a king, or a dictator. [Renewed cheers.]" [6] James G. Blaine, at a later date recalling Butler's picturesque campaigning, wrote that "he went through the country . . . at the head of a triumphal procession." [7]

On the eve of the election Butler attempted to speak in New York's City Hall Park in the interest of Horace Greeley for United States Senator. A Tammany mob, collected for the occasion on the steps of the City Hall, howled him down with cries of "Spoons." "Put him out!" "How are you, Cock-Eye?" "We don't want to hear you!" Greeley supporters on the platform surrounding the speaker responded with three cheers for General Butler, while, as reported by the Boston *Journal,* General Butler, "coolly picking his teeth with a golden tooth pick, and looking quite complacently upon the crowd," remarked "Very well! You have taken your time and I will take mine." There were cries of "Good!" "Good!" [8] But when he attempted to commence his speech, someone threw an apple which caught him in the stomach. Butler picked up the fruit, bit into it and bowed to his antagonist as though he had received a favor instead of an insult. Although his gesture won their applause, the rowdies resumed their heckling when once again he tried to speak.

Butler declined to release his speech to the reporters seated about him on the platform, as Greeley suggested that he do, but returned three weeks later to deliver it before an audience in the Brooklyn Academy of Music who had paid fifty cents each admission and were as well behaved as "a congregation drawn from Plymouth Church."

Butler's maiden speech as a Congressman-elect was a spirited excoriation of President Johnson and a call for impeachment under the following charges:[9]

(1) Drunkenness in office. When he "mumbled the oath" as Lincoln's successor, he "slobbered the Holy Book with a drunken kiss."

(2) Making inflammatory harangues, "unbecoming and in derogation of his high office." "Shall the spectacle remain forever unrebuked of the President debasing himself so as justly to draw from the crowd witnessing the exhibition, such expressions as 'Go it, Andy!' 'Keep your temper, Andy!' 'Don't get mad, Andy!' And for the President to reply, 'I left my dignity at Washington!' " " 'Why' he says, 'with the Freedman's Bureau with agents and satraps in every town and school district, with fifty million of dollars in my pocket, and the army at my back, I could proclaim myself Dictator.' This was at Cincinnati . . . Shall we loiter till a wicked 'humble individual' has actually overturned our Government, and 'by his satraps and backed by the army' made himself Dictator, and then attempt impeachment?"

(3) Usurping the rights and powers of Congress. Johnson had taken over the power of forming State constitutions and of deciding who should or should not vote.

(4) Corrupt use of the appointing power. He had "kicked out"

some 200 postmasters who would not oppose Congress, and had illegally filled vacancies.

(5) Abuse of the pardoning power. Since the President had pardoned John T. Monroe, wartime Mayor of New Orleans, he bore a part of the responsibility for the "riot, bloodshed and murder" that had occurred in New Orleans since Monroe had returned to the mayor's chair. Johnson had exempted "whole classes of criminals [ex-Confederates] from the penalties of their crimes."

(6) Appointing disloyal men to office. Seven provisional governors of States had been appointed who had aided the rebellion.

(7) Refusing to execute the laws. The Civil Rights Bill, passed over the President's veto, was being openly flouted. "Do we not hear daily of wrong and outrage and murder done upon the freedmen and Union men in every rebellious State? In Texas where there were 500 untried indictments for murder and where a dozen Negroes on the average were being murdered every day, General Sheridan has asserted that United States troops are unsafe in reconstructed Johnsonian Texas outside of their own camps."

(8) Complicity in the New Orleans massacres. When Union sympathizers in New Orleans attempted to hold a convention to consider constitutional amendments to the State government, Johnson "did incite, move and permit John T. Monroe and his rebellious and wicked associates to disperse and break up such lawful convention and [incite] the members thereof to kill, assassinate and murder." "We have paid 5,000,-000,000 (five billions) of dollars and a half a million lives to preserve our free government," Butler concluded. "We will not yield it to usurpation now."

In Congress Butler's avant-garde liberalism was displayed in his advocacy of woman suffrage at a time when short-haired women, pantaloons for females, and "petticoat government" were distinctly unpopular. He threw in his lot with the advocates of greenback paper currency — cheap money for the masses — when such "soft money" ideas terrified the bankers of the country as "financial heresy." In line with his early battles in Massachusetts for a ten-hour day, Congressman Butler became an earnest sponsor of the eight-hour day for Government workers. If private industry could not afford so expensive an experiment, Butler felt that the Government could and should perform the experiment and pioneer in this development. In its navy yards, where work was done comparable to that in heavy industry, the issue could be empirically tested as to whether a man in eight hours, by working more efficiently and energetically, could not accomplish as much as a man working the long hours required in industry. His advocacy of equal political rights for Negroes was derided by the conservative press as a belief in "miscegenation" and gave rise to a flurry of cartoons showing Butler's new race of blue-eyed and fair-skinned people with woolly hair.

It was, however, as prosecutor in the Impeachment Trial that Butler won his spurs in Congress. When Johnson in the spring of 1868 openly broke with Congress over the removal of Stanton, the impeachment for which Butler had long clamored was resolved upon and Butler as the ablest and best-fitted lawyer on the Board of Managers was selected to lead the prosecution.

To prepare his case in time for the opening on March 30, Butler for three days worked around the clock, allowing himself but a few hours for cat naps. "When I entered the Senate chamber from the Vice President's room the scene was almost appalling," Butler recorded in his autobiography. "The floor of the Senate chamber was filled because the House attended in committee of the whole . . . and the ladies' gallery shone resplendent . . . I came as near running away then as I ever did on any occasion in my life." [10]

Butler's opening speech, the Brooklyn Music Hall arraignment brought up to date, lasted for two hours. "It struck me as a very forcible argument," wrote a young Boston Brahmin who was so fascinated that he subsequently missed not a day of the proceedings. "It was not a very elevated speech, sometimes he sacrificed the dignity of the occasion to get in a joke, but it was always a good one, and the part about the speeches at St. Louis and Cleveland was very amusing." [11]

In cross-examination of witnesses Butler ingeniously developed the significance of testimony that at first seemed irrelevant. The defense, led by the Attorney General, Henry Stanbery, fought every bit of testimony. The Attorney General boasted to a bystander that he was "not afraid of Ben Butler," but the way he said it convinced the bystander that he was.[12]

Concerning General Butler, Journalist W. S. Robinson, whose nose Butler had once pulled, wrote, "it is not to be denied, that the General showed greater resources as a trier of the case than any other man there.

Indeed, I understand that he declares that the President's counsel are quite unfit to try the case, and that, in Essex and Middlesex and Suffolk, he has met with much more dangerous opponents. Of course he is depreciated, and cried out against as an 'Old Bailey' practitioner; and this cry would do very well if he had not also shown great readiness and power in the argumentative work assigned to him." [13]

Ben Butler, in the verdict of history, made a mistake in judgment in sizing up the nature of the Impeachment Case. "As to myself," he recorded in his autobiography, "I came to the conclusion to try the case upon the same rules of evidence, and in the same manner as I should try a horse case, and I knew how to do that. I therefore was not in trepidation. When I discussed that question with the managers they seemed to be a good deal cut up. They said: 'This is the greatest case of the times, and it is to be conducted in the highest possible manner.' 'Yes,' I said, 'and that is according to law; that is the only way I know how to conduct a case.' Finding me incorrigible, they left me to my devices." [14] As the trial progressed Butler's cleverness and wit impressed the galleries, but there were some who found his dealings with opposing counsel and witnesses in bad taste. "The fencing and sparring between the two sides is very amusing and Butler is master of the situation," Moorfield Storey wrote to his sister Mariana on April 12: "He is the most cool and impudent man I ever saw, and had the effrontery to tell Stanbery yesterday that the argument he had just finished was the best he had ever made in his life, because it was borrowed from himself [General Butler] . . . He also charged him with malpractice, unworthy, or only pardonable in a very young counsel. His effrontery positively takes Stanbery's breath away, and the expression of bland impudence with which Butler stares at him when he rises to reply seems to excite him as much as a red cloth does a turkey cock. Butler is amusing and able, but his taste is very bad, and he is, I think, unnecessarily brutal in cross-examination. It was almost pitiable to see him make [General Lorenzo] Thomas confess that his testimony was wrong, that he himself had bragged, and he let him expose himself in the most dexterous manner . . . Thomas is a handsome, well formed, soldierly looking man, with snow-white hair, and he made a very good appearance when he took the stand, but he was utterly crumbled by Butler's cross-examination." [15]

Toward the close of the trial the tempers on both sides flared. If one of General Butler's speeches could be condemned as "outrageous," the Attorney General's riposte that the Managers were "not gentlemen" was equally out of place. "Nothing," wrote young Storey, "could have been in worse taste than to taunt General Butler as he [Stanbery] did for his failures during the war." [16] During the trial Butler employed agents to search the wastebasket in Stanbery's office in the hope of turning up discarded notes or copies of correspondence that might be useful to himself in prosecuting the case, and upon his own mandate as a Congressman he caused his agents to seize a file of telegrams at the Telegraph Office to discover what might be gleaned from them in the way of evidence. The verdict of not guilty, by the narrow margin of one vote, so infuriated Ben Butler that he never forgave the Radical Senator Ross of Kansas who at the last minute had switched his vote.[17]

Had impeachment succeeded, Butler would have moved at once to try Jefferson Davis, in the belief that a few examples of stern punishment meted out to Southerners prominent during the war would do much to repress the "malignant lawlessness" of the Ku Klux Klan. The Civil War, as Ben Butler and other Radicals saw it, was now being lost through namby-pamby administration in Washington.

In spite of his hard words about Andrew Johnson, Ben Butler had no feeling against him personally, and at the next New Year's reception at the White House, Butler was seen to shake hands with President Johnson as cordially as though his bitter anti-Johnson speeches of the past two years had never been made.[18]

Butler's relations with General Grant underwent a metamorphosis after the war. Grant's report as General-in-Chief of July 1865 referred to Butler at Bermuda Hundred as "in a bottle strongly corked," [19] and the picturesque idea, though used inadvertently by General Grant, afforded wonderful ammunition for Butler's enemies. Political cartoonists had a field day showing the Butler features corked in a bottle, and "Bottled up" Butler became almost as popular as the sobriquets "Beast" Butler or "Old Spoons."

On January 20, 1866, a year after Fort Fisher, when Butler received a belated invitation to Grant's reception, he severed all personal relationships with Grant in a formal note.[20] Nevertheless in the spring of 1868

George Wilkes, a New York publisher and a mutual friend of Grant and Butler, succeeded in bringing the two together for a clearing of misunderstandings. Grant explained to Butler that in his general report he had simply copied General Barnard's phrase "in a bottle strongly corked" without attaching any special significance to it, and that the delay in issuing General Butler's invitation to the reception had been due to the clerk's using an old Congressional list that antedated Butler's election to Congress. On the afternoon of the reception day Mrs. Grant had noticed the omission and Grant had at once directed the invitation to be sent. Butler accepted the explanations and good relations were restored between them on the eve of Grant's elevation to the Presidency.[21]

In championing the cause of the underdog — the civil rights of Southern Negroes and poor whites, or the rights of labor to reasonable working hours, or the rights of farmers to fair freight rates, or the rights of the nation to a satisfactory form of currency, Congressman Butler was always ready with hard-hitting fusillades of acrid argument. In New Orleans a mildly blasphemous Texan stepped up to a group of men who were damning Butler and accosted them in his friendly drawl: "Strangers, I am acquainted with Benjamin F. Butler . . . If there was a vacancy — mark me, I say, if there was a vacancy, — I would vote for Ben Butler for God." [22] The forthrightness which so appealed to many ordinary men constituted a fetish with Butler himself. "I shall always remain in the rear when Miss Nancyism is in the lead of the hosts," Butler wrote his friend Senator Chandler of New Hampshire. "But when true earnest republicanism is in line of battle fighting for the rights of men of every degree, color and race, fighting to rescue from monopolists, the sharks, the blood-suckers of the country . . . then if any man strikes harder or more vigorous or more determined blows or advances more readily to the conflict than I, it is because he has more ability and more power than I have." [23]

Goldwin Smith, the English reformer, in a visit to the United States recognized General Butler as a leader in the crusade for the Negro's rights. "This, to give the Beast, as well as the devil, his due, is the work of Gen. Butler. That man's indomitable energy and iron will (qualities written on his face more plainly than on any face I ever beheld, unless it be the portraits of Cromwell) have crushed the obstacles that stood in the way of the great moral and social revolution." [24]

Butler's work as Chairman of the House Committee on Reconstruction, his struggles against the Ku Klux Klan and crusade for Civil Rights, are his most important achievements as a Congressman. For convenience in disentangling the complex story, as well as to give them the emphasis they deserve, these matters will be treated in later chapters.[25]

Congressman Ben Butler could seldom resist a chance to amuse the gallery. Once he replied to a critic by pantomime. "Mr. Speaker," he began. Then followed a long silence. When expectancy had almost reached the breaking point, he raised his arms over his head and wrung his hands in the gesture peculiar to his critic. "That is all, Mr. Speaker. I just wanted to answer the gentleman from Ohio." [26]

His friend and political mentor J. W. Shaffer in Freeport, Illinois, once thought it necessary to caution him: "I know the temptation for you to pitch in was great, and with your temperament it would of [sic] been hard to withhold but I think there is no earthly use in your increasing the number of your enemies. You have fights enough on hand. Don't hunt for any more . . . I know in Washington you have many earnest & warm friends who like to see you stir [sic] up the animals, and constantly advise it. Now while I believe the country is the better for this being done, and I want some one to do it, I don't want you to do it, however, for the simple reason that you can't afford to." [27]

In private Butler acknowledged the justice of his friend's criticism but in the heat of debate he usually forgot moderation. Both Schuyler Colfax and James G. Blaine on occasion left the Speaker's chair to chastise the liberal firebrand from Massachusetts.

The anteroom to General Butler's office in Washington was always thronged. During the rush seasons he dictated to two stenographers and answered from thirty to fifty letters a day.

Although he operated in a goldfish bowl with the eyes of the press upon him from all angles, he manged to elude the watchers in giving assistance to Mrs. Mary Mumford. The widow of the man hanged in New Orleans for desecration of the flag, although aided by Confederate subscriptions, was destitute by 1869 when she sought assistance from

General Butler. Butler checked her story through a lawyer friend living near her home in Wytheville, Virginia, and using her letter as "a sort of civil service examination" obtained a clerkship for her in the Treasury. When she was turned out by the Hayes administration in 1877, she once more appealed to Butler. Butler wrote a full statement of the case and sent a special messenger to read it to the incoming Assistant Treasurer. "I would deem it the greatest possible favor," he concluded, "if you could give her temporary employment. If you can do so, the gentleman who will hand you this will find her and take the letter of appointment to her. I write this not to be put on file for the same reasons which led me not to file any recommendation originally. I do not desire that the name of the unfortunate lady should get into the newspapers as it might annoy her, and there is nothing that I do but what is put in the newspapers. I trust the peculiar circumstances of this case will be sufficient apology for my troubling you." [28] When the Treasury job was not restored within a reasonable time, Butler went to the ex-Confederate David M. Key, who was Hayes's Postmaster General, and obtained employment for Mrs. Mumford which enabled her to live in Washington the last ten years of her life. Not the least remarkable feature of this episode is that it was managed without publicity of any sort.

As a leader in political reform Butler suffered from his inability to concentrate upon big issues and ignore little ones. The struggles nearest his heart were Civil Rights, curbing the lawless Ku Klux Klan, and Currency Reform, but his active mind reached out and busied itself with such comparatively trivial matters as the "Salary Grab," "Sanborn Contracts," the defense of Oakes Ames, and the appointment of W. A. Simmons as collector of the Port of Boston.

Butler as a Congressman made it a rule to answer all his letters, and to do this he had to maintain an office staff. His pay as a Congressman was only $5000 per annum, which was about his average retainer fee for a case involving a corporation. He estimated that to be a Congressman cost him $30,000 per year in office expense and in fees lost from his law practice. Had he not been independently wealthy he could not have afforded to live in Washington and run the kind of office that he ran as a Congressman. In 1873, accordingly, Butler championed a measure to increase the pay of the President, the Justices of the Supreme Court, and Congressmen. To initiate salary increases for top Federal officials Butler became convinced that he himself, being wealthy, was one of the best fitted Congressmen. The very fact that he did not stand in financial need, as did the average Congressman, he reasoned, placed him beyond petty accusations of personal avarice and greed. Accordingly he advocated a bold schedule of salary increases: The President's salary was to be upped from $25,000 to $50,000; the Chief Justices's from $6500 to $10,500; Associate Justices from $6000 to $10,000; and the pay of Members of Congress from $5000 to $7500. In his eyes the increases were so obviously a matter of justice and good administration that he advocated making the pay raises retroactive. Then he so vigorously publicized the matter by attaching his bill as a rider to other bills that the press cried out against the "salary grab." If Butler looked upon salary increases as a simple matter of good administration, and doubtless he did, the bill fell at a time of general financial depression and was at once branded by the nation's press as "the salary grab." Butler as its foremost proponent was denounced as the chief raider of the Federal Treasury. Many Congressmen who had at first been glad to receive the additional pay suffered attacks of conscience, and returned their increase to the government. The pay raise for the President was allowed to stand, but that for Members of Congress was repealed. Butler had been prepared to receive criticism, however he might vote. Had he opposed the bill, he would have expected to be denounced as a rich man denying the chance for a poor man to go to Congress. "I confess," he wrote after the dust had settled, "that I did not suppose the delightful stream of calumny which I knew would be poured upon me, whatever course I took, would contain an accusation that I regarded it as a question of money to myself; for the hard labor of a long business life has given me the means of living without it." [29] He was consoled at length by a pat on the back by level-headed James Parton who congratulated Butler for "getting the two months extra pay for those 500 discharged clerks . . . your getting the President's salary doubled, the beginning if possible of good government, and your ever glorious salary grab — only defective perhaps in the method. In the substance, most wise, most just . . ." [30]

The Sanborn Contracts "Fraud" was a variation on the old moiety system, whereby the informer was granted by the government a share of the fines collected from delinquents. John D. Sanborn, one of Butler's wartime detectives at Fortress Monroe, came to Congressman Butler with a proposition for collecting for the government the internal revenue taxes which certain corporations were illegally withholding. Butler introduced the man to Secretary of the Treasury George S. Boutwell and obtained for him a contract giving him the legally authorized 50 per cent of all he could collect. What no one foresaw was that the delinquent corporations would put up no fight at all and that inside of two years Sanborn would collect $427,036.49 and receive for himself the princely share of $213,519.24. Sanborn's bonanza was heralded as a fraudulent raid on the nation's treasury, and Butler was gratuitously denounced by political opponents as a politician to whose coattails Sanborn was attached.

Congressman Butler's experience in the courtroom led him to take an unusually humane view of wrongdoing in others. For example, he felt there was something to be said in extenuation of the faults of poorly paid Congressmen who accepted bribes in Crédit Mobilier stock or who speculated in wildcat silver mines and other doubtful ventures. On their salary of $5000 few Congressmen could make ends meet in Washington. Butler himself spent more than his salary in clerk hire alone. Congressmen who could afford it often paid more than their salary for house rent in Washington. "I saw in Congress many faithful, efficient representatives, honest, temperate economical men, unable to bring their families to Washington, or if affection and duty induced them to do so, they lived in the third story of some second or third rate boarding house, in a single room, combining office, parlor, sitting room, and bedroom in one, so that the rest of their means could be used in educating their children or keeping up the homestead . . . I knew that some [Congressmen] . . . were obliged to borrow money and pledge their salaries in advance to pay their way and support their families . . . I saw them exposed day by day, to the pressing temptations of whoever should offer them other means of getting money to supply their wants, and I knew that some of them had yielded, and disgraced themselves and their country by so doing." [31]

When the Crédit Mobilier scandal broke out, Congressman Butler dared say a word in behalf of Oakes Ames — the disgraced villain of the affair. Ames, a fellow Congressman from Massachusetts, had confessed to distributing Crédit Mobilier stock to various members of Congress "where it would do most good." [32] While not condoning Ames's action, Butler pointed out that Oakes Ames was a man of very little education who should scarcely shoulder the entire guilt when he had "sinned with hundreds of others, and these the best business men of this land who took stock in that enterprise." [33] Butler's personal connection with the Crédit Mobilier railroad construction company was not as a receiver of tainted stock as his political enemies would have liked to believe. He was retained by the Union Pacific Railroad to advise them what to do following the debacle, and the only controversy that directly concerned Butler was the amount of his fee. Several Union Pacific directors, with whom Butler had disagreed on a procedural issue, tried to chop his fee in half, but when he suggested that he might sue they paid him the entire $6000.[34]

Sarah's health had been failing for several years. She had sometimes been so troubled by neuralgia in her shoulder and across her chest that she had had to ask Paul or Blanche to write her letters for her.

A newsreporter who obtained entrance into the Butler home on the corner of 15th and I Streets in 1874 reported of Butler that in his domestic life "no man could be more charitable, gentle and pleasing . . . He reads everything, he remembers everything, he knows everything. By the charm of perfect courtesy and the brilliancy of his conversation, he grows almost handsome." Mrs. Butler was described as "a woman of intelligence and cultivation with the manners of an empress." [35]

In 1873 General Butler bought the yacht *America* at an auction for $5000, both to obtain relaxation for himself and to entertain his friends without giving trouble to Sarah. Although he often sailed on weekends, he was too jealous of his time to indulge in lengthy pleasure trips. To a friend who had challenged him to a 160-mile race, Butler retorted, "Why should gentlemen of your age and mine make a toil of pleasure? . . . Men of business pursuits like ourselves make yachting an auxiliary of health and recreation, and not a business." [36] His normal routine was so jammed with professional duties, he explained, that if he should win a dinner in a yacht race, he could not spare the time to go to New York to eat it.

28

THE RADICAL CONGRESSMAN:
RECONSTRUCTION

To cover Ben Butler's campaign for re-election after the Impeachment trial the New York *Herald* sent one of its sharpest reporters to Lowell. "In the minds of many, the Presidential contest [between Grant and Seymour] was insignificant compared with the real or fancied importance of the result in Ben Butler's district." As the chief Radical leader in the Impeachment trial, Ben Butler had inherited from Thad Stevens the mantle of leadership in the fight of the Radical Republican Party to control Reconstruction. "All over the country," reported the *Herald's* observer, ". . . there was an absorbing and lively interest either in triumph or defeat of the renowned and persevering Butler." [1]

In their efforts to defeat Butler, whose campaign was centered on the civil rights of the Negro, the Boston Brahmins persuaded Richard Henry Dana to run on the Democratic ticket against Butler, who was running as a Radical Republican. Dana, a "blue blood" and famous author of *Two Years Before the Mast,* was a Boston lawyer colorless beside Butler, but liberal toward the Negro, having made a specialty before the war of fugitive slave cases. Dana's measure as a politician is suggested by his signature to a "hard money" campaign document name-calling Congressman Butler as "this FIREBRAND of Congress, this MARPLOT of the 19th Century! . . . this Repudiator of a nation's credit!" "this Hero of Fort Fisher, DUTCH GAP, and the BOTTLE!!!" [2]

"The Codfish aristocracy," as Butler termed his banker opponents, and the Hoar brothers, George and Ebenezer Rockwood, in the hope that Dana would make inroads into the abolitionist wing of Butler's Republican party, imported as speakers General George H. Gordon and General Judson Kilpatrick. The former once headed an inquisition into

Butler's military administration in Norfolk and the latter had been a red-legged Zouave at Big Bethel. Instead of facing the civil rights issue, these "foreigners," as the Boston *Journal* reported, beat the tom-toms about General Butler's poor military record during the war, with the result that they became little more than "fall guys" for Butler. Kilpatrick, after painting a sinister portrait of Butler, asked the crowd whether they wished to send such a man to Congress and was answered by uproarious cries of "Yes." Again the speaker charged that Butler was "bitterly opposed to human freedom and human equality," and a voice called out, "That ain't so!"

On the stump for re-election, with Sarah's bouquet pinned to his lapel, Ben Butler answered all charges with zest and wit. No hall was big enough to hold the crowds that flocked to hear him. Huge circus tents were erected for the purpose. Cartoonists and financier-controlled newspapers berated him, and the people — "the men who are not clean in their shirts" — cheered him.

Following his usual practice Butler did not limit himself to speaking inside his own Essex Congressional district, in which he owned the seaside estate of Bay View. He made speeches in Lowell and Boston, but ranged as far west as Corning, New York, and as far south as Richmond, Virginia. The sensationalist who had dogged Andrew Johnson's footsteps in the "swing around the circle" waged an unusually temperate campaign. The congregation of Negroes in Richmond's African Church he reminded that they were not equal to their white enemies, but that they had a right to be (if they could be), by exercise of integrity and by practicing Christian virtues. In answer to the taunt that Negroes have produced no Caesars, no Shakespeares, no Miltons, or Napoleons, Butler pointed out that until about thirty years ago Europeans did not read books by white Americans; whereas now their books were read and their telegraph and their steamships were respected. As to the political rights of the Negro, Butler declared, "I had rather be ruled over by the blackest face and the curliest hair . . . than by the fairest haired, whitest-faced rebel with a black heart." [3]

People from the surrounding countryside poured into Corning, New

York, to hear General Butler on October 13, 1868. Companies of militia and war veterans from all over the state swelled the audience by about 20,000. Butler answered the aspersions of General Kilpatrick by a survey of his dealings with Negro troops during the war. Ordered to hold New Orleans, but being denied reinforcements of troops, Butler recalled that he had been like the man who had the wildcat by the ears. "I could not hold on without danger of being bitten. I arrived at the conclusion that I must call upon Africa for aid." [4] He had, therefore, organized Negro troops. And since these men had borne arms to secure their freedom, fighting necessarily alongside the loyal white men from the North, they had in effect compelled Lincoln to emancipate them. The Negro, therefore, ought now to be protected in his right to vote. "Democrats say they are determined the negro shall not have the ballot, because they don't want to be ruled by black men. I am with them there . . . There are 5,000,000 black people and 35,000,000 whites. I don't think it would be fair for the blacks to rule the others . . . [The Southern Democrats] look at his face. I wish to look at his heart . . ." [5]

At the close of his speech when the crowd kept crying "Go on, go on!" he told the story of the bassoon player in a band. When the crowd kept calling "Play louder," he at last threw down his instrument and exclaimed, "It's easy enough for you to say 'Louder, louder!' but who's to vurnish ze wind?" Butler called for a decisive Radical victory so that rebellion in the South would not take heart again, and deprive the newly enfranchised Negro of his vote.

Butler was re-elected by a landslide (Butler 13,080, Dana 1812, and Lord 4941); but in the national contest Grant polled only 52.67 per cent of the popular vote. The blacks throughout the South, who had been expected to vote solidly for Grant on the Republican ticket, had been bribed, beaten, killed, or otherwise intimidated into keeping away from the polling places. Their voting power as guaranteed by the Fourteenth Amendment had been practically annihilated.

Making the polls unhealthy for the newly enfranchised black man had been chiefly the work of the Ku Klux Klan, a secret society of angry white supremacists which had sprung up in Tennessee and quickly fanned out over the South. When members of such local organizations as "The White Brotherhood," "Heroes of America," "The Red Strings," "The Constitutional Guards," and "The Invisible Empire" donned the robes of the K.K.K., they frequently retained their memberships in the lesser organizations so that if they were ever questioned as to their activities in the Ku Klux Klan they could "truthfully answer" that they were members of "The White Brotherhood," etc! Such were the subterfuges testified to by witnesses before Butler's Reconstruction Committee. Throughout the South these white-sheeted and hooded phantoms with awe-inspiring titles awakened Negroes in the dead of night and warned them against going to the polls. Some Negroes they beat or killed as examples to others. Carpetbaggers who had moved into the South during the Johnson era and a sprinkling of poor whites were warned to leave the country. When interrogated by the press following the election, Congressman Butler predicted that the Grant administration would be thoroughly committed to carrying out the Congressional (Radical) plan of reconstruction, "to give suffrage to the Negro, and fully protect him in its enjoyment." That Louisiana had gone against Grant by 55,000 majority, whole parishes not giving him a single vote under the reign of terror which existed there, where thousands of Negro Republican votes had been thrown before, would force the administration to come to grips with the Ku Klux, Butler predicted. The situation would be difficult in the South because the hiring system had been used to suppress Negro votes. "The contracts everywhere made in the South for the employment of negroes on condition that they will abstain from voting if their masters so desired, are as much purchases of men as were the purchases from the auction block a few years before."[6] Butler was convinced that the spirit of rebellion in the South was reviving and was determined to fight this all he could in Congress.

Another equally difficult problem, as Butler saw it, concerned the currency. Both as a businessman and as a politician who courted the favor of the masses, Butler announced his opposition to the resumption of specie payments for the greenbacks that had been issued during the war. The effect of such a policy was to make money scarce and expensive at a time when the national economy was bursting to expand. The supply of currency in the country needed to be increased, Butler contended, rather than diminished. In other words Congressman Butler, whose personal wealth made him financially independent, was throwing down the glove to the bankers of State Street, as he had done in his youth as a member of the Massachusetts legislature. As Butler saw it, the currency system in the country was such that half a dozen men could create a panic. One problem, said Butler, "is to render impossible such derangement of the currency as that under which the country is now suffering; and the other is to give money to the business of the country at a cheaper rate of interest than is possible under our present financial system. It seems that half a dozen men, by locking up, through the aid of the banks, some twenty million, more or less, of the legal tender notes can so cripple the money market and banks not in the combination as to foil solvent merchants and raise the rate of interest and demand for money to such an extent as to create commercial revolution and to change the entire national securities five per cent in a single day, thus altering their value to the unheard of amount of a hundred and twenty millions." In the future, cornering gold would be easier, Butler predicted, than cornering grain had been in the past; "because the amount of currency in the country can be known to a dollar, and the exact effect of the engrossment can, therefore, be calculated. Advantage has also been taken of the very time when large amounts of money are needed to move the crops to market to carry out this nefarious scheme of plunder, by which the price even of food may be enhanced without any benefit to the producer. This must be stopped." [7]

Butler's proposed remedy was "that the government should issue a large amount, say $200,000,000 or $300,000,000 of legal tenders, which should be convertible and reconvertible into bonds at a low rate of interest, so that when the money market became stringent and currency was worth a higher rate of interest than the bonds, the holders might return the bonds and take the currency; and when the money was worth in the market a less rate of interest than that provided by the bonds, then the money might be returned to the Government and converted into bonds." Cheap money, Butler argued, was good for the country; tight money was bad. He saw no good reason why the rate of interest in Europe should be 2½ percent while in this country "the commercial rate should be not less than eight and from that to thirty per cent in various parts of the country. Eight per cent per annum is the ordinary rate of bank accommodation in Eastern cities, and thirty per cent in the South is the ordinary rate, when, indeed, money can be got there at all." The return to specie payments, he argued, would only increase the difficulty of high interest rates. "Until we have cheap money we cannot have cheap transportation, cheap food, and consequent cheaper labor. It gives capital an unjust advantage over labor." In essence Butler's "automatic balance wheel" for the nation's currency was designed to accomplish much the same ends as the Federal Reserve system that was eventually adopted after his death. His financial ideas were, certainly, in their author's time, anathema to the "hard money" financial interests of the country, and these interests through the newspapers which they controlled waged against Congressman Butler a guerrilla warfare in name-calling reminiscent of the same phenomenon during the Civil War. On the other hand his advanced ideas on currency endeared him to a host of reformers of various kinds, and eventually led to his being nominated for President in 1884 by the Greenback and Anti-Monopoly Parties. Meanwhile, as he announced to the New York press following re-election in 1868, he proposed "to advocate a cheap capital, cheap transportation, the rights of labor and of the people against all monopolies and oppressions whatever. In brief, I mean to stand by the motto under which I fought the canvass — viz: 'Equality of right in all men, equality of power of all men and equality of burdens to all men under the government.' " [8]

Since Grant was clay in the hands of the bankers, Congressman Butler was able to make better headway during the Grant administration as an advocate of civil rights than in currency reform. As chairman of the Committee on Reconstruction one of Butler's chief problems was to maneuver through the House a bill to remand the "back-slidden" state of Georgia to military rule and to bring about Georgia's readmission to membership in the Union following another "reconstruction," with additional constitutional guarantees on civil rights.

As demanded by Congress, Georgia had abrogated the government that had been established by Andrew Johnson, and in its stead had set up a provisional government. In the summer of 1868 this provisional government, having apparently accepted the required constitutional guarantees on civil rights, her newly elected members of Congress were admitted to take their seats in the House of Representatives. After the fall election when Georgia's new senators-elect presented themselves in Washington, they were refused confirmation by the Senate because it had now become apparent not only that Negroes in Georgia had been deprived of their votes but that Negro and carpetbagger members of her state legislature had been ousted from their seats and their places forcibly taken by white supremacists. Governor Bullock of Georgia, although he had managed to cling to his office, was being made the target of a mass of charges ranging from malfeasance to corruption and theft. On their way home from testifying in Washington the two Negro state legislators, as Butler reported to the House, were waylaid and murdered, and although Governor Bullock offered a reward of $5000 for the arrest of the murderers, nothing came of it.[9] Several Northern Democrats on the fifteen-man Committee on Reconstruction opposed Butler on the bill to reconstruct Georgia. They contended that once Georgia had been readmitted as a state Congress could not then declare her to be outside of the Union. Butler took the position that by robbing the Negro of the franchise Georgia had in effect revealed that she had not been truly reconstructed; hence the seating of Georgia's representatives by the House of Representatives had been improper. Congress had to begin the whole process over again by returning the state to military law until she should accept a government in which civil rights should actually be guaranteed to her Negro citizens.

I have no more doubt of the power of Congress to set this great wrong done in Georgia right than I have in the power of Congress to legislate upon any other subject relating to the general welfare of the United States. We admitted this State upon the implied condition that it should have a government to carry out the laws of the United States in good earnest and good faith. On the contrary, the State has undertaken to fly in the face of every just and proper law of the United States. We have now the right to resume the power which we gave when we allowed the State to emerge from rebellion and be admitted as part of the Union, and to require such further conditions and restrictions as to its conduct as wrong doing on its part has made necessary.[10]

Congressman Ben Butler was accused of listening with a too willing ear to "carpetbaggers and idlers . . . in reference to morals and the state of society in Georgia," and his bill to require that state to undergo a second reconstruction was denounced as "another instance of cruelty to be received in the South with indignation." Much of the objection to the bill centered around Butler's provision that the ousted Negro legislators be returned to office to serve the full term for which they had been elected. Northern Democrats thought Butler too dogmatic in his insistence upon this provision. Southern Congressman Beck from Kentucky, having prejudices against Negroes in politics without the handicaps of Southerners from the states which came under the juggernaut of Reconstruction, accused Butler of giving the Georgia carpetbaggers "unbridled license" to plunder the state's railroads, stocks, bonds, in fact "everything that was subject to plunder." Beck feared that if the Georgia bill was passed, Butler, as "the leader of the more radical element of the Republican party," would next "turn Tennessee out of the Union." [11] Congressman Bingham of Ohio stigmatized the Georgia bill as "a bill of abominations"; "Sunset" Cox of New York labeled it "a bill of political servitude." Butler, however, with the conviction that "every giving way here is the death knell of some black or white man of the South," refused to waver or compromise and his Georgia Bill was passed with 125 yeas, 55 nays, 40 not voting.[12]

In her second reconstruction Georgia ratified the Fifteenth Amendment and excluded from office Confederate soldiers and former officeholders whose disloyalty to the Union had not been forgiven in a bill of amnesty. Needless to say the new arrangement did nothing to curb the extra-legal activities of white supremacy organizations, especially the Ku Klux Klan.

In 1870 when his daughter Blanche was married to General Adelbert Ames, Congressman Butler acquired an important personal reason for maintaining law and order in the South. Adelbert Ames was a young West Point graduate when the Civil War broke out.[12a] In the debacle of the First Battle of Bull Run, young Ames was brevetted major and awarded a Congressional Medal of Honor for continuing to direct his battery of light artillery even after he had been wounded. Subsequently he had fought in the Peninsular Campaign, at Antietam, Sharpsburg, Gettysburg, around Charleston, and finally at Fort Fisher, by which time he had risen to the rank of Brigadier General of volunteers. As one of the Federal commanders of Negro troops he had, like General Butler, aroused the ire of the Confederate Government, but he had not dramatized the Negro problem as Butler had done in his declaration that Negroes were "contraband of war," nor had he personally been placed under the ban of outlawry as had his future father-in-law. After the war General Ames had commanded a military department in the South, but by the time of his marriage to Blanche Butler, he had already given up his military career to accept the post of United States Senator from Mississippi. At the age of thirty-five in 1870, he was handsome, idealistic, and short of money. His family moved to Minnesota after the war, and Adelbert had advanced them substantial loans out of his army pay to enable them to operate a waterpowered flour mill. Congressman Ben Butler was fond of his Senator son-in-law. At considerable cost he had the architect change the plans of his new home on Capitol Hill to make an apartment for Blanche and Adelbert, and reflecting upon his own career as a reformer and the pursuit of the milling business by Adelbert and his family, Ben Butler once wrote Blanche that her husband was "much better employed in getting the cockles out of wheat than to be engaged in getting the cockles out of men's hearts and Brains." [13]

One of Congressman Butler's toughest crusades was his fight to curb the Ku Klux Klan. To this end he publicized their outrages and drafted the drastic "K.K.K. Bill." In *The Invisible Empire* Stanley F. Horn tells how Butler dramatized for Congress and the nation the beating of a carpetbagger. A. P. Huggins, an Ohio-born veteran of the Union Army, had become Superintendent of Schools and Assistant United States Assessor of Internal Revenue in Monroe County, Mississippi. In March of 1868 Huggins was ordered by night riders to leave the state within ten days. When he refused they stripped off his coat and "in a calm and deliberate manner" gave him seventy-five lashes. Huggins' bloodstained shirt was sent to Butler by a Lieutenant Picket, U.S. Army. Butler, as though brandishing an exhibit in a courtroom, shook the bloody shirt for his fellow Congressmen to see.[14] The expression "waving the bloody shirt" henceforth entered the language of American politics, and Congressman Butler drew crowds to the galleries whenever men knew beforehand that he was to speak.

Butler's "K.K.K. Bill," as it was called by the press, was first presented to a caucus of Republican Senators and Representatives and was approved by all but two of the eighty-four members present. This sweeping document made night riders "Liable to the party injured." Any person who deprived another of "any rights, privileges, or immunities secured by the Constitution of the United States" could be sued for damages. Lest state courts in the South be too lenient toward Southern white offenders, these cases were to be tried in the several district or circuit courts of the United States. Penalties were drastic. Section 2 of the bill stipulated "that if two or more persons shall, within the limits of any State, band, conspire or combine together to [violate Constitutional rights] . . . whether principals or accessories, [they] shall be deemed guilty of a felony," and upon conviction liable to fines up to $10,000 or imprisonment up to ten years or both. For murder they should suffer death. Should armed forces hinder the execution of the law, the President was authorized to use the militia or the armed forces of the nation, suspending the *habeas corpus,* and declaring martial law.[15] The "K.K.K. Bill" was not intended to apply to past cases or current cases which were not yet decided, but was directed only toward checking future violations.

Not only in the South was Butler's "K.K.K. Bill" damned. Some Northern papers denounced it as too inflammatory. "If in spite of all resistance, this bill passes and is signed by President Grant," declared the New York *World,* "then we will spurn and spit upon it, and counsel a resolute opposition to its enforcement . . . If this incendiary firebrand is flung into the South it will kindle a conflagration which it may require rivers of blood to extinguish." The Washington *Chronicle,* while quoting the *World's* opinion, reminded its readers that the bill's worthy purpose was "to protect Union men at the South from midnight assassins who now have full sway." [16]

When Butler, now chairman of the Committee on the Judiciary, brought the "K.K.K. Bill" before the House, the enthusiasm of his colleagues in the Republican caucus had cooled. "Little was done today," the New York *World* reported on March 18, 1871. "Butler stood up a long time, looked very anxious for [Speaker] Blaine to recognize him, and finally asked leave to have his famous Ku-Klux bill printed. Objection was promptly made on the Democratic side, and the hero of Fort Fisher, with a very mournful expression, subsided." As Butler concluded later, there was a deal being made between Republicans interested in tariff matters and Democrats opposed to Butler's bill to curb the Ku Klux.

Speaker Blaine, with a personal interest in tariff matters (Butler believed) because of his owning stock in a coal mine, had been absent from the Republican caucus, and when Butler's bill came on the floor, he maneuvered to sidetrack it. With the aid of Democratic votes he put through a resolution providing for a House Committee to investigate conditions in the Southern states and appointed Butler as chairman of this committee. This was done at a time when Butler was not on the floor. When Blaine notified Butler, the latter refused to accept the appointment, and the Speaker refused to withdraw it.

The next morning Butler placed on the desk of each member of Congress a printed statement of the situation as the best means of replying to Blaine's maneuver. The entire affair, Butler contended, was "a political trick," with "high tariff Republicans" in temporary alliance with Democrats. The proposed House Investigating Committee had been given no power to call witnesses or to make a report. Its work at best could only duplicate what had already been accomplished by a Senate committee investigating conditions in the South. Butler himself was "not in harmony with the majority of the committee, or the purpose of the committee." The whole thing could only provide "electioneering fodder" for the Democrats because, as was well known, Butler himself was "the most hated man" in the South and only wartime bitterness, rather than truth, would result.[17] The circulation of Butler's statement in the House and its publication in the morning papers were unusual maneuvers and they nettled Mr. Blaine.

Turning over the Speaker's chair to someone else, Speaker Blaine for the first time in two Congresses descended to the floor to denounce Butler for his insinuations against the Speaker that were contained in his "remarkable letter." Blaine, at fifty, was a large and imposing individual, and his friends pressed around him to enjoy the show. He pointed out that Butler had resorted to a mere quibble in saying that the proposed committee was not authorized to report its findings, "the usual power not being inserted in it, 'to report at any time.'" The publication of Butler's protest, declared Blaine, "was intended covertly as an insult to the Speaker of this House."

Butler retorted that in taking his action he had been "painfully aware of the risk he ran in arousing the Speaker's anger." In a versified parody he rapped the Speaker

> *"For ways that are dark*
> *And tricks that are vain,*
> *I name Speaker Blaine,*
> *And that I dare maintain.*

. . . I appeal to the Speaker's fairness — No, I cannot appeal to that. I will state what I said when he came to my seat yesterday and showed me the resolution and asked me to go for it, and said I should be chairman of the committee under it. I said, 'I will be damned if I will. [Great laughter] I will have nothing to do with it' . . . But all this abuse of me, this getting exceedingly wrathy by the Speaker against me, does me no harm, and will not frighten anybody . . . The calling of hard names will do no harm to me here or in the country. If I could have been killed by being called hard names, I should have died long, long ago. [Laughter.] I have withstood the rough side of a rougher tongue than the one just wagged at me." [18]

The debate over the Ku Klux Bill was continued into the next session of Congress which began immediately. Butler, who "carried the whole load and kept the members here in spite of their determination to adjourn," [19] quoted copiously from the testimony recently taken by the

Senate committee investigating Ku Klux activities in the South. Butler was admonished by border state Democrats for "stirring up the old issue of the war . . . by reducing the South to a subjugation more degrading than she has yet endured."[20] Congressman Swann of Maryland verbally cudgeled him for having for weeks "flared in our faces" his "infamous bill," "his barbarous and vindictive war upon the unoffending South."

Butler replied with statistics compiled from the Senate Committee's investigation. Some 40,000 men in North Carolina belonged to extralegal organizations, many of them "half-fledged boys and newspaper 'bummers' who egg them on." In Louisiana a so-called "Innocents' Club" numbering 2000, and "Knights of the White Camellia," 15,000 strong, operated in and around New Orleans. There were too many to be controlled by the handful of United States troops under General Hancock who commanded the Department of Louisiana, although, Butler added, General Hancock now had more troops than Butler himself had had to control New Orleans in wartime. In Louisiana during the sixty days prior to the election of 1868 over 300 "leading and active Republicans [carpetbaggers] white and colored, were killed, wounded and otherwise cruelly maltreated by Ku Klux" and other night riders.[21] Near Murphreesboro, Tennesse, a Negro, "defending his own roof-tree and hearthstone," shot down a night rider who turned out to be the sheriff of Rutherford County. Near Talladega, Alabama, a carpetbagger from Canada was permitted by night riders to write a last note to his wife before being lynched along with four Negroes a half mile out of town.

On April 5 Butler's brief eulogy on John Brown inspired Congressman Ritchie of Maryland to resort to name-calling: the "patron saint of Republicanism" praised by the "living leader of that party." "Think of it! Saint John Brown and Saint Benjamin Butler to be our household gods!"

"Mr. Speaker," rejoined Butler, "I desire not to reply to any personal remarks which have been made, because almost the only thing that elects some of the gentlemen on the other side is abuse of me. [Laughter.] Some of them have been kind enough to tell me that the best card they had in their district was to show their people how they had 'berated Ben Butler!' [Laughter.] Therefore, I am always willing to afford gentlemen just as much as they please of that kind of appeal to the intelligence of their constituents." [22]

Butler's Ku Klux Bill (H.320) after passing the House on April 6, 1871, had still to go over the hurdle in the Senate, where Butler had several good friends like Senator Wilson of Massachusetts, who had personally defended him during wartime against one of the New Orleans "robbery" charges, and Senator Adelbert Ames, of Mississippi, Butler's son-in-law. Blanche Ames coached her husband beforehand, since he had been bred up as a general rather than a public speaker, and his maiden speech in favor of the Ku Klux Bill, which he delivered on April 11, was temperate, and well reasoned. Had it not contained a sharp polemic against Southern Senator Blair of Missouri, one could scarcely have detected the father-in-law's influence. This, however, was not obtrusive.

Senator Ames, himself a fair-minded and even-tempered idealist, although a carpetbagger, and hence anathema to Southern plantation owners and other white supremacists, cited some of his own personal experiences in support of the Ku Klux Bill. Before becoming a Senator, General Ames had served as president of a commission "to try men charged with the murder of some negroes, the burning of their houses, and the expulsion of their families from the neighborhood. These deeds done by a mob were cold-blooded and fiendish, and though many testified to having seen the ruins of the huts and the dead negroes, no one could be found to tell anything of the incendiaries or murderers. Profound ignorance fell upon the witnesses when questioned. All were obliged to be acquitted . . . Previously little versed in matters civil, with ideas of equality and liberty formed in a New England village, I could but resolve, come what might, to pursue the course I did [i.e., to offer military protection to the Negro in Mississippi]." [23] During the last three months, Senator Ames pointed out, there had been sixty-three murders by armed bands, and during the past year thirty churches and schoolhouses had been burned. Ames told of how he and other carpetbaggers "had been given to understand that we must leave," and expressed the firm conviction "that there exists in every town and county in this state [Mississippi] a thoroughly organized band of Ku Klux, and all I can say is 'God help us,' if Congress should fail to enact laws for the protection of our lives and property!" [24]

In the Senate Chamber aging and enfeebled Senator Garrett Davis of Kentucky sought to discredit Butler's Ku Klux Bill by reviving the wartime "robber" charges against him. In the House, Butler replied to the Senator's abuse: "Do the Ku Klux banditti in Kentucky [dominate] that dark and bloody ground, where the savage and brutal passions of men never yet have found restraint . . . so that neither the palsy of years can control [their leaders, nor] grey hairs soften them, insomuch that their untaught and untamed outbursts may break forth even in the Senate Chamber of the United States, their impotent rage exhibiting itself with the whining and piping voice of an imbecile and unhonored old age [?]" [25]

Senator Davis, within the security of the Senate Chamber, now flew into a rage of denunciations but subsided as with shock when he saw Congressman Butler enter the Senate Chamber, seat himself near Senator Wilson, and turn about to face Senator Davis, who though silent, still held the floor. There exist several versions of the pantomime and colloquy that ensued. Davis himself gave the following statement of it. "I then took my seat. He (Butler) continued an earnest and excited look at me, whereupon I turned my seat to face him, and when we had looked each other in the eye for an instant, I said to him: 'You damned old scoundrel, are you here to scowl at and brow beat me?' He made no reply, and I repeated that language. He then responded: 'I have not addressed you, sir, or said a word to you.' I then said, 'What are you here for; why did you scowl at me?' He answered: 'I did not scowl at you; you are an old man.' I rose to my feet and advanced one step toward him and said, 'I am young enough to go with you from the Senate Chamber wherever it is your pleasure.' At this point of time Senator Wilson stepped between us, laid his hand on Butler's shoulder, said a few words to him, and they walked off together." [26]

The Ku Klux Bill was finally passed by the Senate and was signed by President Grant. One of Congressman Butler's greatest parliamentary victories, it had been hard fought and exhausting. After Sarah returned to Lowell and Adelbert Ames went for a visit to his family in Minnesota, Blanche remained in Washington for several weeks to take care of her father. It was a period of relaxation from tension, during which Butler upset domestic arrangements "in a most masterly manner" by bringing in dinner guests without notifying Blanche and made mistakes in keeping score when Blanche outplayed him at billiards. "To my astonishment," Blanche wrote to Adelbert, "he insisted that he had been counting his shots 'one at a time instead of three.' What could I do? I mildly asked him if he meant to cheat his 'only daughter in that way.' I agreed that the last half of the game should prove which was *the humbug.*—Mr. Clancy to be judge. I won by nearly forty points. Father, you know, is very careless about counting. No doubt part of the time he counted one way, part the other. We had a good laugh at his expense." [27]

After winning the spectacular Congressional fight to curb Ku Kluxism, Butler attempted to gain the Republican nomination for Governor of Massachusetts. Immediately the Ku Klux law, Ames wrote Blanche, had "a subduing effect all over the South." [28] The white supremacist, whose property now stood in jeopardy from damage suits in Federal courts, broke off or greatly curtailed his night-riding activities. Congressman Butler stood at the crest of his power as a political figure. Obtaining the governorship, he believed, would put him in line for the Presidency. [29] Butler's candidacy added excitement to the Worcester convention. It was blocked, however, by Senator Charles Sumner who confided to Ben Perley Poore his belief that if Butler "captured" the state, he would next "aim to capture the Presidency," an office to which Sumner apparently cherished a claim of his own. [30] Butler redoubled his efforts for the gubernatorial nomination in 1873. This time, recognizing political realities in Massachusetts, he gambled $10,000 of his own money and $5000 from his friends on winning the nomination. He now had the support of Sumner, who was too ill to participate in the canvass. Butler counted heavily on the help of his friend Boutwell, whose campaign for Congress had had the strong support of Butler and Fisher Hildreth. Not to disturb Boutwell, who represented the Lowell

constituency, Butler had himself gone freewheeling into another district to obtain his own seat in Congress. Butler's influence had backed
Boutwell as Secretary of the Treasury and later as United States Senator. In relying upon his friend, however, Butler failed to take due
note of the fact that Boutwell had also to appease Boston's financial
interests, and that the bankers were dead set against Butler because of
the greenback issue. Boutwell "evidently wished to convey the idea
that he was kindly disposed" toward Butler, but when Butler backed
him for president of the Nominating Convention, Boutwell reneged,
and even refused to make a public statement in favor of Butler until
after the nomination. Butler, losing all patience with such "fair
weather" friendship, gave him "the rough side of his tongue" and
refused for a while thereafter to shake hands with him.

Playing a lone hand in Massachusetts politics, Butler next sought
to build up his own machine. Learning in the spring of 1874 that
the Collector of the Port of Boston wished to obtain a diplomatic post,
Congressman Butler quietly secured for him an appointment as Minister to Venezuela, and with equal absence of fanfare persuaded President Grant to nominate Butler's friend W. A. Simmons as Collector.
The usual practice, of course, in so important a matter of Federal patronage, was to clear the nomination with the Congressmen from the
state concerned, and Butler's cavalier bypassing of Senator Boutwell
and other Massachusetts members of Congress promptly raised a hue
and cry. Butler was accused of getting offices by trickery, of "bulldoz-
ing," of "Butlerism," of setting up a one-man "Butler Party," etc. Thousands of protests descended upon the Congressmen. One of Boston's
leading merchants, John M. Forbes, came to Washington at the head of
a delegation to protest. In the face of anti-Butler prejudice, Grant stood
firm, and the Simmons appointment was ratified. Henceforth, in addition to the temporarily alienated Senator Boutwell, Congressman
Henry L. Pierce from the Boston District, Congressman George F.
Hoar from the Seventh District, and Congressman Ebenezer Rockwood Hoar from the Ninth District were joined in hostility to Butler.
These forces combined to defeat Butler's renomination for Congress in
the 1874 Republican State Convention. At the time of this collapse of

his political fortunes the overconfident Butler was actually absent from the convention and engaged in trying a lawsuit.

Butler was annoyed to be sure. A poor return this for eight years of service in Congress. "Now Massachusetts has no smart man to represent her in Congress," consoled his friends. But such thought did not long occupy the mind of the busy lawyer and politician, for in Mississippi the "whiteliners" joyfully seized upon Butler's defeat as a signal for renewed effort to oust Butler's carpetbagger son-in-law from his post as Governor of Mississippi.

29

THE RADICAL CONGRESSMAN:
CIVIL RIGHTS

WHEN Benjamin and Sarah Butler ordered the architects to partition off a second office with a separate living apartment in their new $125,000 house under construction on Capitol Hill fronting the eastern face of the Capitol building, they doubtless hoped that Blanche with her family might live with them. The transformation of Little Buntie from schoolgirl at the Georgetown convent and "major" of volunteers in wartime Lowell into a young woman of more than ordinary beauty gave her parents a deep feeling of pride. With no great appreciation of the arts, the father was flattered and happy that Blanche should develop a flair for painting in oils. He often escorted her in his carriage to her art lesson, and took uncritical delight in her work. Sarah, too, whose passion for Shakespeare suffered no decline in the years since she quit the theater to marry Benjamin, encouraged Blanche in her art. The mother, indeed, enjoyed the adult daughter as her most intimate friend and companion. Blanche's marriage to Senator Adelbert Ames aroused Sarah's natural apprehensions. There was danger that Blanche might one day move to Northfield, Minnesota, whither Adelbert's family had emigrated and where Adelbert owned an interest in a flour mill. Should the son-in-law's political fortunes continue to hold him in Mississippi, there was an even greater chance that Blanche might move there to live. Minnesota was too cold, Mississippi too hot, and both were too far away from Lowell and Washington. At first Sarah's attitude toward Adelbert was frankly critical. She was pleased with his position as Senator, and although she felt that he lacked initiative and drive, she resolved to suppress and not to show these feelings. Ben on occasion teasingly reminded Sarah of these good intentions as a mother-in-law.

During the first few years of Blanche's marriage, while Adelbert was in the Senate, the young couple lived with her parents. Blanche kept house for her father while Sarah Butler went to Germany to see her sons who were in school there. This was a tremendous boon to the father who had never before been so far separated from Sarah that he could not by an overnight trip return to her at the home base. Blanche wrote her mother in Europe of her father's extreme "homesickness" to see her, and before Sarah's boat was released from quarantine, Ben rushed on board to greet her, and professed himself willing, busy as he was, to accept detention also should she be placed in quarantine.

At Sarah's insistence Blanche came to Lowell for her confinements, and when after two years Senator Ames was elected Governor of Mississippi, Sarah insisted that Blanche and the children spend summers either in Lowell or at Bay View on Cape Ann. Sarah's fear lest Blanche's children catch yellow fever or some other dread Southern disease was intensified by her own ill health and craving for Blanche's companionship.

Blanche loved and adored both mother and husband. Adelbert, despite a feeling that he was accepting too much from his parents-in-law, agreed that Massachusetts did have a healthier climate in summer and acquiesced in his family's annual sojourn in the North. Never willingly did Adelbert and Blanche allow a day to pass without each writing the other an account of the day's occurrences. Not all of Blanche's letters deal with tiny Butler Ames's relayed greetings to his absent parent. Frequently her famous "Father" wins a notice in her letters — his temporary abstinence from cigars, his having fun with the yacht *America,* going with Paul on a fishing trip into Maine, or planning his next political campaign. And Adelbert's letters, postmarked from Jackson, Mississippi, reiterate not only the husband's love for "my Beautiful" and the children. They also tell of the political vagaries of Governor Ames's Negro colleagues in the government of Mississippi and his preparation of the "Mansion" for his family's return South. So much for the summer routine.

During the winter, when Blanche and the children rejoined Adelbert in Mississippi, Blanche and her mother took up their pens. Theirs were affectionate letters, formal, beautifully written, and filled with news. Sarah communicated news about the family — Ben-Israel's difficulty making good grades at West Point, Paul's experiences at Harvard, Father's slight bout with gallstones, his numerous absences from home on law business, and his legal opinions to be relayed to "General Ames" in Mississippi. From Mississippi Blanche, in turn, kept her mother posted on the doings of the grandchildren, and with growing frequency about conditions in Mississippi which concerned herself and Adelbert — the plainness of the dwellings of the Southern planters, the limited social life among the wives of carpetbaggers, society snubbings, "white-liner" impositions upon Negroes, random shots fired into the Governor's "Mansion." Sarah, or "Gran," as little Butler Ames called his grandmother, voraciously absorbed the interesting minutiae about little Edith, Butler, and the new baby and worried about her son-in-law's mounting political problems.

This treasure of letters, which Blanche Ames hoarded and toward the close of her life arranged, was published in 1957 under the title *Chronicles from the Nineteenth Century: Family Letters of Blanche and Adelbert Ames.*[1] This material on the post–Civil War era in Mississippi constituted one of Congressman Ben Butler's chief sources of information. Not a source, to be sure, which he was willing to acknowledge in Congress, but a private pipeline of information, honest, sincere, unofficial, from the wife of Mississippi's governor who was his own daughter.

Concerning the entire business of Reconstruction there were many mistaken impressions fixed in the public mind and about almost any public act or utterance of Congressman Ben Butler there were false notions. The idea that Ben Butler helped his son-in-law obtain office in Mississippi is but one of the widely accepted notions for which there is no evidence. After Ames had himself attained his positions as U.S. Senator and as Governor, Butler advised him on curbing the Ku Klux. In private Butler loaned Ames substantial sums for investment in the West, and when the white-liners regained control of the Mississippi state legislature and threatened Governor Ames with impeachment, Butler advised him on how to present his case before the public and sent lawyers to Mississippi to fight the case.

In *The Story of Reconstruction* the Southern historian Robert Selph Henry rates Adelbert Ames as "an engaging young man of good ability." [2] Certainly Mississippi tolerated him with a better grace than other "carpetbaggers"; although the moment they recovered control of the state legislature they framed impeachment charges to oust him.

As a military man Ames felt that laws were to be obeyed. As a politician he was an idealist and a complete novice. In Mississippi he resisted the black code that denied Negroes the rights of citizenship, which he believed to be theirs under the laws. "I believed I could render them great service. I felt that I had a mission to perform in their interest, and I hesitatingly consented to represent them and unite my fortune with theirs." [3]

After the passage of the Ku Klux Bill, under which violence might bring intervention by Federal troops, the Southern white supremacist resorted to intimidation of the Negro without actual use of force. White men on horseback appeared at the polls just before balloting opened with noosed ropes dangling conspicuously from the pommels of their saddles. Within the hearing of crowds of blacks who came expecting to cast ballots they dropped broad hints that the hangings would commence as soon as the ballot boxes were opened. Most of the Negroes overhearing these threats left the scene. Three Mississippi counties that had each returned thousands of Negro Republican votes when Ames was elected Governor in 1873 cast the ridiculous numbers of 12, 7, and 4 votes respectively in 1874.[4]

President Grant never categorically refused to send Federal troops into Mississippi, as requested officially by Governor Ames and as he was privately urged to do by Congressman Ben Butler, but he procrastinated and ultimately never did send them. In one county Governor Ames enlisted a troop of Negro militia and thereby provoked riots of such magnitude that the Governor could not begin to control them.

With carpetbag rule in the South daily deteriorating, Congressman Butler introduced a bill to guarantee civil rights to the Negro. "This bill of ours," Butler declared in Congress on 7 January 1874, "only removes all impediments to every man in making himself the equal of every other man if God has given him the power to become their equal . . .

We have been told we must respect the prejudices of the South. Pardon me, we must *lament* the prejudices of the South . . . With deep sorrow and not offensively, I say this: Prejudice can never be the ground of legislation in regard to the rights of citizens . . . We must demand that prejudice shall square itself with the law." For Democratic Southern Congressmen on the opposite side of the chamber, Butler interpreted the prejudice against the Negro as a postwar development. "Was there any objection in the [prewar] South to consorting with the negro as a slave? O, no; your children and your servant's children play[ed] together; your children sucked the same mother with your servants' children; had the same nurses; and unless tradition speaks falsely, sometimes the same father. Would you ride in first-class cars with your negroes in the olden time? What negro servant, accompanying its mistress or master, and administering to his or her health, was ever denied admittance to a first-class hotel? . . . You once associated with the slave in every relation of life. He has now become a freeman, and now you cannot associate with him; he has got up in the scale and you cannot stomach him. Why is this? Is it because he claims that as a right [which the law now gives him]? . . . This is not a prejudice against the Negro or any personal objection to him — it is a political idea only." [5]

Social equality, the speaker contended, was not the issue. "Equality! We do not propose to legislate to establish equality . . . I believe that [the word "equal"] in the Declaration of Independence is a political word, used in a political sense, and means equality of political rights. All men are not equal [in other respects] . . . God has not made them equal, with equal endowment. But this is our doctrine; Equality . . . as the true touch-stone of civil liberty is not that all men are equal, *but that every man has the right to be the equal of every other man if he can* . . . and all constitutions, all laws, all custom in contravention of that right is unjust, wicked, impolite, and unchristian, and surely will be brought to naught." [6]

The Civil Rights Bill, like all matters concerning race relations and Reconstruction, provoked bitter wrangling which delayed its passage until the next session of Congress, by which time Butler, preoccupied with law cases and out-of-state speeches had failed of renomination for Congress. In February of 1875, therefore, when Butler next gained the floor as an advocate of civil rights, he was a "lame duck" whose term would expire within a month. He therefore sought to hurry the measure through the House before he himself went out of office, and meanwhile his opponents across the way ungenerously reminded him of his temporary status and plagued him by filibustering. At this aggravated moment in history, records W. E. B. Du Bois, in *Black Reconstruction,* "the campaign of slander against 'carpetbaggers' rose to a climax which included in its denunciation every Northern person who defended the Negro . . . or who admitted the right of the Negro to vote or defended him in any way. It was the general, almost universal, belief that practically without exception these people were liars, jailbirds, criminals, and thieves, and the hatred of them rose to a crescendo of curses and filth." [7]

In Congress this was a period of ill-tempered bluff and bluster. "Much of it was theatrical and in a rude way artistic," writes W. V. Byars who witnessed these quarrels. "In exceptional cases, such as that of General Butler, it was the height of art with little or no passion in it. But back of it were fierce popular hatreds . . . and in the South there was a terror of the future which made logical action difficult and expressed itself from time to time in desperate acts of protest." [8]

On January 27, 1875, during a turbulent session in the House, Congressman Richard P. Bland scribbled a note to his wife: "We are now filibustering on the Civil Rights bill, Butler having reported a new one; we are moving to adjourn, and making all kinds of motions to stave it off. I expect we will be here all day and all night. We have taken three votes on the roll call to adjourn, and now have another. The excitement is getting greater all the time. The galleries are full of fifteenth amendmenters, and all other kinds of people . . . 'Old Ben' looks smiling, and I suppose will call for his dinner again (to be served at his desk in the House)." A week later the same writer noted that the filibuster was still on, "The galleries are crowded full, and back of me there are about five hundred negroes. It is suffocating." [9]

On February 1 Congressman Butler argued to amend the rules so as to curb filibustering. "[W]ith the country almost breaking into civil war, with White Leaguers organized all over the South, and one state disorganized and held by bayonets alone — are we to give up one-half of the remaining time of this House to filibustering?" [10]

Congressman John Young Brown of Kentucky declared that he would continue the filibuster till March 4 if necessary to prevent passage of the Civil Rights Bill. Brown, like Senator Garrett Davis of Kentucky, was a Southerner who accepted as truth the "Beast" Butler propaganda of wartime. Congressman S. S. ("Sunset") Cox of New York voiced a minority view that Civil Rights was now an "abstract, dead, and inconsequential business," but the situation grew tenser by the minute. Speaker Blaine once again descended to the floor to reply to Butler on procedural rules and to oppose the over use of the parliamentary device of calling for the previous question.

The House now amended the rules to curb filibustering by a vote of 157 yeas, 96 nays, 37 not voting. But this was not done until after forty-six hours of continuous session, during which the Members relieved their pent up feelings by name-calling. "This House," complained "Sunset" Cox, "is a sort of reservoir of the intemperance of the country: I simply refer to its intemperate language." [11]

The controversial Civil Rights Bill, as Butler explained it after the filibuster was checked, provided "That all citizens and other persons within the jurisdiction of the United States shall be entitled to the full and equal accommodations, advantages, facilities, and privileges of inns, public conveyances on land or on water, theaters, and other places of public amusement; and also of common schools and public institutions of learning or benevolence supported, in whole or in part, by general taxation; and of cemeteries so supported, and also the institutions known as agricultural colleges endowed by the United States, subject only to the conditions and limitations established by law, and applicable alike to citizens of every race and color, regardless of any previous condition of servitude." [12]

In spite of the prevailing tension Butler could not refrain from further "stirring up the animals." "The bill is necessary," he explained, "because there is an illogical, unjust, ungentlemanly, and foolish prejudice upon this matter. There is not a white man at the South who would not associate with a negro — all that is required in this bill — if that negro were his servant . . . But the moment that you elevate this black man to citizenship from a slave, then immediately he becomes offensive. That is why I say that his prejudice is foolish, unjust, illogical, and ungentlemanly." [13]

Congressman Brown of Kentucky, having listened with only half an ear and caught only the last sentences, assumed that Butler had meant to slander all Southerners, including those who were Members of Congress. Brown struck back in rage. Butler, whose constituency had not re-elected him to Congress, was declared by Brown to have been "outlawed in his own home from respectable society." Such widely distorted facts as Butler's defense of Oakes Ames, the Sanborn contracts, and the "Salary Grab" indicated, according to Brown, that Butler was one "whose name is synonymous with falsehood; who is the champion . . . of fraud . . . the apologist of thieves . . . such a prodigy of vice and meanness that to describe him would sicken imagination and exhaust invective . . . If I wished to describe all that was pusillanimous in war, inhuman in peace, forbidden in morals, infamous in politics, I should call it 'Butlerism.' " [14]

For this diatribe Congressman Brown was immediately disciplined in a vote of censure (161 yeas, 97 nays, 49 not voting). Even Congressman E. R. Hoar defended his old old enemy Butler: "My relations to my colleague from Massachusetts (Mr. Butler) have not been such that I think anyone would suppose I should rush forward to be his champion on any occasion; and in a contest of words I have always found that he is able to take care of himself pretty well and to give anybody as good as they send." "Sunset" Cox tried to smooth it over. "If my friend from Kentucky (Mr. Brown) was wrong, and my friend from Massachusetts (Mr. Butler) was intemperate yesterday — I mean in language only — we are all more or less responsible." The feeling was general that Congress had indeed lapsed too far into Billingsgate. Congressman Butler in a final word on the matter declared that in his eight years in Congress he probably had engaged in debate a great deal more than he ought to have done, but that he had never "commenced a personal attack upon any man in this House . . . I have endeavored with studied courtesy never to attack; and I have endeavored one thing more, sir — when I was attacked never to leave a man until he was sorry he did it. I have no more to say." [15]

Debate over the bill continued until the last day of the session. Two Negro members, Congressman Lynch from Mississippi and Congressman Rainey from South Carolina, offered moderate demands. Said Mr. Lynch, a mulatto preacher of obvious culture, "If I come [to Washington] by way of Louisville or Chattanooga, I am treated not as an American citizen, but as a brute. Forced to occupy a filthy smoking car both day and night, with drunkards, gamblers, and criminals; and for what? Not that I am unable or unwilling to pay my way; not that I am obnoxious in my personal appearance or disrespectful in my conduct, but simply because I happen to be of a darker complexion . . ." [16] Congressman Rainey sought to allay the fears of Southern whites that the Civil Rights Bill would promote intermarriage. "We, the colored people, are not in quest of social equality . . . [The] time has come when it is admitted that the negroes have rights that white men are bound to respect." [17]

As Chairman of the Judiciary Committee Butler presented the final arguments for the bill. "The Negro has been made . . . a citizen of the United States. And were he as black as the black diamond, he has an equal right to every privilege with a citizen who is white as an angel. And upon that ground alone can a democratic republic stand . . . I wonder with amazement when I hear it stated here that this bill is intended as a stab to constitutional liberty . . . What does it do? It simply provides that there shall be an equality of law all over the Union." [18]

Butler caused to be read into the record a letter he had received from a Negro woman in Richmond praising him for his work on the Civil Rights Bill.

I have long wanted to address a few lines to you in regard to your civil rights bill, but could not overcome my timmidity [sic], knowing as I do in my incapacity to write as I ought to such a lurned [sic] person as yourself; but fearing I shall not do my duty to my race if I remain silent, I shall trust these lines to your generosity for the forgiveness of all mistakes. Dear sir, there is one important point which has escaped your notice. Nothing can ever make us the equal with the white race while our daughters are forced to commit adultery by every white man and boy that chose to treat them as dogs; and if we attempt to apply to court one or more white boys will get up in court and say, I know her to be a bad woman or girl long ago; and the police justice calls us all a parcle [sic] of worthless prostitutes, and drives us out of court; and they won't even let the newspapers notice the outrage; just because we are colored people . . . I know (because I live South) that we can never raise virtuous daughters unless there is some law made to protect us from the power of the white man to outrage our little daughters before they reach the age of twelve, and some of them are even outraged at eight, nine, and ten . . . Do all that is in your power for us in this case.[19]

In summarizing, said Butler, "I desire . . . to assure gentlemen on the other side and the men of the South that we are only trying to protect these poor men that we have taken from slavery and made citizens, and I adjure them now that they shall do it for themselves after this bill is passed . . . When I spoke of the South as having a large minority of murderers and night-riders, I spoke of that class of men that make the Ku Klux and White League. It never occurred to me that any man on this floor could suppose for a moment that I referred to men who were here, or to a majority of the men in the South, who I have no doubt honestly desire peace and quiet. I am bound in all fairness to say so much; and it is done without compulsion . . .

"I want [the Civil Rights Bill] to go forth as a thing which I stand upon . . . When we passed the Thirteenth Amendment to the Constitution of the United States we [Republicans] lost Ohio the first year; but we regained it the next. So now if the republican party will finish their great work, pass the civil-rights bill. If, then, we will by bayonet or otherwise bring peace, prosperity, law and good order in the South, and put down those that ride by night there to murder and burn, which the South ought to do for itself, you will find that we will come back here sustained by voices of the loyal union-loving men of the country." [20]

Here the Speaker's hammer fell.

The vote was now taken on the last day of the session and the Civil Rights Bill was passed. It was a strictly party vote, the tally being 162 yeas, 99 nays, and 28 not voting.

For two years following Butler was out of Congress. Though he plunged into his law cases, he was for some weeks as restless as a caged cat. Then, relaxed by frequent trips on the yacht *America,* he even began to toy with the idea of abandoning politics permanently.

From Salem, after a day in court, he wrote to Sarah, "I am quartered with my client at his home, a very handsome one. He is one of the richest men in Salem and [I] am very pleasantly housed and cared for. Barring a slight cold I am very well and have been working like a horse or more properly like an Ass — as I am. Why do I not go out of politics and quit. I suppose that such a little incident as occurred today keeps me in. As I left my house this morning all the boys in the school nearby turned out and gave me three lusty cheers. They were very grateful to me as not one of the little fellows wanted a place in the Custom House . . ." And the next night again — just before taking his bath and going to bed — "Here am I in a large three story house occupying a whole floor with not a soul in it but *two* negros [sic] who sleep in the ell. There you are occupying a whole three story house with nobody else in it but *three* negroes. And this too when we should both be together and not apart. Isn't it funny, although funny it is not pleasant. I feel very lonely . . . Let us think what is gained by all this turmoil and strife. Might we not get more out of life by being quiet [?] I am thinking so more and more day by day, what say you?" [21]

Yet he could no more retire from politics than he could surrender the pleasurable excitement of the courtroom. His family situation — the plight of Blanche and Adelbert, for one thing — never permitted him to forget the old issues he had wrestled with in Congress. The flour mill in which Blanche and Adelbert had invested required further loans, and to enable the children to escape the high interest charges in the West, Butler endorsed Ames's notes. As a foremost advocate of cheap money, he made an address on finance to the New York Board of trade, although aware it would possibly "set the [political] pot to boil with renewed vigor." [22]

The Boston *Herald*'s prompt reaction was to needle Butler in an article "Our Son-in-law in Mississippi." Both Ames and Blanche meanwhile were becoming fed up with Mississippi. While Governor Ames was on his usual summer vacation in the North, the Negro Lieutenant Governor of Mississippi dismissed certain of Ames's appointees from their jobs and accepted money for issuing pardons to criminals. A Negro member of the Republican State Central Committee was convicted of mail robbery. The failure of Federal support at election time persuaded Ames that he could look for no future in Mississippi. On 12 October 1875 Ames wrote his wife that the White-liners had put over their revolution and returned the Negroes to a "second slavery." "The Nation should have acted but *it* was 'tired of the annual autumnal outbreaks in the South' . . . The political death of the Negro will forever release the nation from such 'political outbreaks.' Last night I made up my mind to resign after the election when this revolution shall have been completed. Why should I fight on a hopeless battle for two years more, when no possible good to the Negro or anybody would be the result?" [23]

Sarah Butler, despite an annoying swelling in her throat which interfered with her breathing, wrote letters of encouragement, and once again Ben Butler rode the train to Long Branch, again to beg President Grant to break the log jam of shilly-shally and send troops to Mississippi. Some colored men called at Belvidere, Butler's home in Lowell, to solicit a contribution to purchase rifles for Negroes of the South to defend themselves. "Not one dollar," declared Butler. "I will give you twenty-five cents for a package of lucifer matches, and if you cannot take care of yourselves with that you are not worthy to be freemen. If you and your friends are molested why do you not burn the dwellings and cotton fields of your persecutors [?] Take it when there is a high wind, and you will not have to burn more than four or five before they will be glad to leave you alone." [24] To one H. Adams of Shreveport, Louisiana, Butler wrote, "I see at present no hope of alleviation except in themselves. So long as they will submit to be killed by every marauding white man who will do so, so long there will be no help; nor do I believe there is any aid to be looked for from the United States . . . I should take to killing equally if I were a colored man . . ." [25]

To Ames, when impeachment became a certainty, Butler sent the advice that he should "put calmly, in the most dignified way, a statement of all occurrences in the election in your forthcoming message . . . dwell particularly upon the financial character of your administration." [26] Ames was advised to send an advance copy of his message so that Butler could get it published on the day it was delivered.

Less and less of Butler's time, in the interval when he was out of Congress, was spent quietly at home. "I have got back as far as Boston," he wrote Sarah on October 20, 1875, "and have got to turn on my heel and go back again. I will go at six o'clock. Please come here and go with me. Now, if your health will permit, don't say no. If you can't come, send Paul down with a couple of shirts . . ." [27] Blanche, who had not yet gone south, sent the shirts by express and explained that Paul was away and that her Mother was still too hoarse to leave home. "We are sorry that you are to go back at once, without coming home for a night at least." [28]

Discouraged over his wife's ill health, as well as by the diminishing fortunes of Blanche and Adelbert, Butler offered for sale his new and unfinished four-story granite house on Capitol Hill. The figures he quoted for the prospective buyer, Senator Jones, were $100,000 in its present state or $125,000 finished. Jones declined to purchase, and after Butler had completed the building, he rented it to Jones for $13,000 a year, so that Sarah would not have the bother of furnishing it.

When the impeachment charges against Governor Ames were finally voted by the new white-controlled legislature, Butler engaged two of the best lawyers in the country to go to Mississippi to conduct Ames's defense, Thomas J. Durant and Roger A. Pryor. The latter was an ex-Confederate general and now a law partner in Butler's New York Office. Butler would have gone himself had he not felt that in the inflamed state of public opinion his own appearance in Mississippi would do more harm than good. In confidence Blanche Ames informed Pryor that she and Adelbert really wanted to leave Mississippi, but that Adelbert could not resign while under fire. Pryor now approached the Democratic leaders of the legislature and arranged for the impeachment charges to be withdrawn upon the assurance that Governor Ames would resign. This pleased the legislators, whose interest lay in recovering control of the State and not in pressing dubious charges against Ames as an individual.

Neither Ben Butler nor Sarah was satisfied with this result, but they suspended judgment pending the children's arrival home and in April, Sarah's condition having become grave, Butler broke up housekeeping in Washington to take Sarah to see specialists in Boston. On April 1 he wrote his son-in-law Governor Ames of Mississippi, "Tell Blanche that I start for home on Monday morning, April 3, breaking up house-keeping here, with her mother. She goes home but the house will be open a little while. My stay there will be determined by her state of health, although I have got very pressing matters to call me here, so that if she is able to have me come away I shall come. Meanwhile she intends to have some operation upon her throat, if so advised by her physician, Dr. Cabot whom we shall visit in Boston on our way home. Now, don't be unnecessarily alarmed at this, but yet I do not conceal from you that Mrs. Butler would be exceedingly gratified if Blanche could be with her and relieve her from the care of the household during this painful and perhaps dangerous operation . . . Everything goes well with me except, the one thing, and that is Sarah's health, and the thought of her suffering and possible danger makes everything bad." [29]

On April 6 the surgeons operated on Mrs. Butler in the Massachusetts General Hospital and discovered a fibrous cancer filling the throat. They estimated that she might live three weeks. She died in less than three days. Paul and Ben-Israel were with their father. Blanche was summoned by telegraph. To his half sister Mrs. Betsy Morrill Stevens of Nottingham, New Hampshire, Butler wrote on the 9th, "My Dear Betsy, Sarah died at one o'clock and thirty minutes this morning at Boston. She will be buried Wednesday at the earliest, perhaps not until Thursday. Won't you and such of your family as can come down? If Mr. Batchelder is with you have him and Lizzie come. I will send to Chelsea for them. I hope when you do come you will make it convenient to stay with us some time. We are very lonely here. Blanche will come home. Give my love to Daniel, Amanda and Thomas. Perhaps Thomas will come down. Brother, Benj." [30]

30

THE REFORM GOVERNOR

AFTER the calamity of Sarah's death Butler plunged into a political grapple with his old enemy Judge Ebenezer Rockwood Hoar and wrested from him the Congressional seat for the Lowell district. Election to this final term in Congress "vindicated" him, and wiped out the sting of his defeat in 1874, and at its close in 1878, having rounded out ten years in the House of Representatives, Butler gave up running for Congress and shifted his sights to the governorship of Massachusetts.

This office he had long coveted. In 1860 he had run for Governor on the Breckinridge Democratic ticket, but Massachusetts, overwhelmingly abolitionist and furious over his having voted fifty-seven times for Jefferson Davis at the Charleston Convention, had defeated him by a landslide. In 1871 he had campaigned unsuccessfully for the Republican nomination. His candidacy was sponsored by labor reformers who organized Butler clubs, packed caucuses, systematically outcheered and outjostled their opponents, but had not been able to outvote them. In the Republican State Convention Butler found the party machinery against him, with George Frisbie Hoar in the chairman's seat and his brother Ebenezer at the head of the Committee on Credentials. Butler delegates from several areas were refused seats, and their candidate lost the nomination. In 1878, Butler left the Republican Party and without asking consent of the Democratic Party announced his return after sixteen years to its fold. He was now an acknowledged national leader of currency reform, a unique role among New England Congressmen, and one of the counsel in the legal tender case (Julliard Vs. Greenman) which Butler had devised to test Congress's constitutional power to regulate the currency. While this role rendered him anathema to Boston bankers, it made a wide appeal to men in the West whom Butler in view of his ambition to be President never forgot.

From San Francisco came an unkempt advocate of greenbacks named Dennis Kearney to stump Massachusetts in favor of Ben Butler for Governor. Often this brass-kettle orator to crowds of workingmen on street corners shook his fist at the "lecherous bondholders" and shouted "Bullets, if ballots fail!" [1]

Butler, meanwhile, spoke to out-of-state audiences in Maine, New York and Connecticut, explaining his shift from Republicanism to Democracy and outlining his views on currency and on the relations of capital and labor. "The whole legislation of this country for the past sixteen years has been in favor of money and not in favor of enterprise or labor." Overproduction should be regulated by cutting hours of labor "to one hour a day, if necessary." The wrongs of the laboring classes, Butler told a New York audience, could be righted by electing proper men to office. Their safety lay "in organization and standing together." At New Haven he declared that his fight against paper currency issued by banks was "the same fight that Andrew Jackson had fought." Accepting as a mandate a petition signed by 51,874 voters, he became a candidate for Governor, and proclaimed his basic policy to be: "Equal rights, equal duties, equal burdens, equal privileges and equal protection, by the laws to every man everywhere under the Government, State or Nation." [2] In the interest of the workingman he demanded new laws covering education, health and safety precautions in factories.

The Independent-Greenback Convention held in Boston on September 11, 1878, chose Butler as its candidate for Governor, after which Butler men began popping up in Democratic caucuses all over Massachusetts and electing members to the State Democratic Convention to be held in Worcester on September 17.

Since Butler had not made a formal request for readmission to their party, the Executive Committee of the State Democratic Central Committee adopted a rule "That no person not a recognized member of the party is to be nominated for Governor." And the day before the convention met, a cartoon was circulated representing General Butler as a tramp, looking wistfully over a garden fence at a melon marked "nomination."

On September 17, the day of the Worcester convention, Butler did not appear in person; however, his friends arrived before daylight, 973 of them. They forced the door with a crowbar and took possession of Mechanics Hall. There they waited, puffing tobacco, chewing, spitting, laughing, breakfasting on barrels of crackers, cheese and milk tins filled with coffee, making nominating speeches for Ben Butler until eight o'clock when the regular Democratic officials arrived.

When Mayor Charles B. Pratt of Worcester ordered the Butlerites out of the hall, they defied him. At 8:25 Mayor Pratt and 276 other delegates managed to squeeze inside the hall. After two hours of not ill-natured wrangling — during which Mayor Pratt was "nominated" for a place on Ben Butler's ticket — the Regular Democrats withdrew to meet later at Faneuil Hall in Boston and draw up their slate of "regular Democratic" nominees. The Butlerites, meanwhile, went through the usual formalities of organizing and nominating their candidate.

How far Butler was responsible for the excesses of his friends it is not possible to say. Newspapers of all party affiliations showered upon him the usual abuse, which one is tempted to believe he relished.

In the campaign that followed, Butler waged a restrained, even-tempered fight. "If I catch myself saying a word against Thomas Talbot [the Republican candidate], I shall consider myself as showing signs of insanity." [3] Republican Senator George Frisbie Hoar, stumping against Butler, denounced the latter's "worthless rag" currency ideas, charged him with coveting the governorship as "a stepping stone for his national ambitions," and damned his whole political record as one of "swagger, quarrel, failure." [4] Dennis Kearney, on the other hand, mounted a railing at the Frog Pond in Boston to hail General Butler as "the liberator of the people" and to belittle the Regular Democratic leaders as "honorable bilks," "respectable snides" and "lop-eared mackerel." [5] For six weeks Butler himself traveled over the state speaking every day but Sunday with "moderation, caution and carefulness" to two or three audiences a day.

Again his record as lawyer, businessman, general, and Congressman was raked with a fine-tooth comb, and cartoonists had a field day.

At the polls, where the voters were monitored by their employers, as the law permitted the candidates to use ballots of distinctive colors, the score ran: Talbot (Republican) 134,725; Butler (Butler-Democrat) 109, 435; Abbott (Regular Democrat) 10,162; Minor (Prohibition) 1913. Although he lost in the state, he carried Boston by a plurality of 4283. He was, indeed, so encouraged that he tried again the following year, but with approximately the same results, the Democratic Party split continuing. Failing to win the governorship in time for such victory to have an effect on the National Campaign of 1880, and having spent on the elections of 1878 and 1879 (according to the estimates of opposing newspapers) some $275,000, Butler refrained from running for Governor for the next two years.

His famed racing yacht became his chief means of escape and relaxation. He clothed his crews in smart uniforms, mounted a salute gun on the *America*'s bow and on national holidays dressed the craft with bunting and opened her to visitors. Most often he engaged in short races or ran down to Newport and New York to view other yacht races. Several times he poked up the St. Lawrence, and along the Labrador coast where he had fished for cod the summer after his graduation from Waterville. Once he cruised as far as Havana with his sons Paul and Ben-Israel. On board the *America* in rough clothes and rubber coat he loved to ride out a nor'wester. With advance notice from the Coast Survey he would hurry out to sea in order to catch a storm. "I suppose you know the qualifications of a yachtsman," he wrote a prospective guest, "to wit, to be able to eat and drink unlimitedly, not be seasick more than one-half of the time and keep good natured under difficulties, if any occur, especially in drizzly weather and to be able to play any ordinary game of cards except Kino, which is strictly forbidden on the ground that it requires so much mathematics as to be inadmissible. The outfit will need to be the thickest possible clothing and roughest clothing, a rubber overcoat and cap if you desire to be on deck when it rains and a reasonable supply of the latest novels in case the yacht library should not be sufficient." [6]

After Sarah's death he had to adjust himself to a new existence. "Bay View," his granite cottage overlooking Ipswich Bay, he gave up living in altogether, preferring to turn it over for summer occupancy to Blanche or to one of his nieces. Occasionally he would nose the *America* into Ipswich Bay for a brief visit. His Washington home was kept for him by his nieces, Harriet H. Heard, daughter of Sarah's sister Harriet, and Charlotte B. Stevens, daughter of the only surviving member of his boyhood household, his half-sister Betsy Morrill Stevens. At "Belvidere," overlooking the Merrimack near Lowell, he kept Sarah's room exactly as she had left it, with reading and needlework scattered around, and surrounded himself with a veritable museum of family trophies — swords, powder horns, landscapes painted by Blanche, bearskin rugs, lawbooks and busts of famous lawyers. Here in purple velvet dressing gown and carpet slippers he felt most at home, keeping bachelor hall with his son Paul.

Blanche Ames, with her family, returned from Mississippi soon after her mother's death. Now more than ever a favorite, Blanche looked after her father as much as his crowded business schedule and her own increasing family would permit. In short visits at Thanksgiving and Christmas Butler renewed acquaintance with his older grandchildren and met the new ones. When his namesake Butler Ames, Blanche's oldest child, got diphtheria one summer and could not come to Bay View, the grandfather was amazed to find that he could worry so much about "a young gentleman of his size." [7] Butler offered the services of his yacht to transport his daughter's "division of the Grand Army" from New York to Bay View, and on May 29, 1881, he replied in jest to her request for a lock of hair: "In the matter of the lock of hair, I am inclined to believe from the context that it is a pious fraud on your part to get my hair cut. But I had it cut the very Sunday morning after I left you but not short enough so that by the time you get to Bay View it will not want cutting again, and then I shall find out whether this hair business is a matter of affectionate desire or simply a delicate way of calling my attention to a lax personal appearance." [8]

His son Paul became his mainstay after Sarah's death. Following Paul's graduation from Harvard — or obtaining, as Butler termed it, "a patent of Massachusetts nobility" — Butler turned over to him the management of the United States Cartridge Co.[9] Paul's boyhood injury to his spine had left him a cripple with short legs, though from the waist up he was thickset and muscular. Skilled in handling a canoe, he would occasionally take a ten-day trip up the Concord River, probably without realizing what pangs of loneliness his busy father would suffer during his absence. Paul had a laboratory in the attic at Belvidere in which he invented improvements for the cartridge manufacturing machinery. He also built an ingenious sliding seat for use on his ice-sailboat to enable him to shift his weight readily and compete in races with men who had the full use of their legs. Paul made business trips over the country and in 1877 at the time of the Russo-Turkish War went to Russia to sell cartridges. On January 3, 1881, while Paul was away traveling at company expense — his father and himself being the company — General Butler wrote his son: "The members of the company voted with great unanimity that a committee be appointed to examine the accounts of our traveling agents and see to it that there was no expenses for swallow-tail coats and white gloves concealed under the head of stationery. As your friend I give you notice of this, — Perhaps I ought not to do so — that you may have your vouchers in proper form. My kindness of feeling may lead me into a partial betrayal of trust in this regard, but I know you will excuse it on the ground of natural affection." [10]

Ben-Israel Butler was a likable but not an industrious youth. Upon his return with Paul from preparatory school in Heidelberg, his father obtained for him an appointment to the Military Academy — the father was determined that the son should not be handicapped as he had been for want of a West Point education. Ben-Israel had been Sarah's favorite child, and Butler watched his progress anxiously. As the youth was an average cadet who cared little for grades and less for drill, his father was moved to write him "fetch up your standard as high as possible . . . I do not speak the language of blame, but ask you as your dear Mother would if she was here to work a little more continuously." [11] And a month later he wrote, "I do not see what always ought to accompany a school boy's letter, a request for money. Where do you get yours, and how much are you using and what do you want? It is not often a father writes these questions to his son when away at school . . . Paul and I are keeping house in Lowell, all alone with one servant; a little short commons, but we shall get on after we get going." [12] In

1878 while Ben-Israel was a junior officer on monotonous Indian-patrol
duty in the Southwest, and the possibility loomed of a war between
England and Russia, Butler offered to get Ben-Israel a commission on
either side — if he felt "warlike" — but the young man preferred to resign his commission to study law at Columbia. In the fall of 1881, after
completing his bar examination, he was all set to enter the law office
with his father. In anticipation of the new partnership Butler moved
into roomier quarters at 16 Pemberton Square. But on September 1
Ben-Israel died suddenly of Bright's disease, at Bay View, where he had
been spending the summer with Blanche. The great shock hit General
Butler the next day upon his return from a vacation cruise.

In 1881, when his prospect of becoming Governor was brightened
by a country-wide sentiment for reform, Ben Butler at sixty-four was
persuaded once more to run for Governor. Both Democratic and the
National Greenback-Labor State Conventions nominated him.

Butler's decorum during the campaign was a disappointment to the
Boston *Journal*. "There is a disagreeable suspicion creeping through
the Democratic ranks that Butler does not care to be elected Governor;
that he will not make one of his old-fashioned fights, and that while he
soars for higher game he cares little what becomes of the Massachusetts
Democracy." [13] The Cape Ann *Advertiser* tried prodding the candidate.
"Put him today at the head of the nation, give him a procession with
banners flying and bands playing, and the world looking on with admiration, and while all that procession is going on let there be a dog or
cat fight up some back alley and he will jump off to run to it." [14]

Reform, despite detractions, was in the ascendant. At last on November 8, 1882 — after many disappointments — Benjamin F. Butler
was elected Governor of Massachusetts, by a plurality of 14,000 in a total
vote of 250,000.

From all quarters came congratulations. "In your new career," wrote
his friend and biographer James Parton, "I hope you will wreak a full
revenge upon your traducers by doing every good and wise act which
they ought to have done, but had not the courage to do." [15] Clara Barton's message read: "Glad. God Bless you General, now and always." [16]
One enthusiastic Confederate veteran assured Butler that he now be-

lieved "that you did not get those spoons." [17] Another sent "Three cheers and a tiger *for grand Old Ben Butler* for the next Democratic President of the U.S." [18]

The liberals who flocked to congratulate the Governor-elect and encourage him in sponsoring their several causes included Wendell Phillips, civil rights crusader; Burnham Wardwell, prison reformer; and the suffragette Susan B. Anthony. Mrs. Anthony wrote to Phoebe Couzins, "I had an hour, a splendid one, with 'brave Old Ben Butler' a few days since, and I believe he is going to say a splendid word for woman suffrage in his address to the Mass. Legislature." [19]

At 11:35 A.M. on Thursday, January 4, 1883, General Butler stepped out of the Revere House and into his private carriage. He was accompanied by his son-in-law General Adelbert Ames and his grandson Butler Ames. At the State House five minutes later he removed fur cap and coat and in black broadcloth, with white tie and kid gloves, and wearing a flower in his buttonhole, "without which he would not be Gen. Butler," entered the Executive Chamber to be introduced to Governor Long, ex-Governor Talbot, President Eliot of Harvard College and other dignitaries.[20] At 12:55, receiving notification of committees from the two branches of the legislature, the Governor-elect entered the Chamber, carrying the same gold-knotted oak staff which Governor Hancock had used. When he took the oath he bent over very close to sign, and Secretary of State Pierce noting his nearsightedness, guided his hand to the proper place for the signature. The Secretary of State now announced that General Butler was Governor of Massachusetts and the applause of the legislature was echoed outside by a saluting battery on the Common.

At 1:03 P.M. Governor Butler moved to the rostrum to give his inaugural address. "Lifting the printed copy to his eye," reported the Boston *Journal,* "as if he would analyze every letter, and beginning in a low, measured tone, he broke at once to his full force of voice and earnestness." [21] In a speech lasting two hours and thirty minutes, he covered relations between capital and labor, reform of the criminal law code, reform of the management of almshouses and penal institutions.[22] He advocated woman suffrage, eliminating the poll tax, prohibiting the sale of liquor on election days. Hours of labor should be lowered, wages increased. Railroad employees, in the interest of public safety, should not be required to work more than ten hours a day. Antiquated blue laws, he declared, should be stricken from the books. His most sensational charges concerned the management of the Tewksbury Almshouse, whose officials were accused of supplying themselves with luxury goods at the expense of the inmates, and of ghoulish traffic in the sale of cadavers to medical schools.

While some Massachusetts editors shuddered at the unflattering criticism, out-of-state journalists hailed his liberalism with delight. "It is a remarkable paper, such as might be expected from so remarkable a man," wrote Dana of the New York *Sun:* "It is uncommonly long, yet nothing commonplace, no nonsense. Brave, shrewd, patient, persistent, clearsighted, quick-witted, level-headed, the bluff General goes right to the heart of every question he touches. There is not an idea or suggestion or recommendation that is not inspired by an honest purpose to serve the State of Massachusetts. Yet his message could not have created a greater stir in certain quarters if he had proposed to paint Bunker Hill monument green or to hang Frisbie Hoar for piracy." The *Times* wrote, "Most vigorous and suggestive document . . . Butler evidently intends to be a live Governor, and if there is not a raking up of old business and breaking to pieces of routine methods, and the infusion of new vigor tempered with economy in the administration of affairs, it will not be his fault!" The *Tribune* commented, "No more readable public document has been issued anywhere for many years. It is thoroughly Butlerish throughout . . . , he tells a great deal of truth which his immediate predecessors have lacked either the courage or the inclination to utter." [23] Butler was hailed as a second Andrew Jackson whose road to the White House could no longer be blocked by Lilliputian opponents.

After such a buildup it was unfortunate that the Democratic reform governor should have been hamstrung by hostile Republican majorities in Legislature and Executive Council. Even Lieutenant Governor Oliver Ames, Butler's second in command, was a Republican. A great deal, nevertheless, was done to publicize reform. A committee of the Legislature listened to Julia Ward Howe and other witnesses assert that votes for women would not increase the number of female insane as some male politicians contended. There was an overhauling of the state's budget and upon the invitation of the Joint Committee of Expenditures, Butler appeared before it to advocate a single purchasing agency for all the state's reformatory and charitable institutions.

State office workers, since the new Governor was an early riser, began getting to their desks on time. Clara Barton accepted Butler's offer of the Superintendency of the Women's Reformatory Prison. Butler sent Dr. William B. Goldsmith, superintendent of a mental hospital, to England and France to visit institutions there with a view of improving methods of treating the insane in Massachusetts. Breaking precedent he appointed a Negro lawyer to be judge in the Bunker Hill district.[24]

Butler invited the prisoners of the State Prison at Concord to send complaints to him in sealed envelopes with which prison authorities were forbidden to tamper. When Warden Earle opened the letters anyway the Governor ousted him. After a new warden had been installed, the Governor inspected the prison, talked with the men, quietly pocketed some letters that were handed him, had lunch with the new warden and made a speech to the prisoners. The Boston *Journal* noted that he was "greeted with round after round of plaudits, and then with tumultuous shouts that were not half as noisy as they were cordial." [25]

When the Saturday Club of New York entertained Governor Butler, and Chauncey Depew hailed him as "the political evangel of the future," Butler laughed heartily, and running his hands over his shoulders, felt for his wings.[26]

In issuing his Fast Day Proclamation, Butler, remembering the trouble that clergymen had made for him in some of his campaigns, urged ministers "to feed their flocks with the Divine Word," and avoid political topics, an admonition, which, needless to say, none of them observed.[27]

As Governor, Butler gave up his law practice within the state of Massachusetts, but he had cases elsewhere that had been on the dockets for a number of years which he could not readily turn over to other counsel.

Since he often found it necessary to cancel his appearances before legislative committees, the *Journal* suggested that he publish in advance a schedule of his movements to enable clients, courts, and legislators to make their arrangements. Disgruntled legislators of the opposing party questioned the legality of a veto mailed in from out of the state. Was Butler still Governor when he was in New York or was the Lieutenant Governor temporarily the Chief Executive?

The most notorious of Governor Butler's investigations was that of the Tewksbury Almshouse. Charges of maladministration had been brought against the Superintendent at Tewksbury ten years earlier and nothing had been done to correct abuses. Butler's information was obtained from Burnham Wardwell, a professional reformer, through Milo Hildreth, a trustee of Northboro Reform School, and a Dr. A. N. Blodgett.

The charges against the management of the Almshouse were:[28]

1. That infant mortality in the institution was scandalously high,
2. That inmates had been robbed of their clothing,
3. That funeral services had been held over coffins filled with blocks, while the corpses had been spirited away and sold to the Harvard Medical School,
4. That Harvard medical students had tanned the skins of cadavers and turned the leather into footwear and purses.

Chicago's liberal *Inter-Ocean* declared on April 12, "The Governor may make a name for himself as a reformer, but he is hopelessly disgracing the name of Massachusetts. He might have corrected all the parsimonious errors, even hung the officials, without blowing a horn so loud that all the world would have paused to observe the shame and humiliation of the good people of the State over the iniquity."[29] "Verily the man of Beacon Hill has become the Dick Deadeye of American politics," declared the Philadelphia *Telegraph*.[30]

The Boston *Journal* in May wondered whether Harvard College would offer Governor Butler the degree of LL.D. even though so honoring the Chief Magistrate had become a tradition at Harvard. The question had been posed by President Eliot, and the Harvard faculty voted to grant the degree, but the Board of Overseers — of which Governor Butler's ancient enemy Judge E. R. Hoar was president — voted 15 to 11 against.

In secret Ben Butler took Harvard's refusal as a slap in the face. In two pages of foolscap notes which he never used but filed among his papers he blew off steam in private.

To minimize as far as possible the snub offered Governor Butler by the Board of Overseers, President Eliot invited him to be his personal guest at the Alumni dinner following the commencement exercises, and offered his home to the Governor and his staff during the interval between the graduation and the dinner. Senator G. F. Hoar, president of alumni, now declined to attend the dinner.

Governor Butler drove out to Cambridge in an open barouche drawn by six horses. He did not wear his major general's uniform as some close friends advised, but was accompanied by a major general's honor guard mounted and in full uniform. The Governor was in formal dress with boutonniere and silk topper which he continually doffed to cheering crowds along the route. In his pocket he carried as a speech a historical story about the ungenerous lobbying in the Legislature by Harvard College prior to the founding of Williams College.

But the anti-Harvard anecdote never left its dark pocket. President Eliot and the faculty made the Governor feel that he was at home and among friends. Merriment was created at President Eliot's table when someone produced a cartoon from the current issue of the humor magazine *Life* which represented Butler in the bow of a Harvard boat at the Yale race, vainly trying to reach a balloon marked "LL.D." In his introductory remarks Toastmaster Choate referred with tact and humor to his own delicate position between two horns of the dilemma, and he brought down the house by a reference to Senator Hoar, who had taken fright and run away from the dinner.

In reply to the chairman's toast to the Commonwealth Governor Butler improvised a short and appropriate talk, in which he mentioned his own boyhood envy of a group of bright young freshmen who were entering Harvard and the fact that he had sent his own son Paul there.

Pleased by the outcome of an affair so painful in the anticipation, But-

ler gathered a sheaf of newspaper clippings for his daughter Blanche
and followed it with a letter: "I suppose you have got the papers I sent
you all about the Harvard matter. It was only a little game of skill
between Self and brother Hoar. It is all described in the old nursery
rhyme:

> *He digged a pit*
> *He digged it deep*
> *He digged it for his brother*
> *But he fell in*
> *And was drowned therein*
> *And died instead of t'other.*

I hope you liked the Speech. It was a poor one not by any means up
to concert pitch. But [I] had a real good speech carefully prepared because I supposed I should have a row and then you know one must be
prepared and say on the *spur of the moment* the worst possible things
in matter but manner the most cool and faultless. But I was so kindly
received by President & Fellows and the Post Graduated alumni that I
had to throw all the preparation away and grope about for the speech I
did deliver which was honor bright ex tempore. Alas! There was a
good speech, that other one, lost to the world . . . Love to all the babies
including the General from Father." [31]

31

NOMINATION FOR PRESIDENT: 1884

EVER since his early fights over the secret ballot and the ten-hour law Ben Butler had backed causes that would help the little man. "If I had been the firm, ardent . . . advocate of the hard-money views of the money-lenders of State Street," he once wrote S. W. Hopkinson, "I should have been their pet and not their aversion, and Massachusetts would have given me anything on earth that was in her gift. But following my convictions I suffer the penalties of all reformers."

In Congress he demanded that the national legislature come to grips with such fundamental problems as working conditions and the re- lations of capital and labor. "There is little time or interest expended upon the conditions of labor." "The laborer supports the capitalist and the 'better classes' with the sweat of his brow and the toil of his hands." [1]

In 1878 Congressman Butler introduced an appropriation bill to send workingmen and women, one from each state, to represent Amer- ican labor at the Paris Exposition.

America, he declared, was far behind England in the boxing and housing of machinery for the protection of workers. When fire broke out in the granite mill at Fall River, men and women burned to death for want of suitable fire escapes or dashed their lives out by jump- ing from upper stories of the building. Butler brought suit for one of the sufferers in order to test the question of responsibility for the safety of the worker, but there was no clear decision in the case.

Like some self-appointed Moses seeking to lead his people out of bondage, Ben Butler denounced "the thraldom of King Gold." [2] He condemned the return to specie payments after the war, as a procedure which "made the rich richer and the poor poorer." He opposed either gold or silver money, since these metals, being desirable commodities in the world market, were on occasion drained off by foreigners, with disastrous results to the United States. In California, he estimated, coolie labor annually sent back to the Orient about sixty millions of United States hard currency, the capricious drainage of its money supply adversely affecting the nation's economy. "There is no magic, witchery, mysticism or obscurity in the laws which govern finance any more than the law of gravitation," Butler declared.[3] The solution, in his opinion, was for the Government to coin money of materials having the least possible intrinsic value. The wartime greenback, fiat money, not backed by gold, but simply by the word of the Government, was the money he advocated. He fought specie payments, the return to hard money after the war, in the belief that a currency based on precious metal tempted speculators to corner gold and panic the nation. When Congressman Chittenden, a hard-money man, questioned him about his belief in the constitutionality of greenbacks, Butler mapped out the procedure for bringing up the test case of Julliard Vs. Greenman, and himself wrote the brief which won the case in the Supreme Court, thereby establishing the fact that Congress possessed the constitutional right to issue greenback currency. A monetary system capable of expansion and contraction was needed, claimed Butler, pointing out how the limited hard-money supply affected the country. In New England money could be borrowed at 8 per cent, whereas in the South it often cost the planter as high as 25 per cent, at a time when cotton planters in Egypt could borrow from London at 3 per cent. The disadvantages to the American producer and in turn to the little man, the factory worker and field laborer, were obvious. Butler suggested a system of convertible low-interest-bearing bonds, which the holder could at will convert into legal tender and which at the close of the harvest or other rush season might be turned back again into bonds. His ideas were listened to with rapt attention by workingmen over the country, while he was denounced by bankers, bondholders, and other businessmen.

In the spring of 1876, a month after Sarah's death, Butler declined to have his name put before the Greenback Convention for the nomina-

tion to the Presidency. "I aspire to no honors of that sort," he wrote
T. B. Buchanan, of Indianapolis; "I am content to be a soldier of the
ranks . . . and will do all that within me lies to change what I believe
to be a most vicious and destructive system of finance . . . I am too old
to have any maiden coyness, if I had any wish for that place, nor would
I refuse if I believed I could do any good to the cause by taking it." [4]

His election as Reform Governor in 1882, together with his victory
for the Greenback movement in the Supreme Court, touched off a
flurry of Presidential hopes among liberal friends. "It is my present
determination to vote for you for our next Pres't if possible — & it
hardly makes any difference who or what party nominates you. I am
your sincere friend," wrote E. S. Pope of Indianapolis.[5] Thomas V.
Peck of Hot Springs, Arkansas, sent the first "rebel yell" of the Southwest in the hope that the Governor might now go on to the Presidency.

Editor McClure of the Philadelphia *Times* hailed Butler as "the
only Reform Governor who seems to comprehend his situation — or
who has advanced one step on the road to the White House"; and R. M.
Griffin, editor of the Albany *Evening Post,* wrote Butler that a new
party known as the National Party had just been organized in Albany.
"Among the candidates spoken of for President of the new party is
Gen. B. F. Butler, of Massachusetts, the ablest man, lawyer and statesman to be found in all the New England States." [6]

For twenty years Ben Butler had been receiving fan mail from all
over the country urging him to run for President. Now a new Presidential "boom" inevitably followed his election to the Governorship.

To defeat Butler's re-election as Governor in the fall of 1883, bankers
and merchants attended protest meetings in Faneuil Hall. Moorfield
Storey compiled a campaign pamphlet entitled *The Record of Benjamin F. Butler,* a mass of newspaper quotations and misquotations that
had been attributed to Butler over a period of years. A hodgepodge of
the genuine and the false, and published anonymously, the document
was an accurate reflection only of the unreasoning anger of the Hoars,
the R. H. Danas, and their friends.

To get publicity in Boston, Governor Butler resorted to a paid advertisement in the *Herald,* for which the editor, apparently under pres-

sure, apologized in the next issue. Charles Francis Adams, spokesman of an aroused Beacon Hill, denounced Butler in Faneuil Hall.[7]

The Boston *Transcript* interpreted Butler's defeat in the 1883 election as "more than a simple gubernatorial defeat for the General," but Butler refused to accept the failure as an indication of his Presidential chances.[8] To Charles A. Dana of the New York *Sun* Butler pointed out that his total vote had increased by 40,000 in three years. There was a "tidal wave" quality about it that gave him hope that Massachusetts would go Democratic in 1884.[9]

Other political observers shared Butler's optimism when early in 1884 several bank failures seemed to presage a panic. "As to his chances for the Presidency, I think he has them," wrote George P. Cowlam of Madison, Wisconsin, "and they may become very great . . . But I think the Anti-Monopolists and Greenbackers will nominate him. Their support amounts to only a drop in the bucket, but there is likely to be a *great falling off in both parties this year.* Butler will get the 'usafruct' . . . [If a panic comes] here is where Butler's chance comes in . . . I don't think the man lives today who can ride the whirlwind ahead as Butler can." [10]

On March 4, 1884, an informal conference of Anti-Monopoly, National and Labor organizations, meeting in Chicago, appointed a committee to ascertain whether General Butler would accept the Presidential nomination if tendered him.

General James B. Weaver, Greenback candidate for President in 1880, was chairman of the committee that in secrecy waited upon the General in New York City the night of March 13, and received assurance that their offer would not be spurned. "There are certain good friends of yours residing in this city," Weaver explained next day by letter, "members of the National G. B. [Greenback] Party who entertain strong feelings of jealousy towards what they term 'outside organizations' such as 'Anti-Monopoly,' 'labor organizations,' etc. Now wishing to retain their active support it is thought best by the Committee who visited you last evening *that our visit should not be made known* to them." [11]

About this time the Detroit *Evening Press* predicted that if Ben

Butler were nominated by the minor parties his candidacy would be "a formidable one." Thousands of voters in every state "look upon him as the model leader and the bravest and boldest champion of popular rights . . . Many are dazzled by his singular career; many have an abounding faith in his luck; all are confident that if he were in the White House he would 'stir things up' generally as they have never been stirred up . . . since Jackson's time." [12]

In 1884 both the Anti-Monopoly and the Greenback parties nominated Ben Butler for President.

The two small-party nominations, Butler hoped, would enhance his chances inside the great Democratic circus tent. He was himself chosen a delegate-at-large to the Chicago Democratic National Convention, and a majority, though not all, of the members of the Massachusetts delegation were committed to vote for him as their party nominee.

Butler declined to subsidize newspapers whose editors now offered him their services. "No private fortune could answer the calls I have," he wrote S. H. Jennings, "and I find it very difficult to convince people that the newspaper lies about my fabulous fortune are of the same class as the other lies that are printed about me. I have that fortune only which I have fairly earned in a business life by hard work, less what I have spent in living generously and properly. I have not money enough to buy a Presidential Election, and I would not have a seat in the Presidential Chair if it was to be purchased." [13]

With his own money, however, he sent several henchmen into the field in advance of the convention to pledge delegates to vote for him. Noah A. Plympton, his recent campaign manager in the state election, finding the Detroit delegates committed to Cleveland, reported that although he "could not get a direct expression in your favor," he had rallied the Butler men in the area to exert pressure on the delegation. "It was so successful that all resolutions in his [Cleveland's] favor were laid on the table and three-fourths of the delegation are friendly to your nomination and seven will be OK on the 1st ballot." Western delegates, Plympton found, were looking to New York State: "A great deal depends on smashing Cleveland and that done we have a chance." [14] Plympton cashed a $500 draft on Butler and pushed on to Missouri and

Kansas. As it was now June 20, and late, the Democratic Convention having been called for early July in Chicago, Plympton authorized Charles S. Hampton to make a similar canvass for Butler in Iowa and Nebraska. On the 24th Plympton reported from Topeka that two-thirds of the Kansas delegates would support Butler if it were clear that he could be nominated. In Iowa and Michigan, "The majority of each [delegation] would rather it should be Gen. Butler but fear to take positive ground. There is a general impression that if N.Y., N.J., and Conn. come to Chicago united for Cleveland that they will all go for him. Boiled down the situation is this. Cleveland must be smashed or he will win against the field. With those states split up, you have more friends among these delegations than all the rest put together." Throughout the West Cleveland's manager Daniel Manning had agents at work, "and it is apparent that somebody has opened a 'bar'l' in Cleveland's interest." [15] Winding up in Chicago on the 28th, Plympton wrote: "I have expended the 250. you gave me and most of the 500. for which I made a draft. The distances are long here in the West and I have given in Mich. 100. the same in Iowa, Nebraska and Kansas to parties whom I have sent to get work put in on the various delegates so that I have used together with my own expenses about $650." He offered to open a campaign headquarters in Chicago, order badges, etc., if Butler wished him to. "If you leave it to my discretion I shall do as I always have for you try and make a dollar answer the purpose of two but I should much prefer to have explicit instructions." [16]

Butler sent the necessary authorization, and Plympton arranged for hotel accommodations for the Massachusetts delegation and got in touch with the Chicago labor organizations of shoemakers, brickmakers and typographers, arranging for them to parade the streets and serenade candidate Butler in front of the Palmer House on Saturday July 5. On June 30 he telegraphed his chief, "Yes, demonstration all arranged for Saturday night at nine at Palmer House. Leave Boston at eight-thirty Friday morning." [17]

A reporter, meanwhile, caught Butler as he arrived in Boston.

"General Butler, I believe you have just returned from Washington?"

"I have been to Washington upon professional business."

"What did you do while there, General?"

"I had excellent luck: I argued two cases."

"What is the opinion about politics?"

"I have none. Everybody is all at sea and I am more at sea than anybody else."

"Are you going to Chicago?"

"Yes, I mean to obey the wishes of my constituents, and I hope to do service in the matter of tariff reform."

REPORTER (finally getting to the point): "Are you going to be nominated?"

GENERAL BUTLER (ending the interview): "Did you ever hear the story of the negro who said he wished everybody would die and then he would keep tavern?" [18]

John Kelly, boss of Tammany and at outs with Cleveland, sent word through Roger A. Pryor, Butler's law partner in New York City, that Tammany was "all for Butler." "Kelly will meet you at General Ames' as you may direct. Keep yourself free, you are important in this crisis. Your friends here are resolute and defiant." [19] On June 10 Pryor wrote that August Belmont "is very friendly to you," that if Cleveland and Flower should wear themselves out in the Convention there would then be a good chance for Butler to come to the front. [20]

Here and there over the country amateur politicians promoted Butler booms in advance of the convention. Ex-Confederate General W. H. Parsons, now a sort of health faddist in Baltimore engaged in "the Galvanic-Magnetic treatment of disease," and lately a delegate to the Greenback Convention, began publishing manifestoes on the evils of the times and offering his assistance to Butler. Charles Robert of Sherman, Texas, printed a poster:

> *Hurrah for Ben Butler*
> *Did he steal the Spoons?* [21]

to advertise his own speeches favoring Butler for President. And in Grand Rapids, Michigan, lumberman J. M. Carr ornamented his vest buttonhole with a silver spoon inscribed "Benj. F. Butler," the spoon presumably having sluffed off its wartime connotation and become the symbol for some more prosaic concept like "feeding the oppressed little man." [22]

If Ben Butler hoped that wartime bitterness against him had begun to die out in the South, he could not be too sanguine. Several Southern editors wrote him that they would try to overcome their prejudice in case he were nominated.

Butler reached Chicago a day late, missing the scheduled demonstration by labor organizations. Word of his arrival spread quickly, however, and by ten o'clock Sunday night there gathered outside Butler's hotel, the Palmer House, several thousand of the lean kine of Pharoah's dream — "all bellowing for Butler and moving on the fat-fleshed Democrats in party convention on the banks of the Chicago River." [23] There were brass bands, Butler portraits, and transparencies proclaiming "The Workingman Welcomes Butler," "Butler will Sweep the Country," and "Labor Needs a Statesman." [24]

Finding it impossible to make himself heard from the steps of the ladies' entrance, Butler and his party made their way through an upstairs bedroom to a window overlooking the crowd. "When his well-known figure appeared," reported the New York *Sun*, "wild cheers rent the sky." Scarcely had Butler begun speaking when a horrified Cleveland man protested that Butler had entered and was now speaking from the bedchamber of Daniel Manning, Cleveland's manager. Butler's bodyguard fended the man off, but could not prevent him from shouting in a voice loud enough for the crowd outside to hear; "Mr. Manning courteously gives you the use of his parlor until 11 o'clock. Be so good as to leave it at that hour, as he wishes to retire." [25] Butler concluded his speech unconscious that he had been standing under a portrait of his rival Cleveland and was whisked back to his headquarters where he sat for an hour fanning himself and picking his boutonniere to pieces while receiving the congratulations of his admirers.

On the floor of the Democratic National Convention Butler's Tammany friends, Boss Kelly and New York State Senator Grady, lost their battle with Cleveland men to break up the unit rule. This meant that New York's undivided vote would be cast for Cleveland and that that vote, as Plympton had discovered, would influence Western delegations. Butler, nevertheless, enjoyed the spotlight as a leading contender. Chairman William F. Vilas had scarcely mentioned the name of Cleveland in his keynote address when Butler stole the show by making his entrance into the convention hall. The Massachusetts delegation in the fifteenth and sixteenth rows leaped to their feet, the galleries shouted, and Ben Butler, wearing a light suit with a black tie, was escorted to his chair on the platform.[26] This sort of thing, reported the Chicago *Tribune,* "made the veteran Bourbons who foam at the mouth at the mere mention of Butler turn pale with dismay." [27]

In the platform committee Butler met a second reverse when his ideas for a "laboring man's" tariff were voted down. Such a tariff, Butler explained, would promote American enterprise and American industry . . . cherish and foster American labor, and not create monopolies." [28] But the committee, bound by the money interests, as Butler believed, now struggled for thirty-six hours to phrase a plank "that should appear to say what mine said, and yet not say it; like the western hunter who tried to shoot his rifle at something he saw dimly stirring in a bush, so as to hit it if it was a deer and miss it if it was a calf." [29]

Butler carried his difference before the convention in a minority report in which he proposed liberal aims which the larger parties had hitherto shied away from. Since under existing laws controversies including labor and capital could be settled only by brute force, Butler wanted the Government to set up "tribunals in which these great controversies may be settled." He proposed that laborers be permitted "to combine and organize for their own protection, as capital may be incorporated and combined for its protection," and that laws restraining labor be changed. He denounced the importation of cheap contract labor. "America ought never to be a Lazar house for the reception of pauper labor of other countries." He offered a resolution "that all monopolies, as they tend to make two classes, the very rich and the very poor, were hurtful to the people of the republic." [30]

After the clerk had read "General Butler's platform," the candidate himself, in white cravat and dress coat with "a bunch of pansies in his lapel," [31] stepped to the front of the platform and began speaking "in his customary jerky, forceful way, gesticulating freely, and facing the audience at the right, the left, and in front of him." [32] It was crowding on to midnight and in the thirty minutes allotted to him he could argue only a single plank — the tariff for the protection "of the American laborer and producer." There was some isolated pro-Cleveland shouting here and there. Several Southern delegates stepped out of the hall for a few minutes and returned "smelling of cloves and coffee," but most of the delegates listened attentively.[33] In the gallery, applauding the liberal champion of their cause, were the prim Frances Willard and the colorful feminist and actress Anna Dickinson.

"If you refuse to stand by the workingmen," Butler shouted as his time ran out, "God help you, I cannot." [34] His liberal proposition was voted down 712½ to 97½.

Butler, finding the adopted platform unacceptable, and seeing that he could not be nominated, forbade the Massachusetts delegation to advance his name and returned to New York. Throughout the month of July he withheld public announcement of his plans. Should he support Cleveland? Should he run independently? Should he refuse to run at all? Cleveland men claimed he had promised to support the Democratic nominees. To go over to Cleveland, Butler felt, would be to betray the liberals of the minor parties that had nominated him.

On July 21, E. G. Afgar, Cleveland's Assistant Treasurer, went to Boston to see Butler's friend John Boyle O'Reilly. Afgar hoped that Butler would not run independently and assured O'Reilly that Governor Cleveland "regarded Butler in high estimation." "Has any courtesy been shown Gen. Butler by Cleveland or the leaders of the party?" demanded O'Reilly. "If not, why do they [not] do it without a moment's delay?" Afgar asked what they should do. O'Reilly suggested that he see Butler's friend P. A. Collins. Collins then came to consult O'Reilly, and both agreed that "as we were quite ignorant of your views, & only aware that you ought to receive all their courtesy and consideration, we said that they ought to send their most important men to see you." [35] Butler's failure to respond to this overture led Collins himself shortly to desert him and line up with Cleveland. On July 25 Butler's law partner Roger Pryor telegraphed: "Is it still an open question with you, whether you shall support Cleveland or not? If so, I would beg the privilege of an interview, and to that end would come to Boston. I have on the supposition that your mind is still undetermined, something of importance to communicate. If I need *not* come, telegraph *no.* If I need come telegraph *yes.*" [36] W. A. Simmons, the shrewd politician in the Boston Customs Office, wrote Butler: "You cannot support Blaine. It would be suicide for yourself and murder-for-your-friends to run independent; and therefore there is nothing left but to take the turkey and go for Cleveland." [37]

But Butler was not interested in Cleveland's "turkey." According to an interview given by Noah A. Plympton to the Buffalo *Times* six years later, "three prominent Democrats" offered Butler a choice of the attorney generalship, a foreign mission or the political patronage of New England. Butler thrashed the matter out in private with Plympton.

Take the attorney generalship. What is there in that? Who recalls the cabinet ministers of the last two administrations? . . . What opportunities has any one of them for individual assertion and distinction? What are they but a species of upper servants in thin disguise? Why, I can hire clerks myself for $2,500 who will be entirely competent to discharge all the duties of cabinet officers . . .

Now take No. 2. Only one foreign appointment has any attraction for me. I would like the place of American Minister at St. James. If I were in that place I could warrant an end of humbuggery and the surrender of American interests by incompetent commissions. But the appointment is impractical. No President would make it and no Senate would confirm it. The English would not tolerate the suggestion . . .

Now for No. 3. The patronage of New England is offered me. I do not want it. The control of patronage carries no inducement to be compared with its plague. Every appointment makes nine enemies and one ingrate . . .[38]

According to Plympton, Butler offered to support Cleveland if the latter would adopt the essentials of Butler's liberal program. And, as nothing came of this offer, Butler decided to accept the Greenback and Anti-Monopoly nominations and to wage an independent campaign. Plympton now presented the obvious arguments opposed to this course, "but the General said he didn't expect to win." "It will be the close of my political life," Plympton quotes Butler as saying. "But I shall be able to draw the attention of the American people to certain principles which I hold to be essentially democratic and vital to the well being of the republic. These will be the fully deliberated conclusions of my life long experience and judgment. I would have them stand as my memorial and legacy . . ."

In his decision to break with the Democratic Party a second time Butler assured Plympton that he had no wish to sacrifice his friends. "You are not called to break with your party by the considerations which move me. You can remain at your post [Chairman of the State Central Committee of the Democratic Party] and carry on the campaign against me without the slightest breach in our personal friendship." [39] Plympton, however, unlike Pryor, Simmons, Collins and Maguire who remained with the Democrats, elected to play the role of faithful squire to assist Butler in his forthcoming tilt with the windmills of the two old parties.

32

THE PEOPLE'S PARTY CAMPAIGN

For two months Butler delayed his acceptance of the nominations by the Anti-Monopoly and the National Greenback-Labor parties. So long, in view of the fact that he in the meantime had become a delegate to the Democratic Convention, that some of his supporters felt he had used them only to advance his cause in the larger party. A group of irate Greenbackers in Morgantown, Kentucky, passed a resolution that Butler's "betrayal" of their interests "has no parallel since the days of Judas Iscariot and Benedict Arnold." [1] "How shall I answer inquiring and impatient Greenback editors, who desire to start at the word 'go'?" wrote Ohio Greenbacker Peter Herold; "What shall I say to Butler & West clubs of the Buckeye State? What shall I tell the outraged miners of the Hocking Valley . . . who have been on the ragged edge of despair and almost starvation for nearly 6 months?" [2] Editor C. H. Hanson of Cleburne, Texas, solicited no job, asked for no funds, but did wish to know Butler's plan of campaign.

In his lone-wolf fashion Ben Butler was working to find the answers. To the queries of an impatient Anti-Monopoly leader in New York he replied on July 29, "Has the Anti-Monopoly Party enough money to keep up a hot campaign from now until the 1st of November? . . . When you begin your meetings, ratification or others, you have got to keep them going . . . If I was intending to make the most vigorous campaign I could for my life's sake, I would not begin before the first of September, if then, and yet everybody seems to be perfectly wild to begin now in the heat of summer, and I am not allowed to enjoy a moment's vacation because my table is piled with letters from people wanting to know when the campaign is to begin, and every other question that can be asked. These men that write these letters are well meaning, earnest and honest men, but they have no more idea of conducting political campaigns than they have of the New Jerusalem." [3]

As Butler was well aware, the reform parties were scarcely parties at all in the accepted sense. They possessed only the flimsiest of organization, had national officials but no local ward heelers, treasuries but no funds. Their rank and file, high in ideals and low in bank accounts, were apt to look upon their party as the debating society that it primarily was. Their leaders, having so little chance to win, took pride in the fact that they were "not office seekers." How could Butler handle his unpromising materials in the forthcoming contest? What should be his plan of campaign? How might he finance the venture?

During the last few weeks of July he decided to consolidate the minor parties into a third party to be called the "People's Party," into which he would invite all other voters who, like himself, were discontented with the two older parties. Granted that he could not win, he might yet throw the election into the House of Representatives — witness the Hayes-Tilden situation in 1876 — and force acceptance of the principles in the "Butler platform."

To make every vote count Butler conceived a scheme for changing the normal procedure in the Electoral College. Instead of each party submitting to the voters its own list of electors, and the victorious party acquiring all the electoral votes of a state, Butler invented a system for the "fusion" within a state of his own minority party with whichever of the great parties happened to be weaker. The two weaker parties within a state having "fused," would vote for a common list of electors, or a "fusion" ticket, upon the gentleman's understanding that in the Electoral College the electoral votes from the state would be cast in proportion to the number of votes actually received by each of the parties entering into the fusion.

In West Virginia, where the Democratic Party was dominant, Butler on July 29 advised S. H. Piersall of Parkersburg to fuse with the weaker Republicans. "Fusion is . . . capable of being done in any electoral ticket with a distinct, positive and honorary understanding which would bind gentlemen that the electoral vote is to be cast according to the head of the ticket. For example, don't claim that we must have so many Greenbackers, and so many Republicans on the ticket, but say we will make a ticket of respectable gentlemen who shall agree to give their votes in the Electoral College according to the number of votes each party casts . . . Every vote thrown by a Greenbacker will count for a Greenbacker and will not count for a Republican." [4] This procedure was possible in 1884 because the uniform printed ballot had not yet been adopted. Each candidate in 1884 printed his own ballot and passed it out to voters at the polls. In West Virginia, then, under fusion, the printed Greenback vote would read "Ballot for Butler," followed by the list of electors, and the Republican vote would read "Ballot for Blaine," followed by the same list of electors.

Dana of the *Sun* held Butler's plan to be "entirely feasible." "If, for instance, a State has ten Presidential electors, and casts 100,000 votes for the successful [fusion] ticket, of which 60,000 are contributed by the regular Democrats and 40,000 by the People's Party, then, in pursuance of their compact, the Democratic electors would cast six votes for Cleveland and four for Butler." [5] The *Sun* felt "absolutely certain" that Cleveland-Butler fusions could carry such Republican strongholds as Connecticut, New Jersey, Indiana; and "probably" Massachusetts, New Hampshire and Ohio; with a "fair chance" in Michigan, Wisconsin, and Illinois. In the solidly Democratic South, they thought there was a "reasonable prospect" of Blaine-Butler fusions carrying Virginia, West Virginia, North Carolina, South Carolina, Florida, Mississippi and Louisiana. The idealist Dana, while counting on Butler's appeal to Negroes in the South, was shutting his eyes to actual conditions there; and his roseate predictions presupposed for the People's Party a strength of party organization and finances very different from the fact. With no party organization at the start and with limited and uncertain funds, Butler found it impossible to campaign actively outside a few crucial states, and even then, he overextended himself.

The financing of his campaign was a problem which both Anti-Monopoly and National Greenback-Labor parties left completely to Butler, in the belief that the "millionaire lawyer" could handle this matter in his own way. Noah A. Plympton, Butler's manager, estimated that the candidate paid $200,000 out of his own pocket.[6] William A. Fowler, who served as Treasurer in the central headquarters at the Fifth Avenue Hotel in New York City, was compelled to borrow from personal friends when sudden emergencies arose and the candidate-and-check-signer was away on speaking tours. Francis D. Moulton, of Beecher case fame, stretched his own credit and that of his company in order to lend $8500. Several Greenback and Anti-Monopoly editors and self-appointed organizers who could ill afford to do so spent from $300 to $500 each of their personal funds and nearly bankrupted themselves in "the noble fight for the people." [7] Boss Kelly of Tammany contributed early in the campaign, then switched to Cleveland, leaving $838 of Tammany's pledge to Butler's coffers unpaid. Telegrams and letters sent to Butler from his national headquarters in New York City speak guardedly of other contributors who for reasons of their own did not wish their names to be made public. Precisely what roles were played by "the man in Washington," "your friend at Saratoga," "W.F.S.," and "S.B." cannot be deduced from the contexts of headquarters' correspondence to Butler. His "fusion" system by its very nature brought Butler into political deals with both Republican and Democratic leaders. Whether Democrats who fused with him in Michigan to fight Blaine subsidized Butler in that state is not known. That he was privately and secretly subsidized in the fight against Cleveland in New York State is indicated by Butler's letter of September 24 to his longtime friend Secretary of the Navy William E. Chandler, who served Butler as go-between in negotiations with these unknown parties.

Butler had a number of conferences during the summer with Secretary Chandler, and on June 8 the latter wrote a letter to Blaine about conditions in New York in which he referred to Butler: "B. F. Butler is an important factor. If he continues to run, the independents will be important . . . Republicans can offer him nothing. His vanity, his desire to see how many votes he can get and his hope of getting electoral votes enough to hold the balance of power are all that I can think of to keep him firm. Can you do or suggest anything? He told me the above desire and hope influenced him." [8] Butler saw Chandler at the

Fifth Avenue Hotel on July 18, and later in the month, when the latter was receiving the polar explorer Greely at the Portsmouth Navy Yard, Butler thus invited himself to the ceremonies: "When is the show to come off? If possible I might like to run down and see it, and, if I could get time, invite myself to a sail with you around to Portsmouth or Boston, but I reluct at the thought of the time that sail would take. You see, while I make no 'bones' of trespassing upon your hospitality, you are quite at liberty to tell me you don't want me without the disturbance of any relations between us." [9] Chandler sent the requested invitation and Butler in the yacht *America* went to Portsmouth. After viewing the ceremonies from the deck of the Secretary of the Navy's steamer, Butler prevailed upon his former colleague Congressman Samuel J. Randall and Mr. Chandler to return with him to his cottage at Cape Ann to address a reunion of the Thirty-first Massachusetts who were having a picnic at Butler's summer place. At some odd moment during the activities of these first few days of August it was possible for Butler to have come to an agreement, as was later charged, although the precise nature of that agreement and the names of its parties were kept secret.

On August 6, Butler wrote Charles A. Dana of his intention to run "for better or worse" and enclosed a letter for publication in the New York *Sun* which announced "I do intend to stand by the nominations of the Greenback and laboring men, and the Anti-Monopolists." [10] Butler said he would wait until Cleveland had published his acceptance before stating his own compelling reasons. But Cleveland, by keeping quiet, refused to give Butler the ready ammunition he craved, while Butler's impatient followers strained at the leash to force their candidate to declare himself.

Numerous "Butler-for-President" clubs which sprang up in industrial cities swamped their standard-bearer with questions and advice. The ex-Confederate General W. H. Parsons, with no warrant from the candidate, presumed to launch a campaign for Butler by a rabble-rousing speech in Washington, D.C.

Nettled by too much assistance, and prone to play a lone hand, Butler was not always precise enough in his instructions to other people. From the start he had assumed that Plympton would manage his campaign, and so he did; although as late as August 27, to dispel all uncertainty, Plympton finally brought the matter specifically to his chief's attention. Most sorely Butler needed the services not of two men merely — Plympton, his manager, and William A. Fowler, treasurer. He needed a secretarial staff to winnow his vast incoming correspondence, to answer questions, to scotch rumors. To a well-meaning zealot in Scranton, Pennsylvania, Butler retorted: "Perhaps I speak too strongly upon this matter, but for weeks I have been thorned and prodded and goaded and pricked in every way by a thousand people, good and true men, who seem to think it was their mission to give me advice and to direct me what to do. If I had been a drifling [sic] idiot I should not have been more thoroughly coached than I have been." [11]

In a press release on August 12, Butler surveyed the aims of the new party and explained how the "fusion" technique was designed to operate. "It seems to me certain that at worst, even in the infancy of our organization, we can hold the balance of power between the two old parties; so that if we cannot wholly prevent bad and unjust legislation, we can force them to band together to enact it." "You have one advantage in your candidate," he told the two parties who had nominated him, "you will have to spend no time in defending him. His doings have been known to the country for more than a quarter of a century. Every act of his life has been under a microscope lighted by the lurid fires of hate and slander . . . Of personal advantage to myself nothing can accrue. I am too old to make selfish plans for the future; yet I hope as my last political act, if it so be, to do some service to the people and mankind." [12]

In a precampaign speech to 3000 laborers near Providence, Ben Butler sought to allay the workingman's distrust of himself, an employer of labor, in the role of the laboring man's friend. "Politics should be the highest exhibition of the human intellect in favor of the greatest number of men and for the greatest good of the greatest number." [13]

On August 29 he opened his campaign with a pilgrimage to Harrisburg, Pennsylvania, to see his octogenarian political friend Simon Cameron, who in the fateful spring of 1864 had come to Fortress Monroe to offer General Butler the Vice-Presidential position on Lincoln's ticket, and whom Butler had later defended in the Oliver-Cameron extortion suit. Having received the elder statesman's blessing, he rode on the cars out to the Grangers' picnic at Williams Grove, doffing his "Granger" straw hat to ladies in answer to their waving of handkerchiefs. Butler, bareheaded in the broiling sun, emphasized that his main objective was to found a new "People's Party" to replace the old parties. "Don't you go away and say General Butler wants you to vote for him," he charged the Grangers. "You could do me no good. If you elected me you would do me great harm. I am an old man, and could do no good without the cooperation of the Senate and House. I would only be annoyed and fretted to death. But you may say the Presidency gives a man fame. Well, if he is as lucky as Hayes he will be remembered about three years. [Applause and laughter.] I will be remembered long after some men who have been Presidents are forgotten. My object is to lay the foundation for a people's party." [14]

As the mass meeting in Union Square arranged for the night of August 30 was rained out, the few hundred who appeared were herded into the small hall of the Masonic Temple. When Butler entered the hall the band leader struck up "Hail to the Chief" and the cheering audience, waving hats, canes, umbrellas, handkerchiefs and newspapers, climbed upon chairs and tables to shout their welcome. The *Herald* reporter, disliking the tenor of Butler's anti-monopoly speech, jeered the "horny handed son of toil";[15] but the liberal *Sun* applauded Butler's denunciation of the sewing machine monopoly for holding up the domestic price of their machines to $75, while selling them abroad for $15, a practice "obviously unfair to American labor." Petroleum, "the poor man's light," was similarly described by Butler as a necessity which the Government should not permit a private individual to monopolize.

Butler left New York on September 1st for a two-week trip into Michigan, Illinois, Minnesota, Iowa, Nebraska and Kansas. Large crowds greeted him in the West, where old-timers were reminded of political gatherings for Clay, Webster and Calhoun. Everywhere people lighted red flares and fireworks and raised bright-colored flags and bunting from Butler's U.S. Bunting Company with Butler's principles painted on them. At Detroit, where he had difficulty clearing spectators away from the railing around the speaker's platform so he could see the audience, Butler announced that a tariff to protect the American worker would eventually succeed, "whoever is elected." [16] "My cause will win," he declared, "and what will happen to me isn't of the slightest possible consequence." [17] In Grand Rapids he spoke to 10,000 and shook hands with 3000 in a two-hour reception at Sweet's Hotel. At Chicago's Battery D Armory there was not the exaggerated fanfare of two months ago "but Bay State Ben," reported the Chicago *Tribune,* "is always a whole circus in himself and certain to draw a good house." [18]

In Des Moines 10,000 people in the Court House park heard him excoriate the two old parties. "If I do not come in and through the agency of the People's Party break up these useless and offensive organizations, they will curse the country with years of humbug politics. I have them in my power, and I am using them for their own destruction. In their place the people will build up a new party. Don't ask me for an apology for being an humble instrument in accomplishing that." [19] Speaking to large audiences in the open air in public squares and fairgrounds strained his voice but he held to his schedule of two and three speeches a day. At the fairgrounds in Omaha his popular theme was the railroad monopoly and speculators in the commodity market. "Transportation should be made cheap. A man can steal $3,000,000 of pork in Chicago and go unpunished, while one who steals enough to support life is sent to jail . . . The cry of overproduction should be changed to underconsumption. People are starving while Nebraska granaries are overflowing with grain. The railroads will not allow grain and consumers to be brought together so as to live." Butler urged Western farmers to "liberate themselves as the abolitionists liberated the slaves." [20]

Back in New York City on the 15th, Butler this time enjoyed good weather for his monster laboring men's rally in Union Square. Three platforms faced the plaza. On the front of the main stand was a large sign: "Jackson, Lincoln, Butler." F. D. Moulton and Senator Thomas F. Grady spoke from the side stands, while Butler, arriving late, found the crowd so massed around the main platform that he had to approach it from the rear, where, as the *Herald* jocularly depicted the scene, "two stalwart policemen grasped a stout, bald-headed man by the wrists, two others clutched him by the broad part of his pantaloons and with a mighty tug the General was hoisted onto the platform." [21]

At the Lowville, New York, fairgrounds 500 crowded wagons were packed around the speaker's stand. "The New York *World* accuses me of making a canvass in favor of Blaine, and when I went out in Michigan and fused with Cleveland's people to give him some electoral votes in a Republican State, they began abusing me because I was trying to help Cleveland. They both abuse me so that I know I am pretty nearly right . . . As I have no secrets I will tell you what I am about. I am founding a people's party that shall last when I am gone." [22]

On September 21 a formal "notification" ceremony was held at the Skating Rink in Lowell. The building held a capacity crowd of 7000 while four times that number lined the flare-lighted streets outside to watch the Butler parade of workingmen and Civil War veterans. And in Worcester, Massachusetts, a few days later the first People's Party convention met and organized. Noah A. Plympton, Butler's manager, was chosen as its national president. Ben Butler's liberal program was adopted as the platform. After rallies in Plymouth, New Hampshire, at Faneuil Hall and the Tremont House in Boston, and in Springfield, Butler returned for more canvassing in the crucial State of New York.

At this point a financial crisis developed, and Butler, in response to frantic messages from his treasurer, W. A. Fowler, wrote an appeal to Secretary William E. Chandler in Washington. So urgent was this message and so great the need for secrecy concerning it, that Butler sent it in care of his private secretary, Mr. Clancy, to be read by him to the Secretary of the Navy and personally returned to Butler. This letter, dated September 24, read:

> My Dear Chandler: I am anxious to have a communication made to you and I have sent Mr. Clancy in whom you have the most implicit confidence I know, as I have, to read the communication and then you will take such action as you think the thing demands. The more I hear from the West — the more I think there is danger in the West of very serious import unless New York is carried. We have now been engaged three weeks in organizing New Jersey, Connecticut and New York. We

may lose the two first without disaster. We cannot lose the last without uncontrollable disaster. This is my deliberate judgment. We have been at this business of organization for three weeks and if we can organize the State thoroughly I feel sure of success. Now, then, the friends with whom you consulted in New York have not even come up to the pittance which they promised in aid, and we are seriously crippled now for want of funds. We have already spent more money than we have received from any other source in that State alone, although the money was sorely wanted for the general purposes of the campaign; that is, for general organization outside in the interests of the People's Party. Now before the first day of October we should have at least $35,000 beyond what was understood, i.e., $5,000 a week. This is imperative to success. I have done all that I can do and more than you thought I ought to do. Will you see to it that this is done? I cannot attend to it because I speak every night and sometimes twice a day, and on the first day of October I start through the State of New York and State of Indiana to make as many speeches as my health will permit, and it is good now. I shall be accompanied by Senator Grady to every place. I propose to go into Indiana where we are to fuse with your people as arranged by Mr. Plympton, who is now there. We do not use money by pageants and shows and I have a weekly audit of accounts. I know where the money goes and so far I approve all that has been done. In the latter three weeks of the campaign we shall not have the draft upon us that we have now, which is very large, for distributing documents, for I hold that documents distributed in the last three weeks of the campaign are thrown away, so that we shall not in any event need to exceed the sum in the whole which I have allotted as necessary for the campaign. I leave it in your hands. I shall be in New York on Sunday next [28 September] and must then, of course, cut my coat according to my cloth. I shall take care of Massachusetts, so that I do not believe there will be any need of fireworks or plumed knights or other like appliances there, although the defection is larger than I thought from the Republican party, but that is largely going for St. John [Prohibition candidate]. Please answer at New York. If I cannot see you there Sunday. Yours truly. Benj. F. Butler.[23]

Apparently Butler received assurance that the matter would be attended to and so informed Fowler; but that the problem of finances continued to bedevil the treasurer is indicated by the following undated communication to Butler from Fowler:

W.F.S. came to me today just after you left & was quite rampant, saying that the understanding was 5 [$5000] per week, & that was all, his tone was unpleasant, but I kept my good nature. Now, where they are wasting money, we are doing practical service, & I would respectfully state that I understood that since your communication to Washington recently, that embargo was taken off, & that what was *necessary* should be done, as I wrote you fully at Boston last week, I understood the sum named would be provided, & of course have arranged accordingly with full approval of friends here & that Washington had pledged that what was required viz 15 per week should be supplied. It is with extreme reluctance that I write, but it is a duty I owe you that I should do so, & that this matter be settled once and for all. I told them how generously you had acted, but they seem to be blind to their position. Now I write this, but don't think I will do any thing indiscreet whatever happens, only if Washington can *order* I think Washington ought to be peremptory. This is written after consultation with Plympton who came thro. here today on his way to Penna. With respect & true regard I am Faithfully Fowler.[24]

The financial crisis occurred during a series of major speeches in Brooklyn, Albany, Troy, Rochester and Buffalo. After this, although his financial backers had probably already shown their heels, Butler made a second western trip to Fort Wayne, Indianapolis, Cincinnati and Pittsburgh. Returning to New York State, he averaged two speeches a day in this critical battleground for the last two weeks of the campaign.

"Brave Old Ben" was one of the hardiest campaigners in history. At hotels he rose early, ran through a pile of newspapers and letters, and greeted callers. Dressed plainly in black broadcloth with waistcoat of old-fashioned cut resembling evening dress and decorated with his boutonniere of red and purple flowers against a background of green leaves, he seemed in the bloom of health. He spoke rapidly to callers and got to the point without waste of words. "He lays his hand on the shoulder of a man as if he admired him for his good quality — winds up the interview and dismisses him with a good-natured shake of the hand." [25] A reporter who entered the candidate's bedroom late one night found him "in an easy chair, with a crimson flower in his coat lapel and his feet crossed comfortably." Butler laid aside his newspaper and rolling a cigar in his fingers expressed his pleasure over the recent People's Party

Convention in Worcester and the workingmen's meetings in Boston.[26]

In Albany Butler spoke for thirty-five minutes to a crowd of 10,000 in a circus tent on Hudson Street and the same evening rushed to nearby Troy to address another 10,000 from the steps of the City Hall.

"What has brought this great crowd here?" he asked the Trojans.

"Ben Butler!"

"No," admonished the General; "it is not mere idle curiosity; it is the deep feeling you have on the political questions to be discussed . . . You are here for the purpose of hearing what I am trying to establish, a People's Party."[27]

As he was leaving, while people flocked beside his carriage, a saloon-keeper handed him a glass of lager which he downed with relish.

Toward the close of the canvass, when it appeared that his whole plan to win the balance of power might be wrecked unless he could force a People's Party-Republican Party "fusion" victory in New York State, Butler rented for $150 per day the boudoir car "Etelke Gerster" which had dining and sleeping accommodations for a party of fifteen. If he could save the time required for living in hotels he might increase the number of speeches on the road. The luxurious appointments of the new sleeper-diner, however, attracted crowds, and unhappily for Butler drove home to many voters the difference in economic status between the People's Party candidate and the people themselves. "The car is furnished with a royal dining room, four magnificent sleeping rooms . . ." reported the Syracuse *Journal*. "The walls and ceilings are covered with heavily embossed leather, and the General has a writing desk of carved Spanish mahogany. He can also look at the people's candidate in a large number of mirrors and can keep out the light by dropping costly tapestry." It was decorated outside with "examples of Landseer in stained glass," and its lavatories were fitted with "lustrous nickel-plated toilet apparatus."[28] The car was stocked with provisions for fifteen people for two weeks and, according to one reporter, with every kind of liquor, including a case and a half of Medford rum for Butler's personal use.

But the cookstove heated the new varnish and spoiled the food in the refrigerator which sat alongside, producing "an unbearable stench."[29]

Worse still, the car's journals heated up and Butler lost time trying to repair the fault. He later complained to the car's owner "if it had had less elegance and more mechanical perfection in its running gear, it would have been much more to the purpose." He missed connections and finally abandoned the car at Elmira, "because I could not get along with it and get to New York at the same time that the slow running trains on the Erie road could get there." [30]

T. E. Major, Butler's trusted stenographer and secretary who at 16 Pemberton Square in Boston disbursed the thousands that flowed from the General's private means into the campaign, was the only person privileged to scold the strenuous campaigner. On October 8 he appended to a letter dealing with bad checks and protested notes the caution "You have beaten everybody else's record now, according to the morning papers, which said you made twenty speeches yesterday, and I wish you could be content from now out, having done twenty men's work in one day, to work somewhat as other men do." [31]

Candidate Butler aimed his blows at the parties and not the men, and he pounded impartially both Republicans and Democrats. The Republicans he flayed as "kept alive by the cohesive power of public plunder" and the refrain of one of his campaign songs called on the voters to "Throw the rascals out!" [32] The Democratic Party platform he believed had been shaped by monopolistic big business — the Erie Railroad, the Rockefeller oil interests, the Southern employer who underpaid Negro labor.

Butler's prediction that he was personally invulnerable to attack, since his past had been so thoroughly scrutinized, was not borne out in the campaign. Cleveland men revived a Civil War legend by throwing tin or wooden spoons onto the speaker's platform. Butler was wrongly credited with having suppressed the draft riots in New York City in 1863. Some feeling flared up in the South when the case of the Reverend James G. Bain of Norfolk, whom Butler had sent to Cape Hatteras, became a pulpit topic with Southern Methodists. But the most damaging anti-Butler charge sprang from the complexities of his strategy in his present campaign. Many people who scarcely knew what the Electoral College was, were mystified by Butler's "fusing" with the Republicans in one state and with Democrats in another. As the most critical state for Butler's plans happened to be New York, his major effort being expended there, the situation was ideal for the spawning of rumor.

As early as August 18, B. F. Clayton wrote Butler, "Your present attitude is that of Pilot-fish to the Blaine shark. Surely none but the veriest simpleton can fail to see that your canvass can have only one effect: namely to help Blaine and hurt the Democracy." [33] A secretarial staff would have caught such rumors early and explained to such men as Clayton that "fusion" with the Republicans in New York was designed "to hurt the Democracy," just as fusion with Democrats in Michigan aimed to hurt Republicans. Had Butler enjoyed the aid of a steering committee, such earnest and sincere men as General W. H. Parsons who had begun a free-lance Butler campaign in Washington, D.C., might have performed useful service for the People's Party. After failing to persuade Butler to try fusion in Maryland, General Parsons went to New York, saw Plympton and Fowler and offered to stump for Butler in eight Northern states. He wanted Butler to speak in Baltimore and follow up his Civil War conquest by a "moral victory" over that city. Butler, attending to too many matters himself, and considering Parsons an interloper, instructed his managers to have no dealings with him.

Newspaper rumors remaining unanswered, Patrick J. Ford of Yonkers, who had spoken in eight towns for Butler, wrote him a few weeks before the election: "It has been said by many here and there, that you have undoubtedly been bought by Blaine supporters. If so, Sir, my aid in your behalf ceases. If not so, you will do me a favor and gain many votes by sending me a straight denial of the truth or falsity." [34] This letter, apparently buried under the thousands that poured in, could hardly have been seen by Butler until after the contest was over.

On October 19 the New York *Times* denounced Butler's "treachery." "Every workingman, anti-monopolist, every laborer and friend of labor who votes for Benjamin F. Butler becomes the dupe of the basest conspiracy that has ever disgraced a Presidential canvass in the United States." Butler was called a "decoy duck managed and paid by the Republican Party." "A few days ago Gen. W. H. Parsons, who is chairman of the National Greenback-Labor Committee for Maryland, went to

New York to get Butler to come here [to Baltimore] and speak. He was referred by the Butler managers in New York to the Republican Committee. He went to the Committee, and was told that the Republicans could not afford to send Butler to Maryland, as it was not a doubtful State and that they had no money to spend in experiments." [35]

On October 20 Butler in Syracuse issued the following denial: "I have read Parson's statement. There is not one word of truth in it. He applied to me some weeks ago for money to organize in Maryland, I declined and told him my plan of campaign had been placed in the hands of Mr. Plympton, whom I warned against him afterward. I refused to see Parsons." But the *Times,* thumping for Cleveland, continued its outcry against Butler as "the Benedict Arnold of American politics." [36]

A few days later *Harper's Weekly* thus garnished the tale: "He [Butler] and John Kelly waited together in New York to be approached by Governor Cleveland, but without success. Then General Butler came home, and still continued glum and sour. In a few days he announced that he was going off on a yachting tour. He started, but didn't go far. He suddenly put into Portsmouth, and there he met the man who has been Mr. Blaine's go-between for twenty years for all his scheming in the lobby and out of it, William E. Chandler. They briefly conferred in that city for several days, after which Blaine is said to have agreed to pay Butler $25,000 down and $25,000 in later installments." [37]

To this charge Butler made reply in a letter to I. B. Abbott of North Brookfield, Massachusetts, who ran it in the *Times* on the 27th. "The story of meeting Mr. Chandler on the *Tallapoosa* is a very plain one. Lieut. Greely, who was an old friend and constituent of mine, and one whom I tried to assist when in Congress to carry out his ideas of the North Pole expedition, had returned home from that perilous and important voyage and was to be received by the citizens in my native state of New Hampshire. Mr. Chandler invited several gentlemen of prominence to go to Portsmouth to do honor to Greely and his brave associates. I went. The first man I met was the Hon. Samuel J. Randall, with whom I was many years in Congress, and I went on board the *Tallapoosa* with him, and there met Mr. Chandler and other gentlemen of distinction . . . I made no bargain with Chandler on board the *Tal-lapoosa* about anything. I certainly did not make a bargain with Mr. Blaine, because he was not there. Mr. Chandler had not seen Mr. Blaine since the nomination, as I understood." [38]

Parson's telegram of November 1 to Cleveland's national headquarters was published the next day in the *Herald*:

> The culminatory evidence of the coalition and price between Mr. Blaine and General Butler, in addition to the facts which still remain unchallenged that $22,000 were drawn by the political manager of the former in favor of the political manager of the latter, it has just come to our knowledge, and we directly challenge James G. Blaine and Benjamin F. Butler to invoke the books of the First National Bank of New York City to prove it, that each week during this Presidential campaign, except the last two, checks of $5,000 each, have been drawn by Mr. Blaine's manager, Mr. Jones, to the order of Noah A. Plympton, General Butler's campaign manager, which are accepted by the latter and cashed by the above named bank. General Butler accepts the nomination of the national party on the one hand, and $10,000 weekly from the Republican campaign funds on the other, the consideration of which is that Butler will canvass in States exclusively doubtful between Mr. Cleveland and Blaine to assist the election of a man and the continuance to power of a party through whose legislation Butler declares, in his address of August 12, that workingmen are out of work and starving, after a quarter of a century of Republican rule. I directly charge James G. Blaine and B. F. Butler as parties to the contract, whereby the third, or People's Party, is to be made the instrument of this iniquity . . . W. H. Parsons.[39]

That some sort of bargain was made to which Chandler was a party or an intermediary cannot be doubted. What Butler literally denied was that a bargain had been made with Chandler *"on board the Talla-poosa."* Whatever the arrangement was between Butler and "the man in Washington" or "your friend in Saratoga" or "S.B." or "W.F.S.," it was an agreement in which the parties were committed to secrecy. Ben Butler, Chandler and the other party or parties held to this clause in their "bargain" despite provocative needling by the press.

To Ira E. Perkins of Minneapolis, who in an apparently honest letter charged Butler with a desire "to rule or ruin," the defeated third-party candidate on November 24 replied: "I did endeavor to put before the country a platform of principles, and to inaugurate an organization, which will sooner or later, succeed in crushing out monopolies, and speculators in the necessaries of life, such as grain, by whom the farmer, the producer and the laboring men, the consumers are alike robbed, by wholesome laws. Your suggestion that the suspicion that I sold myself for a consideration will never be eradicated, is noted . . . The mole can never compehend the beauties of the landscape but supposes the whole world is as dark as his world is to him." [40] Having said apparently his last word on the matter, he sent copies of Perkins' letter and his own reply to the editor of the Minneapolis *Mirror*.

What effect the story of the alleged sellout to Blaine had upon the voters is difficult to judge. From the beginning of the campaign it was recognized that a vote for Butler was a protest vote, and in a practical sense was thrown away. Charles A. Dana defined the appeal Butler had for the intelligent liberal in an editorial in the New York *Sun* of September 12: "Butler is a disturbing and health-giving force wherever he appears in politics. Many people do not agree with him and many heartily detest him; but the agitation which he brings is salubrious. He leaves the political atmosphere in a better state than when he finds it." [41]

Butler, however, was deeply disappointed in his low vote of 175,000 in a total of 10,000,000. The laboring men — he had expected at least 1,500,000 of them — had failed to stand up and be counted for him. There were the usual indications that a number of Butler votes had been counted for Cleveland; but it was hardly worth litigation. Fairly exhausted from overwork, and saddled with campaign debts that would take months to straighten out and settle, Ben Butler went home and spent several days in bed, as did his faithful manager Noah Plympton.

From Highlands, New Jersey, his daughter Blanche Ames sent him a heartening note of sympathy: "Dear Father; The thought of the election gives me a mental sensation, which may quite properly be compared to the physical one experienced when eating unripe persimmons." She was sending him some field-plum preserves "like those you and Mother used to eat at the farm." [42] And she invited him for Thanksgiving.

33

BUTLER'S BOOK

In his declining years Ben Butler became increasingly concerned over his reputation. Paul and Blanche, having grown up with the legends, knew how to discount what they saw in newspapers concerning their famous father, whose every word or gesture was seized by penny-a-liners and fictionized. For his children the often garbled and grossly exaggerated account which they got from the daily press had shortly been corrected by the parental letter. They had followed the nuisance trials, had seen the spoons story refuted by evidence.

But what idea of their grandfather might Blanche's children acquire, growing up in the post–Civil War world of rumor and travesty, of lie and legend? Butler spoke of his election to the governorship as "a vindication," a sort of refutation of the abuse his enemies had heaped upon him over the years. The point seems to have been emphasized in his taking young Butler Ames to witness the inaugural. Then had come criticism over the Tewksbury investigation, Harvard's refusal of the degree and defeat for re-election as Governor in 1883. His presidential race was a sort of reply to his critics. He took Butler Ames with him on the first western trip when the shower of tin spoons rattled down on the stage in Detroit. Then at the close of the campaign there were the cacophonous cries of "Judas Iscariot" and "Benedict Arnold of American politics." "The New York *Herald* publishes so much of my address as is against the Republicans," Butler complained to O. H. Worth, "and the *Tribune* publishes that which is against the Democrats and conceals the rest. If the age of miracles was not passed and the Lord would come down and punish as he did in the time of the Apostles the suppression of truth in the same way, he would stop the majority of the newspapers in the United States until a new set of editors at least were procured." [1]

Ben Butler was fond of his eldest grandson. He puzzled over the boy's conundrums when he was in high school, and obtained for him an appointment to West Point. In one of his letters, the grandfather suggested that Cadet Butler Ames get acquainted with a new boy whom he had recommended: "You know how far a kind word goes to a boy when he is away from home." [2] "I don't think you need to have written me that you had passed the examination at West Point. Who ever doubted that you would?" [3]

His six Ames grandchildren — Butler, Edith, Sarah, Blanche, Jesse and Adelbert — could see and be proud of the life-size portraits of their grandfather which hung in the State House on Beacon Hill and in the capitol of his native New Hampshire. They could feel pride in the red brick Butler School on Central Street in Lowell which had been named for the Governor. Other honors fell to him in the later years. Dartmouth College granted him the degree of LL.D. in 1888. A Benjamin F. Butler Post of the G.A.R. was formed in Lowell. Butler Clubs kept alive the liberal traditions which Butler had always championed. In New Orleans, although Butler predicted a short life for it, a "Butler tree" was planted in Audubon Park.

But the favorable side of the picture is seldom so colorful and memorable as the unfavorable. On his world tour General Grant told John Russell Young that while he had always found General Butler a likable, able and patriotic man "of courage, honor and sincere conviction," he was nevertheless "a man it is the fashion to abuse." [4] Murat Halstead, a famed journalist, once told a novice in his profession, "If there comes a time when there is an absolute dearth of news, when you can't think of anything to make an interesting letter, there is always one thing you can do, and that is to pitch into Ben Butler." [5] In Congress, too, pitching into Ben Butler had been a recognized tactic about which Butler himself had jested with fellow Congressmen.

But late in life it was vexing to find that by many the spoons story was still seriously believed. "It is not a copper's consequence to anybody what such a fellow as Slayback may say," Butler exploded when he read a newspaper interview of an ex-Confederate in St. Louis. "If anybody would believe that I would put spoons in a coffin he would believe the rest of the story . . . The only two horses I brought away were those I took to New Orleans from Massachusetts." [6]

In Butler's house on Capitol Hill in Washington there were, according to legend, cupboards behind secret panels which were filled with gold, silver and jewelry. In the cellar, sealed by immense blocks of Cape Ann granite, were popularly believed to be vaults of treasure guarded by the ghosts which had followed the riches north from New Orleans. Somewhere in the building, it was said, was a hidden room with a secret staircase, and underneath the building, a cistern in which, secreted in a chamber concealed by water, were spoons and plate and coins minted in France by the ancestors of the Creoles of New Orleans. [7]

During a meeting of the Jefferson Club in Boston at which Ben Butler's name was proposed for Governor, Thomas Jefferson suddenly appeared in velvets and snuffbox. After a tirade against changes in the Democratic Party and particularly against "the apostate Ben Butler," the Sage of Monticello, as reported by the Boston *Journal,* heaved a decanter at the chairman of the meeting, walked through the table and out through a closed window, where, mounting his horse, he shook his fist at the state of Massachusetts and disappeared from view! [8] Daniel Webster, shocked that Ben should presume to run for President, commented that "he [Butler] has the impudence of the devil with a conscience to match." [9] A certain eeriness was imparted to this legend by the fact that the "God-like" Daniel had departed this life some thirty-two years earlier.

A Washingtonian unfamiliar with the case of Mrs. Phillips and General Butler at New Orleans introduced the two at a reception. "I already know the man," said Mrs. Phillips; while Butler retorted, "Yes, I believe we have met before, under very different circumstances." [10] As reporter after reporter exercised his wit in the retelling of this incident, the fiery little ex-Secessionist lady shook ever more vigorously with rage until at length she caught the Beast on the side of the face with a resounding slap. [11]

Butler denounced the "blatherskite" press on the floor of the House, on the platform, in formal interviews, on the sidewalks, in his office, and no doubt in his sleep, but he never found a satisfactory way to combat "calumny fostered and prompted by those who should know better." [12]

James Parton offered perhaps the best advice in 1877 when he suggested that the General "leave all these law cases to young men, and amuse yourself by writing your Memoirs. Gracious what a hit you could make, if you spoke without reserve." [13]

On November 13, 1883, he read in the Boston *Herald* a fictionized story which portrayed Butler as carrying to New Orleans several hundred barrels of whiskey for his own use.

Butler did not forthwith rush to the newspaper office to pull the editor's nose, as in 1842, or hail the editor into court as in 1852. He brought suit for libel, but having instituted it he left it dangling as a threat to guarantee future good behavior, and eventually the editor publicly explained the flimsiness of his source in a manner tantamount to an apology.

Ten years after Sarah's death he advised a retired friend whose wife had just died "to plunge into some occupation, some affair that shall be urgent and exacting, which will command your withdrawal from self introspection," and he followed his own advice by practicing law to the end of his life.

With several hundred cases on the dockets in Boston, New York and Washington, he was reluctant after the Presidential campaign to accept new business. Troubled by rheumatism, he was compelled to travel always with his Negro valet, Albert West, at his side. An extraordinarily heavy eyelid now practically closed his left eye, leaving him only the nearsighted right eye. Although he was self-conscious about it, he was forced to answer even his personal mail by dictation. In 1886 he instructed his Washington secretary to locate for him a new and quiet office. "But I don't want one in a place where it will draw custom. If a man don't want me enough to find me out, I am not going to have him got by my sign." [14]

On Thursday, February 25, 1887, he slipped in the Philadelphia railroad depot and dislocated his arm at the shoulder. "The injury was exceedingly unpleasant," he wrote his Washington law partner, "but I concluded that I would go through to New York before I had it set, and I did go in great pain and agony. I got to New York and found a competent surgeon and he found another very competent one. I rather objected to taking ether and they pulled away on the arm to stretch the muscles and get the head of the humerus into the socket, but the muscles were too strong for them, and they hurt me like thunder, as they told me they would. They then gave me ether and that relaxed the muscles and they put it in, in a second or two, did it up nicely and I took the boat for home with but little pain. Fortunately, or rather unfortunately, I had the roughest night but one that I ever saw on the sound, but I reached home in good order and condition Sunday morning and have been quite comfortable ever since." [15]

Blanche with the younger children came to Lowell to take care of him and get his weight down. "You would be surprised," he wrote Charlotte, "to learn that for the first three weeks I was not allowed to eat anything but fish and bread; that my weight has been reduced to 220 pounds, and that I now have to live very plainly . . . Blanche and the children are all well. They have just finished their dancing school, and had two wind-up balls, the last of which, in the classic language of young girls, Sarah called 'lovely.' They had about fifty children and they have got all the nice things since I have been sick." [16]

To Judge Hugh L. Bond, who wrote him a letter of condolence and suggested that he give up practicing law and write his memoirs, Ben Butler insisted that to him the law was not work in the usual sense. "I suppose you would not object to an old man's playing chess for amusement, would you? Well I am doing that, with men and women, judges and statesmen, as my pawns, knights, bishops, kings and queens, with lives, fortunes and personal liberty for stakes, which make the game interesting. This to me is not labor, in the fatiguing sense of the word. You may think me foolish, but I really try some cases without much pecuniary reward or the hope of it . . . I am warned by increasing years, however, that I must soon be driven from this class of relaxation." [17] As for writing a memoir, "I abhor the labor of looking up dates," he confessed to Judge Bond, "verifying authorities, reviewing facts, troubled all the time lest I may do injustice to somebody in a statement which may have weight against him or his memory. There is so much to correct in what is now supposed to be history that I must find myself day by day contradicting and staying the current of fables." [18]

The most notorious criminal case in which Ben Butler was active in his last years was that of the Haymarket Anarchists, a prototype of the Sacco-Vanzetti case. On May 4, 1886, as a squad of Chicago police advanced down Desplaines Street to disperse a crowd near the Haymarket, a bomb thrown by some unknown person killed Police Officer Mathias J. Degan.[19] Within the next few days a number of soapbox orators were rounded up and tried in the Cook County Criminal court. A defense committee took up the cause of the doomed men in the belief that they were the victims of a witch hunt, and Butler was retained to appeal the case to the Supreme Court of the United States. It was a hopeless case, for it had been carefully managed by counsel in the state courts. One of the condemned men was a younger brother of W. H. Parsons who had figured so prominently against Butler in the late Presidential campaign. On the theory that it was his duty as a lawyer to defend any man whose life was at stake, Butler made several trips to Washington and worked late hours as the deadline for the execution approached. The Supreme Court, however, ruled against the Haymarket radicals, and the spectacular character of the case brought adverse newspaper criticism against Butler himself. "Don't misunderstand me, madam," he concluded after explaining the case to a feminine critic, "I will defend upon proper occasion if his life is in question, even the editor of a newspaper who has abused me for twenty years if I think that there is a chance of saving his life." [20]

During the last ten years General Butler enacted the role of pawn as well as chessplayer in the lawsuit of The National Home for Disabled Volunteer Soldiers Vs. Benjamin F. Butler. Butler had served as President and Acting Treasurer of the Board of Managers of the Soldiers' Home from 1866 to 1879 and thereafter had continued to serve as Acting Treasurer until 1881. The funds of the Home, small at first, had increased as time went on to a sizable amount. All told in the fourteen years, General Butler handled approximately $10,000,000 of the Home's funds. Aside from interviewing hundreds of applicants for admission, Butler personally did little more than sign checks and direct the investment of its surplus funds or the sale of its securities. Record-keeping he left entirely to his financial clerk and his banker George J. Carney of Lowell. From time to time the books had been audited as the Board of Managers saw fit. In September, 1881, the accounts were given a final audit before being turned over to General Butler's successor General William B. Franklin. A year later the second Auditor in the Treasury Department discovered a discrepancy in the account amounting to $15,000, and this was called to General Butler's attention.

Although Banker Carney's bookkeeping was now exposed as antiquated, Butler found what appeared to him to be the source of the error. The sum of $15,000 had been allotted to the Eastern Branch Home to set up a shoe factory. Carney had made no entry of the total cash outlay, but had written off $9838 of the amount against a bill for supplies owed by the Eastern Branch Home, and then had entered in his account book a receipt for $5162 in cash which he had paid out to General W. S. Tilton, superintendent of this branch.

This explanation not being held satisfactory, Butler in September 1883, on the eve of his race for re-election as Governor, was threatened with a lawsuit to recover the $15,000 for the Home. Butler told the District Attorney to go ahead and sue. "If I paid under threat, I would be considered culpable." [21] The case was fought and lost by Butler both in the Superior Court of Massachusetts and in the United States District Court. Judge George M. Carpenter, convinced that General Butler was honestly mistaken, charged the jury accordingly.

"I need not say to you, gentlemen, that nothing has occurred in this testimony which in the slightest degree reflects upon the integrity, honesty, or upright conduct of anybody who is concerned or who has been at any time concerned in this transaction. It is, so far as the testimony goes here, a bookkeeper's puzzle, a problem, which feeling clear what the right of the matter is, I have judged it was my duty to take the responsibility of instructing you must be solved in favor of the Soldiers' Home." [22]

General Butler excepted to the Court's charge to the jury. The jury as directed brought in a verdict against Butler of $16,537, that being the principal of $15,000, plus accrued interest. Butler as plaintiff in error now carried the case to the Supreme Court of the United States. Not until after the General's death was the case finally settled out of court, when the heirs paid a total of $18,000 to bring the matter to an end.

After he passed seventy he wrote more frequently to his eighty-year-old sister Betsy Morrill Stevens at Nottingham, New Hampshire. He provided her gentle carriage horses and in turn received from her supplies of sausages like the ones he remembered as a boy. He treated as members of his family his two wards, Rowena and Florence Hildreth, daughters of the best friend of his early years, Fisher Ames Hildreth, continuing to look after their estates after they had married. When Florence's daughter came down with scarlet fever and was quarantined at Hygeia Hotel beyond reach of good doctors, Butler procured assistance for her from the nearby Hampton, Virginia, branch of the Soldiers' Home and had the Pennsylvania Railroad dispatch a special car to bring her and her child to Boston. Next to Charlotte Stevens — Betsy's daughter who kept house for him in Washington — he seems to have been fondest of Hattie, daughter of his favorite sister-in-law Harriet Hildreth Heard who had died of cancer in 1866. While Hattie and her husband Lanier Dunn were living in Warm Springs, Virginia, her uncle had her send him a barrel of Virginia hams, lean razorbacks bred in the forest on roots and beech mast. Almost as fond of these hams as he was of Betsy's sausages, Butler keeping house with Paul in Lowell gave his imagination free play and decided that a wisp of clean fresh hay added to the water in which they were boiled improved their flavor! In July of 1885 Butler gave Hattie an apartment in his Washington home, and she was with him during his last eight years.

Now as ever his law business kept him so constantly engaged that he was not free to accept as often as he wished Blanche's hospitality or that of his nieces. In summers, after courts were closed he still enjoyed cruising on the *America,* though compelled now to forego cruising in stormy weather. "Going to sea," he wrote Dillwin Smith, "is the secret of my good health." [23]

In September of 1889 the J. C. Jewett Publishing Company of Boston persuaded him to sign a contract for publishing a 1000-page autobiography. Blanche had urged him to do it. "The papers credit you with the intention of book writing. Why not?" wrote Blanche. "It seems to be the mania of the age, and there surely would in your case, be no lack of material, or capacity." [24] James Parton had been pressing him for years. Editor A. T. Rice, for whose *North American Review* Butler had written an article on "The Presidential Campaign of 1864," had praised Butler's style as having "all the vivacity and sparkling qualities of the best French writers." [25] "You do not seem to have the genius to write any article which the reader will not wish to be longer." [26]

The book was not to be entitled *The Dark Secret,* as a Chicago publisher had suggested, nor "Confessions of Ben Butler," as the Baltimore *Daily News* had recommended, but simply *Butler's Book* and was to be based primarily upon his memory and the wartime documents and letters he had saved. "We preserve all letters," Butler had once written, "as scrupulously as does the Mohammedan under the faith that when he shall pass over the red hot grate to paradise all the pieces of paper that he had preserved through all his life will fly under and protect his feet." [27]

Many old friends — Paul R. George, Godfrey Weitzel, George C. Strong — whom he would have liked to consult as a check against his own recollections — had died. "I admit frankly that this book should have been written before," he stated in his preface, "so as to reap the advantage of being able to apply to my compatriots in their lifetime, and to verify the facts. But being still in active business in the ardent pursuit of my profession, which has always been the pleasantest occupation of my life, I could not find the time." [28] He wrote to Union officers who still survived, requesting their reminiscences on various points, among them Colonel E. F. Jones of the Sixth Massachusetts, which had been mobbed in Baltimore, and General E. V. Kautz, who had led the cavalry in the unsuccessful attempt to isolate Petersburg. The War Records Office in Washington was besieged for statistical data that in 1890 had not yet been compiled. He asked General Beauregard for his estimate of the strength of the Confederate forces that had been opposed to him in the early days at Bermuda Hundred and applied to Colonel William Lamb for information on the Confederate garrison at Fort Fisher at the time of the first attack.

The reading necessary for the Book, added to his full schedule of legal work, weakened his eyes. His farsighted left eye having almost closed, he underwent an operation to remove a section from the lid. Dr. O. G. Cilley, his family physician, and Dr. David Hunt, performed the operation at his home in Lowell. He refused an anesthetic, declaring later that it had pained him less than removing a splinter from his hand, and after the operation he entertained the doctors at dinner.

To the feminist Phoebe Couzins, who sent him a newspaper clipping about his operation, he returned his thanks for "the printed nonsense" and explained that his operation had not been made "for any cosmetic purpose." "My looks are beyond improvement in any regard as I view them, and one lady looks at them, to wit, my daughter, in the same way. She thinks her father's face cannot be improved." [29] To Blanche he wrote exulting in the operation's success: "How do you suppose that I had my eye operated upon to improve my looks? I really did think you knew me better than that. Good gracious! I have gone through life like Mirabeau, 'Let me get a chance to shake my boar's head at them.' He was not quite as homely as I am . . . I don't think it improves my looks, but I know it has improved my sight and the strength of my eye." He assured her that she should pay no attention to the press notices about his health; "I do not make jokes with you when there is really anything important." [30]

He had barely brought his story down to the Civil War and sent in his first two chapters when C. F. Jewett, head of the publishing firm, absconded, leaving the firm in debt. Butler now investigated the firm's solvency and canceled the contract, on the score that Jewett had misrepresented the condition of the company. He signed a new contract with A. M. Thayer & Co., another publishing house in Boston, and as he forged ahead with his autobiography he fended off at the same time two lawsuits brought by lesser officers of the Jewett firm.

While he desired particularly to throw light upon the years 1860–1880

— his career in the war and as a Congressman — he aimed also "to correct much of the wrong done to myself by a prejudiced misrepresentation of facts." He wished to "set down naught in malice," but reserved to himself the privilege of saying "in regard to any man personally what I think it is right to say of him, however hard the criticism may be." [31]

Butler's Book is at its best in its full-length portrayals of Butler's dealings with Lincoln and Grant. With both of these men his wartime relations had at times been very much strained. The circumstances of his recall from New Orleans and his being relieved from command after Fort Fisher had stung him sorely at the time and after twenty-five years they still stung. Able now to see the complexities that had faced the President and the Lieutenant General, he still could feel that injustice had been done him in the first case by Seward, who had listened to the New Orleans consuls, and in the latter by Admiral Porter, whose integrity Butler directly impugned.

Against Scott, McClellan and Halleck who had consistently withheld from Butler troops for offensive purposes he made a good case. His bitterness toward the "West Point" crowd during the war was never softened, for they, more than any other factor, in Butler's opinion, ungenerously exaggerated the importance of the Big Bethel skirmish and by denying him troops, deprived him of military success.

He was compelled by his slow and shaking hand to dictate his book and its 1037 pages of proof had to be read back to him by others. Little wonder that errors in dates and spelling crept in. Direct quotations lost or acquired articles, prepositions or new modes of punctuation. Even the date of Sarah Butler's death was wrongly given as 1877 instead of 1876. But in the main the inaccuracies are minor. The autobiography may be said to be generally true without being meticulously accurate. First-draft manuscript was sent to the printer as soon as it was written, the harassed author not bothering to keep a copy, as that would entail delay. As for chapter divisions, he wrote the publisher, he would decide on those after the material had been put into print! He fell behind, and the publisher tried to hurry him. "Now I have told you that I would work on the book all that I possibly could, and no amount of letters can make me work any more," Butler rasped.[32] He would have gone far over the deadline had he not developed an abscessed ear and been confined to his home for six weeks. While thus incapacitated he dictated during the day and listened at nights while the proof was read into his good ear. Little wonder that the transport *Mississippi* which had grounded on a sandbank *abaft* the foremast found herself, on page 339 of the Book, grounding on a sandbank *above* the foremast!

Since three-quarters of the autobiography deals with the Civil War, the prewar and postwar periods of his life are slighted. Of the 161 pages devoted to the first forty-two years of his life, more than half is devoted to general editorial comment. The coverage of his law career is particularly sketchy, for the most part consisting of disconnected stories of his early days. Almost nothing is said about his later experiences.

His health precarious, he arranged to have James Parton complete the Book in case anything happened to himself. But Parton died when *Butler's Book* was midway along. Butler forced himself, filled 918 pages before he got to the end of the war. Then since the written material had already been set up in type, he was not free to give it the recasting and revision that it needed. The crowded postwar career of twenty-seven years was accordingly jammed into a 66-page chapter entitled "Congressman and Governor" and the Book was topped off with a hurried chapter on "The Law" which offered little more than anecdotes on prewar law cases.

He finished the last of the manuscript the first week in January 1892, and *Butler's Book* was published on the 15th, a labor which might well have occupied a staff of research assistants several years. The day after it was finished he escaped from his sickroom in Lowell and dashed to Washington where one of his cases was ready to come before the Supreme Court.

On January 4, 1893, Ben Butler wrote his sister Betsy a note of thanks for the last sausages she had sent him. And on the same day he attended the funeral at Lowell of an old neighbor. Although he had been soaked by rain and had caught a cold, he returned to Washington.

At midnight of the 11th his valet Albert who slept in an adjacent room in the house on Capitol Hill was awakened by the General's coughing. The General told his man to go back to bed, that he was all right, but Albert aroused the General's nieces, Harriet Dunn and Charlotte Stevens. Lanier Dunn summoned a doctor. At one-thirty the General died of pneumonia and heart attack.

Paul Butler with personal friends came down to accompany the body back to Lowell. Of the eight veterans from the District of Columbia chapter of the G.A.R. who escorted the body, two were Negroes, one of whom wore the medal of honor which General Butler had awarded him.

At home in Belvidere, in the drawing room facing the east, the General lay, with a faint smile under his waxed mustache, and a red rose in his lapel. The scene was rather more gay than solemn. Under the wreath of white lilies and ferns which had been sent by President Harrison were the bright folds of the United States flag. Portraits of Sarah Butler and Ben-Israel in his uniform as a lieutenant in the U.S. Army hung on the walls. After a brief ceremony at the house attended by the family, the body was removed to Huntington Hall.

In this auditorium which had so often been filled with his rasping staccato, Ben Butler lay in state while thousands of his fellow townsmen filed past. The catafalque stood under a canopy of heavy black draperies hung from the center of the ceiling. Gas fixtures were so arranged as to shed light only upon the half-smiling face, above the rose in the lapel. A special train brought Governor Russell, the Executive Council and a 37-man delegation of the Legislature from Boston. People poured into Lowell from all over New England. Seventy-five policemen and firemen directed the crowds that passed through Huntington Hall from 7:30 A.M. until 1 P.M. on the day of the funeral.

A cortege a mile and a half in length carried the body to the St. Anne's Episcopal Church, past business buildings and dwellings draped in black. Stores were closed throughout the city by proclamation of the Mayor. It was bitterly cold but clear. "All morning streets were crowded," reported the Lowell *Evening Star* on January 16. "At noon they were blocked. At 1 o'clock they were jammed. All windows that looked upon streets through which the funeral was to pass were filled with serious faces." [33] Several people were injured in the crush. Dr. Chambre, rector of St. Anne's, read the service.

To the cemetery lot in Dracut, whose six-foot iron fence had been freshly painted for the occasion, the General's remains were carried in a hearse drawn by six black-plumed horses. The cortege, including old G.A.R. men, businessmen wearing Butler medallions, and several brass bands, stretched all the way from Merrimack Street across the river to the cemetery. Bells tolled. Bands played funeral marches. After the body had been lowered into the grave beside Sarah Butler's, and near the graves of his two sons Ben-Israel and the first infant, Paul, the military escort fired a final volley.

His death evoked over the country a varied comment. The Lowell *Evening Star,* paying tribute to the "dearly beloved . . . People's Champion," wrote: "There are men and women living in Lowell who . . . remember how the mill-hands went to work before daylight and did not complete their tasks until half-past seven at night. They remember the early movements for shorter hours . . . that Benjamin F. Butler, then a young and struggling lawyer, was the central figure in those movements." [34] Wrote the New Orleans *Times-Democrat:* "In this section of the country Butler was the most cordially despised and hated man that ever lived." [35] The *Iowa State Register* of Des Moines declared Butler to have been "one of the most picturesque Americans . . . a rugged Titan." [36]

The fairest and most sympathetic judgment was that of Charles A. Dana of the New York *Sun.* As Assistant Secretary of War, Dana was familiar with Butler's war record, and as a liberal editor he had long been keenly interested in Butler as a leader in reform. "For the last quarter of a century at least," wrote Dana, "Benjamin Franklin Butler has stood out as the most original, the most American and the most picturesque character in our public life. He had courage equal to every occasion; his given word needed no brackets; his friendships and his enmities knew no variableness or shadow of turning; his opinions were never disguised nor withheld; his devotion to his country was without qualifications; his faith in the future of liberty and democracy was neither intoxicated by their victories nor disheartened by their defeats; his intellectual resources were marvelous; his mind naturally adhered to the poor and the weak; and his delight was to stand by the underdog in the fight. In these qualities he was a great and an exceptional man, and his friends valued him and loved him as truly as his foes detested him. But was he great in everything? Were his thoughts always thoughts of reality, and his utterances and acts always the utterances and acts of wisdom? Who would say so? No man attains to that height, and no man ever scorned the impostures of sham goodness and unattainable perfection more than Benjamin Butler. He was no pretender and no hypocrite. He lived his life, a life of energy and effort, of success and of failure and he has passed to the allotted reward while we who remain may well be grateful to heaven such a man has lived." [37]

BIBLIOGRAPHICAL NOTES

1. BUTLER PAPERS. The Library of Congress holds practically all the Butler papers. The collection is housed in several hundred shelf-boxes, which have not yet been organized and cross-indexed. A large number of these boxes contain material on special topics, like the Impeachment Trial. Some boxes are chronologically arranged and may be called for by date. Other unlabeled boxes Dr. Powell of the Division of Manuscripts kindly marked for the convenience of the author, "W1, W2 . . . W65." Then there is the most recent accession, that of 1954, which contains about 10,000 items relating to the period of the Governorship and the Presidential Campaign of 1884. A most useful source of reference in this accession of 1954 is the bound volumes of Butler's outgoing correspondence, each volume of which contains an index. This material, however, relates to the later period of his life.

Comparatively few papers of the pre-Civil War period have survived, owing to the fire in Butler's law office in 1856. Beginning with 1861, however, Butler made a practice of saving every scrap of paper, apparently in the belief that it might one day be useful in clarifying the many controversial issues in which he became involved. The Butler papers in the Library of Congress from 1861 to 1893 are magnificently complete; although as yet the shortest cut through the mountain to any particular type of research ore cannot always be easily discovered until the collection as a whole has been cross-indexed.

2. The Massachusetts Historical Society has a card file of 25,000 references to Butler to be found in the Boston Public Library. These, prepared by Henry Jefferson Moulton, are chiefly quotations from newspapers, magazines, and books. They were helpful primarily in making an overall survey of Butler's life and in developing a useful bibliography.

3. Jesse Ames Marshall (ed.), *Private and Official Correspondence of Gen. Benjamin F. Butler*. During the Period of the Civil War. 5 vols., privately issued, 1917. In this most valuable collection Mrs. Marshall has included

the most important items from the Butler papers and the *War Records*. Competently edited, the collection has been of inestimable usefulness. Cited hereafter as *Correspondence*.

4. *Autobiography and Personal Reminiscences of Major-General Benj. F. Butler. Butler's Book: A Review of His Legal, Political, and Military Career,* Boston: A. M. Thayer & Co., 1892. Poorly organized and peppered with minor inaccuracies of fact, its aging author being acutely aware of pressure for time and of physical illness, it nevertheless has merit as an attempt to present controversial issues as they appeared to the writer after a lapse of years. Cited hereafter as *Butler's Book*.

5. James Parton, *General Butler in New Orleans,* New York, 1864. Parton, the competent biographer of Andrew Jackson and others, took the initiative and approached Butler with his idea of writing a biography of the latter. Butler consented on condition that Parton examine the entire record and do an independent piece of work. This Parton proceeded to do, refusing even to permit the general to examine galley proofs in advance of publication. Parton's book is invaluable as a full-scale, near-contemporary, narrative of events of the occupation of New Orleans. It is generally pro-Butler. Cited hereafter as Parton.

6. *War Records. The War of the Rebellion: A Compilation of the Official Records of the Union and Confederate Armies.* Series I, II, III, and IV, 130 vols., Washington, D.C., 1880–1901. These have been examined for all of Butler's military operations and for his conduct of the prisoner-of-war exchange. Cited hereafter as *War Records*.

7. *Official Records of the Union and Confederate Navies in the War of the Rebellion,* Washington, D.C., Series I, vols. 1–27, 1894–1917; Series II, 3 vols., 1921–1922. Indispensable for the tie-in of military and naval operations in the amphibian campaigns of New Orleans, Fort Fisher, and on the James River. Cited hereafter as *O.R. . . . Navies*.

8. Newspapers
    Lowell *Advertiser.* The Lowell Public Library has a complete file of this paper. Edited by Butler's brother-in-law, Fisher A. Hildreth, it throws much light on Butler's law career in the 1840's and 1850's.
    Lowell *Daily Courier and Journal.* The file of this paper, also in the Lowell Public Library, was extremely interesting as it was usually hostile to Butler.
    Boston *Journal.* The Boston Public Library has a complete file of this paper. It was consulted primarily for the postwar election campaigns.

Although it contains some impartially written material about Butler, it tends to reflect the prejudices of the conservative Boston banker toward Butler's radical views on currency and labor reform.

New York *Times*. *Times* reporter H. J. Winser, assigned to cover Butler's headquarters in Virginia, gives an unusually thorough and generally pro-Butler account of happenings there.

New York *Herald*. Anti-administration during the Civil War, this paper often joined with the Secessionist Richmond *Examiner* and other Southern papers in berating Butler.

NOTES

Chapter 1. Never Pull a Journalist's Nose
(pages 3–6)

1. *Butler's Book*, p. 986.
2. Lowell *Advertiser*, July 13, 1842.
3. Lowell *Courier*, July 7, 1842.
4. *Ibid.*, July 9, 1842.
5. Lowell *Advertiser*, July 13, 1842.

Chapter 2. Cross-Eyed
(pages 7–16)

1. Butler Papers, Library of Congress.
2. *Ibid.*
3. For genealogical data see *Butler's Book*. Also, Blanche Butler Ames, *The Butler Ancestry of Gen. Benjamin Franklin Butler* (Lowell, 1895).
4. John Butler Papers. New Hampshire Historical Society, Concord, N.H.
5. *Ibid.*
6. *Ibid.*
7. Butler Papers. *Exeter News Letter*, July 31, 1885.
8. *Butler's Book*, p. 57.
9. *Ibid.*, pp. 48–49.
10. Scrapbook, "Butler as Governor, 1883," vol. IV. Massachusetts State House Library.
11. *Ibid.*

12. *Day Book* is quoted in Lowell *Advertiser,* April 13, 1852.
13. *Butler's Book,* p. 51.
14. Boston *Journal,* March 2, 1876.
15. George F. Kenngott, *The Record of a City: A Social Survey of Lowell, Massachusetts* (New York, 1912), pp. 12–13.
16. *Ibid.,* p. 17.
17. Charles Dickens, *American Notes* (London, 1842), p. 39.
18. *Old Residents Historical Association* (Lowell, Mass.), p. 123.
19. Early catalogues of Waterville (now Colby) College, Waterville, Me.
20. Butler's essays and declamations while at Waterville, 1834–38. Butler Papers, 1954 Accession.
21. Butler Papers, W10.
22. *Ibid.,* Edson's certification, dated January 26, 1836.
23. Same as 20 above.
24. *Butler's Book,* p. 61.
25. Same as 20 above.
26. *Ibid.*

Chapter 3. Juliet
(pages 17–24)

1. Butler Papers, W4.
2. *Butler's Book,* p. 63.
3. *Ibid.,* p. 69.
4. *Ibid.,* pp. 71–72.
5. Lowell *Advertiser,* July 8, 1839.
6. *Ibid.*
7. Butler Papers, 1839.
8. *Butler's Book,* pp. 76–77.
9. *Ibid.,* p. 79.
10. *Ibid.,* p. 72.
11. *Ibid.,* p. 989.
12. Lowell *Advertiser,* April 4, 1842.
13. *Butler's Book,* p. 987.
14. *Ibid.,* pp. 988–89.
15. *Ibid.,* pp. 1014–15.
16. Lowell *Advertiser,* July 20, 1842.
17. Butler Papers, W4, newsclipping.

18. *Correspondence,* IV, 256.
19. *Ibid.,* IV, 507.
20. *Ibid.,* I, 1.
21. *Ibid.,* I, 203.
22. Butler Papers, c. 1856.

Chapter 4. Radical Reform
(pages 25–29)

1. Lowell *Advertiser,* November 3, 1849.
2. *Ibid.,* September 4, 1844.
3. Butler Papers, W5.
4. Lowell *Advertiser,* February 25, 1850.
5. *Ibid.,* June 27, 1850.
6. *Ibid.,* February 8, 1851.
7. Butler Papers. 1847, 1954 Accession.
8. *Ibid.*
9. Lowell *Advertiser,* c. November 7, 1848.
10. *Ibid.*
11. *Ibid.*
12. *Ibid.,* November 14, 1848.
13. *Ibid.,* November 28, 1848; quotes the Lowell *Courier.*

Chapter 5. Ten-Hour Day
(pages 30–38)

1. *Butler's Book,* p. 92.
2. *Constitutional Convention, Massachusetts, Report of Debate and Proceedings* (1853), II, 148.
3. Lowell *Advertiser,* October 29, 1850.
4. *Ibid.,* November 8, 1850.
5. *Ibid.,* November 20, 1850.
6. Charles Cowley, *Illustrated History of Lowell* (Boston, 1868), p. 144.
7. Lowell *Advertiser,* November 22, 1851.
8. *Ibid.,* November 25, 1851.
9. *Butler's Book,* p. 103.
10. *Ibid.,* p. 104.
11. For November 21, 1851.

12. Pamphlet in B. F. Butler Papers, New Hampshire Historical Society.
13. *Ibid.*
14. *Ibid.*
15. New York *Day Book*, quoted in Lowell *Advertiser*, April 13, 1852.
16. Resolution of the Middlesex County Democratic Convention in 1846. Butler was a member of the Committee on Resolutions.
17. See note 15 *ante*.
18. *Ibid.*
19. Lowell *Advertiser*, November 5, 1852.
20. *Ibid.*, November 8, 1852.
21. Springfield *Republican*, February 19, 1853.

Chapter 6. Political General
(pages 39–47)

1. *Butler's Book*, p. 1019.
2. *Idem*, p. 109.
3. *Correspondence*, V, 24.
4. Butler Papers, Scrapbook.
5. *Correspondence*, I, 204.
6. Boston *Transcript*, August 26, 1897.
7. Butler Papers, W5.
8. New York *Herald*, June 17, 1900.
9. Butler Papers, W58, Scrapbook, "Portrait."
10. Butler Papers, W28, dated December 24, 1872.
11. Boston *Atlas and Bee*, February 8, 1859.
12. *Butler's Book*, p. 93.
13. Parton, pp. 42–43.
14. *Correspondence*, I, 1–2.
15. Parton, p. 52.
16. New York *Herald*, June 17, 1900.
17. *Butler's Book*, p. 168.

Chapter 7. Relief of Washington
(pages 51–63)

1. *Butler's Book*, p. 190.
2. Frank Moore, *The Rebellion Record*, 11 vols. (New York, 1861–64), I, 34.

3. *Butler's Book*, p. 189.
4. *Correspondence*, I, 18 and 45.
5. *Atlantic Monthly* (June 1861), p. 774.
6. *War Records*, Ser. I, vol. 2, pp. 588–90.
7. Baltimore *Sun*, April 23, 1861.
8. *Butler's Book*, p. 193.
9. *Correspondence*, I, 47.
10. *Ibid.*, pp. 47–48.
11. *Atlantic Monthly*, VII, 774ff.
12. *Ibid.*
13. *Correspondence*, I, 28.
14. *Ibid.*, p. 28.
15. *War Records*, Ser. I, vol. 2, p. 593.
16. Moore, *Rebellion Record*, I, "Diary," 45.
17. *Atlantic Monthly*, VII, 774ff.
18. *Correspondence*, I, 32.
19. *Ibid.*, p. 43.
20. New York *Times*, April 27, 1861.
21. *Correspondence*, I, 36–37.
22. New York *Times*, May 3, 1861.
23. Carl Schurz, *Reminiscences*, 3 vols. (New York, 1907), II, 225.
24. *Correspondence*, I, 51–52.
25. *Ibid.*, pp. 52–53.

Chapter 8. Butler Seizes Baltimore
(pages 64–75)

1. Theodore Winthrop, *Atlantic Monthly*, VIII, 108.
2. *Butler's Book*, pp. 222–23.
3. *Correspondence*, I, 64.
4. New York *Times*, May 11, 1861.
5. *Correspondence*, I, 72.
6. *Butler's Book*, p. 228.
7. *Correspondence*, I, 65.
8. *Ibid.*, p. 71.
9. *Ibid.*, p. 263; and New York *Tribune*, May 9, 1861.
10. *Correspondence*, I, 40.
11. *Ibid.*, p. 76.
12. *Ibid.*, p. 75.

13. *Butler's Book*, p. 230.
14. *Correspondence*, I, 81.
15. New York *Times*, May 16, 1861.
16. *Ibid.*
17. *War Records*, Ser. I, vol. 2, pp. 637–38.
18. *Correspondence*, I, 85.
19. *War Records*, Ser. I, vol. 2, p. 28.
20. Frank Moore, *Rebellion Record*, 11 vols. (New York, 1861–64), I, "Documents," 254–55.
21. *Butler's Book*, pp. 238–39.
22. *Ibid.*, p. 242.
23. *Ibid.*
24. *Correspondence*, I, 96–97.

Chapter 9. Butler's Fugitive Slave Law
(pages 76–86)

1. *Atlantic Monthly*, VIII, 105ff.
2. Butler Papers, B. F. King to Butler, May 16, 1861.
3. *Correspondence*, I, 78.
4. New York *Times*, May 18, 1861.
5. Quoted in Baltimore *American and Commercial Advertiser*, June 10, 1861.
6. New York *Times*, May 20, 1861.
7. *Ibid.*
8. New Orleans *Picayune*, May 22, 1861.
9. *War Records*, Ser. I, vol. 2, p. 907.
10. *Atlantic Monthly*, VIII, 250.
11. *Ibid.*
12. *Ibid.*
13. *War Records*, Ser. I, vol. 2, p. 35.
14. *Ibid.*, p. 871; and *Butler's Book*, pp. 257–58.
15. *Ibid.*
16. New York *Times*, May 27, 1861.
17. *Atlantic Monthly*, VIII, 248–51.
18. *Correspondence*, I, 119.
19. *Ibid.*, p. 116.
20. *Ibid.*, pp. 112–13.

21. *Ibid.*, p. 128.
22. Parton, pp. 132–33.
23. New York *Times,* May 31, 1861.
24. *Ibid.*
25. Butler Papers. J. Q. A. Griffin's "portrait," first published in Charlestown, Mass., *Advertiser,* September 7, 1859.

Chapter 10. Enough Rope
(pages 87–96)

1. *Correspondence,* I, 95.
2. *Ibid.*, p. 121.
3. *Ibid.*, p. 130.
4. *Ibid.*, pp. 129–30.
5. *Ibid.*, p. 113.
6. *Ibid.*, pp. 109–10
7. *War Records,* Ser. I, vol. 2, p. 76.
8. New York *Times,* June 13, 1861.
9. *Correspondence,* I, 133.
10. *Ibid.*
11. Parton, p. 151.
12. *War Records,* Ser. I, vol. 2, p. 86.
13. New York *Times,* June 14, 1861.
14. Battle reports on Big Bethel, *War Records,* Ser. I, vol. 2, pp. 77ff.
15. *War Records,* Ser. I, vol. 2, p. 87.
16. New York *Times,* June 15, 1861.
17. *Ibid.*, June 12, 1861.
18. *War Records,* Ser. I, vol. 2, pp. 79–80.
19. Philadelphia *Inquirer,* June 21, 1861.
20. *Ibid.*

Chapter 11. Recovery After Big Bethel
(pages 97–107)

1. *Correspondence,* I, 177.
2. *Ibid.*, pp. 162–63.
3. *Ibid.*, pp. 172–73.
4. *Ibid.*, p. 194.

5. *Ibid.*, p. 203.
6. *Ibid.*, pp. 208–9.
7. *Ibid.*, p. 191.
8. New York *Times*, August 19, 1861.
9. *Correspondence*, I, 212.
10. New York *Times*, July 2, 1861.
11. *Ibid.*, July 20, 1861.
12. *Ibid.*
13. *Ibid.*, August 1, 1861.
14. *Correspondence*, I, 183.
15. *Ibid.*, p. 207.
16. *Ibid.*, pp. 186–88.
17. *Ibid.*, pp. 206–7.
18. *Ibid.*, p. 215.
19. *Ibid.*, p. 218.
20. *Ibid.*, p. 223.
21. *Butler's Book*, pp. 287–88.

Chapter 12. Launching the New Orleans Expedition
(pages 111–118)

1. *Correspondence*, I, 210.
2. *Ibid.*, p. 239.
3. *War Records*, Ser. III, vol. 1, p. 816.
4. *Ibid.*, p. 826.
5. *Butler's Book*, p. 307.
6. *Ibid.*, p. 312.
7. For the feud between Governor J. A. Andrew and Butler over recruiting in Massachusetts, see *Correspondence*, I, 264ff.; Parton, Ch. XI; and *War Records*, Ser. III, vol. I, pp. 819–66.
8. *Correspondence*, I, 251.
9. *Butler's Book*, p. 297.
10. New York *Times*, November 20, 1861.
11. *Correspondence*, I, 318.
12. *Ibid.*, p. 319.
13. *War Records*, Ser. III, vol. I, p. 862.
14. *Ibid.*, p. 863.
15. *Correspondence*, I, 341.

16. *Ibid.*, p. 332.
17. *Ibid.*, p. 323.
18. *Ibid.*, pp. 330–31.
19. *Ibid.*, p. 363.
20. *Ibid.*, pp. 360–62.

Chapter 13. New Orleans Campaign
(pages 119–128)

1. *Butler's Book*, p. 336.
2. Parton, p. 203.
3. *Correspondence*, I, 365.
4. *Ibid.*, p. 367.
5. *War Records*, Ser. I, vol. 6, p. 701.
6. *Correspondence*, I, 382–83.
7. *Butler's Book*, p. 355.
8. Richard S. West, Jr., "The Relations Between Farragut and Porter," U.S. Naval Institute *Proceedings* (July, 1935); and "Admiral Farragut and General Butler," *Proceedings* (June 1956).
9. New Orleans *Picayune*, April 5, 1862, quoted in Parton, p. 209.
10. Parton, p. 225.
11. *O.R. . . . Navies*, Ser. I, vol. 18, p. 136.
12. *Ibid.*, p. 160.
13. *Butler's Book*, p. 366.
14. *Correspondence*, I, 420.
15. *Ibid.*, p. 422.
16. *Ibid.*, p. 423.

Chapter 14. The Woman Order
(pages 129–143)

1. Parton, p. 265.
2. *O.R. . . . Navies*, Ser. I, vol. 18, p. 698.
3. *Butler's Book*, p. 480.
4. *Correspondence*, I, 438.
5. New York *Times*, May 22, 1862.
6. Parton, p. 279.
7. Thomas E. Dabney, "The Butler Regime in Louisiana," *Louisiana Historical Review* (April, 1944), p. 495.

8. Parton, p. 281.
9. *Correspondence*, I, 433–36.
10. Parton, p. 286.
11. *Ibid.*, pp. 286–88.
12. *Ibid.*, p. 288.
13. *Correspondence*, I, 439.
14. Parton, p. 295.
15. *Ibid.*, pp. 295–96.
16. *Correspondence*, I, 443.
17. *Ibid.*, p. 491.
18. *Ibid.*, pp. 490–91.
19. New York *Times*, May 30 and June 23, 1862.
20. *Atlantic Monthly*, XII, 105.
21. *War Records*, Ser. I, vol. XV, p. 426.
22. Parton, p. 327.
23. *Ibid.*, pp. 327–28.
24. *Correspondence*, I, 486–87.
25. New York *Times*, June 2 and 19, 1862.
26. Parton, p. 339.
27. *Ibid.*, pp. 339–41.
28. *Correspondence*, I, 381–83.

Chapter 15. Military Government Reforms
(pages 144–157)

1. *Correspondence*, I, 456–67.
2. *Ibid.*, pp. 457–58.
3. *Ibid.*, p. 458.
4. *Ibid.*, pp. 497–98.
5. *Ibid.*, p. 498.
6. *Ibid.*, p. 499.
7. Marion Southwood, *Beauty and Booty* (New York, 1867), p. 182.
8. *Butler's Book,* p. 395.
9. Southwood, *Beauty and Booty,* p. 182.
10. New York *Times,* June 30, 1862.
11. *Correspondence*, I, 571–72.
12. *Ibid.*, pp. 568–69, and Parton, p. 349.
13. *Correspondence*, I, 428.
14. *Ibid.*, p. 453.

15. New York *Times,* June 19, 1862.
16. *Correspondence,* I, 485.
17. Moore, *Rebellion Record,* 11 vols. (New York, 1861–64), I, "Documents," 190.
18. *Butler's Book,* p. 440.
19. Moore, *Rebellion Record,* V, "*Documents,*" 190.
20. New York *Times,* June 19, 1862.
21. *Butler's Book,* p. 547.
22. New Orleans *Picayune,* July 11, 1862.
23. Parton, p. 439.
24. Southwood, *Beauty and Booty,* p. 149.
25. Parton, p. 441.
26. *Ibid.*
27. *Ibid.,* p. 442.
28. *Correspondence,* II, 152–53; *War Records,* Ser. I, vol. XV, pp. 538–42.
29. *Ibid.*
30. New York *Herald,* June 26, 1862.
31. *Ibid.,* September 11, 1862.

Chapter 16. Shoestring Offensive
(pages 158–170)

1. New York *Times,* July 3, 1862.
2. *Ibid.,* July 25, 1862.
3. *Ibid.,* August 25, 1862.
4. *Ibid.,* June 17, 1862.
5. *Ibid.,* June 26, 1862.
6. *Ibid.,* September 11, 1862.
7. Wickham Hoffman, *Camp, Court and Siege* (New York, 1877), p. 52.
8. *War Records,* Ser. I, vol. 15, p. 23.
9. *O. R. . . . Navies,* Ser. I, vol. 18, p. 531.
10. *Correspondence* I, 547–48.
11. *O. R. . . . Navies,* Ser. I, vol. 18, p. 535.
12. *Ibid.*
13. *Correspondence,* I, 585–86.
14. *War Records,* Ser. I, vol. 15, p. 25.
15. Parton, p. 567.
16. New York *Times,* May 23 and 24, 1862.

17. Parton, p. 556.
18. New Orleans *Picayune*, June 29, 1862.
19. New York *Times*, July 3, 1862.
20. *Correspondence*, II, 32.
21. *Ibid.*, p. 323.
22. New York *Times*, September 29, 1862.
23. *Correspondence*, II, 187.
24. *War Records*, Ser. I, vol. 15, pp. 124–26.
25. *Ibid.*, p. 158ff.
26. New York *Times*, December 1, 1862.
27. *War Records*, Ser. I, vol. 15, p. 171.

Chapter 17. Reconstruction
(pages 171–185)

1. *War Records*, Ser. I, vol. 6, p. 832.
2. *Correspondence*, I, 502.
3. *Ibid.*, p. 434.
4. Boston *Journal*, January 13, 1863.
5. *Correspondence*, I, 487.
6. *Ibid.*, p. 575.
7. New York *Times*, June 23, 1862.
8. *Ibid.*, June 19, 1862.
9. *Correspondence*, I, 596.
10. New York *Times*, July 14, 1862.
11. *Ibid.*, June 19, 1862.
12. *Ibid.*, July 21, 1862.
13. Parton, p. 469.
14. *Correspondence*, II, 305.
15. New York *Times*, September 29, 1862.
16. *Correspondence*, II, 332–33.
17. Parton, pp. 481–82.
18. *Ibid.*, p. 484.
19. New York *Times*, October 20, 1862.
20. *Correspondence*, I, 553–54.
21. *Ibid.*, pp. 516–20.
22. Parton, p. 499.
23. *Correspondence*, I, 614–15.

24. *Rebellion Record*, V, 559.
25. *Correspondence*, II, 109.
26. *Ibid.*, pp. 125–26.
27. *Ibid.*, pp. 126–27.
28. *Ibid.*, pp. 148 and 154.
29. Parton, p. 493.
30. New York *Times*, November 3, 1862.
31. *Correspondence*, II, 426.
32. *Ibid.*, pp. 488–89.
33. *Ibid.*, p. 447.
34. *Ibid.*, p. 450.
35. New York *Times*, December 19, 1862.

Chapter 18. Commerce, Consuls and the Recall
(pages 186–204)

1. *Correspondence*, I, 579.
2. *Ibid.*, p. 493.
3. *Ibid.*, p. 533.
4. *Ibid.*, pp. 612–13.
5. *War Records*, Ser. I, vol. 15, pp. 493–94.
6. *Correspondence*, II, 92.
7. *Ibid.*, p. 354.
8. *Ibid.*, p. 305.
9. *Ibid.*, pp. 229–30.
10. *Ibid.*, pp. 270–1.
11. *Ibid.*, p. 356.
12. *Ibid.*, pp. 422–23.
13. *Ibid.*, pp. 423–25.
14. *Ibid.*, p. 527.
15. *Ibid.*, p. 529.
16. *Ibid.*, p. 390.
17. *Diplomatic Correspondence*, 1862, p. 527.
18. *War Records*, Ser. III, vol. 2, p. 124; *Diplomatic Correspondence* (1862), p. 621.
19. *Correspondence*, I, 553.
20. *Ibid.*, p. 636.
21. *Ibid.*, p. 580.

22. *War Records,* Ser. III, vol. 2, p. 245.
23. New York *Times,* November 5, 1862.
24. *Correspondence,* II, 389.
25. *Ibid.,* p. 375.
26. New York *Times,* November 3, 1862.
27. *Correspondence,* I, 600.
28. Thomas A. Bland, *Life of Benjamin F. Butler* (New York, 1879), p. 126.
29. New York *Times,* June 26, 1862.
30. *Ibid.*
31. *Ibid.,* June 21, 1862.
32. *Ibid.,* November 10, 1862.
33. *Correspondence,* II, 469.
34. *Ibid.,* pp. 499–500.
35. *Ibid.,* pp. 512–13.
36. *Ibid.,* p. 541.
37. *Ibid.,* p. 461.
38. New York *Times,* January 3, 1863.
39. *Correspondence,* II, 554–55.
40. *Ibid.,* pp. 555–57.
41. Boston *Journal,* January 5, 1863.

Chapter 19. Politics Behind the Lines
(pages 205–216)

1. *Correspondence,* II, 557–62.
2. *Ibid.,* p. 553.
3. *Butler's Book,* pp. 533–34.
4. Parton, pp. 613–14.
5. New York *Times,* January 3, 1863.
6. *Butler's Book,* pp. 550–51.
7. *Ibid.,* p. 552.
8. New York *Times,* January 8, 1863.
9. *Ibid.,* January 9, 1863.
10. Boston *Daily Courier,* January 14, 1863.
11. New York *Times,* January 14, 1863.
12. *Ibid.,* February 20, 1863.
13. *Correspondence,* II, 574.

14. New York *Times,* January 22, 1863.
15. *Correspondence,* II, 589–90.
16. *Ibid.,* p. 582.
17. *Ibid.,* p. 583.
18. Quoted in Milton E. Flower, *James Parton: the Father of Modern Biography,* (Durham, N.C., 1951), p. 67.
19. *Ibid.,* p. 68.
20. *Correspondence,* II, 587.
21. *Ibid.,* III, p. 15.
22. *Ibid.,* pp. 21–27.
23. New York *Times,* February 4, 1863.
24. Springfield *Republican,* April 11, 1863.
25. New York *Times,* April 3, 1863.
26. *Butler's Book,* pp. 563–64.
27. *Ibid.,* pp. 567–68.
28. New York *World,* January 15, 1863.
29. *Correspondence,* III, 58.
30. *Ibid.,* p. 106.
31. *Ibid.,* p. 115.
32. Butler Papers, March, 1863.
33. *Ibid.,* October, 1863.

Chapter 20. The Virginia Front
(pages 219–231)

1. *War Records,* Ser. I, vol. 63, p. 333.
2. *Correspondence,* III, 183.
3. *Ibid.,* p. 186.
4. *Ibid.,* pp. 183–90.
5. Edward A. Pollard, *Observations in the North* (Richmond, 1865), p. 102.
6. New York *Times,* January 9, 1864.
7. *Ibid.*
8. *Ibid.*
9. *Correspondence,* III, 315.
10. *War Records,* Ser. I, vol. 48, p. 913.
11. *Correspondence,* III, 227.
12. New York *World,* January 11, 1864.

13. *Ibid.*, February 11, 1864.
14. *War Records*, Ser. I, vol. 49, p. 596.
15. Butler Papers, telegram from B. to Lincoln, January 16, 1864.
16. *Correspondence*, III, 489.
17. *Idem.*
18. *Correspondence*, III, 319n.
19. *Ibid.*, p. 381.
20. *Ibid.*, p. 397; New York *Times* of February 10, 1864, quotes the Richmond *Examiner* of February 8, 1864.
21. *Correspondence*, III, 400.
22. *Butler's Book*, p. 662.
23. *Ibid.*, p. 627.
24. Benjamin F. Butler, "Vice Presidential Politics in 1864," *North American Review*, vol. 141, pp. 331–34; *Butler's Book*, pp. 631–35.
25. *Ibid.*
26. *Ibid.*

Chapter 21. Bermuda Hundred
(pages 232–250)

1. *Butler's Book*, p. 1059.
2. *War Records*, Ser. I, vol. 68, p. 392.
3. *Ibid.*
4. New York *Times*, May 9, 1864.
5. *Ibid.*
6. Quoted in the New York *Times*, May 11, 1864.
7. New York *Times*, May 11, 1864.
8. *Correspondence*, IV, 172.
9. Clarence Buel and Robert Johnson (eds.), *Battles and Leaders of the Civil War*, 4 vols. (New York, 1884–88), IV, 208.
10. New York *Times*, May 20, 1864.
11. *War Records*, Ser. I, vol. 68, p. 12.
12. *Ibid.*, vol. 69, p. 43.
13. *Ibid.*, p. 77.
14. *Correspondence* IV, 256.
15. *Ibid.*, pp. 257–58.
16. *Ibid.*, pp. 262–63, Butler to Sarah Butler, May 24 and 25, 1864.
17. New York *Times*, June 1, 1864.

18. *Correspondence,* IV, 275.
19. *Ibid.,* p. 276.
20. *Ibid.,* p. 277.
21. *War Records,* Ser. I, vol. 68, p. 282.
22. New York *Times,* June 28, 1864.
23. *War Records,* Ser. I, vol. 81, pp. 299–300.
24. *Ibid.,* p. 300.
25. *Ibid.*
26. *Ibid.,* p. 559.
27. *Ibid.,* p. 598.
28. *Butler's Book,* p. 1088.
29. *War Records,* Ser. I, vol. 82, p. 31.
30. *Correspondence,* IV, 472.
31. Quoted from Dana in James H. Wilson, *Life and Public Services of William Farrar Smith* (Wilmington, Del., 1904), p. 113.
32. *Correspondence,* IV, 481.
33. *Ibid.,* pp. 481–82.
34. *Ibid.,* p. 513.

Chapter 22. Prisoners and the Exchange
(pages 251–262)

1. Richmond *Examiner,* November 21, 1863.
2. *Correspondence,* III, 147
3. *Ibid.,* p. 149.
4. *War Records,* Ser. II, vol. 6, p. 659.
5. *Ibid.,* p. 683.
6. *Ibid.,* p. 769.
7. *Ibid.,* p. 768.
8. *Ibid.,* pp. 770–71.
9. "Report of Major General Hitchcock," *Report of the Joint Committee on the Conduct of the War,* Supplement No. 2, p. 11.
10. New York *World,* February 12, 1864.
11. *War Records,* Ser. II, vol. 6, p. 768.
12. Tyler Dennett (ed.), *Lincoln and the Civil War in the Diaries and Letters of John Hay* (New York, 1939), p. 150.
13. *Ibid.,* p. 151.
14. Richmond *Examiner,* March 8, 1864.

15. *War Records,* Ser. II, vol. 6, p. 839.
16. *Butler's Book,* p. 592.
17. *Ibid.,* p. 594.
18. *War Records,* Ser. II, vol. 7, p. 691.
19. New York *Times,* September 8, 1864.
20. New York *World,* September 7, 1864.
21. Richmond *Examiner,* September 16, 1864.
22. New York *Times,* June 25, 1864.
23. Richmond *Examiner,* February 10, 1864.
24. New York *Times,* June 25, 1864.
25. Edward A. Pollard, *Observations in the North* (Richmond, 1865), p. 105.
26. New York *Times,* October 17, 1864.
27. *Ibid.,* October 18, 1864.
28. Quoted in the Richmond *Examiner,* October 25, 1864.

Chapter 23. Military Vs. Civil Government
(pages 263–278)

1. Francis H. Pierpont, "Letter of Governor Peirpont [sic] to His Excellency the President. . . ," 60 pp. (Washington, D.C., 1864), p. 11.
2. *Correspondence,* III, 309.
3. Portsmouth, Va., *Old Dominion,* December 25, 1864.
4. *Correspondence,* III, 321–24.
5. *Ibid.,* pp. 450–60.
6. Thomas J. Wertenbaker, *Norfolk: Historic Southern Port* (Durham, N.C., 1951), p. 249.
7. Quoted in the New York *World,* March 5, 1864.
8. Butler Papers, transcript dated March 5, 1864.
9. *Correspondence,* III, 357.
10. *Ibid.,* IV, 104–5.
11. Pierpont, "Letter . . . ," p. 23.
12. *Correspondence,* IV, 159–60.
13. *Ibid.,* p. 306.
14. Butler Papers, General Order No. 50, June 30, 1864.
15. *Correspondence,* IV, 567.
16. *Ibid.,* p. 574.
17. *Ibid.,* pp. 575–76.

18. *Ibid.*, pp. 576–86.

19. John G. Nicolay and John Hay, *Abraham Lincoln, a History*, 10 vols. (New York, 1890), IX, 442–43.

20. Howard K. Beale, (ed.), *The Diary of Edward Bates, 1859–1866* (G.P.O., Washington, D.C., 1933), p. 394.

21. *Correspondence*, V, 52–53.

22. *Ibid.*, pp. 65–66.

23. *Ibid.*, p. 72.

24. *Ibid.*, p. 78.

25. *Ibid.*, pp. 108–9.

26. Butler Papers, J. K. Herbert to Butler, September 13, 1864.

27. New York *Times*, November 8, 1864.

28. *Ibid.*, November 9, 1864.

29. New York *Tribune*, November 16, 1864.

30. New York *Times*, November 16, 1864.

31. *Ibid.*

32. New York *Herald*, November 16, 1864.

33. Nicolay and Hay, *Abraham Lincoln*, IX, 443.

Chapter 24. Finale at Fort Fisher
(pages 279–292)

1. *Report of the Joint Committee on the Conduct of the War* (Washington, D.C., 1865), II, 3. Hereafter cited as *Report*.

2. *Ibid.*, p. 51.

3. *Correspondence*, V, 299.

4. New York *Times*, August 13, 1864.

5. Richard S. West, Jr., *The Second Admiral, a Life of David Dixon Porter, 1813–1891* (New York: Coward McCann, 1937), p. 277.

6. *Report*, II, 69.

7. *Correspondence*, V, 379.

8. *Ibid.*

9. *Ibid.*

10. *Report*, II, 66.

11. *Ibid*, p. 113.

12. *Ibid.*, p. 95.

13. *Ibid.*, p. 52.

14. *Ibid.*, p. 216.

15. *Correspondence*, V, 436.
16. *War Records*, Ser. I, vol. 42, Part I, p. 967.
17. *Report*, II, 17.
18. *Correspondence*, V, 430.
19. *Ibid.*, pp. 432–33.
20. *Report*, II, 30–31.
21. *War Records*, Ser. I, vol. 42, Part I, pp. 971–72.
22. *Report*, II, 72.
23. *Ibid.*
24. *Ibid.*, p. 23.
25. *Ibid.*
26. *Ibid.*, p. 96.
27. *Ibid.*, pp. 24–25.
28. *Ibid.*, p. 24.
29. *Butler's Book*, p. 797.
30. *Correspondence*, V, 438.
31. *Ibid.*, p. 450.
32. *Ibid.*, p. 455.
33. *Ibid.*, pp. 467–68.
34. *Ibid.*, pp. 468–69.
35. *Ibid.*, p. 471.
36. *Report*, II, 33.
37. *Correspondence*, V, 473.
38. *Report*, II, viii.

Chapter 25. The Legend of the Spoons
(pages 295–308)

1. Butler Papers, W60.
2. William Dana Orcutt, "Ben Butler and the 'Stolen Spoons,'" *North American Review* (January 1918), pp. 66–80.
3. *Correspondence*, III, 21.
4. *Ibid.*, p. 527.
5. *Ibid.*, p. 526.
6. *Ibid.*, p. 523.
7. *Ibid.*, p. 525.
8. *Ibid.*, p. 533.
9. *Ibid.*, p. 528.
10. *Ibid.*, p. 529.

11. *Ibid.*, pp. 531–33.
12. *Ibid.*
13. *Ibid.*, pp. 531–32.
14. *Ibid.*, p. 534.
15. *Ibid.*, p. 535.
16. *Ibid.*, pp. 560–63.
17. *War Records,* Ser. I, vol. 15, p. 513.
18. *Correspondence,* III, 595.
19. *Ibid.*, V, 417.
20. *Ibid.*, p. 243.
21. *Ibid.*, p. 280.
22. *Ibid.*, p. 342.
23. *Ibid.*, p. 410.
24. *Ibid.*, p. 519.
25. *Ibid.*, pp. 519–20.
26. *Ibid.*, p. 519.
27. New York *Times,* January 24, 1865.
28. *Ibid.*
29. *Ibid.*
30. Parton, pp. 467–68.
31. Butler Papers, Butler to Mrs. W. T. Sherman, February 13, 1878.
32. *Correspondence,* II, 570.
33. Butler Papers, C. Black, Sr., to Butler, April 14, 1870.
34. *Correspondence,* III, 535–36.
35. Butler Papers, W3, unidentified newsclipping.

Chapter 26. Return to the Law
(pages 309–319)

1. Charles Cowley, *Illustrated History of Lowell,* Boston, 1868, p. 54.
2. *Correspondence,* V, 565.
3. Butler Papers, March 14, 1865.
4. Thomas A. Bland, *Life of Benjamin F. Butler* (Boston, 1879), p. 319.
5. Butler Papers. Bound copies of Butler's outgoing correspondence are available for most of the period 1866–93. Where the name of the addressee is unimportant, the author cites merely volume and page. References to these bound volumes are indicated by *italicized* inclusive dates, to distinguish them from references to the loose, original papers. This reference is to *January–June, 1876, p. 397.*

6. *Contributions* (local history of Lowell), 1879, vol. I, p. 329.
7. Butler Papers, George Wilkes to Butler, July 20, 1867.
8. Butler Papers, W36.
9. *Butler's Book*, p. 991.
10. Butler Papers, W58.
11. *Ibid.*, W7, "Argument of Benjamin F. Butler in behalf of the Government in the cases of Lambdin P. Milligan and others, petitioners for a writ of Habeas Corpus, before the Supreme Court of the United States at Washington, D.C., December Term, 1865," Lowell, 1866, pp. 13 and 60.
12. Butler Papers, Butler to Farragut, c. June, 1867.
13. Butler Papers, W36.
14. *Ibid.*, Butler to W. McAdoo, February 12, 1884.
15. *Ibid.*, Butler to W. E. Chandler, December 31, 1871.
16. *Ibid.*, W40.
17. George W. Stimpson, *A Book about American Politics* (New York, 1952), p. 211.
18. Campaign leaflet, "Them Spoons! What General Butler Said, etc.," 1876.
19. Butler Papers, W4.
20. *Ibid.*, Butler to Mrs. Butler, January 1, 1867.
21. *Ibid.*, W27, Mrs. Butler to Butler, no date (c. 1870).
22. *Ibid.*, Butler to Mrs. Butler, February 26, 1870.
23. *Ibid.*, Butler to Mrs. Butler, March 23, 1871.
24. *Ibid.*, Butler to Mrs. Butler, April 17 (1871?).

Chapter 27. The Radical Congressman: The Impeachment Trial
(pages 320–333)

1. *Correspondence*, V, 361.
2. *Ibid.*, p. 364.
3. *Ibid.*, p. 560.
4. New York *Herald*, September 4, 1866.
5. Boston *Journal*, September 10, 1866.
6. Butler Papers, W45.
7. James G. Blaine, *Twenty Years of Congress*, 2 vols. (Norwich, Conn., 1884), p. 289.
8. Boston *Journal*, November 5, 1866.

9. Butler Papers, W9, pamphlet reprint of Butler's "Speech at the Brooklyn Academy of Music."

10. *Butler's Book*, p. 929.

11. Mark A. DeWolfe Howe, *Portrait of an American: Moorfield Storey*, Boston, Houghton Mifflin, 1932, p. 87.

12. Mrs. W. S. Robinson (ed.), *"Warrington" Pen Portraits: A Collection of Personal and Political Reminiscences from 1848 to 1876 from the Writings of William S. Robinson, with Memoir, and Extracts from Diary and Letters never before Published* (Boston, 1877), p. 315.

13. *Ibid.*

14. *Butler's Book*, pp. 929–30.

15. Howe, *Portrait*, p. 92.

16. *Ibid.*, p. 103.

17. Butler Papers, outgoing letter, November 10, 1885.

18. Boston *Journal*, January 2, 1869.

19. *War Records*, Ser. I, vol. 36, Part I, p. 20.

20. Louis T. Merrill, "General Benjamin F. Butler and the Campaign of 1868" (University of Chicago Library, 1939), p. 207, quotes Butler to Grant, January 29, 1866.

21. *Butler's Book*, p. 854.

22. Butler Papers, W40, newsclipping, n.d., unidentified.

23. *Ibid.*, Butler to W. E. Chandler, January 4, 1877.

24. *Ibid.*, largest scrapbook, article by Goldwin Smith in *The Palladium*, January 25, 1865.

25. Chapters 28 and 29.

26. Louis T. Merrill, "General Benjamin F. Butler in Washington," quotes San Francisco *Argonaut* of April 6, 1903, *Records of the Columbia Historical Society*, p. 87.

27. Butler Papers, J. W. Shaffer to Butler, March 28, 1868.

28. Butler Papers, Butler to Governor MacCormack, July 21, 1877.

29. Butler Papers. Pamphlet, *Salaries of Public Officers*, p. 41.

30. *Ibid.*, James Parton to Butler, November 12, 1882.

31. Butler Papers. Pamphlet, *Salaries of Public Officers*, p. 42.

32. *Ibid.*, "Crédit Mobilier, February 27, 1873."

33. *Ibid.*

34. William S. Robinson, *The Salary Grab*, New York, 1873, pp. 69–70.

35. Butler Papers. Unidentified clipping included in a letter from R. H. Bacon to Butler, March 26, 1874.

36. Butler Papers.

Chapter 28. The Radical Congressman: Reconstruction
(pages 334–351)

1. Quoted in the *Boston Morning Journal,* November 19, 1868.
2. Boston *Journal* Supplement, October 31, 1868.
3. Butler Papers, W45.
4. *Daily Advertiser* of Elmira, N.Y., c. October 13, 1868.
5. *Ibid.*
6. See footnote 1 above.
7. *Ibid.*
8. *Ibid.*
9. *Congressional Globe,* December 20, 1869.
10. *Ibid.*
11. *Congressional Globe,* vol. 90, p. 1720.
12. *Ibid.,* February 1, 1871.
12ª. See *Adelbert Ames, 1835–1933,* by Blanche Ames Ames (North Easton, Massachusetts, 1964).
13. Butler to Blanche Ames, March 1877.
14. Stanley F. Horn, *The Invisible Empire,* The Story of the Ku Klux Klan, 1866–1871 (Boston, 1939), p. 151.
15. Butler Papers, W58.
16. Washington *Chronicle,* March 20, 1871.
17. Butler Papers, W58.
18. *Ibid.,* pamphlet, *Controversy between Speaker Blaine and General Butler.*
19. Blanche Ames to Sarah Butler, April 6, 1871. *Chronicles from the Nineteenth Century, Family Letters of Blanche Butler and Adelbert Ames,* compiled by Blanche Butler Ames, privately issued in two volumes (1957), I, 243.
20. *Congressional Globe,* April 4, 1871.
21. *Ibid.*
22. *Ibid.*
23. Ames, *Chronicles,* I, 255.
24. *Ibid.,* I, 258.
25. *Congressional Globe,* April 20, 1871.
26. Butler Papers, W58, printed and written speeches.
27. Ames, *Chronicles,* I, 268.

28. *Ibid.,* I, 345.
29. *Ibid.,* I, 653.
30. *Ibid.,* I, 319.

Chapter 29. The Radical Congressman: Civil Rights
(pages 352–365)

1. In two volumes, copyright, 1957, by Jessie Ames Marshall and privately issued. Cited hereafter as *Chronicles.*
2. Robert S. Henry, *The Story of Reconstruction* (Indianapolis, 1938). Henry's appraisal of Ames, p. 326.
3. William E. B. Du Bois, *Black Reconstruction, An Essay toward a History of the Part which Black Folk Played in the Attempt to Reconstruct Democracy in America,* 1860–1880 (New York, 1935), pp. 439–440.
4. Henry, pp. 548–49.
5. Butler's speech on Civil Rights, *Congressional Globe,* January 7, 1874. Butler Papers, W60.
6. *Ibid.*
7. Du Bois, *Black Reconstruction,* p. 348.
8. William V. Byars, *An American Commoner* (Columbia, Mo., 1900), pp. 87–88.
9. *Ibid.,* pp. 94 and 96.
10. *Congressional Globe,* February 1, 1875, p. 897.
11. *Ibid.,* p. 987.
12. *Ibid.,* p. 938.
13. *Ibid.,* p. 987.
14. *Ibid.,* February 4, 1875, p. 986.
15. *Ibid.,* p. 991.
16. *Ibid.,* p. 945.
17. *Ibid.*
18. *Ibid.,* p. 1005.
19. *Ibid.,* p. 1006.
20. *Ibid.,* p. 1009.
21. Butler Papers.
22. Blanche Butler Ames (ed.), *Chronicles from the Nineteenth Century: Family Letters of Blanche Butler and Adelbert Ames* (privately issued, 1957), II, 213.

23. *Ibid.*, II, 216–17.
24. *Ibid.*, II, 245.
25. Butler Papers, November 28, 1875.
26. Ames, *Chronicles,* II, 516.
27. Butler Papers.
28. Ames, *Chronicles,* II, 227.
29. Butler Papers, Butler to A. Ames, April 1, 1876.
30. *Ibid.*, Butler to Betsy Morrill Stevens, April 9, 1876.

Chapter 30. The Reform Governor
(pages 366–378)

1. Boston *Journal,* August 13, 1878.
2. *Ibid.*, August 20, 1878.
3. *Ibid.*, September 21, 1878.
4. Boston *Daily Evening Traveller,* October 2, 1883.
5. *Ibid.*
6. Butler Papers, Butler to S. Webster, June 26, 1879.
7. *Ibid.*, Butler to Adelbert Ames, April 1877.
8. *Ibid.*, Butler to Blanche Ames, May 29, 1881.
9. *Ibid., December, 1876,* p. 528.
10. *Ibid.*, Butler to Paul Butler, January 3, 1881.
11. *Ibid.*, Butler to Ben-Israel Butler, February 14, 1877.
12. *Ibid.*, Butler to Ben-Israel Butler, March 17, 1877.
13. *Ibid.*, October 27, 1882.
14. *Ibid.*, November 6 and 7, 1882.
15. *Ibid.*, James Parton to Butler, November 12, 1882.
16. *Ibid.*, Clara Barton to Butler, November 10, 1882.
17. *Ibid.*, R. T. Owens to Butler, November 8, 1882.
18. *Ibid.*, W. F. G. Young to Butler, November 10, 1882.
19. *Ibid.*, Phoebe Couzins to Butler, December 22, 1882.
20. Boston *Journal,* January 5, 1883.
21. *Ibid.*
22. "Address of His Excellency Governor Benjamin F. Butler to the two Branches of the Legislature of Massachusetts," January 4, 1883.
23. Comments by New York papers (*Sun, Times,* and *Tribune*) quoted in the Boston *Journal,* January 5, 1883.
24. Butler Papers, Butler to W. S. Taylor, June 21, 1886.

25. Boston *Journal,* February 20, 1883.
26. *Ibid.,* February 28, 1883.
27. *Ibid.,* February 24, 1883.
28. Butler Papers, W51.
29. Quoted in the Boston *Journal,* April 19, 1883.
30. Quoted in the Boston *Journal,* April 20, 1883.
31. Butler Papers, Butler to Blanche Ames, June 29, 1883.

Chapter 31. Nomination for President: 1884
(pages 379–390)

1. Butler in House of Representatives, May 21, 1878, "Relief to Labor."
2. Butler Papers, *July 2–December 31, 1878,* p. 292.
3. Butler Papers, Butler to R. H. Williams, November 4, 1875.
4. *Ibid.,* Butler to T. B. Buchanan, May 12, 1876.
5. *Ibid.,* E. S. Pope to Butler, April 16, 1883.
6. *Ibid.,* 1954 Accession, R. M. Griffin to Butler, June 1, 1884.
7. Boston *Transcript,* November 5, 1883.
8. *Ibid.*
9. Butler Papers, Butler to C. A. Dana, December 3, 1883.
10. *Ibid.,* G. P. Cowlam to S. V. Powell, April 28, 1884.
11. *Ibid.,* J. B. Weaver to Butler, March 14, 1884.
12. *Ibid.,* clipping from Detroit *Evening Press,* n.d., prior to March 23, 1884.
13. *Ibid.,* Butler to S. H. Jennings, June 9, 1884.
14. *Ibid.,* N. A. Plympton to Butler, June 20, 1884.
15. *Ibid.,* N. A. Plympton to Butler, June 24, 1884.
16. *Ibid.,* N. A. Plympton to Butler, June 28, 1884.
17. *Ibid.,* telegram, N. A. Plympton to Butler, June 30, 1884.
18. *Ibid., January 1–December 30, 1884,* p. 397½.
19. *Ibid.,* R. A. Pryor to Butler, March 17, 1884.
20. *Ibid.,* R. A. Pryor to Butler, June 10, 1884.
21. *Ibid.,* drawer "R" for 1884.
22. *Ibid.,* J. M. Carr to Butler, June 20, 1844.
23. Chicago *Tribune,* July 5, 1884.
24. New York *Herald,* July 6, 1884.
25. New York *Sun,* July 7, 1884.
26. Chicago *Tribune,* July 9, 1884.
27. *Ibid.,* July 6, 1884.

28. Indianapolis *Sentinel,* August 8, 1884, clipping in Butler Papers, 1954 Accession.

29. *Ibid.*

30. *Ibid.*

31. Chicago *Tribune,* July 11, 1884.

32. New York *Herald,* July 11, 1884.

33. New York *Sun,* July 11, 1884.

34. Butler Papers, W3; also Henry Watterson, *'Marse Henry,' An Autobiography,* 2 vols. (New York, 1919), vol. II, p. 252.

35. Butler Papers, J. B. O'Reilly to Butler, July 26, 1884.

36. Butler Papers.

37. *Ibid.,* July 23, 1884.

38. Buffalo *Times,* August 23, 1890.

39. *Ibid.*

Chapter 32. The People's Party Campaign
(pages 391–407)

1. Butler Papers, unidentified clipping sent to Butler by C. H. Hanson, Cleburne, Texas, c. July 23, 1884.

2. *Ibid.,* P. M. Herold to Butler, n.d.

3. *Ibid.,* Butler to J. F. Henry, July 29, 1884.

4. *Ibid.,* Butler to S. H. Piersall, July 29, 1884.

5. New York *Sun,* August 22, 1884.

6. Buffalo *Times,* August 23, 1890.

7. Butler Papers, J. H. Mooney to Butler, August 21, 1884.

8. Chandler Papers, New Hampshire Historical Society, W. E. Chandler to J. G. Blaine, June 8, 1884.

9. *Ibid.,* Butler to W. E. Chandler, July 22, 1884.

10. Butler Papers, Butler to C. A. Dana, August 6, 1884.

11. *Ibid.,* Butler to J. E. Barrett, August 21, 1884.

12. New York *Herald,* August 19, 1884.

13. New York *Sun.,* c. August 30, 1884.

14. *Ibid.*

15. New York *Herald,* August 31, 1884.

16. New York *Sun,* September 5, 1884.

17. Chicago *Tribune,* September 2, 1884.

18. *Ibid.,* September 4, 1884.

19. *Ibid.,* September 9, 1884.
20. New York *Herald,* September 10, 1884.
21. *Ibid.,* September 16, 1884.
22. *Ibid.,* September 18, 1884.
23. Butler Papers, Butler to W. E. Chandler, September 24, 1884.
24. *Ibid.,* W. A. Fowler to Butler, n.d.
25. New York *Sun.,* September 29, 1884.
26. *Ibid.*
27. *Ibid.,* September 30, 1884.
28. New York *Herald,* May 21, 1908, quotes an article by Charles Davis in the Syracuse *Journal.*
29. Butler Papers, W. D. Mann to W. A. Fowler, November 11, 1884.
30. *Ibid.,* Butler to W. D. Mann, December 30, 1884.
31. *Ibid.,* T. E. Major to Butler, October 8, 1884.
32. *Ibid., January–December, 1882,* p. 504.
33. *Ibid.,* B. F. Clayton to Butler, August 18, 1884.
34. *Ibid.,* P. J. Ford to Butler, October 8, 1884.
35. New York *Times,* October 19, 1884.
36. *Ibid.,* October 20, 1884.
37. *Harper's Weekly,* October 25, 1884.
38. New York *Times,* October 27, 1884.
39. New York *Herald,* November 2, 1884.
40. Butler Papers, Butler to I. E. Perkins, November 24, 1884.
41. New York *Sun,* September 12, 1884.
42. Butler Papers, Blanche Ames to Butler, November 10, 1884.

Chapter 33. *Butler's Book*
(pages 408–422)

1. Butler Papers, Butler to O. H. Worth, August 27, 1884.
2. *Ibid.,* Butler to Butler Ames, September 6, 1884.
3. *Ibid.,* Butler to Butler Ames, July 10, 1884.
4. Clarence E. Macartney, *Lincoln and His Generals* (Philadelphia, 1925), p. 61.
5. Washington *Evening Star,* January 23, 1899.
6. Butler Papers, Butler to T. W. Snyder, February 20, 1883.
7. Washington *Sunday Star,* May 1, 1927.
8. Boston *Journal,* September 22, 1883.

9. Butler Papers, unidentified Richmond paper, April 3, 1896.

10. Chicago *Record,* May 11, 1897.

11. Butler Papers, *January 8–December 31, 1897,* p. 386.

12. *Ibid.*

13. *Ibid.,* James Parton to Butler, November 30, 1877.

14. *Ibid.,* Butler to W. P. Clarke, July 26, 1886.

15. *Ibid.,* Butler to O. D. Barrett, March 3, 1887.

16. *Ibid.,* Butler to Charlotte B. Stevens, March 25, 1887.

17. *Ibid.,* Butler to H. L. Bond, June 25, 1887.

18. *Ibid.*

19. Chicago *Tribune,* November 11, 1887.

20. Butler Papers, Butler to Mrs. A. Elmore, October 23, 1887.

21. *Ibid.,* Butler to G. P. Sangar, September 29, 1883.

22. U.S. Supreme Court, October Term, 1891, No. 170. *Benjamin F. Butler, Plaintiff in Error* Vs. *The National Home for Disabled Volunteer Soldiers,* Boston, 1892, p. 10.

23. Butler Papers, Butler to Dillwin Smith, August 17, 1888.

24. *Ibid.,* Blanche Ames to Butler, December 28, 1884.

25. *Ibid.,* A. T. Rice to Butler, August 14, 1885.

26. *Ibid.,* A. T. Rice to Butler, June 27, 1885.

27. *Ibid.,* Butler to J. F. Dore, April 9, 1878.

28. *Butler's Book,* p. 15.

29. Butler Papers, Butler to Phoebe Couzins, May 5, 1890.

30. *Ibid.,* Butler to Blanche Ames, February 25, 1890.

31. *Butler's Book,* p. 14.

32. Butler Papers, 1954 Accession, Butler to Jaros, December 8, 1891.

33. Lowell *Evening Star,* January 16, 1893.

34. *Ibid.,* January 14, 1893.

35. Quoted in Lowell *Evening Star,* January 26, 1893.

36. Quoted in Frederick E. Haynes, *Third Party Movements Since the Civil War* (Iowa City, State Historical Society of Iowa, 1916), p. 152.

37. New York *Sun,* quoted in Lowell *Evening Star,* January 13, 1893.

INDEX

Abbott, J. G., 27, 37, 369
Adams, Charles F., 382
Advertiser, Lowell, 18, 23, 25, 27
Afgar, E. G., 388
Alden, James, 282
Allen, William H., 95, 101
America, yacht, 333, 353, 362, 369, 395, 415
Ames, Adelbert, 318, 341, 347, 349, 352–354, 363–65
Ames, Adelbert, Jr., 409
Ames, Blanche (dau. of Adelbert and Blanche Butler Ames), 409
Ames, Mrs. Blanche Butler, 25, 40, 44, 62, 276, 318, 341, 347, 370, 407, 412, 416
Ames, Butler, 353, 370, 373, 408
Ames, Edith, 354
Ames, Jesse, 409
Ames, Oakes, 533
Ames, Oliver, 374
Ames, Sarah, 409
A. M. Thayer & Co., 417
Andrew, John A., 46, 47, 69, 111, 112, 114, 115, 208, 209
Annapolis, 54, 56, 59
Annapolis, Department of, 61
Anthony, Susan B., 373
Anti-Monopoly Party, 391ff.
Arkansas, C.S.S., 166
Armstrong, George D., 266, 267, 268
Astor, William B., 62
Avendano Brothers, 193

Bailey, Theodorus, 313
Bain, George M., 264
Bain, James G., 403
Ballot, Secret, Controversy, 29, 31

Baltimore disorder, 51
Bancroft, George, 18
Banks, Nathaniel P., 200, 201, 298
Barker, Jacob, 150, 186
Barnard, John G., 239, 240
Bartlett, Washington, 88
Bates, Edward, 271, 272
Baton Rouge, 164
"Bayview," 309, 335, 370
Beauregard, Pierre G. T., 78, 158, 236, 237, 416, 417
Beck, Congressman (Ky.), 341
Beecher, Henry W., 226, 277, 278, 315
Bell, Joseph M., 157, 158, 220
Belmont, August, 385
"Belvidere," 40, 210, 263, 270, 420
Ben Deford, S.S., 287
Bendix, John E., 91
Bermuda Hundred, 229, 239, 242
Big Bethel, 92, 94, 243
Bingham, Congressman (Ohio), 341
Birge, Henry W., 173
Black, C., 307
Black Prince, S.S., 186
Blaine, James G., 329, 344, 358
Blair, Montgomery, 83, 87, 104, 105
Blake, Captain George S., 54
Bland, Richard P., 357
Blasco de Garay, Spanish warship, 197
Bliss, George, 37
Blodgett, A. N., 376
Bond, Hugh L., 412
Boston, S.S., 55
Botts, John Minor, 321
Bouligny, Ex-Congressman, 185
Boutwell, George S., 31, 304, 305, 322, 332, 349, 350
Boyle, William, 226

Brackett, E. A., 211
Breckinridge, John C., 46, 166
Breese, K. R., 282
Bright, Daniel, 224
Brooks, James, 303, 304
Brother, Alexander, 296
Brown, George W., 52, 71
Brown, John Y., 358, 359
Bryant, William C., 275
Buchanan, James, 46
Buckingham, Gov. (Conn.), 111, 112
Bullock, Gov. (Ga.), 340
Bull Run, 94
Burnside, Ambrose B., 216
"Butler-for-President" Clubs, 395
Butler Guards, 170
"Butlerism," 350, 359
Butler's Book, 416, 418, 419
Butler School, 409
Butler, Andrew Jackson, 9, 12, 51, 54,
61, 97, 99, 101, 114, 122, 187, 189, 190,
274, 276
Butler, Ben-Israel, 25, 41, 318, 354, 365,
371, 372
Butler, Benjamin F.: ancestry, 7; An-
drew, J. A., clash with, 112, 113, 115;
Ames, A., advises on impeachment
charges, 364; Annapolis, relieved of
command of Dept. of, 73; Anti-Mo-
nopoly Party, nominated for President by in 1884, 383; Baltimore, seizure of, 70; Bermuda Hundred, his
troops withdrawn from, 241; birth, 8;
Blaine, J. G., tilt with, 344, 345; "bottled up" charge, 244; business ventures, 40, 310, 311; canards, 76, 194,
195, 359; cartoons, 308, 367, 377;
charity, contributions to, 156, 310;
Charleston Convention, 1860, 44;
Chase, S. P., offered nomination for
Vice Presidency with, 230, 231; Civil
Rights, 321, 322, 335, 355, 356, 357;
Congressman, 310, 324, 328; contempt,
jailed for, 28; "contraband" decision,
82, 85; cotton, 186; currency reform,
338, 367, 379, 380; discipline, 100;
doggerel on, 102; education, 10, 13,
15; Fast Day Proclamation, 375;
financial matters, 189; "fusion" system, 391, 403, 404; "Galvanized

Butler, Benjamin F., *cont'd*
Yanks," 255; as a general, 243, 244,
250; Gillmore, Q. A., removed, 243;
Governor of Mass., elected, 372;
Greenback Party, nominates for President, 1884, 384; Harvard refuses
LL.D. to, 377; Hatteras Inlet Expedition, 107; home life, 333; house on
Capitol Hill, 352; honorary degree,
409; Impeachment, prosecutor in
Johnson's trial, 325; Judiciary, Chairman of House Committee on, 344,
360; law cases, 3, 21, 26, 27, 39, 42,
312, 313, 315, 366, 413; lawyer, 4,
312; legends concerning, 256, 259,
295, 296, 410; Lincoln, offered nomination for Vice Presidency with in
1864, 231; marriage, 25; militia, 20,
36, 42, 47; militia, elected brigadier
general of, 42; Negroes: enlists, 180,
181; Negroes, hires free laborers, 182,
183; Negroes, policy on, 105, 166,
177; New England, commands Department of New England, 112, 113;
New Orleans: consuls, 138, 194; New
Orleans, food problem, 136; N.O.
"nuisance" cases, 296, 300, 302, 305;
N.O. recall from, 192, 200, 202; N.O.:
relief problem, 145, 155, 180; N.O.
trade revival, 180, 186, 187, 188;
newspapers, 409; New York, during
election of 1864, 275; outlawed by
Jefferson Davis, 205; party shift, 207;
"People's Party," 391; politician, 350;
politics, 31, 32, 36, 44, 367; President,
urged to run for in 1864, 274, 275;
prisoner exchange, 251; Radical, 327;
Reconstruction, 213, 320–21; Reconstruction, Chairman of House Committee on, 329; reformer, 312; reputation, 131, 143, 408, 409, 410; reputation
as a military commander, 243; reputation in the South, 86, 96, 141, 151,
156, 175, 198, 199, 214, 253, 258; "salary grab," 331; Senator (Mass. State),
43; Smith, W. F., difficulty with,
245, 246; speeches, 172, 202, 207, 208,
212, 277, 320, 322, 323, 325, 335, 356,
361, 367, 373, 397, 398, 399, 401; Supreme Court, admitted to practice in,

Butler, Benjamin F., *cont'd*
27; teaches school, 18; ten-hour day, 29, 30; Tewskbury Almshouse, 376; troops, authorized to raise, 111; troops, difficulty obtaining, 104; Virginia, commands Department of Virginia and North Carolina, 105, 219, 291; West Point, 42; "Woman Order," 138–40
Butler, Blanche. *See* Ames, Mrs. Blanche B.)
Butler, Mrs. Charlotte Ellison (mother of B.F.B.), 7, 10, 11, 26
Butler, George, 51, 97, 99
Butler, John (father of B.F.B.), 8, 9
Butler, Nicholas, 8
Butler, Paul, 25, 41, 318, 353, 365, 376, 420
Butler, Sarah (Mrs. B.F.B.), 19, 20, 23, 25, 40, 41, 62, 79, 98, 99, 106, 117, 118, 131, 134, 147, 158, 183, 189, 204, 241, 273, 276, 283, 333, 352, 363, 365
Butler, Zephaniah, 8, 9
Byars, W. V., 357

Cabot, Dr., 365
Cadwallader, Maj. Gen., 72
Cahill, Col. (9th Conn.), 114
Callejon, Spanish Consul, 198
Cameron, J. D., 315
Cameron, Simon, 46, 65, 74, 83, 98, 111, 112, 214, 231, 315, 396
Camp, B. F., 215
Camp Chase, 112
Camp Parapet, 169, 176, 180
Cardenas, S.S., 198
Carney, James G., 25, 46, 187, 318, 414
Carpenter, George M., 414
Carr, Col., 95
Cartter, David K., 315
Cary, J. B., 81
Cataline, S.S., 79
Chamberlain, U.S.S., 288
Chambre, Rev., 421
Chandler, William E., 315, 320, 328, 394, 399
Chase, Salmon P., 65, 74, 168, 181, 183, 189, 190, 200, 201, 212, 216, 230
Chesapeake Female Seminary, 81, 103, 318

Chittenden, Simeon B., 380
Choate, Rufus, 377
Chronicles from the Nineteenth Century, Family Letters of Blanche Butler and Adelbert Ames, 2 Vols., compiled by Blanche Butler Ames, 1935. Privately Issued 1957, Copyright 1957 by Jessie Ames Marshall, 354
Cilley, Abigail, 8, 9
Cilley, Joseph, 8
Cilley, O. G., 417
Citizens Bank of New Orleans, 137
Civil Rights, 329, 330
Civil Rights Bill, 356, 358, 360–62
Clancy, Mr. (B's secretary), 318, 399
Clark, Thomas M., 13
Clarke, Haswell C., 158, 168, 220, 304
Clayton, B. F., 464
Cleveland, Grover, 384
Colfax, Schuyler, 304, 329
Collins, P. A., 388
Constitution, S.S., 114, 117, 122
Constitution, U.S.S., 54, 56, 58, 59
Couturié, Amadié, 137, 193, 194
Couzins, Phoebe, 373, 417
Cowley, Charles, 309
Cox, S. S., 214, 358, 359
Crédit Mobilier, 333
Crosby, Nathan, 28
Crosby, Pierce, 167
Currency Reform, 330
Cushing, Caleb, 14, 112

Daily Advertiser, Boston, 21
Daily Advertiser, Lowell, 5
Daily True Delta, New Orleans, 136
Dana, Charles A., 246, 334, 393, 407, 421
Daniels, J. T., 268
Davis, Charles H., 164, 165
Davis, Garrett, 296, 348
Davis, Jefferson, 42, 43, 45, 96, 205, 254, 327
Davis, Robert S., 160, 220
Dean, A. F., 27
DeKay, George C., 153, 164
Denison, George S., 181, 182, 189, 191
Depew, Chauncey, 375
Devereaux, Capt., 55
Dickens, Charles, 12

Dickinson, Anna, 388
Dimick, Justin, 79, 88
Dimon, A. R., 255
Dismal Swamp Expedition, 222
Douglas, Stephen A., 44
Dow, Neal, 114, 119
Draper, Alonzo G., 224
Drewry's Bluff, 237
DuBois, W. E. B., 357
Dunn, Harriett, 420
Dunn, John M., 270
Dunn, L., 415
Dunn, Lanier, 420
Du Pont, Samuel F., 52
Durant, Thomas J., 364
Duryea, Abram, 90, 92
Dutch Gap Canal, 250, 261, 281

Edison, Thomas A., 315
Edson, Theodore, 14, 24
Eighth Massachusetts, 53, 55, 58
Eliot, Charles W., 373, 376, 377
"European Brigade," 137, 138

Fairbanks, Gov. Erastus (Vt.), 111
Farr, A. W., 34
Farragut, David G., 117, 119, 122, 124,
    125, 130, 164, 165, 183, 192, 313, 314
Farragut, Prize Cases, 313
Fay, Richard S., Jr., 40, 186–89
Federal Hill, 70
Felton, S. M., 52
Ferguson, Mrs. S. G., 296–98
Field, D. C. G., 152, 298, 307
Flanders, B. F., 185
Foote, Andrew H., 164
Forbes, John M., 350
Ford, Patrick J., 404
Fort Fisher, 279, 284, 286
Fort Fisher Expedition, 280
Fort Jackson, 123–25, 128
Fort St. Philip, 123–26
Fortier, Polycarpe, 177
Fortress Monroe, 74, 76, 79
Foster, General, 216, 244
Fowler, William A., 394, 396, 399
Fox, Gustavus V., 13, 87, 171, 280, 310
Fox, S.S., 192
Franklin, William B., 414
Freeman, E. W., 13

French, Jonas H., 112–14, 147, 158
Fulton, Captain, 120

"Galvanized Yanks," 255
Gardner, Henry J., 41
Garrison, William Lloyd, 200
Gavinzel, G., 226
General Butler in New Orleans, 211
George, Paul R., 25, 122, 187, 200, 214,
    416
Georgia, Reconstruction in, 339, 341
Getty, George W., 219
Gillis, John, 297
Gillmore, Quincy A., 230, 233, 234,
    236, 238, 243
Glisson, O. S., 120, 287
Goldsmith, William B., 375
Gooch, G. W., 320
Gooding, O. P., 131
Gordon, George H., 334
Grady, Senator (N. Y. State), 386
Graham, Charles K., 221, 279, 288
Grand Gulf, 164
Grant, Ulysses S., 229, 230, 233, 238,
    241–46, 248, 257, 258, 279, 281, 290,
    327, 355, 409
Graves, William D., 8, 14
Grayhound, S.S., 234
Greble, John T., 91–93, 96
Greeley, Horace, 35, 275
Greenback-Labor Party, 391
Griffin, John Q. A., 42
Griffin, R. M., 381
Guerrillas, 164

Hackett, John K., 303
Haggerty, Peter, 54, 70, 82, 92, 168, 220
Hahn, Michael, 185
Halleck, Henry W., 220, 227, 239, 247
Halstead, Murat, 42, 409
Hanson, C. H., 391
Harrison, C. J., 114
Harvey, Judge, 21
Hatteras Inlet Expedition, 107
Haven, Nathaniel A., 10
Hay, John, 255
Haymarket Anarchists, 413
Hayne, Paul H., 141
Heckman, Charles A., 219, 236, 237,
    273, 370, 415

Henly, Mr., 261, 262
Henry, Robert S., 355
Herbert, J. K., 269, 275
Hicks, Thomas H., 54, 56, 59
Highland, John, 307
Hildreth, Fisher A., 19, 23, 25, 187, 214, 309
Hildreth, Florence, 415
Hildreth, Israel, 19
Hildreth, Lote, 84
Hildreth, Milo, 376
Hildreth, Rowena, 415
Hildreth, Sarah Jones. *See* Sarah Butler, Mrs. B.F.B.
Hildreth, Susan, 27
Hill, Isaac, 14, 18
Hinks, E. W., 58
Hitchcock, Ethan A., 251
Hoar, Ebenezer R., 34, 35, 43, 334, 350, 359
Hoar, George F., 334, 350, 366, 368, 377
Hodges, W. H. W., 264
Holabird, Samuel B., 298
Homans Charles, 58
Hudibras, 77
Humphreys, A. A., 247
Hunt, David, 417

Inquirer, Phila., 96

Jackson, Andrew, 8, 12
Jewett, C. F., 417
Johnson, Andrew, 322
Johnson, Reverdy, 194, 195, 301
Joint Committee on the Conduct of the War, 292
Jones, E. F., 47, 64, 114, 200, 416
Jones, Samuel, 256
Julliard Vs. Greenman, 366, 380

Kautz, August V., 233, 234, 237, 416
Kearney, Dennis, 367, 368
Keim, W. H., 72
Kelly, John, 385, 386, 394
Kensel, George A., 220
Key, David M., 330
Kilpatrick, Judson, 93, 334
King, B. F., 76
Kinsman, J. Burnham, 113, 220, 221
Kruttschmidt, Prussian Consul, 197

K.K.K. Bill, 342, 347, 348, 355
Ku Klux Klan, 329, 330, 336, 345

La Blanche, Babilliard, 178
Lamb, William, 417
La Mountain, John, 89
LaRue, Mrs. John, 152
Leacock, W. T., 153, 175
Lee, Robert E., 262
Lee, Samuel P., 221, 233, 235
Lefferts, Marshall, 53, 55, 58, 64
Limburg, Joest van, 194
Lincoln, Abraham, 61, 74, 83, 104, 107, 111, 115, 179, 183, 187, 194, 201, 205, 206, 208, 211, 214, 225, 226, 246, 254, 265, 271, 272, 278, 280, 290, 291, 306
L. L. Davis, Schooner, 191
Long, John D., 373
Louisiana, U.S.S., 282
Lovell, Mansfield, 127, 129
Lower California Corporation, 311
Lynch, Congressman (Miss.), 360
Lyons, Lord, British Minister, 192

Magruder, John B., 92
Major, T. E., 403
Mallory, Charles K., 81
Malvern, U.S.S., 284
Manning, Daniel, 384
Marine Brigade, 221, 223, 233, 234, 279, 287
Martin, A. D., 225
Maryland, S.S., 52, 53, 56, 62
Mason, Jeremiah, 17
Mazurean, M. Adolphe, 148
McClellan, George B., 114, 116, 117, 118
McClure, John W., 298, 381
McCrae, Major, 261, 262
McMillan, D. W., 169
Meade, George M., 230
Meigs, Montgomery C., 95, 188, 239, 240
Méjan, Count, 196, 298
Mercer, W. N., 174
Merrill, Joshua, 12
Merrimack, C.S.S., 123
Middlesex Corporation, 40, 46, 189, 309
Milligan, Lambdin, P., 312
Mississippi, S.S., 117, 119, 120, 131
Monroe, John T., 130, 133, 134, 135, 145, 146

"Monroe Guards," 146, 148, 149
Moore, Thomas O., 130
Moulton, Frances D., 315, 394
Mountain Mining Company, 311
Mumford, William B., 127, 149, 150, 151, 205, 313
Mumford, Mrs. W. B., 151, 256, 259, 329, 330
Myers, Mrs. Marion Twiggs, 308

Nast, Thomas, 211
National Home for Disabled Volunteer Soldiers, 316, 317, 318, 413
Naval Academy, U.S., 57
Negroes: Cavalry, 236; Civil Rights, 208; "Contraband," 85; free labor, 182; fugitive to Fortress Monroe, 83, 84; infantry, 168, 169, 180, 205, 221–225, 228, 238, 248, 250, 252, 258, 261; Office of Negro Affairs, 221; recruitment, 220; miscellaneous, 103, 129, 131, 165, 168, 175, 181, 184, 219, 265
Negro Question, 199
New Orleans *Delta,* 167
New Orleans Expedition, 116
New Orleans, description, 127; destruction of property, 129; food problem, 136, 169, 181; relief problem, 145, 155, 182; sanitation, 146, 147; trade, 190
Newport News, 81
Ninth Connecticut, 112
Norfolk, 263

Oliver, Mrs. Mary, 315
Opdyke, George, 275, 276
O'Reilly, John B., 388
Ould, Robert, 252, 253, 257, 258, 264

Pack, Frank H., 169
Pack, John J., 219
Page, Edward, 134, 176
Parker, J. M. G., 300
Parr, A. W., 27
Parsons, William H., 385, 395, 404, 406
Partisan Rangers, 169
Parton, James, 210, 214, 291, 331, 372, 411, 416
Patterson, Robert, 72

Pentuchet Navigation Company, 311
People's Party, 391, 393, 397–99, 401
Phelps, J. W., 82, 97, 104, 114, 122, 126, 161, 171, 176, 178, 179
Philadelphia Convention, 1866, 321
Phillips, Mrs. Philip, 152, 153, 154, 155
Phillips, Wendell, 209
Picayune, New Orleans, 77
Pickett, George E., 256
Pierce, Ebenezer W., 89–94
Pierce, Franklin, 18, 36, 39
Pierce, Henry L., 350
Pierpoint, Francis H., 263, 265, 269, 270
Pierrepont, Edwards, 301, 302
Plympton, Noah A., 383, 384, 389, 393, 396, 399
Point Lookout, 220, 253
Polk, James K., 27
Pollard, Edward A., 222, 260
Porter, David D., 117, 119, 126, 128, 148, 165, 281–83, 285, 289, 314
Portsmouth, 264
Powder boat, 280
Pratt, Charles B., 368
Press, Phila., 76, 77
Prisoner of War Exchange, 231ff., 257
Pryor, Roger A., 285, 288, 364
Puffer, Alfred F., 220

Rainey, Congressman (S.C.), 360
Raymond, Henry J., 98, 275
Reconstruction, 354
Reconstruction Committee, 337
Record, Elbridge, G., 3, 5
Reichard, Prussian consul, 197
Reid, Charles, 266
Relay House, 65–68
Reynaud, French Admiral, 183
Rice, A. T., 416
Rinaldo, S.S., 197
Ritchie, Congressman (Md.), 346
Robinson, William S., 3, 5, 23, 26, 37, 69, 325
Rogers, Henry, 270
Rowena Rutherford Vs. B.F.B., 305, 307
Russell, Gov. (Mass.), 420

"Salary Grab," 330
Samuel Smith & Co., 168, 300

"Sanborn Contracts," 330, 332
Sanborn, J. D., 215, 332
Saxon, S.S., 125
Schouler, William, 5, 6, 26, 37, 76
Schurz, Carl, 62
Scott, George, 90, 93
Scott, Winfield, 42, 61, 64, 65, 68, 72, 73, 74, 80, 83, 87, 95, 103, 104, 116, 207
Sedgwick, John, 227, 228
Selfridge, Thomas, 281
Seventh New York Militia, 53
Seward, William H., 192, 194, 206
Sewell, Hartley W., 270
Shafer, J. Wilson, 209, 220, 248, 253, 275, 329
Shed, Zachariah, 3
Shepley, George F., 114, 117, 127, 147, 158, 173, 179, 194, 199
Ship Island, 114, 121, 122
S. H. Kennedy & Co., 196
Simmons, William A., 330, 350, 389
Sixth Massachusetts Militia, 51, 65, 72
Smith, Goldwin, 328
Smith, William, 18
Smith, William F., 230, 233, 236, 237, 241, 242, 244, 248, 249
Snead, Edward K., 271, 272
Soulé, Pierre, 134, 135, 148
Southwood, Marion, 147, 153
Spaulding, S.S., 204
Stanbery, Henry, 325
Stanton, Edwin M., 116, 117, 179, 188, 195, 206, 211, 252, 265, 303
Stevens, Mrs. Betsy Morrill, 9, 365, 370, 415
Stevens, Charlotte, 415, 420
Stevens, Charlotte B., 370
Stevens, Thaddeus, 275, 334
Storey, Moorfield, 326, 381
Stringham, Silas, H., 104, 107
Strong, George C., 115, 123, 140, 416
Sumner, Charles, 31, 349

Talbot, Gov. (Mass.), 369, 373
Taylor, Richard, 170
Ten-Hour Controversy, 33
Terry, Alfred H., 243, 244, 291
Tewksbury Almshouse, 374

Thomas, Armand, 157
Thomas, Lorenzo, 115, 326
Thorpe, T. B., 147, 214
Tilton, W. S., 414
Townsend, Frederick, 91, 93
Twiggs, David E., 306
Tyler, John, 80

Union Pacific Railroad, 333
U.S. Cartridge Co., 370

Van Buren, John, 37
Van Lieu, Elizabeth L., 226–28
Varney, Samuel J., 34
Vicksburg Campaign, 162 ff.
Vilas, William F., 387
Villeneuve, Adolphe, 297

Wade, Benjamin F., 275, 320
Wadsworth, James, 277
Walker, W. S., 239
Wardwell, Burnham, 373, 376
Warland, John H., 32, 34, 35
Warren, Judge, 168
Washburne, Gov. (Me.), 111
Weaver, James B., 382
Webster, Sue Hildreth, 318
Webster, W. P., 27, 75, 309, 318
Weeks, Pender, 256
Weigel, Lieut., 168
Weitzel, Godfrey, 119, 122, 153, 170, 237, 279–81, 287–88, 416
Welles, Gideon, 314
West, Albert, 411, 419
West, Robert, 234
Wetmore, Prosper M., 276, 277
White, James W., 290
Whitney, B. D., 317
Wild, Edward A., 223, 225, 256
Wilkes, George, 328
Willard, Frances, 388
Williams, D. H., 72
Williams, Thomas, 119, 132, 133, 161, 164, 166
Wilson, Henry, 214, 225, 226, 296, 347, 348
Winans, Ross, 68
Winser, H. J., 236, 260

Winthrop, Theodore, 55, 60, 65, 76, 82, 90, 92, 93
Wistar, Isaac J., 228
Woman Order, 129ff, 139–42, 146, 198–199, 207
Wool, John E., 104

Yeadon, Richard, 152

Zantzinger, Francis, 268
Zantzinger case, 270